The Political Economy of Manitoba

Edited by James Silver and Jeremy Hull

Canadian Plains Research Center
University of Regina
1990

Canadian Plains Research Center
University of Regina
Regina, Saskatchewan S4S 0A2
Canada

∞

Printed on acid-free paper

Canadian Cataloguing in Publication Data

Main entry under title:

The Political economy of Manitoba

  1st ed. --

  (Canadian plains studies, ISSN 0317-6290 ; 19)
  ISBN 0-88977-059-X

1. Manitoba - Economic conditions - 1870-*
2. Manitoba - Politics and government - 1870-*
3. Manitoba - Social conditions - 1870-*
I. Silver, James, 1946-   II. Hull, Jeremy, 1949-
III. University of Regina.   Canadian Plains Research
Center.   IV. Series.

HC117.M3P64 1990   330.9712703   C90-097060-X

Cover Design: Ann K. McCrorie
Printed and bound in Canada by
Hignell Printing Limited, Winnipeg, Manitoba

The Political Economy of Manitoba

CONTENTS

FIGURES

TABLES

ABBREVIATIONS

ACCL	All Canadian Congress of Labour
ACTU	Amalgamated Clothing and Textile Union
AFL	American Federation of Labour
BNA	British North America
CAIMAW	Canadian Association of Industrial, Mechanical and Allied Work
CAP	Canada Assistance Plan
CARAL	Canadian Abortion Rights Action League
CCF	Co-operative Commonwealth Federation
CCL	Canadian Congress of Labour
CFI	Churchill Forest Industries
CIO	Congress of Industrial Organizations
CLC	Canadian Labour Congress
CLP	Canadian Labour Party
CMA	Canadian Manufacturers' Association
CNR	Canadian National Railway
CPC	Communist Party of Canada
CPR	Canadian Pacific Railway
CUPE	Canadian Union of Public Employees
DIAND	Department of Indian Affairs and Northern Development
DLP	Dominion Labour Party
DREE	Department of Regional Economic Expansion
EPF	Established Programs Financing
FOS	Final-Offer Selection
FTA	Free Trade Agreement
GDP	Gross Domestic Product
GNP	Gross National Product
HBC	Hudson's Bay Company
HESP	Health, Education and Social Policy
IAS	Industrial Adjustment Service
ILO	International Labour Organization
ILP	Independent Labour Party
ILGWU	International Ladies Garment Workers Union
INAC	Indian and Northern Affairs Canada
INCO	International Nickel Company
IUS	Institute of Urban Studies

LLP	Labour Progressive Party
LMRC	Labour-Management Review Committee
MACSW	Manitoba Action Committee on the Status of Women
MCS	Manpower Consultancy Service
MDC	Manitoba Development Corporation
MDF	Manitoba Development Fund
MECS	Manpower and Employment Committee
MFL	Manitoba Federation of Labour
MGEA	Manitoba Government Employees Association
MLA	Member of the Legislative Assembly
MP	Member of Parliament
NDP	New Democratic Party
NPR	Northern Pacific Railway
OBU	One Big Union
POWER	Prostitutes and Other Women for Equal Rights
RCMP	Royal Canadian Mounted Police
RED	Resource and Economic Development
RRSP	Registered Retirement Savings Plan
SDP	Social Democratic Party
SPC	Socialist Party of Canada
TLC	Trades and Labour Congress
TUEL	Trade Union Educational League
UGWA	United Garment Workers of America
UIC	Unemployment Insurance Commission
WLS	Winnipeg Lesbian Society
WPC	Workers' Party of Canada
WUL	Workers' Unity League
WWLM	Winnipeg Women's Liberation Movement

ACKNOWLEDGEMENTS

We would like to acknowledge the assistance of numerous people in bringing this project to fruition. Jim McCrorie, Executive Director of the Canadian Plains Research Center, has supported our efforts from an early stage. Derek Cook made a valuable contribution in getting the project off the ground. The University of Winnipeg provided the funding for a conference in October 1986, at which most of the chapters were initially presented. Participants in that conference offered many constructive criticisms. And our fellow contributors were patient with our impositions of deadlines and requests for revisions. Brian Mlazgar of the Canadian Plains Research Center did the copyediting and formatting of the book.

PERMISSIONS

Every effort has been made to contact the copyright owners of material quoted in this volume. The editors and publishers would be grateful if any errors or omissions were brought to their attention so that suitable acknowledgements could be made in future.

Permissions to quote from the following previously published materials are gratefully acknowledged:

Alan Artibise, Winnipeg: A Social History of Urban Growth, 1874-1914 (Montréal: McGill-Queen's University Press, 1975), 25, 152; Ruben Bellan, *Winnipeg's First Century: An Economic History* (Winnipeg: Queenston House, 1978), 77-78, 109-10; V.C. Fowke, *The National Policy and the Wheat Economy* (Toronto: University of Toronto Press, 1973), 110, 135-36, 191-92, 263; Gerald Friesen, *The Canadian Prairies: A History* (Toronto: University of Toronto Press, 1984), 92, 93, 128, 293; Marcel Giraud, *Le Métis Canadien* (St. Boniface: Editions du Blé, 1984), 1271-72; James McAllister, *The Government of Edward Schreyer* (Kingston and Montréal: McGill-Queen's University Press, 1984), 7, 24-25, 69-70, 122-23, 141; Robert Miles, *Racism and Migrant Labour* (London: Routledge and Kegan Paul, 1982), 32; Bryan D. Palmer, *Working Class Experience: The Rise and Reconstitution of Canadian Labour, 1800-1980* (Toronto: Butterworth, 1983), 211; Norman Penner, *The Canadian Left: A Critical Analysis* (Scarborough: Prentice-Hall, 1977), 138-39; Doug Smith, *Let Us Rise: An Illustrated History of the Manitoba Labour Movement* (Vancouver: New Star Books, 1985), 32, 59; Nelson Wiseman, *Social Democracy in Manitoba: A History of the CCF/NDP* (Winnipeg: University of Manitoba Press, 1983), 12.

Introduction

Jeremy Hull and Jim Silver

The chapters contained in this volume analyze selected aspects of Manitoba's political economy. While they are not the first such attempts, we believe that the study of Manitoba's political economy is at a relatively early stage because of insufficient attention in the past. We hope that this book will stimulate further such work, either as an extension or as a critique of our collective efforts.

The gaps in the existing knowledge of Manitoba's political economy hinder both the efforts of activists to wage successful popular struggles, and those of governments to initiate progressive policy. We believe that these gaps create a need for analysis in two broad areas. First, a clear sense of the historical development of the political economy of Manitoba is needed to advance the efforts of activists, and to develop progressive policy initiatives. Second, more debate is needed about the practice of a socialist politics appropriate to the province's political economy, and to the specific circumstances of the social democratic party that formed the provincial government for most of the 1970s and 1980s.

A common theme that links the following chapters is the centrality of political struggle, and its relationship to the origins, development and structure of the political economy of Manitoba. Both those who have long since been marginalized by the process of capital accumulation in Manitoba, and those who have been the central antagonists in the process of capital accumulation, have engaged in various forms of political struggle throughout the history of Manitoba. Many of the chapters in this volume analyze important aspects of the origin and historical development of those struggles. Others focus on more recent developments, particularly the gradual transformation of the social and economic structure of Manitoba, within which a wider variety of struggles has emerged, including those relating to the restructuring of the family, the redefinition of the role of women, the recomposition of the working class, and the renewed vitality of the struggles of Natives. All of these issues raise questions about the pragmatic politics of Manitoba's New Democratic Party (NDP), and about a politics of the Left. Many of the essays address the constraints upon, and limitations of, the NDP's brand of social democracy and raise, albeit tentatively and inconclusively, the question of alternatives. We return to speculate on these issues in the Conclusion.

The Political Economy of Manitoba

While the metropolis-hinterland model yields considerable insight into our historical experience, it also obscures much that is important. We know, for example, that Manitoba is not just a resource-based hinterland whose economy has been distorted and underdeveloped, and whose surplus has been extracted to serve the needs of a distant metropolis. Winnipeg itself became a metropolis a century ago, with a vast hinterland of its own, and highly developed financial, commercial and manufacturing sectors.

Consequently, many Manitobans have enjoyed the benefits of a more stable and diversified economy than the term "hinterland" would suggest.

At the same time, and consistent with the uneven fashion in which capitalism develops everywhere, many Manitobans have not so benefited. In fact, the origins of Manitoba's modern political economy can be located in the process of primitive accumulation by which the original Indian and Métis inhabitants of the region were pushed off the land, often by nefarious means.[1] Their subsequent marginalization is moved closer to centre stage in this volume with descriptions of several aspects of the bitter legacy of that process.[2] This focus is not only consistent with recent scholarly approaches to Manitoba's past,[3] but also reflects a traditional socialist concern with social and economic inequality, and the steady and significant development of political activity in Manitoba's Native community.

In the wake of the dispossession of the original inhabitants, the Prairies filled with farmers and railways, and Manitoba experienced the phenomenal turn-of-the-century wheat boom which would shape its economy and class structure well into the last quarter of the twentieth century. But again, the achievements of this great capitalist boom were bought dearly. The several hundred thousand men and women who poured onto the Prairies prior to World War I in order to farm the land faced exceptional hardship. Many were defeated — witness the very high failure rate of homesteads. Those who stayed fought the formidable natural obstacles inherent in clearing bush and breaking sod in a harsh and unpredictable climate, and the human obstacles created not only by a plethora of middlemen, but also by the irrational and unyielding world market which set prices for their produce without regard for their needs. Out of their hardship emerged a class struggle against middlemen and markets which was long at the centre of Manitoba politics.[4]

To grow and transport the wheat required a massive infrastructure of railways, bridges, grain elevators and towns, the construction of which created an industrial boom centred in Winnipeg. At the heart of the boom were the railways: vast rail yards, repair shops, freight sheds, office buildings, powerhouses, stores, scrap yards and stations were constructed in the city. Construction materials and work clothes were made in Winnipeg to supply the needs of farms and railways, and the city became a major wholesale centre, supplying a hinterland stretching from the Lakehead to the Pacific. Metal shops and foundries manufactured the machinery for country elevators and structural steel for railways and bridges, while the produce of the farms became the raw material for flour milling, meat packing and a host of related industrial activities.[5]

Immigrants flooded the province to fuel the boom, the differential pattern of their distribution across Manitoba reinforcing the emergent class structure. In Winnipeg especially, and to a lesser extent in Brandon, a substantial working class took shape. Many of the skilled workers were British, and their moderate ideas of politics and trade unionism had a disproportionate influence on the ultimate political direction of the fledgling trade union movement.[6] But the majority of the working class was composed of European immigrants, jammed into the teeming, multilingual north end of Winnipeg, where conditions in the early part of the century were shocking.[7] Poverty, disease and appalling housing conditions were part of the daily experience of Winnipeg's working class, and added to the intensity of the class conflict which led to the Winnipeg General Strike of 1919.

The province's capitalist class, centred largely in Winnipeg, deserves more attention than it has received in this book. The basis of the capitalist class was the wheat-railway nexus. The grain itself, the ultimate source of most of the province's economic activity, was moved by farmers to country elevators owned by grain firms centred in Winnipeg. Thousands of Winnipeg's citizens were employed in grading, marketing, shipping, financing, accounting for and speculating in grain. By 1909 Winnipeg had become "the greatest grain centre on the North American continent"[8] and a significant financial centre as well. "By 1914 more than 25 buildings used exclusively for banking and stockbroking were concentrated in Main Street just north of Portage Avenue."[9] Here, in the heart of Winnipeg's booming business district, was the other pole of the great class conflict in which the farmers were engaged — against the middlemen and financiers who moved and financed their crops.[10]

Unlike a "typical" hinterland, Winnipeg's business class was largely local, having moved to Manitoba from Ontario and elsewhere, and having settled in the south end of Winnipeg to raise families and fortunes. Aggressively self-confident, narrow-mindedly growth-oriented and profoundly antilabour, this business class directly controlled Winnipeg's city council, using it effectively to promote business-class interests while ignoring the needs of the massive influx of immigrant workers.[11] The resultant poverty and destitution was not an unfortunate side effect of, but a principal contributor to, the boom. The consequent gulf between the classes was strikingly symbolized by the virtual apartheid between the working-class north end and the plush south end mansions of the businessmen.[12] The physical separation of the classes by the "longest [railway] yards in the world"[13] was replicated at the cultural and ideological level, as described in intriguing fashion by Reg Skene. In "C.P. Walker and the Business of Theatre," he includes a revealing description of the attitudes of the business class to those who created its profits.[14]

Economically and socially, the wheat boom created modern Manitoba. The linkages from grain to railways, and thence to manufacturing, wholesaling and financing, laid the basis for a relatively stable and diversified economy. The typically uneven development of capitalism, accentuated by the boom conditions of the period, created a class structure whose lines of demarcation and whose politics were strikingly clear.

By 1914 the boom was over. The best prairie land was occupied, most of the railways were built, and the insatiable demand for new supplies and infrastructure was largely filled. The dynamic for growth — a wheat-railway "megaproject" of immense proportions — was exhausted. The shape of Manitoba's political economy and its class structure were largely determined for the next fifty years. Economic changes after World War I were incremental for the most part, and largely consistent with developments elsewhere: there was a relative decline in the importance of agriculture, notwithstanding its continued central role in Manitoba's economy, and a relative increase in the importance of the service and public sectors.[15] During this long postboom period the working class, assembled during the wheat-boom era, took on its political colouration through the struggles described by Black, as did farmers through the struggles described by Phillips, while those who had been marginalized to make way for the boom in the first place continued to pay the price long after its exhaustion.[16]

Northern Manitoba became a resource hinterland. Exploited primarily for its minerals, forests and hydroelectric power, the north's traditional fish and fur economy became relatively unimportant. Native residents, marginalized by the process of capital accumulation, and long the victims of poor living conditions and high mortality rates, were generally ignored in the process of industrial development, apart from the activities of the churches and fur traders.

After World War II, and particularly after 1960, the welfare state was extended north and services to northerners were gradually rationalized, providing somewhat improved health and education. Falling Native mortality rates led to dramatic population increases, which added to the poverty of marginalized rural Native communities, and increased urban Native migration. But in the cities Natives have fared little better than in rural communities and in some respects, as shown by Falconer, they have become worse off.[17]

While much has remained the same since 1914, much has changed. The social and economic structure of Manitoba, largely shaped by the turn-of-the-century wheat boom and relatively unchanged for fifty years, is undergoing a significant, though largely silent, transformation. Traditional sectors of the provincial economy — meat packing, flour milling, metal fabricating, manufacturing — appear to be in relative decline and new sectors are emerging. This is part of the worldwide restructuring of capital. It has potentially serious implications for Manitoba's traditional economic diversity and stability, though precisely where these changes may be leading is difficult to tell, given Manitoba's peripheral position in the world economy. Nor can we predict with certainty the trajectory and outcome of the wide variety of struggles that have emerged in recent years — around family, women, Natives, and the recomposition of the working class, to name but a few.

The governmental expression of political conflict has also experienced a long evolution. A political party with its roots in the working class formed the provincial government for most of the 1970s and 1980s, while post-World War II prosperity and the growth of employment in bureaucracies and professions softened the demarcation between classes. In addition, the welfare state and a prosperous economy reduced the numbers of people affected by extreme poverty, although these sources of stability may also be eroding.

This reality, with its many contradictions, and with its gains and limitations, is a focal point of Manitoba politics in the 1990s. This is especially so for socialists, for whom it raises complex questions about the nature of a socialist politics in a single province. Answers to such questions require an analysis which is rooted in an empirically detailed understanding of the specifics of Manitoba's political economy. We hope that this volume can contribute to such an understanding.

NOTES

1. Chapters 1, 3 and 4 in this volume; see also Gerhard Ens, "Métis Lands in Manitoba," *Manitoba History* 5 (Spring 1983): 2-11.

2. Chapters 3, 4, 9 and 12 in this volume.

3. Gerald Friesen, *The Canadian Prairies: A History* (Toronto: University of Toronto Press, 1984).

4. Alan Artibise, *Winnipeg: A Social History of Urban Growth, 1874-1914* (Montréal: McGill-Queen's University Press, 1975); Ruben Bellan, *Winnipeg First Century: An Economic History* (Winnipeg: Queenston House, 1978).

6. Chapter 5 in this volume.

7. Alan Artibise, *Winnipeg*; J. Marlyn, *Under the Ribs of Death* (Toronto: McClelland and Stewart, 1957); Doug Smith, *Let Us Rise: An Illustrated History of the Manitoba Labour Movement* (Vancouver: New Star Books, 1985).

8. Alan Artibise, *Winnipeg*, 152.

9. Ibid.

10. Chapter 1 in this volume.

11. J.M.S. Careless, "The Development of the Winnipeg Business Community," *Transactions of the Royal Society of Canada* 8, no. 4 (1970): 239-54.

12. J. Marlyn, *Under the Ribs of Death*.

13. Doug Smith, *Let Us Rise*, 29.

14. Chapter 6 in this volume.

15. Chapters 1 and 2 in this volume.

16. Chapters 3, 4 and 12 in this volume.

17. Chapter 9 in this volume.

SECTION ONE

Structural Change and Political Struggle in Manitoba: An Introductory Overview

The period from 1870 to 1900 witnessed the death of the preindustrial culture of the Prairies. The original Indian and Métis inhabitants were dispossessed so that the west could be opened to the interests of capital. Relegated to reserves, or dispersed to scattered Métis villages, the aboriginal peoples eked out an existence on the margins of the emergent mode of production. Much of Manitoba's political economy and political struggles can best be understood in the context of the marginalization of indigenous peoples that followed upon the process of primitive accumulation. Some of the negative consequences are described later in this volume by Bailey, St.-Onge, Falconer, Hull and Loxley.

With the "clearing of the commons" and the establishment of the preconditions for a new mode of production, the great wheat and railway boom of the late nineteenth and early twentieth centuries burst across the Prairies. This boom established the agrarian character of Manitoba's political economy, which Phillips argues prevailed until after World War II, and set the stage for the fundamental class conflict in Manitoba: between farmers on the one hand; and commercial, financial and industrial, largely monopoly capital on the other.

Winnipeg emerged as the "Chicago of the North," the commercial, financial and industrial metropolis of the Prairies. Its development gave rise to a substantial industrial working class and an intense class struggle which peaked in the Winnipeg General Strike of 1919.

The 1919 strike is a watershed in Manitoba's history. Following its defeat, a rurally based, fiscally conservative, antilabour regime gained control of the provincial government and remained in power until the late 1950s. This was a period of overall structural stability, reinforced by an exceptionally inert government with a minimalist view of the role of the state. The agriculturally based, relatively diversified economy, with strength in manufacturing, commerce and finance, changed little over this period, apart from a long, slow decline in Winnipeg's importance as a western regional metropolis.

A new era began with the election of Duff Roblin in 1958, whose provincial government assumed a more activist role, assisting entrepreneurship and attracting capital. This activism was extended, along much the same lines, with the election of the first Manitoba NDP government in 1969. Gonick argues that while the differing economic policies of successive postwar provincial governments have had an impact — for better or for worse — on Manitobans' quality of life, none of these governments has been able to reverse Manitoba's long-term relative decline. The extent of the problem has been partially masked by large-scale public investment, particularly in hydroelectric developments in the 1970s and 1980s. But the current global restructuring of capital and the Canada-United States Free Trade Agreement (FTA) are likely to accelerate it again, unless Manitoba can find a place for itself in the new world economy. Gonick concludes, therefore, not only that the structure of the Manitoba economy is fragile, but also that the largely defensive economic strategy traditionally adopted by NDP governments may no longer be adequate to Manitoba's needs.

The two-sided question of the extent of the weaknesses of Manitoba's economic and social fabric, and the ability of the NDP to address these weaknesses, is taken up in the chapters in the rest of the volume, particularly those by Silver, Loxley, Tudiver, Hull and Reinart.

Manitoba in the Agrarian Period: 1870-1940 1

Paul Phillips

Since that part of the North American central plains and Pre-Cambrian shield which now comprises Manitoba first came within the orbit of European capitalism in the second half of the seventeenth century, the region's political economy has undergone several transformations.

The first period, the fur trade era, lasted until the prairie region became an internal colony of central Canada, with Confederation, the first Riel Rebellion and the creation of Manitoba as a province in 1870. This period, for all its importance, will not be treated here, due to limitations of time and space. In any case, it is brilliantly recounted elsewhere.[1] But the legacy of the destruction of the fur/buffalo economy remains with us in the form of a marginalized Native population, the reserve system, and legal disputes over land claims and aboriginal rights.

The second period, which lasted until the end of the nineteenth century, can be defined as the age of primitive accumulation, analogous to enclosure in Britain and the "end of the commons." Capital, in the form of land, was expropriated from the Native population and converted into capitalist form; while the state's credit was used to create the Canadian Pacific Railway (CPR) and to accumulate capital in the period of railway construction. The period encompasses primarily the stagnation phase of the long economic wave in Canada (1873-96), though extending back to the design and implementation of Confederation.

The third period of economic development and change was the great wheat boom. It was a brief period in Manitoba's history, from approximately 1896 to 1912, but one which placed an indelible imprint on the province's political economy. In this expansionary phase of the long wave, the dominance of agriculture in the provincial political economy was strengthened, a dominance that was to prevail until well after World War II. Despite the prominence given to the increasing conflict between capital and labour during this and the subsequent period, it was the rising conflict between independent commodity producers (farmers) and commercial, industrial and financial capital, both local and national, that was the more fundamental. This conflict was for control of the economic surplus from agricultural production, and despite the eventual success the farmers achieved in eliminating the open market system of grain marketing and establishing a modicum of control over the trade, they remained at the mercy of world market forces. It was also in this period that Winnipeg reached its apogee as the regional metropolis in a dependent prairie economic region, before beginning its gentle decline, victim not only of these same world market forces but also of political and institutional changes in transportation and the grain marketing system.

The fourth period, during the stagnation phase of the long economic wave from 1912 to 1939, was one of regression and relative decline. The economic stimulation of World

War I proved both temporary and insubstantial. In an era marked by the rising hegemony of industrial monopoly capital, Manitoba's main characteristic was retrenchment of agriculture and of the commercial capital supported by it. The result, with the collapse of international trade and grain prices in the 1930s, was economic crisis and Winnipeg's metropolitan decline.

The Transition Period: Primitive Accumulation

In the late 1840s, the British government began the task of dismantling the regulations protecting its commercial empire, as mercantile imperialism gave way to industrial, free-trade imperialism. One casualty of the repeal of the Corn Laws, the timber duties and the Navigation Acts was the "commercial empire of the St. Lawrence," that economic foundation of the Montréal Tory elite that dominated the commercial economy of central Canada.[2] The first alternative strategy pursued by the central Canadian elite was integration into a continental economy: first, and most crudely, as expressed in the annexation movement; second, in the form of trade reciprocity, a strategy that proved relatively successful for a decade before being abrogated by an increasingly protectionist United States; and third, a strategy aimed at uniting the Atlantic economies of the Maritimes with the continental economies of central Canada to exploit the commercial potential of a new internal colony, the prairie agricultural region.[3]

This strategy was the National Policy, "collectively the group of policies . . . which were designed to transform the British North American territories of the mid-nineteenth century into a political and economic unit."[4] The legal framework of the National Policy was the British North America (BNA) Act and Confederation. Its three pillars were a transcontinental railway uniting the regions (and providing an unbroken British link with the Orient), a land and immigration policy opening the west to agricultural settlement, and a system of tariffs to protect the industrial interests of central Canada and, simultaneously, to protect the commercial and railway interests of central Canada by guaranteeing a western market.

This strategy did not augur well for indigenous interests in the fur trade and the supporting buffalo hunt. In the two or three decades prior to the region's absorption into Canada, its economic base lay in provisioning and providing transport for the fur trade, carried out primarily by French Métis centred on the Red River Colony. Friesen describes three measures of the transformation of the economy over this period:

> Perhaps the simplest index to the new order was the health of the buffalo hunt . . . .
> In the 1840s and 1850s, the Red River métis challenged Indian hegemony and probably became the most important processors of pemmican for the Hudson's Bay Company trade. By the 1860s, both Indians and métis were travelling farther and farther west in search of buffalo herds and were coming into conflict over this once seemingly infinite resource. By the end of the 1870s, the herds had disappeared forever. The Indians were on reserves, the métis in disarray, the whites in control.[5]

A second measure of the transformation was the creation of a capitalist labour market:

At the start of this era, most Indians hunted and travelled according to the rhythms of the seasons and the demands of the resource cycle. . . . Some Indians and many more métis participated to a limited degree in the wage labour system of the Hudson's Bay Company. . . . This labour system might be described as typical of a non-industrial society and, in its informal work discipline and rough measures of time, not far removed from that of the casual farm labourer or cottage artisan in seventeenth-century England. If this system was common in the 1840s, it was in retreat in the 1880s.[6]

A third measure was the transformation in attitudes to property. It marks the change from land as a *common* resource to that, with the arrival of European ideas and institutions, of exclusive private property:

> Henceforth, one could possess the land and the water, the animals and the plants; one could require that others not ''trespass'' or ''steal''; if ever land was to be in short supply, one could make rules to ensure that the first in the race — the shrewd and the competitive — would be rewarded.[7]

The political dimension of the transformation is best manifested in the transfer to the federal government of the Hudson's Bay Company's (HBC) charter rights to Rupert's Land. This removed a barrier to westward expansion, and provided extensive Crown land both for settlement and the financing of a western railway. The confrontation of the new property relations — represented by the arrival of land survey crews in 1869 — with the buffalo hunt culture precipitated the first Riel Rebellion. The rebellion did result in provincial status for the tiny ''postage stamp'' province of Manitoba, but this was to prove a short-lived reprieve for the dying political economy of a pre-industrial culture. As Friesen concludes:

> The métis had made their presence felt by means of the resistance and had defended their right to an equal start in the incoming order, but they could neither hold back the tide of newcomers nor guarantee the integrity of their community. Their ability to command political and economic power would determine how they fared in the new order.[8]

Unfortunately they commanded little power in the new order, leaving a legacy of marginalized indigenous and Métis peoples.

In the 1870s, following the annexation of the west to the new confederation, the pieces of the National Policy were put into place. In 1872 the Dominion Lands Act was passed, which provided a free quarter section of land for settlers plus preemption rights to the adjoining quarter section at a low, government-set price. It was ''a magnet to attract the immigrants necessary to produce wheat, the key staple of the economy for the next four decades.''[9] In 1880, agreement was finally reached on the contract and the level of public subsidy which permitted the construction of the CPR to begin. Finally, in the 1878 election, the Conservatives ran on their famous National Policy, a policy of comprehensive tariffs (implemented in 1879) designed to achieve multiple ends: revenue to support public and railway finance; protection for the nascent manufacturing industries of central Canada; and protection for the railway in terms of promoting an east-west flow of goods rather than the more geographically natural north-south flow. Indeed, the first shipment of grain from Manitoba to Britain in 1878 had followed the American route through St. Paul. As political economist Irene Spry noted:

> With the achievement of access by railroad to the markets of the world and a dependable all-year-round route across the open plains of the Palliser Triangle, where before only nomads could survive, the Canadian west was equipped for the inrush of settlers and surge of grain exports which came about when, in the mid-nineties, there was a favourable shift in the relationship of the price of grain and the cost of shipping it across the Atlantic.... After forty years of gradual preparation the country was ready for the great surge of economic growth of the first decades of the twentieth century.[10]

One reason for the delay between the establishment of the preconditions for expansion and the rapid growth that characterized the wheat boom was the great worldwide deflation and economic stagnation between 1873 and 1896. Federal immigration policy in this period, however, was important to the subsequent social and ethnic composition of Manitoba. Land reserves were offered to attract ethnic colonies: the Icelandic reserve on the west shore of Lake Winnipeg (1875-81), the East and West Mennonite reserves (1874), and the French-Canadian settlements for New England emigrants (beginning 1874). Other ethnic groups established informal settlements in Manitoba and the then North-West Territories during this period.[11]

The expropriation of the commons in western Canada was a precondition of this settlement. Much of the land granted to the Métis was acquired by purchase, theft or manipulation by speculators and land grabbers. This appropriation of land was a complex process. Métis residents on river lots were required to obtain clear (British) title, a process that necessitated land settlement and improvement. This was incompatible with participation in the buffalo hunt and as a result the majority of Métis claims were unsuccessful. Adult Métis were granted scrip, redeemable in cash or in title to dominion lands, but that pattern of dominion land settlement was alien to the Métis culture and economy and most of the scrip quickly became an article of speculation rather than a settlement claim. The children of the Métis were ostensibly guaranteed a reserve of 1.4 million acres but, with the connivance of the courts, most of this land passed into the hands of land speculators. The Métis were driven west to follow the diminishing buffalo herds or into marginalization.[12] Indian lands were, by and large, expropriated by treaty, but the bargaining power of Natives in these treaties was minimal. The plight of the Indian and the Métis involved in the buffalo hunt became increasingly desperate in the 1880s with the expansion of western settlements, the predations of American hide hunters, and American attempts to extinguish aboriginal opposition to the expansion of capitalist agriculture and settlement in the United States.

Were these processes leading to the marginalization of the aboriginal population deliberate on the part of the government? The answer is almost assuredly "yes," although perhaps not reflecting an explicit intent to discriminate against the aboriginal population as much as to extinguish its claim, which was incompatible with capitalist control of the western economy.

Facing starvation, Métis and Indian remnants made their last stand in the abortive second Riel Rebellion in 1885. Riel's execution in Regina later that year symbolized the extinction of the commons and of a political economy based on commercial fur-trade capital, pre-industrial work organization, and pre-capitalist land ownership.

Out of the ashes of the fur/buffalo economy of the Red River Colony rose the phoenix of Winnipeg as the commercial, financial and industrial metropolis of the prairie political economy; a consequence of the construction of the CPR through Winnipeg rather than the more suitable route through Selkirk.[13] With this construction in the early 1880s began a period of significant growth for Winnipeg and its environs, interrupted only briefly by the collapse of a speculative land boom in 1883.

In 1881 the population of the prairies was 119,000. A decade later it had more than doubled, to 251,000. The development of the infrastructure of railways and communities provided the impetus for Winnipeg's expansion — in building materials, clothing firms, packing plants, flour mills and, of course, the railway shops. Industrial workers in Winnipeg increased during the decade by almost 150 per cent, and the first unions appeared. The Knights of Labour were active in the mid-1880s and were instrumental in the 1886 formation of the first Winnipeg labour council; Smith reports their membership at between 1,500 and 2,000.[14] The number of international union locals in the prairie region, mainly locals of the railway brotherhood but also printers and building trades, rose to sixteen during the decade,[15] while a similar or slightly smaller number of local unions formed in and around Winnipeg, primarily among construction workers, teamsters and draymen, but with an occasional organization of service workers. However, expansion came to a halt in the depression of the early 1890s.

The Wheat Boom Period: 1896-1914

The depression of the early 1890s slowed the pace of western development, which was already considerably less than that anticipated a quarter century earlier by the Fathers of Confederation. Economic historians have debated the reasons for the sluggishness of western Canadian settlement and agricultural development in the last quarter of the nineteenth century without achieving consensus. A number of factors were undoubtedly relevant, the most important being the great deflation in raw material prices on world markets arising from secular stagnation of the major European economies. In addition, the drylands of the great American desert and its Canadian counterpart, the Palliser Triangle, resisted settlement until less arid lands were completely taken up, dryland technology was developed and grain prices had improved.

Expansion of the world money supply with new gold discoveries in the Yukon, and the evolution of a new social structure of accumulation (monopoly capital),[16] initiated an era of secular expansion around the capitalist world. In Canada it was marked by explosive growth in new raw material staples, the product of the forests, the mines, the seas and, on the prairies, the agricultural lands.

The subsequent expansion of the prairie grain economy was manifested in two major phenomena. The first was the construction of not one, but two additional transcontinental railway systems which also funnelled through Winnipeg. One of them, the Winnipeg-based Canadian Northern, represented the first major challenge by a regional capitalist elite to the hegemony of eastern capital.[17] The second phenomenon was the massive wave of immigration, including many eastern Europeans of peasant background, that flooded the region in the first decade of the new century. Population growth was phenomenal: immigration to Canada was 50 percent higher than natural increase in 1901-1911, the highest ratio in the history of Canada (see Table 1).

TABLE 1
POPULATION AND POPULATION GROWTH, 1891-1911
(Thousands)

	Region*	% Growth	Manitoba	% Growth	Winnipeg	% Growth
1891	251.5	—	152.5	—	25.6	—
1901	419.5	66.8	255.2	67.3	43.3	69.1
1911	1,328.1	216.6	461.4	80.8	90.2	108.3

*Note: Manitoba and North-West Territories in 1891 and 1901; Manitoba, Saskatchewan and Alberta in 1911.
Source: *Census of Canada, 1911*.

Winnipeg's strategic position was considerably enhanced by these developments. The National Policy tariffs increased the protection afforded Winnipeg by the Canadian Shield by greatly reducing the potential of competition in industrial and construction goods from American sources. Transport rate structures blatantly favoured Winnipeg wholesalers over those in other prairie centres: in 1890 Winnipeg received preferential rail rate reductions; in the 1898 "trader's tariff" the advantages were extended. In addition, by 1890 Winnipeg had persuaded the federal government to switch control of grain inspection and grading from Toronto to Winnipeg. With the creation of the Grain Exchange in 1887 and the convergence of three railways and attendant shops on the city, its dominance over the grain trade, and the supporting financial and commercial industries, was complete. One indicator of Winnipeg's metropolitan commercial status was its domination of wholesale trade, comprising well over one-half of the wholesale employment in the entire prairie region.[18]

Manitoba also enjoyed industrial supremacy. By 1910 Manitoba's share of prairie manufacturing approached 70 percent (see Table 2); Winnipeg alone contributed nearly 50 percent. Moreover, the predominance was broadly based, both in processing agricultural products for export, and in manufacturing for the regional market.

The social and class implications of this expansion were important:

> As the metropolis of the Prairies, Winnipeg was the main Western repository of entrepreneurial capacity, skilled and unskilled labour. . . . Because of its size and

strategic location, Winnipeg was the central clearing house for Western labour. Private employment agencies, located in shacks near the CPR station, received the demands for labour from farmers, railway contractors, building contractors, bush camp operations, and, through crude wall posters, obtained the required hands from the great throngs of immigrants newly arrived in the city and from men just arrived from jobs in the West, seeking employment during the coming season.[19]

In Winnipeg, the resultant division between capital and labour was manifested in the division between the poor north end with its immigrant working class, and the bourgeois, affluent south end. But not all the immigrants or the working class were non-English speaking. Many were skilled British artisans, mainly of English and Scottish origin, who were influenced by the emerging British labourism and socialism, and who manned the railway, metal and printing shops and dominated the skilled building and railway running trades. Outside the urban centres, where the unskilled workers toiled in the railway construction camps, the mining and lumber camps of the Canadian Shield, and the harvesting operations, the living and working conditions were "sheer hell."[20] The capitalist labour market provided no safety net:

> The employment system was a striking illustration of the capitalist labour market in action. The employer took no responsibility for the worker beyond the bounds of the job; when the contract ended, or when the worker was found wanting, employment ceased. When it rained, there was no pay. Not for these contractors the paternalism that accompanied long-term employment and loyal retainers.[21]

TABLE 2

MANITOBA'S SHARE OF PRAIRIE MANUFACTURING ACTIVITY, 1910
(Percentage of Total Prairie)

	Manitoba	Winnipeg
Employment	62.3	57.3
Value Added	65.7	51.0
Gross Value of Output	68.7	48.2

Source: Phillips, "Prairie Urban System: 1911-1961," in Alan Artibise, ed., *Town and City* (Regina: Canadian Plains Research Center, 1981), 13.

Tensions between capital and labour were exacerbated by several factors: periodic price increases, which reduced real incomes or kept them relatively stagnant, particularly in the second half of the first decade;[22] recurring unemployment, particularly in the 1907 financial depression and the general depression after 1912;[23] and the resolute opposition to trade unions by many employers. Still, the expansion of the wheat economy and Winnipeg's metropolitan status as gateway to the west had produced a significant industrial labour force:

> By the outbreak of the First World War there were 82 union locals in Winnipeg representing 10,000 members. This made Winnipeg the third largest centre of union activity in the country. The majority of union members were concentrated in three areas: construction, the railway running trades, and the metal trades. The Winnipeg work place had undergone a drastic transformation; in 1891 the average

manufacturer employed eight people, by 1911 he employed 60. It was the age of the skilled craftsman, and it was coming to an end.[24]

Of course, the working class/capital division, while important, was secondary to the primary division between the rural, agricultural population of independent commodity producers, and commercial and financial capitalists who controlled the grain trade and the sources of finance for prairie agriculture, including mortgages on land. This class conflict was rooted in the expropriation of surplus and rents that accrued to agricultural land by the railways, the grain trade, speculators and banks through the monopoly control of commercial and financial capital in the grain handling system and mortgage markets. As Fowke has noted, "joined with the grain trade were the milling interests and eastern consumers generally."[25] Hence the class element of conflict was early connected to a western regional grievance that has persisted.

The battleground shifted over time, increasingly focussing on the "open-market" system of the grain trade, epitomized by the commercial grain companies and their central institution, the Winnipeg Grain Exchange, which began futures trading in 1904. But the fundamental issue remained the imbalance in market power between the "competitive" farmers and the "monopoly" commercial, industrial and financial elements, collectively considered by the farmers to be "central Canadian business." Particular targets of agrarian discontent were the monopoly of the CPR (even after the introduction of controlled grain rates and the construction of the other two transcontinental railways), and the private "line elevator companies" which not only warehoused the grain but also bought and sold it in the terminal market, and who connived with the railways to monopolize the handling of grain:

> The persistent agrarian belief in the early decades of the present century was that inequality of bargaining power in grain markets, associated with monopoly of line elevators, lay at the root of injustice in the determination of these items [the weight of grain, dockage and shrinkage, grading and above all, price].[26]

Farmers responded to these abuses initially by exerting pressure through political agitation, utilizing the traditional party structures. The first tangible result was the appointment of a royal commission in 1899 "on the shipment and transportation of grain in Manitoba and the North-West Territories" which led to the passage of the Manitoba Grain Act of 1900. But dissatisfaction with its implementation and enforcement led to the formation of the Territorial Grain Growers' Association in 1901. Less than two years later the Manitoba Grain Growers' Association was formed. These were only the first in a series of farmer organizations designed to exert political pressure on federal and provincial governments for reform of the grain-handling system. In 1906 they joined to found the Grain Growers' Grain Company, a cooperative, alternative grain-handling organization, and in 1908 launched the *Grain Growers Guide*, which for decades was the influential voice of agrarian interests in western Canada.

The Manitoba Grain Act and the Canada Grain Act of 1912 led to federal regulation of grading and a requirement by the railways to provide for loading platforms where farmers could load grain independently of the elevator companies. Farmers also attempted to break the monopoly of the elevator companies (which had combined in the NorthWest Grain Dealers Association to regulate prices paid to farmers) by the establishment of farmer-owned elevators. However:

> Locally owned and managed farmers' elevators were no match for the monopolistic elements which increasingly dominated the Canadian grain trade over the turn of the century. The powerful grain companies represented substantial aggregations of capital directed into the various areas of the grain marketing business on the basis of both integration and combinations. The line elevator companies individually owned many country elevators, they were integrated in the field of terminal operations and the export business, and operated as commission agencies as well. The substantial chains of country elevators owned by the milling companies represented but one stage in the integrated operations of the wheat processing concerns. Much of the capital was American, and the Canadian organization in certain important areas represented foreign investment of a direct or "branch plant" nature. Trade association of the open price variety further restricted whatever competition might otherwise have survived among the few dominant groups in the grain trade. Neither locally owned farmers' elevators nor independent private elevators could operate effectively within such an environment.[27]

In Manitoba, farmers' organizations pressured the provincial government to counteract the monopoly power of the grain companies by establishing a publicly owned elevator system.[28] Facing an election in 1910, Conservative Premier Rodmond Roblin agreed, and a provincial elevator system was established for the 1910 crop. It lasted only two years before it was liquidated as a result of massive losses and debt. Its failure was due less to the power of the line elevator companies than to the incompetence of the province, which managed the system so as to discredit the demands for public ownership.[29]

More successful in the long run, at least in providing a farmer-owned alternative to the private grain trade, was the formation of a cooperative grain-marketing organization, the Grain Growers' Grain Company. It quickly joined the Winnipeg Grain Exchange but was almost immediately expelled because it practiced the cooperative principle of paying patronage dividends to its members. It was ultimately readmitted with the help of pressure from the provincial government, but only when it abandoned the patronage dividend principle and paid dividends on investment by its owner-members. Nevertheless, the company did grow and prosper and took over most of the viable elevators from the Manitoba government system in 1912. In 1917 it amalgamated with the Alberta Farmers' Co-operative Elevator Company to form the United Grain Growers.

However, open market (futures) trading, the Winnipeg Grain Exchange and the major private companies maintained primary control of the system despite the gains farmers had achieved in the regulation of transportation and grading, and in providing an alternative farmer-owned grain company. This was the situation on the eve of World War I.

Watershed: World War I

The World War I period proved traumatic for Manitoba. Most of the cards were already on the table before the war, but had yet to be played. Indeed, the war to some extent delayed the impact. The extensive period of settlement and railway construction was coming to a close. This was presaged by a depression after 1912.[30] Urban areas were much more affected than were the rural ones, since grain harvests and prices remained buoyant, and preplanned rail construction continued until the eve of the war. Winnipeg was most affected by the ending of the extensive settlement frontier, partly as a result of the economic consequences, and partly as a result of external developments and policy decisions.

The slowing of western growth reduced demand for the manufacturing, handling and retail trading in agricultural and construction materials, camp supplies, settlers' effects, and work clothing. This had a multiplier effect on commercial construction in Winnipeg. Between 1912 and 1914, building permits in Winnipeg declined by 40 percent,[31] and with the outbreak of war the collapse of construction was intensified. By 1915 building permits had dropped to less than 10 percent of their 1912 value. Winnipeg's population declined, retail sales dropped and, despite heavy army enlistments, unemployment soared. War demand had little influence on the Winnipeg economy until almost halfway through the conflict, partly because the lucrative armaments contracts were heavily concentrated in central and eastern Canada. Only when capacity there became strained did war contracts spill over into Winnipeg and the west. The westward spread of wartime economic activity was accompanied by a major threat to the welfare of the working class. The failure of federal economic policy with respect to the financing of the war led to rampant inflation after 1916. The fundamental problem was that the government was unwilling to tax business and the rich to pay for the war and resorted to inflationary financing.[32] Throughout the west, the inflation ate away at workers' incomes. This, combined with political repression (see Chapter 5), the refusal of employers to recognize or bargain with unions, and the institution of conscription, exacerbated class conflict. But it also contributed to intraclass conflict between western Canadian labour, conditioned by the economic structure and short industrial history of a resource hinterland, and central Canadian labour, conditioned by a diversified manufacturing structure and a longer history of craft-based work organization.

This latter conflict came to a head at the 1918 Trades and Labour Congress (TLC) convention in Québec when, defeated on many contentious issues on the convention floor, most western delegates, including those from Winnipeg, formed a separate caucus to press for the radical western agenda which included the demand for industrial rather than craft-based unionism. This caucus led directly, via the March 1919 Western Canadian Labour convention in Calgary, to the formation of the One Big Union (OBU), formally inaugurated in Winnipeg later in 1919. Before the OBU could be constituted, however, the Winnipeg General Strike broke out.

The fundamental issues of that great confrontation were economic and political — inflation, falling real wages, war profiteering, political repression, conscription — but the immediate issue that precipitated the strike was the refusal of employers in the metal and building trades to bargain collectively with union bargaining councils. This refusal, symptomatic of rising class conflict, prompted a class response. Approximately thirty thousand workers walked out in Winnipeg, only about one-half of them unionized. They were joined in sympathy by hundreds more in Brandon, as well as countless thousands in cities from Amherst, Nova Scotia, to Vancouver and Victoria in British Columbia. The Winnipeg General Strike was met with the combined repressive power of the employers and the state.[33] Strike leaders were arrested and, after almost six weeks, the strike collapsed in defeat. Two days later the Brandon sympathy strike ended.

The consensus of most students of the Winnipeg General Strike is that the repressive actions of the employers and the state were aimed more at the OBU in particular, and at radical unionism in general, than at the orthodox and relatively conservative craft unions. Initially, the employers' strategy had little success. The OBU consolidated and grew, but now it faced the combined opposition, not only of employers, government and the press, but also of the TLC and the international unions which opposed the OBU's radical and industrial policies. Ultimately, as Smith notes, "what the fratricidal war between the OBU and the TLC could not destroy, the high unemployment of the twenties did."[34] Indeed, the sharp postwar depression which began in 1920 started the precipitous decline of the OBU in Winnipeg and throughout the west, though its one remaining centre of strength for almost four decades lay with the Winnipeg Street Railway employees. But the postwar depression marked the beginning of a new and generally dismal period in Manitoba's political economy.

Wartime economic conditions had a very different impact on Manitoba agriculture. If the role of the working class was to supply cannon fodder and cannon shells to the war effort, the role of the agrarian class was to supply food, and wheat in particular.[35] The result was that "the price of wheat (basis Fort William) rose from ninety five cents per bushel in May 1914 to $1.65 per bushel in May 1915, to $2.21 in 1917 and to $2.24 in 1918."[36] Though poor growing conditions reduced quantities after 1915, this was more than offset by high prices. This situation encouraged renewed agricultural expansion, investment and the expansion of debt. Indeed, pressure on grain supplies, rising prices and faulty speculation on grain futures forced the government to establish the first Canadian Wheat Board in 1917, when futures trading was suspended on the grain exchange and a buying pool was established. The Canadian Wheat Board became the exclusive purchaser of wheat, though handling was conducted by the established companies. Returns from sales by the wheat board were pooled and distributed to farmers on the basis of deliveries.

Prices continued to rise after the war due to the devastation of European supplies. The government's move to abolish the board in 1919 had to be aborted as prices continued to climb, eventually reaching $2.85 a bushel in 1920. But the government eventually prevailed and, after handling the 1916-19 crops, the board was abolished despite strong opposition from the farmers of western Canada. Ideology had triumphed over practicality and efficiency. Within months, wheat prices began a precipitous decline, from the peak of $2.85 before the 1920 harvest to $0.81 a bushel in 1921. As with the defeat of the Winnipeg General Strike in 1919 and of the OBU in the subsequent depression, the destruction of the wheat board and the collapse in wheat prices in the depression ushered in a new era for Manitoba's independent commodity producers.

Winnipeg's position as commercial and transportation metropolis for the prairie region was also changing. In 1914 the Panama Canal was completed, enabling Vancouver to compete for grain exports and merchandise imports into the region when ocean freight rates declined sharply after the war.[37] This situation was compounded by changes in the railway regulatory structure, which began in 1907 and continued until after the war, and eliminated freight rates that discriminated in favour of Winnipeg as a wholesale and distribution centre.[38] Even without these changes, Winnipeg's dominance was being eroded. As Bellan observed:

> As early as 1914, the small village store was losing ground, as rural merchandising came to be concentrated to an increasing extent in larger centres which, incidentally, were better able to withstand mail order competition. Bigger retailers, however, tended to purchase their supplies directly from manufacturers and importers, in contrast to the smaller stores which purchased primarily from wholesalers ... Winnipeg wholesalers, heavily dependent for their custom upon small retail stores which purchased too little to justify direct dealing with manufacturers or importers, suffered the repercussions of developments which weakened the economic basis of such stores.[39]

Additionally, the war precipitated an economic crisis in Canada's second and third transcontinental railways, the Grand Trunk and the Canadian Northern, which resulted in their nationalization and consolidation as the Canadian National Railway (CNR) with headquarters and control in Toronto, not Winnipeg.[40]

The Interwar Years

The interwar period in Manitoba's history, from the 1920 depression to the renewal of military hostilities in Europe in 1939, can best be described as dismal, with only a limited, brief respite of relative economic buoyancy in the late 1920s. The regional political economy was characterized by several trends: stagnation of, and factional feuding between, the province's working-class economic organizations (though this was offset to some degree by an uncertain advance in political organization); the increasing emergence of right-wing populism with a regional, not class, consciousness as the dominant ideology of the agrarian movement; a consequent decline in the identification of common interest between the working class and the farmers; and the decline of Winnipeg as the regional metropolis in response to the economic malaise of the wheat economy, regulatory changes and the dispersal of commercial functions around the region.

The 1920s

The alliance of employers, state and the TLC combined with the postwar depression to defeat the OBU:

For all intents and purposes the OBU was dead by 1922. While many workers continued to show support for its ideas by electing OBU supporters to political office, the union had been crushed in its infancy by a coalition it had not yet had the power to confront.[41]

But the OBU was not the only loser. By helping to destroy their more radical challengers, the craft unions weakened their own legitimacy and left themselves vulnerable to employer attacks, particularly given the depressed labour market and the institutional and technological changes that weakened the strategic position of the skilled worker. The virtual collapse of Winnipeg's construction industry after the war particularly threated the construction unions. Union membership fell dramatically, by over 50 percent from 1920 to 1923, while employer assaults on wage levels, hours of work limitations and union recognition intensified. Union fortunes revived somewhat in the short-lived recovery from 1926 to 1929, as membership climbed back to immediate postwar levels. However, comparable advances in collective bargaining were not achieved.

One industrial sector that did expand significantly during the 1920s, and again during the depressed 1930s, was the garment industry, in part stimulated by the abundance of suitable, low-cost manufacturing space made available by the decline in Winnipeg's wholesaling and warehousing function.[42] With this expansion, the garment unions began aggressive organizing that flared sporadically in the 1920s and 1930s.

On the political front the working class had considerably more success, at least initially. In the 1920 provincial election, labour elected eleven members, including three of the gaoled strike leaders. The following year, J.S. Woodsworth, also associated with the strike, was elected to the federal Parliament from working-class Winnipeg. Municipally, labour elected seven Winnipeg aldermen in 1919, though its candidate for mayor, S.J. Farmer, was defeated. Three years later, in 1922, Farmer did become mayor of Winnipeg, a post he held for two years. Though without majority labour support in the city council, Farmer was able to achieve the establishment of a municipally owned power utility for the city. In Brandon, three Independent Labour Party (ILP) aldermen were also elected in the immediate postwar period.

This initial success, however, could not be maintained. One reason was the mobilization of antisocialist, antilabour coalitions of the "old-line parties" at the municipal level. The second was the rise of populist, farmer-dominated parties which, though initially sympathetic to labour's reform stance, became increasingly conservative and antilabour regarding social change, or became absorbed into the old-line parties. A third factor was the establishment, in 1921, of the Canadian Communist Party, which institutionalized internal division between the "soft" (social democratic) and "hard" Left.

The trials and tribulations of the urban working class in the first half of the 1920s had parallels among the farmers. The collapse of grain prices after the abolition of the wheat board in 1920, particularly given the heavy debt structure of western agriculture, brought an urgent demand for the restoration of the board and its pooling system for marketing grain:

> There was no longer any possibility of harmony between the views underlying agrarian protest and those of any substantial section of federal leadership. The conviction of the western wheat grower that the Winnipeg Grain Exchange ought to be abolished because of inherent unsoundness was, even on the surface, a radical conviction. Far down it rested upon a belief — diametrically opposed to the free enterprise tenets underlying the national policy — that the open market or competitive system, the system of freely moving prices, ought not to govern the marketing of western grain. . . . It was not, however, a question of abolishing the Exchange and leaving the grain trade otherwise intact. The proposal was that the free enterprise grain trade should be removed, and replaced by a governmental agency with power to control prices. The western wheat farmer reasoned that there was serious inadequacy in national policies which assured the subsidization of transportation interests by land and money grants and security guarantees, provided for the protection of industry by tariff walls, permitted to economic interests generally the greatest possible freedom in their efforts to avoid the hazards of competition by combination and agreement, and, at the same time, left the agricultural producer exposed to the full rigours of competition both nationally and internationally.[43]

The failure of the western agrarian movement to convince the federal government to reestablish the Canadian Wheat Board led the farmers to initiate a campaign to establish cooperative, preferably compulsory, pooling.[44] In 1924 the Manitoba Pool was established (the same year as Saskatchewan and one year after Alberta), and together with the other prairie pools set up a central selling agency and expanded into elevator operations. By the end of the decade the pools handled approximately one-half of the prairie wheat crop.

The success of the pools in capturing some of the economic surplus, the recovery of wheat prices after 1925, the legislative entrenchment of the Crowsnest Pass freight rates on grain, and the generally prosperous cattle industry stimulated the further filling in of settlement, branch line construction, renewed homesteading and the resumption of construction on the Hudson Bay Railway. The political power of the agrarian movement also peaked. In Manitoba the United Farmers had captured office in 1922. For two decades, under the unimaginative, conservative and generally antilabour leadership of Premier John Bracken, the farmers' party held power. Federally, the agrarian-dominated Progressives elected sixty-five members nationally in 1921, becoming the second-largest party in the House of Commons. Although they never acted cohesively as a party and rapidly declined in popularity in subsequent elections, the Progressives retained the balance of power in Parliament in 1926, giving them more influence in achieving western farm interests than their declining electoral support might otherwise have warranted.[45]

How can we reconcile the apparently radical, antimarket demands of the farmers' movement with respect to grain marketing with the increasingly right-wing, antilabour stance which led it, in the late 1920s, along "responsible, cautious, even conservative" paths?[46] Certainly economic recovery and a measure of apparent political power was a contributing factor. So too was the farmers' response to the Russian Revolution and the subsequent "Red scare" campaign, which identified radical reform with the confiscation of farmers' land. Perhaps most important was the ambiguous position of independent commodity producers in a capitalist economy and a consequent ideological mystique, "a Physiocratic conviction that the productivity of the farmer has been the basis of all other (essentially parasitic) wealth . . . " which led to the development of hostility towards labour as the farm movement became more consolidated and successful.[47] In any case, the demand for abolition of the open-market system was not radical in the eyes of most farmers, but merely an elimination of parasitic middlemen and an equalization of economic power within the capitalist system. This did not compare with the labour radicalism that challenged the capitalist system itself.

Winnipeg's decline as a commercial,transportation and financial metropolis was attributable to a number of forces. The first, obviously, was the slowing rate of expansion of the agricultural frontier. The 1920s were a period of filling in, rather than expanding into new regions. This greatly undermined Winnipeg's function as supplier and wholesaler of construction materials and settlers' effects, and as the regional pool for unskilled construction labour. This latter effect was exacerbated by the move to mechanization on farms and the adoption of farm machinery propelled by the internal combustion engine, which reduced the demand for seasonal unskilled labour. Consequently, the regional urban economy tended to stagnate.[48]

Second, the opening of the Panama Canal, the increased density of population and hence of demand in the western Prairies, the evolving urban structure in Saskatchewan and Alberta which created competitive wholesale systems, and the ending of the railway rate regulations that favoured Winnipeg all encouraged the emergence of Vancouver as an alternate commercial gateway to the west. In addition, the CPR built alternative yards and workshops in Calgary in 1912.

Third, the rise of the wheat pools reduced the control of the grain trade by Winnipeg's commercial and financial elite. To some extent, therefore, the surplus expropriated through the monopoly power of the grain trade was redistributed back to the farmers themselves, thereby lessening the tendency towards uneven rural and urban development.[49]

This is not to say that capital in Winnipeg suffered a significant retrenchment in the period. The high level of agrarian indebtedness, some contracted in the buoyant economic conditions of the late war period, shifted the locus of economic control from commercial to financial capital. At the same time, however, there was a tendency for control to pass from regional to central Canadian interests, as with the 1925 takeover of the Winnipeg-based Union Bank by the Montréal-based Royal Bank. This contributed to a regional grievance which was strengthened by changing marketing practices and the resurgence of protectionism in the disorganized markets of Europe and North America in the wake of the international trade and financial dislocations caused by the war and the punitive provisions of the peace. This sense of regional grievance against the National Policy tariff structure was summed up in the farmers' protest slogan against ''buying on a protected market and selling on a competitive market.''

The late 1920s also saw the emergence of a new kind of economic frontier in the Canadian Shield area of northern Manitoba and Ontario: mineral exploration and development, particularly at Flin Flon (copper, zinc, and gold), Bissett (gold), and Red Lake, Ontario (gold); and of hydroelectric development in the Whiteshell region. This encouraged the emergence of new, service-type industries based in Winnipeg, such as Richardson's Western Canada Airways founded in 1926, as well as new markets for industrial goods. Further technological change and the rise of new consumer goods industries led to expansion of small, new manufacturing industries in Winnipeg in addition to the garment industry.

Nevertheless, in relative terms Winnipeg stagnated. Employment in the city in the second half of the 1920s lagged well behind the rate of regional employment growth, as did bank clearings, construction and population growth. Still, it was prosperity compared with what was to come.

The 1930s

The onset of the Depression is popularly associated with the collapse of the New York stock market. But the crash was a symptom, not a cause. For western Canada, the Depression is better symbolized by the collapse of agricultural prices, which was a major cause and which preceded the stock market crash. In the popular conception, as well, the Depression in the prairie region is closely associated with the drought. This is doubly unfortunate. The drought was never general, either in all years or in all places. Manitoba, for instance, never suffered the same devastation as Saskatchewan and Alberta. In fact, for the whole of Canada from 1929 to 1933, agricultural production remained relatively constant while prices fell by one-half.[50] However, in the prairie region average crops in the worst years of the drought, between 1933 and 1937, averaged only two-thirds of what they had been in the 1920s.[51]

Second, the identification of the Depression with drought disguises the fact that the economic suffering of the Depression was not primarily a natural phenomenon but rather was the result of human agency, indeed of the capitalist economic system, though certainly made worse by natural calamity.

Agriculture and its marketing institutions were profoundly rocked by the crisis. As grain prices fell the prairie pools, which had paid a high initial price of $1.00 a bushel for their members' crop, saw the difference between this price and the selling price increase, and they became insolvent. The government was forced to step into guarantee the financial viability of the pools and of the banks that had advanced them money. Though virtual government management of the trade and the Central Selling Agency was not intended to replace the open-market (or futures) system, but only to sterilize the market by orderly selling of the pools' stocks, political events intervened. Pressure from the prairie provinces and the farmers' organizations, and the prospect of an upcoming federal election, led the Conservative Prime Minister R.B. Bennett to establish the second Canadian Wheat Board in the autumn of 1935, just before the defeat of his inept and arrogant government by the Liberals.

The new Wheat Board did not initially involve the abolition of futures trading despite repeated demands by farm organizations to do so:

> Whatever preference the growers had for a wheat board over a voluntary co-operative — and the preference varied from time to time — the one insistent element in the western viewpoint after 1920 was the belief that the open market or speculative system was detrimental to the producers and therefore could not be tolerated. A national board with a monopoly of the wheat market meant the entire removal of the futures market and for that reason if for no other had much to commend it.[52]

In fact, however, the Board's main function was to guarantee a minimum price for wheat by setting an initial price. If the world price fell below that level, the Wheat Board would handle most of the crop and the government would, in effect, subsidize the price by absorbing the deficit. If, however, the world price was higher, the private trade and the futures market would prevail. Indeed, the federal Liberals were no more supportive of government involvement in the grain trade or of subsidies to prairie agriculture than were the Conservatives, and in 1938 moved to abolish the Board. But western protest, in part engineered by Manitoba's Premier Bracken, led the Liberals to recant.[53] Politically, in the face of western (regional) and agrarian (class) pressures, the government proved unable to get out of the grain-selling business. However, as with the first Wheat Board, it was only the exigencies of war that prompted the government in 1943 to make the Wheat Board the *monopoly* agency for deliveries of wheat, completely eliminating the futures market and the grain exchange in the buying and selling of wheat.

Thus government action, reluctant though it was, saved the wheat pools and increasingly usurped control of the grain trade from private capital, in the process significantly reducing the expropriative power of commercial capital. Also, by the late 1930s, Manitoba agriculture had shown a considerable measure of recovery. Prices had improved somewhat, Manitoba had escaped the drought of 1937, cattle prices had improved, access to the American market had been eased by a Canadian-American tariff agreement, and government agricultural stabilization and public works programs had aided the wheat economy.[54]

These improving conditions helped sustain Premier Bracken's ostensibly non-partisan coalition of Manitoba's elite, residing in south Winnipeg, and the conservative (and heavily British) farmer class of southwestern Manitoba, despite the fact that his party was no longer officially a United Farmers' Party. In maintaining this political hegemony, Bracken was also aided by his skillful exploitation of regional grievances against restrictive federal monetary policies and the tariffs favoured by central Canadian capital.[55]

Among the working class, in Winnipeg and in the northern resource frontier, the Depression was hard and long. The agricultural collapse reverberated through the urban economy, resulting in declining demand for manufacturing, wholesale and retail services, transportation and construction. In Winnipeg, for example, the value of building permits declined by 80 percent between 1931 and 1933.[56] In addition, the decline in demand for agricultural labour flooded the Winnipeg labour market with further unemployed despite increasingly restrictive immigration policies. At the same time, the punitive protectionism of the American Smoot-Hawley tariffs, plus the industrial slowdown, decreased demand for mine and forest products, thus throwing more unemployed on the market. At the height of the Depression the rate of unemployment in Winnipeg reached approximately 25 percent. As a result, while in the depression of the early 1920s, 5 percent of Winnipeg's population had been on relief, in the 1930s this percentage rose to about three times that level — some thirty to forty thousand people annually. And despite the slow recovery in the second half of the Depression, there was little decline in these numbers.

In the absence of any coherent national or provincial unemployment or relief program, responsibility for the unemployed fell on municipal governments that did not have the fiscal base to provide adequate levels of support. Even when labour and a lone Communist controlled a majority of Winnipeg's city council in 1935, there was little they could do to ease the severity of the crisis, particularly when they faced the organized opposition of the middle and upper classes.[57]

Given the level of unemployment, most unions became moribund, particularly those associated with the craft union congress, the TLC. Only the unions affiliated with the Communist central organization, the Workers Unity League (WUL), showed any measure of aggressiveness, particularly among the miners in the newly developed Flin Flon mine, where the company's policy of hiring farmers and immigrants could not prevent the emergence of a Communist-led union, and in Winnipeg's garment industry where, between 1929 and 1935, there were twenty-two strikes, most Communist-led.[58] The provincial and civic governments (except during labour's brief control of the Winnipeg council) were acutely hostile to unionism in general, and Communist-led unions in particular, leading to frequent state involvement in defeating strikes. Nowhere was this more evident than in the 1934 Flin Flon mine strike, when Bracken ordered the arrest of the strike leaders and brought in the Royal Canadian Mounted Police (RCMP) to assist in breaking the strike and the union.[59]

Public employees and teachers were also the targets of repressive state action, particularly in the form of wage cuts. Worst affected were Winnipeg's female teachers, whose salaries were cut dramatically in 1933 on the grounds that, being women, they did not have dependents to support.[60] Only with the outbreak of war were pay packets brought back to 1931 levels.

In 1935, as a result of a change in policy in Moscow, the WUL was dissolved and its members instructed to rejoin the TLC unions. One result was the emergence of the International Ladies Garment Workers Union (ILGWU). The leading union in the needle trades, it was under the control of Sam Herbst whose highly unorthodox organizing methods, involving collaboration with the employers and opposition to strikes, brought a measure of cooperation from employers in obtaining collective, albeit, critics would maintain, inferior, agreements.[61]

There was also substantial organizing action among the unemployed during the Depression. The burden of relief for the jobless was too heavy for the municipalities and the province to bear, forcing the federal government to establish work camps for the single unemployed in 1932. It was among the relief camp workers that the WUL had its greatest success in organizing. However isolation and military control of the camps limited industrial action. Nevertheless, discontent with unemployment and with camps, fanned by radical agitation, led to the On-to-Ottawa Trek of the unemployed in 1935. Beginning in Vancouver, thousands of trekkers boarded CPR and CNR freights and, picking up recruits on the way, headed for Ottawa, only to be stopped in Regina on the orders of the federal government. After a fruitless meeting of the trek leaders with the arrogant and uncompromising Prime Minister Bennett in Ottawa, police raided a trekker rally in Regina, causing a riot that killed one policeman and injured hundreds of other people. But the trek was stopped and the men were shipped back to the camps.

Approximately one thousand unemployed Manitobans waiting in Winnipeg (supported by a city council controlled by the ILP members and the lone Communist) thus never got the opportunity to join the trek, particularly after Premier Bracken refused to allow the men to leave Manitoba for Ottawa by truck or bus. Despite the immediate failure of the trek, however, it was a factor in the crushing defeat of the Bennett government and in the subsequent reform of the work camps by the Liberals. As well, the radicalizing influence of the camps and the WUL leadership contributed to electoral support, primarily in Winnipeg, for the ILP, the Co-operative Commonwealth Federation (CCF), and for the Communist Party which elected its first provincial member in 1936. And when war rescued the economy from its continuing doldrums, membership increased in the young industrial unions, which consolidated around a new, central labour organization, the Canadian Congress of Labour (CCL).

It was not all bad news for the provincial economy, particularly in Winnipeg in the late 1930s. The garment industry grew rapidly and, notwithstanding the fall in manufacturing employment, the number of small local manufacturers of all types increased. And although Winnipeg's control of grain exports was further eroded by Vancouver's increased importance as a grain port, its metropolitan status was reinforced by the establishment in the city of the headquarters of the new, government-owned Trans-Canada Airlines in 1937.

Conclusion

Though it is tempting to see in the more spectacular confrontation of labour and capital, and of socialist and conservative politics, a classic case of class conflict in an industrial society, one must rather recognize that the dominant political economy in the period from 1870 to 1940 was agrarian, not industrial. Further, though the class conflict between labour and industrial capital was perhaps most visible, the conflict between independent commodity producers (farmers) and commercial, industrial and financial capital with its regional dimension was most fundamental to the province's political economy. It is this that delineates the period.[62]

By the outbreak of World War II, the structure of the Manitoba economy was little different from what it was a half-century earlier. True, the metropolitan domination of Winnipeg in the grain economy had declined somewhat. True also, the farmer's movement had succeeded in eliminating the open-market system of grain marketing and in obtaining a modicum of control over grain handling through the pools and government regulation. But farmers remained at the mercy of competitive international grain markets, the protected home market, and the monopolized transportation and financial systems. Nevertheless, the economic havoc created in the province by the collapse of agricultural prices in the Depression is a testimonial to the primacy of agriculture in Manitoba prior to World War II.

NOTES

The author wishes to acknowledge his gratitude to Gerald Friesen and Irene Spry for their critical reading and helpful suggestions on an earlier draft of this chapter.

1. Gerald Friesen, *The Canadian Prairies: A History* (Toronto: University of Toronto Press, 1984), chapters 2-6.

2. Donald Creighton, *The Empire of the St. Lawrence* (Toronto: Macmillan, 1935).

3. To serve imperial interests, it was also intended to create a continuous "red line" of unimpeded commerce from Britain to the Orient.

4. V.C. Fowke, "The National Policy — Old and New," in W.T. Easterbrook and M.H. Atkins, eds., *Approaches to Canadian Economic History* (Toronto: McClelland and Stewart, 1967), 242.

5. Friesen, *The Canadian Prairies*, 92.

6. Ibid.

7. Ibid.

8. Ibid.

9. W.T. Easterbrook and H.G.J. Aitken, *Canadian Economic History* (Toronto: Macmillan, 1956), 390.

10. Irene Spry, "The Transition from a Nomadic to a Settled Economy in Western Canada, 1856-96," *Transactions of the Royal Society of Canada* 6, series 4 (June 1968): 201.

11. Friesen, *The Canadian Prairies*, 186.

12. Ibid., 197-201. By "marginalization" we mean the relegation of the Native population to a peripheral role in the dominant society, destined to participate only "on the margin" of the political economy.

13. Ruben Bellan, *Winnipeg's First Century: An Economic History* (Winnipeg: Queenston House, 1978), 19-23. He concludes that "Winnipeg's economic and political strength had proven superior to Selkirk's natural advantages." This was the result of the astute bribery of the CPR with public money by Winnipeg's land-owning city councillors.

14. Doug Smith, *Let Us Rise: An Illustrated History of the Manitoba Labour Movement* (Vancouver: New Star, 1984), 16.

15. Eugene Forsey, *Trade Unions in Canada: 1812-1902* (Toronto: University of Toronto Press, 1982), 502.

16. David Gordon, Richard Edwards and Michael Reich, *Segmented Work, Divided Workers* (Cambridge: Cambridge University Press, 1982), 9. They define social structure of

accumulation as "the specific institutional environment within which the capitalist accumulation process is organized."

17. T.D. Regehr, "The Canadian Northern Railway: The West's Own Product," *Canadian Historical Review* 51, no. 2 (1970).

18. Paul Phillips, "The Prairie Urban System: 1911-1961," in Alan Artibise, ed., *Town and City* (Regina: Canadian Plains Research Center, 1981), 20 ff. Winnipeg's share was still one-half as late as 1931, well after the city's dominance of the region was in decline.

19. Bellan, *Winnipeg's First Century*, 77-78.

20. Friesen, *The Canadian Prairies*, 294.

21. Ibid., 293.

22. Harry Sutcliffe, "The Economic Background of the Winnipeg General Strike: Wages and Working Conditions" (Master's thesis, University of Manitoba, 1972).

23. Bellan, *Winnipeg's First Century*, 125.

24. Smith, *Let Us Rise*, 32.

25. V.C. Fowke, *Canadian Agricultural Policy* (1946; reprint, Toronto: University of Toronto Press, 1978), 247.

26. V.C. Fowke, *The National Policy and the Wheat Economy* (1957; reprint, Toronto: University of Toronto Press, 1973), 110.

27. Ibid., 135-36.

28. There was a parallel antimonopoly campaign among farmers and labour for public ownership of the telephone and electrical utilities, a movement that led to the formation of the Manitoba Telephone System and, ultimately, the Winnipeg and Manitoba Hydro Companies.

29. Fowke, *The National Policy and the Wheat Economy*, 142-43.

30. Bellan, *Winnipeg's First Century*, chapter 8.

31. Ibid., 125-27.

32. R.T. Naylor, "The Canadian State, the Accumulation of Capital, and the Great War," *Journal of Canadian Studies* 16, nos. 3 and 4 (Autumn-Winter 1981).

33. Details of the strike and its repression are too well reported elsewhere to require repetition here. For an extended bibliography see Craig Heron and Greg Kealey, "Labour Conflict and Working-Class Organization," in Daniel Drache and Wallace Clement, eds., *The New Practical Guide to Canadian Political Economy* (Toronto: Lorimer, 1985), 62-70.

34. Smith, *Let Us Rise*, 59.

35. See Fowke, *The National Policy and the Wheat Economy*, 164-65.

36. Bellan, *Winnipeg's First Century*, 131.

37. Ibid., 154.

38. Ibid., 110-13, 154-55.

39. Ibid., 109-10.

40. Ibid., 137.

41. Smith, *Let Us Rise*, 59.

42. Ibid, 61; Bellan, *Winnipeg's First Century*, 175.

43. Fowke, *The National Policy and the Wheat Economy*, 191-92.

44. Friesen, *The Canadian Prairies*, 336-37.

45. Ibid., 367, 374; Bellan, *Winnipeg's First Century*, 163.

46. Friesen, *The Canadian Prairies*, 373.

47. H.C. Pentland, *A Study of the Changing Social, Economic and Political Background of the Canadian System of Industrial Relations* (Ottawa: Task Force on Labour Relations, 1968), 23.

48. Derek Hum and Paul Phillips, "Growth, Trade and Urban Development of Staple Regions," *Urban History Review* (October 1981).

49. Paul Phillips, "Staples, Surpluses and Exchange," in Duncan Cameron, ed., *Explorations in Canadian Economic History: Essays in Honour of Irene M. Spry* (Ottawa: University of Ottawa Press, 1985), 39.

50. Fowke, *The National Policy and the Wheat Economy*, 101.

51. Friesen, *The Canadian Prairies*, 387.

52. Fowke, *The National Policy and the Wheat Economy*, 263.

53. Ibid., 270 ff.

54. Bellan, *Winnipeg's First Century*, 213-14.

55. Friesen, *The Canadian Prairies*, 401-3.

56. Bellan, *Winnipeg's First Century*, 203.

57. Smith, *Let Us Rise*, 85.

58. Ibid., 83.

59. Ibid., 81-82.

60. Ibid., 84-85.

61. Ibid., 82-83.

62. As Cy Gonick has pointed out, this feature of Manitoba's political economy did not really change with the war but rather awaited the modernization of the Manitoba economy in the 1960s.

The Manitoba Economy Since World War II 2

Cy Gonick

This chapter describes the structure and dynamics of Manitoba's political economy since World War II. It is divided into two sections. The first describes the economic strategies of successive postwar governments, and their implications. The argument developed is that differing provincial government policies — which have been in large part a function of Manitoba's changing class structure — have been able to modify, but not to reverse, the long-term decline of Manitoba's economy relative to Canada as a whole. The second section describes the current structure of Manitoba's economy, emphasizing those emergent features which make it fragile, and thus particularly susceptible to further erosion in the face of the global restructuring of capital and the FTA with the United States.

Provincial policy is an important factor in economic performance. But it is only one factor, and in small jurisdictions like Manitoba its impact is modest. Certainly no Manitoba government could ever subjugate market forces. Government policy can be entirely passive, as during the Campbell regime (1949-58). But it need not be so, as the governments of Duff Roblin (1958-67), Edward Schreyer (1969-77) and Howard Pawley (1982-88) exemplify. Within limits, it can bend and shape market forces and modify their effects.

To illustrate, the government of Howard Pawley could have done nothing to lessen the impact of the global crisis on Manitoba's economy. But because of its social democratic commitments, it designed its fiscal regime and capital spending strategies to protect social services and minimize unemployment. Public sector investment was largely responsible for holding up the provincial economy through the mid to late 1980s. These policies, together with the diversified character of the provincial economy, gave Manitoba the lowest unemployment and highest job creation rates in the country; and Manitobans were spared the Draconian cuts in social services experienced in neighbouring western provinces. But by the time the Pawley government was forced from office, these expansive forces had been all but depleted. Having established no alternative economic strategy, the province's economy was bound to deteriorate, and its ability to protect social services to dissipate.

So while surface statistics indicate Manitoba's superior performance through the 1980s, a closer look reveals a fragile economy (see also Chapters 11 and 12). Beyond the cyclical depression, global and national restructuring have affected all sectors — service as well as goods producing — and all locations — rural, urban and northern. Agriculture remains in secular decline, with farm closures causing a continuous drop in the number of farms; important mines have closed with more likely to follow, while technological change has drastically reduced the size of the work force required in the mines that remain in operation; manufacturing has seen major closures and scaling down in important traditional industries like meat packing, agricultural implements and metal fabrication; financial and distribution services continue their long-term decline with a spate of recent head-office departures — Hudson's Bay Company, parts of Richardson- Greenshields, Great West Life, Monarch Life and Citadel Life. Shrinkage of such industries inevitably forces a reduction in auxiliary service businesses and employment.

In sum, while Manitoba has benefited from the diversity of its economy, it is doubtful that future growth can be sustained by its resource endowments and its existing manufacturing, financial and service base. Massive global restructuring and the FTA threaten Manitoba's economic viability. Whether Manitoba can develop a niche in the global economy of the future is not certain. In the absence of any alternative program, failure would mean that in the twenty-first century provinces like Manitoba and Saskatchewan will await the twentieth-century fate of Atlantic Canada.

Party, Policy and Economy

Manitoba has been in relative decline for the past seventy years. At the height of its importance during the wheat boom, Manitoba accounted for 9 to 10 percent of all income earned in Canada. By 1926, when official statistics first became available, Manitoba's total income had already fallen to 7.3 percent of the national total.[1] By 1945 it had fallen to 6.1 percent, and by the time Douglas Campbell left office in 1958, Manitoba could claim only 5.1 percent of national income.

The Progressive Conservatives under Duff Roblin adopted an approach advocating more state intervention, but succeeded only in slightly slowing the rate of decline, so that by 1969 Manitoba's share of national income had fallen to 4.4 percent. Edward Schreyer nearly managed to halt the decline. Manitoba outperformed the national economy until 1975, but by the time of Schreyer's defeat in 1977, the province had slipped to 4.1 percent of national income. With the worst record in Canada under the one-term Progressive Conservative government of Sterling Lyon, by 1982 the figure had slipped further, to 3.9 percent. Howard Pawley's government finally halted the decline. When Pawley left office in 1988, Manitoba's share of national income was still 3.9 percent. This result is indicative of his government's superior performance in protecting provincial incomes from the global economic crisis. Whether it indicates that Manitoba is now in a position to enjoy a growing or even stable share of national income in the global economy of the future is more doubtful.

The Campbell Era, 1949-1958

In 1949 Manitobans elected a Liberal-Progressive government headed by Douglas Campbell. Campbell had represented the rural constituency of Lakeside since 1922, and his government was another in a long line of rural-based, conservative coalitions headed by Premiers Bracken and Garson. Campbell's ultracautious, pay-as-you-go economic philosophy reflected the still rural orientation of the province.

Farmers were seen to require little more from the provincial government than rural electrification, improved roads and low taxes, and this was to be Campbell's legacy to the province. When he left office in 1958, Manitoba had the lowest per capita tax rate in Canada and the lowest per capita public expenditures.[2]

The Campbell government's fiscal regime reflected two dominant rural characteristics: self-reliance and uncertainty. Functioning in a world commodities market that was very competitive and volatile, farmers could neither pass their taxes on to their customers, nor count on their ability to repay current debts at a later date. Moreover, their needs were limited to those relatively few goods and services which they could not produce for themselves. This was in essence a nineteenth-century world. Until the late 1950s, Manitoba Liberalism was "as pure an expression of the small '1' liberalism of the 19th century as was to be found in any area of the world."[3]

The government's major fiscal objectives were to relieve the debt that had accumulated during the Depression, to balance current budgets, and to maintain a tax regime that would minimize the burden for farmers and maximize business incentives. The Campbell regime fulfilled these objectives, enjoying a substantial surplus in all but one year of its legislative life. Obsessed with the fear that a depression could reoccur at any time, it followed a fiscal regime of caution and prudence. All current and capital expenditures — except those which were self-financing, such as hydroelectricity — had to be financed from tax revenues. Since the government opposed any increase in tax rates, and since a large part of tax revenues was earmarked for debt retirement, it was a fiscal regime that placed very strict limits on expenditures for public services. This was a result that perfectly satisfied Campbell's rural electorate, but it was inconsistent with the changing demography and class lines of the province.

On the eve of Campbell's victory as premier, over 30 percent of all gainfully employed Manitobans were either independent proprietors or small employers. By 1958 this total had fallen to less than 20 percent.[4] Manitoba may still have had something of the flavour of a rural *petit bourgeois* society, but its substance was increasingly urban and working class. Between 1941 and the late 1950s, Manitoba lost a quarter of its farms. Due to increased mechanization and ample off-farm opportunities, thirty thousand Manitobans left their rural roots and moved into cities and towns.[5] By the end of the decade, Winnipeg accounted for over one-half of the provincial population, a shift reflected in the 1958 electoral redistribution. With urbanization come a variety of needs: new streets and water works, schools and recreation — all of which had been badly neglected.

Moreover, despite increased economic activity, Manitoba's growth over the decade was well below the Canadian average: 63 percent compared to 79 percent.[6] This was the common theme of the Conservative opposition in the 1958 election campaign. Its new leader, Duff Roblin, charged that the government was "an old lackadaisical limping administration . . . with a debt depression complex."[7] Development in Manitoba had lagged, he argued, because expenditures on social overhead capital such as roads, power facilities, transport facilities and education had not been made. The government lacked a development policy and thus the province's growth had suffered. The Conservatives promised a development policy based on expenditures on social overhead capital ''sufficiently in advance [of demands by existing industry] to stimulate and attract new economic development.''[8]

The Roblin Era, 1958-1967

Duff Roblin's goal was to secure a place for Manitoba in the postwar era of transnational capital, and he had no reservations about using the state to do so. His government was a significant advance over Campbell's Liberals, so aptly described by Roblin himself as the government of ''yesteryear.''

However, Roblin's modernization efforts were blunted by the class composition of his party and caucus. In the elections following the formation of his minority government in 1958, the Conservatives came to control much of rural Manitoba along with the suburban ring around greater Winnipeg. Constrained by his electoral dependency on a farm element that still insisted on low taxes, while pressed to increase the supply and quality of public goods demanded by his urban supporters, Roblin had to resort to borrowing and a flexible debt policy.

The Roblin administration rejected Campbell's pay-as-you-go fiscal policy, with Roblin blaming Manitoba's backwardness on this type of fiscal conservatism:

> We have consistently maintained that inadequate capital investment in recent years has handicapped the growth of the Province. Not only is the government now faced with the present day needs for capital improvements, it is also faced with a formidable accumulation of unfilled capital needs, inherited from a period of governmental inactivity and stringency. With statesmanlike foresight these capital charges could have been met at very much lower costs. Parsimony is rarely true economy. When such parsimony operates to inhibit normal growth, it can become the very opposite of true economy.[9]

Government expenditures nearly tripled between 1958 and 1965. Roblin showed no reluctance to finance new public facilities by borrowing and paying off the debt with the growth dividend earned from the increased productivity. The notion of dead-weight public debt was put to rest:

> Who can say what the monetary cost is of *not* building a road, a school, or a hospital? Must we assume that investment for growth can only be justified when it can be supported by a statement of profit and loss? Nevertheless, this factor is as real as any reflected in a profit and loss statement . . . All factors must be weighed and the direct and indirect benefits offset against the costs.[10]

The major expenditure expansion was in health and education (see Tables 3 and 4). Roblin often justified these expenditures on the grounds that, at least indirectly, they promoted economic growth. Altogether, government contributed nearly 30,000 new jobs during the Roblin era — 12,000 in education, 9,000 in health and social development, and 8,000 in public administration (mainly provincial).[11]

But Roblin's was more than a welfare state. He saw the state as catalyst and promoter of economic growth. As he told the legislature in 1963, Manitoba was an underdeveloped region whose modernization could not be left to "the natural play of economic forces. . . . While Manitoba is primarily a free enterprise and private initiative economy, the growing importance of provincial government activity in terms of economic growth must be accepted and understood.''[12]

TABLE 3
PERCENTAGE CHANGES IN PROVINCIAL GOVERNMENT
EXPENDITURES BY FUNCTION, 1958-1969

Function	Percentage Change
Health, Social Welfare	367
Education	591
Transportation and Communication	56
Natural Resources and Primary Industry	302
Other (including debt charges and contributions to municipalities)	309

Source: Dominion Bureau of Statistics, Provincial Government Finance, 1957 and 1968.

In the 1960s, economic growth became accepted as the official goal of all governments; all competed to attract industry to their provinces. Roblin's government wasted little time in adopting ''Growing to Beat 70'' as the provincial motto, and dramatically expanding the provincial Department of Industry and Commerce, giving it a new mandate to undertake feasibility, location and marketing studies.

TABLE 4
EXPENDITURES BY FUNCTION AS A PERCENTAGE OF
GOVERNMENT EXPENDITURES, 1958, 1969

Function	1958%	1969%
Health, Social Welfare	20.2	23.3
Education	22.8	38.9
Transportation and Communication	33.9	13.1
Natural Resources and Primary Industry	8.4	8.3
Other (including debt charges and contributions to municipalities)	15.9	16.4

Source: Dominion Bureau of Statistics, Provincial Government Finance, 1957 and 1968.

But the key instrument of the Conservative interventionist strategy was the Manitoba Development Fund (MDF). When the MDF was established in 1958, the minister of industry and commerce reassured an anxious business community that it would not be any sort of socialist planning agency: ''It's the opposite of socialist — it's strongly anti-socialist, to help the small business to be successful.''[13] Set up as a ''lender of last resort'' to small enterprises, the MDF soon graduated into something more ambitious. When the lending power of the MDF was raised to $100 million in 1966, it was heralded as the first step in ''Operation Industrial Breakthrough.'' Rex Gross, head of the MDF, told a Minneapolis audience in 1967:

We are going "flat-out" to attract U.S. capital . . . the provincial government is
willing to use its influence where appropriate to create a profit opportunity where
none might otherwise exist.[14]

Loans amounting to $123.5 million went to ten foreign companies, accounting for over
three-quarters of the capital loaned by the MDF since its inception.[15]

The most infamous example of MDF largesse was the $92 million loan to Churchill
Forest Industries (CFI). When first announced in 1966, a government spokesman said
that upon completion the new pulp and paper complex would create four thousand
direct and indirect new jobs. An overjoyed Premier Roblin proclaimed:

> We're just beginning folks. We've two major permanent resources in Manitoba,
> water and forest. We've been working four years to bring these two to the stage
> where they can go ahead. We are at that stage now.[16]

Besides the $92 million loan, CFI was given timber rights to forty thousand square miles
of Manitoba (16 percent of the area of the province), free fire prevention services, free
reforestation, free aerial photographic surveys, free sand and gravel for roads, up to $1
million for road construction, and a twenty- year tax exemption from the city of The Pas.
In the end, the mysterious Austrian owners absconded with most of the money, leaving
behind a partially built, flawed mill inherited by the NDP government upon its
assumption of office in 1969.

As the CFI example illustrates, the government had become more than just a catalyst:
"The new government, with the full weight of the public purse at its disposal, became
an entrepreneur extraordinaire; wheeling and dealing in the province's resources,
enticing new industry and underwriting not only the costs of social overhead capital,
such as roads, power, education and training directly essential to the success of new
industrial enterprises, but providing much of the risk capital itself."[17]

While manufacturing output grew steadily, increasing by about 75 percent and
adding twelve thousand new jobs in the Roblin decade, Roblin's major thrust was his
northern development strategy. It included the mega-hydroelectric development along
the Nelson, the opening up of the rich INCO mine in Thompson, and the CFI forestry
complex at The Pas. Utilities (mainly hydroelectric) alone accounted for 36 percent of
all new investment in the province during the 1960s. Government institutions like
schools and hospitals accounted for another 25 percent with construction and primary
industries, mainly mining, contributing 20 percent.[18]

These investments spurred substantial if temporary manufacturing and service-
related activities. But what was important about manufacturing was not merely its
steady growth, but also that for the first time it included significant volumes of industrial
goods — electrical products, machinery, metal fabrication and transportation equipment. Some of these substituted for industrial components formerly imported into
Manitoba. Largely as a consequence, provincial manufacturing became somewhat
more diversified. Whereas in 1951 the food and beverage and clothing industries

together accounted for 57 percent of the work force employed by the ten leading industries, in 1969 they accounted for 42 percent, while the proportion of the work force increased in certain heavy industries, such as electrical products, machinery and metal fabrication.[19]

The 1960s were a period of rapid growth and development for Manitoba, for which the Roblin government could take some credit. But measured in terms of the government's own yardstick, it came up short. The Roblin administration failed to reverse, halt or even slow Manitoba's deteriorating national position.

Changing technology, federal policy and much more rapid growth in neighbouring western provinces were major factors. Winnipeg suffered a serious loss in the 1960s when Air Canada's repair and overhaul base was moved to Montréal. Other large firms also relocated, such as John Deere, which moved its parts depot to Regina. Many firms which had located in Winnipeg because of its strategic railway location found no reason to remain with the relative decline of rail transport, while the volume of repair and maintenance work in local railway shops also declined. Replacement of the steam engine by the diesel, which required less maintenance, further reduced activity in the shops. To a minor extent, these losses were offset by Winnipeg's emergence as a major long-distance trucking centre. Generally, however, the faster growth of Calgary, Edmonton and Vancouver, as well as Regina and Saskatoon in the 1970s, fostered enterprises that supplied what had once been bought in Winnipeg.

Many warehousing and manufacturing firms previously located in the central business district moved to suburban industrial parks. This move, in tandem with new housing tracts and the springing up of dozens of suburban shopping centres, gave rise to significant construction activity. But it also decimated the city's downtown, with Portage Avenue shops languishing, and old warehouse and industrial buildings falling vacant.

Two other obstacles blocked Roblin. First, Manitoba remained relatively unattractive to investors. Government giveaways may have been effective at first, but once the giveaway game began, Manitoba could not keep up with the prizes offered by provinces like Ontario and Alberta. Second, Roblin was restricted by the political instrument at his disposal — the Progressive Conservative Party of Manitoba. When he took over the party in the mid-1950s, it still reflected the old political economy. However much he remade the party over the next five years, he still had to drag along a reluctant, doubting, hesitant association of small businessmen, farmers and senior citizens. Resentment built up, even in his own caucus, as he bullied them into accepting his modernizing measures. And when the government had to pay the price — a sudden rise in taxes — of a modernization program that had not yet yielded large economic returns, many in the party withdrew their support. By the time Roblin resigned as premier in 1967, Manitoba's personal income tax was matched only by that of Saskatchewan, while its corporate tax rate was exceeded only by that of Ontario.[20] As far as his party was concerned, the ''experiment'' had failed.

The Conservatives replaced Roblin with Walter Weir, a rural conservative more to their liking. There was to be no more experimentation, just stability and maybe even a return to the old order. But Manitobans did not agree, and the Weir government did not survive the next election.

The Schreyer Years, 1969-1977

Ed Schreyer inherited the mantle of progressive reform from Duff Roblin. It has long been said that Schreyer was more liberal than socialist, which made it logical that his administration would choose to fully implement and cautiously advance Roblin's modernization strategy, rather than attempt to leap ahead of it.

James McAllister argues that the NDP's record of reform, while adequate, was undifferentiated from other contemporary provincial governments, and that since virtually all of the policies it introduced could be found in other parts of Canada governed by non-social democratic governments, the NDP *per se* made only a marginal impact on Manitoba's political economy.[21]

This conclusion is offered as substantiation for various theories which argue that socioeconomic structures, rather than the party in government, determine policy outcomes. Among these is the Marxist hypothesis that what social democratic governments can do to improve the conditions of the working class is constrained by the fact that ''they are tolerated in power only as long as they refrain from attacking or reducing the position and privileges of the dominant class. . . . They are allowed to use an egalitarian rhetoric but have rarely translated this into effective policy.''[22]

Left-wing critics of the Schreyer government will hear the ring of truth in this kind of argument, but it is more than a little off key. For example, it insists on measuring the NDP record against a socialist doctrine that had been abandoned by the party mainstream at least twenty-five years earlier. Schreyer never lost an opportunity to specify that his long-term goal was to promote the equality of the human condition, but he ruled out social ownership of industry as a means of democratizing wealth and power. On the eve of taking office, he assured the *Winnipeg Tribune* that ''the notion of government ownership of production, distribution and exchange which is mouthed so glibly, should be looked upon by a social-democrat almost as uncomfortably as by a liberal.''[23] Conceding capitalist ownership and direction of the economy means that the only reforms possible are those that can be paid for from capitalist prosperity. This is the meaning and limitation of social democracy. Acceptance of this compromise places social democracy at the left end of the spectrum of parties that compromise the post-World War II welfare state consensus.

Manitoba, for so long ruled by parties whose philosophical viewpoint lay outside this consensus, was still in the backwoods concerning progressive reform, public facilities and state regulations. Roblin's party did not permit him to make up all the lost ground, but Schreyer's did. The Schreyer government appropriated for Manitoba the most progressive tax and social reforms in Canada. His administration pioneered nothing, but by selectively adopting the most advanced programs in other jurisdictions, it pushed

Manitoba into the forefront of reform. The question is, did Schreyer's achievements approach the outer limits of the parameters of social democracy?

The NDP government faced few of the ideological restrictions that had hindered the interventionist Roblin administration. At the same time, it was rarely pressed to adopt measures that would place it in conflict with capital. What pressures there were to introduce reforms outside acceptable parameters, or even up to its limits, were well contained by cabinet and caucus control of all aspects of party affairs. As McAllister observed,

> A highly organized mass-based, social democratic party could have been a strong force in Manitoba politics, pushing both the Schreyer government and the political dialogue as a whole to the left. Such a party organization did not exist. Its absence must be viewed as a contributing factor in explaining the lack of strong policy initiatives by the Schreyer government.[24]

Reducing the party to an electoral machine affects social democratic governments in three important ways. First, the party is not available as a resource to develop policies. Social democratic governments have to rely on the bureaucracy not only to evaluate and implement policy options, but to generate them as well. Second, the party is not available as a means of widening its ideological core beyond its historical base, which in Manitoba never exceeded 15-20 percent. By not engaging in grassroots activism and education, it loses the opportunity to build a more popular social democratic consciousness within the electorate. With the party's small ideological core, NDP governments are always placed in a position where they must avoid policies that could antagonize the swing, ''liberal'' vote. Third, by not becoming an activist organization with deep roots in the community, the party never develops the capacity to mobilize the population in defence of measures strongly opposed by the Right. By keeping politics out of the streets and confined to the legislative chambers, it undermines the possibility of social change.

The goal of the Schreyer administration was to incorporate reform measures in pursuit of equity, but in a manner that would minimize conflict with capital. Public housing, for example, benefited those at the bottom end of the housing market, without challenging the hold of private entrepreneurs on the more profitable middle and upper price range. The government considered but dropped plans to set up a drug manufacturing corporation and a government-owned central drug purchasing and distribution agency. Instead, it set up drug substitution, which allowed pharmacists to substitute equivalent brand-name categories, and Pharmacare, which reimbursed families for 80 percent of their prescription drug costs over fifty dollars. These are cost-control devices and social welfare programs that leave the industry untouched, and are a good example of what James O'Conner called the ''socialization of costs and the private appropriation of profits.''[25] The government commissioned but never seriously considered the Kierans report, which recommended a staged government takeover of the mining industry. Instead, it imposed a tax on mining income that would rise and fall with fluctuations in mineral prices. From the reform packages available to it, the government consistently chose those elements least likely to offend capital. As a consequence, change was minimized.

Government programs accounted for a rising proportion of the gross provincial product, increasing from 12 percent under Roblin to almost 15 percent under Schreyer.[26] Nevertheless, the Schreyer administration boasted that "government expenditure increased significantly less, in percentage terms, than the average of all ten provinces."[27] All governments were playing a larger economic role through most of the 1960s and 1970s, and there was little distinctive about the Schreyer administration in this regard.

Moreover, it proved possible to increase expenditures with but one increase in income tax rates, no addition to sales taxes, and with a current account budget in the 1969-77 period that was almost balanced. This was attributed to growing revenues generated from an expanding provincial economy and, even more importantly, large infusions of federal transfer payments (see Chapter 14). The deficit in capital account was almost entirely due to hydroelectric construction.

Between 1971 and 1975, agricultural, mining and manufacturing output all more than doubled when measured in current dollars, and forest products, from a much smaller base, tripled. All investment expanded, and public investment accounted for 46 percent of the total, slightly less than during the Roblin years.[28]

In 1974, the NDP government launched Manitoba Hydro on its second huge hydroelectric development project. It absorbed a massive amount of capital investment, was the dominant influence over the economy to nearly the end of the decade, and compromised the government's main economic development strategy. By 1977 the Manitoba Hydro debt constituted 60 percent of the entire provincial debt.[29]

Until the 1975 recession, the NDP government could use its growth dividend to introduce reform measures. These included the elimination of health insurance premiums, the introduction of the Education Property Tax Credit Plan and the Cost-of-Living Tax Credit, an increase in the provincial share of education costs from 70 percent to 80 percent, a guaranteed minimum monthly income for seniors, Pharmacare for the elderly, free legal aid, day care, and employment training for the disadvantaged. Tax reforms saved the average working-class family $590 a year, or 6 percent of income, relative to what it would have paid in 1969. Altogether, these new tax and expenditure programs accounted for 20 percent of the 1974-75 provincial budget. Also, the government increased the stock of public housing units from 669 in 1969 to 11,712 in 1976, and took the automobile insurance industry into public ownership. Only in the latter instance did the government threaten the interests of private capital, but because public automobile insurance reduced rates and operation costs for both firms and individuals, it was quickly accepted.

The Manitoba government ended up by owning dozens of other enterprises, including Saunders Aircraft, Flyer Coach, and the hopelessly overcapitalized CFI (renamed MANFOR), as a result of policy changes adopted by the Manitoba Development Corporation (MDC), the NDP's version of the old MDF. Once loans reached a certain size they were converted into equity, but since the MDC was a lender of last resort, the economic position of these enterprises was always precarious. As a result, the Schreyer government ended up by socializing losses. Many of these companies fell into receivership, leaving a sour taste for public entrepreneurship. Under a barrage of criticism, the role of the MDC was sharply curtailed in the final years of the regime.

Having run out of steam, the NDP fell victim to the same forces that defeated many other social democratic governments in Canada and around the world. The reforms extracted from capital had come cheaply over the previous half-dozen years, having been pieced off with minimum concessions. But in the face of the emergent crisis of profitability, capital resisted further concessions. Unwilling to raise taxes or its operating deficit beyond nominal levels, and having no capital base of its own, the Schreyer government capitulated. New reform plans were shelved; existing social services were allowed to run down. Schreyer was one of the first premiers to support the wage controls introduced in 1975. And, during the explosive strike against Griffin Steel (1976-77), his government displayed that when conflict erupted between labour and capital, its allegiance was to capital. Pleas from labour to introduce antiscab legislation were ignored.

In the end, like the Roblin government before it, Schreyer's government was defeated by its own internal contradictions. Given the class base of his party, Roblin exceeded the boundaries of acceptable intervention. Given the existing economic conjuncture, Schreyer could not satisfy his party's pursuit of reforms without challenging capital. But given the confined character of his party, he had neither the ideological nor the organizational resources to do so. It was a frustrated and demoralized party that Schreyer led into the 1977 election campaign. Not surprisingly, it could not deliver the vote.

The Lyon Interlude, 1977-1982

The choices governments make say a great deal about their priorities. Of course, external constraints set limits on what governments can do: international financiers can impose a heavy price on governments that allow expanding deficits; debt charges which absorb growing proportions of the budget limit what is available for government programs; taxes that get too far out of line with nearby jurisdictions can cause capital flight; and stagnant growth limits what social services can be offered by governments. But until they are reached, no one knows for certain what the parameters are, and within them the choices are still significant.

The Schreyer government had expanded its spending in line with the revenue generated by the existing tax structure. Its fiscal strategy paralleled the Roblin administration's, with expenditures and revenues almost balanced between 1969 and 1974. It was not prepared to fully offset lower revenue growth induced by the 1974-75 recession by slashing social services, but while allowing a modest deficit, it did exercise spending restraint. Given his rural orientation, Schreyer was more comfortable with cutbacks than large operating deficits.

Sterling Lyon, on the other hand, claimed spending was out of control and promised a policy of "acute, protracted restraint." It was a policy rooted in the belief that "government has a limited place in business ... and should have a different, sometimes smaller role in other activities as well."[30]

In one of its first acts, the Lyon government lumped all government spending — day-to-day operating expenditures and capital expenditures — into one amalgamated account. This seemingly innocuous accounting alteration was of fundamental political importance. It bloated the size of the government deficit. Overnight, Manitobans were told that their deficit was not $5 million as previously reported, but $225 million. This served the cause of neoconservatism but had no economic justification.

Homeowners and businesses recognize the distinction between an operating deficit and total budgetary requirements which include capital investment. A new homeowner with $30,000 in annual income who has just bought an $80,000 house does not consider that he or she has incurred a $50,000 deficit. A deficit would be incurred only if annual mortgage payments, plus food, clothing, transportation and other living costs exceeded annual income. Similarly, when a business builds a $5 million plant, it does not charge the full cost against income in the current year. Its current year expenses include the plant's operating costs, as well as depreciation and interest costs — not the full cost of acquisition. The plant is treated as an asset that will bring in future revenues. It is an investment in the future.

Government expenditure to acquire assets with long-term benefits should likewise not be treated as part of net operating deficit, even though it adds to total budgetary requirements, for these debts are self-sustaining. For example, Manitoba Hydro's debt is financed by rates charged to consumers.

Much government debt represents investment in public assets. For example, our network of roads, hospitals, power plants, universities, schools, Crown lands, and natural resources constitute enormous wealth-producing assets. Instead of using the size of the deficit as the indicator of financial health, it would make more sense to follow the business practice of using net worth, which measures the value of acquired assets as well as the size of outstanding debts. The Barber report commissioned by the Pawley government showed that the value of public assets exceeds the outstanding debt by about two to one.[31]

By obliterating the distinction between self-sustaining expenditures or wealth-producing assets on the one hand, and expenditures to carry on current programs on the other, the Lyon government retreated to the pre-Campbell days. Campbell at least had made the distinction between dead-weight public debt and self-sustaining public debt; Lyon pronounced all public debt as dead weight.

However, Lyon was not satisfied to eliminate the annual budgetary requirements. He also wanted to reduce taxes, which could only be achieved by wholesale cuts. In Lyon's first year in office, tax changes reduced government revenues by 6 percent. Yet, by slashing civil service jobs, virtually halting capital spending on hydroelectric development and public housing, and cancelling "pump-priming" spending, the Lyon government managed to reduce the budgetary requirement (combined annual deficit on current and capital account) to $153 million by 1980, compared to the $544 million inherited from the last Schreyer government.[32]

Unfortunately this exercise in "acute, protracted restraint" was imposed just as Canada and the world were about to plunge into the worst depression since the 1930s, and it ensured that Manitoba would have the worst economic performance in Canada. A Statistics Canada and Conference Board of Canada evaluation of the 1979 record of the Lyon government illustrates why it was the only one-term government in Manitoba this century. Manitoba had the smallest increase in gross domestic product (GDP), the smallest increase in jobs, the worst record in housing starts, the smallest increase in private investment, the smallest increase in public investment, and was the only province to show an absolute drop in population.[33]

The Lyon government found itself embroiled in a series of confrontations with groups affected by spending cuts. Strike activity reached a new postwar high as private employers became inspired by Lyon's austerity program. The poor mobilized against real cuts in welfare benefits that exceeded 20 percent over the four-year term. Single mothers, day-care workers, hospital workers, civil servants, university students and faculty demonstrated against the declining level of day care, health and education services.

Staring at imminent defeat, the government began its retreat from austerity by priming the pump in all departments, but it was too little, too late. The NDP swept back into office with a strong majority.

The Pawley Years, 1982-88

The NDP regained office in the midst of the worst economic downturn since the 1930s. Deficits were bound to rise: revenue was dropping and depression-related expenditures were rising, while the province's fiscal position was further aggravated by the federal government's cutback in federal transfer payments.

Other provinces, especially in western Canada, followed Lyon's austerity pattern. But Pawley shielded Manitoba from the impact of the global economic crisis by protecting the social services built up under Roblin and Schreyer. And unlike other governments — which legislated civil service wages — the Pawley administration exchanged guaranteed job security for modest wage and salary increases. This required large increases in taxes and/or deficits. In the face of heated opposition from business and the fourth estate, the Pawley government did both.

But without an alternative strategy that addressed the perennial problem of Manitoba's eroding underpinnings, this approach was not sustainable. Rather than establish a new economic development strategy, the Pawley government constructed yet another hydroelectric megaproject to spark short-term economic recovery, with the hope that in the longer term it would bring in export profits. Other megaprojects, such as aluminum and potash, failed to materialize, while the employment effect of the North Portage reconstruction project and the Core Area Initiative were short lived. Much the same was the case for Manitoba's Jobs Fund, used mainly to subsidize private-sector wages on a short-term basis.

As an interim policy, this strategy proved successful. Until 1987 it gave Manitoba the lowest or second lowest unemployment rate in the country, the third largest population increase, the third best record in private investment and real domestic product, the second best in public investment with an increase of 56 percent between 1983 and 1987 (twice the national average), and the second best in average disposable income, moving it very close (98 percent) to the national average.[34] But by early 1988, this strategy showed signs of unravelling.

From the time it took office in 1982, the NDP government was dogged by the question of the provincial debt. The Conservative opposition made the size of the annual deficit the most debated issue in provincial politics. The deficit was portrayed as the symbol of government waste, inefficiency, meddling and irresponsibility. Matters were not helped by the failure of the NDP to reconvert the provincial accounts to an accounting framework grounded in sound economic principles rather than in neo-conservative ideology. Capital expenditures continued to be counted as part of the annual provincial deficit.

Expenditures on programs rose by 46 percent to 1988, about double the rate of inflation, and just enough to enable the government to avoid serious cuts in social services. Until 1986 most of the resulting operating deficit, along with hydroelectric-driven capital expenditures, were financed by borrowing. Between 1981 and 1986 the total budgetary requirement more than doubled, reaching $560 million. Then the Pawley administration succumbed to the neoconservative agenda: massive tax increases in the 1987 budget, and more modest increases in the ill-fated 1988 budget, would have reduced the total budgetary requirement by 40 percent and all but eliminated the operating deficit. The resulting increase in provincial taxes, coupled with the much bigger federal tax hike, was a major factor contributing to the NDP's defeat in the 1988 election.

Given the government's commitment to maintain social services in the face of a depressed economy, and its dependence on national and international money markets, the Pawley administration had no alternative but to raise taxes. It likely could have chosen a more gradual schedule of deficit reduction, but this may be as much a matter of political as fiscal judgement. Debt service charges were already absorbing 12 percent of provincial revenue.[35] Without a serious effort to reduce the size of the deficit, mounting service charges would have made it impossible for the province to maintain social services.

The Pawley government could congratulate itself on the performance of the Manitoba economy, but only in comparison with more dismal situations elsewhere. Manitoba's strength is uneven: agricultural production has continued to decline, while manufacturing and mineral production have stagnated in real terms, employing fewer workers in 1987 than in 1981. Only services, mainly health and education, provide notably more jobs than in the pre-recession period (see Table 5).

TABLE 5

EMPLOYED LABOUR FORCE, BY INDUSTRY FOR MANITOBA, 1981, 1987
(Thousands)

Industry	1981	1987
Agriculture	43	41
Other Primary Industry	7	8
Manufacturing	66	57
Construction	21	25
Transportation, Communication and Other Utilities	51	46
Trade	80	89
Finance, Insurance and Real Estate	24	29
Service	134	161
Public Administration	35	40

Source: Statistics Canada, *The Labour Force*, Cat.: 71-001.

The Manitoba economy, like all others, is being subjected to a restructuring, the final outcome of which is not yet certain. Due to the depression in agriculture, Canadian Cooperative Implements closed, and reopened on a smaller scale under new ownership. Metal manufacturing firms and foundries linked to agriculture, like Bell Foundry, Canadian Rogers Western and Canadian Steel Tank and Metals Industries, have shuttered their operations. Numerous other multinationals closed their branches to consolidate elsewhere, including Christie Brown, Greb Shoes, Kimberley Clark, Rayovac, Keeprite, General Aluminum Forgings and, most importantly, Canada Packers. Some have left a warehouse/distribution centre in Manitoba. In the wake of the supermarket war between Super Valu and Safeway, Dominion Stores surrendered their share of the market and left the province. Some major mines are threatening to close, which would destroy once thriving communities (see Chapter 11).

Manitoba's comparatively strong economic performance in the 1980s rested almost entirely on provincial government stimulation. Between 1982 and 1986, public investment in Manitoba rose by 60 percent, while declining in every other province except Nova Scotia and Prince Edward Island.[36] This spurred considerable private investment: Manitoba's 61 percent growth between 1981 and 1986 matched that of Québec and Ontario; all other provinces were much lower. However, the North Portage reconstruction was completed in 1987, and construction at Limestone began to slow in 1988 when, not surprisingly, Manitoba's unemployment moved above the national average for the first time since 1981.

In the absence of a new economic strategy and, it might be added, major restructuring in the delivery of expensive social services like health, the Pawley government's efforts were bound to be short lived. In opposition, the NDP was always critical of capital-intensive, resource-based megaprojects as instruments of economic development. In office, it came to be totally dependent on precisely this economic strategy.

Howard Pawley's NDP government was reluctant to confront capital. Except for the payroll tax and final offer selection, none of its programs was offensive to capital. Labour demands for plant closure and antiscab legislation were rejected. The takeover of Inter-City Gas was abandoned. But however modest its achievements, Pawley's defensive posture in maintaining and even extending social services, and fighting privatization, deregulation and free trade, was important.

In the final analysis, however, it was a stalling action, for unless Manitoba finds a place in the global restructuring, it will be unable to maintain present living standards without massive transfers from the rest of the country. This altruism it cannot presume.

Structural and Sectoral Trend Analysis

This section will describe the structural characteristics of the fragile political economy of Manitoba, which for seventy years has been in a gradual economic decline relative to Canada as a whole, and which is likely to decline further as a consequence of the global restructuring of capital.

If, through most of the first half of this century, Manitoba was the financial and distribution linchpin of the Prairies, in the second half it has been transformed into a satellite of Ontario. Its ownership and trade links with Ontario are far more extensive than those with Saskatchewan or Alberta. The prairie economy as a distinct economic region linked by common economic forces no longer exists. This should come as no surprise, for the prairie economy was a euphemism for the wheat economy, and while wheat still plays an important role, especially in Saskatchewan, it is no longer dominant. Manitoba's economy is now driven by market forces quite distinct from those driving the economies of Saskatchewan and Alberta. Manitoba is less dependent on agriculture than Saskatchewan, far less dependent on resource extraction than either Saskatchewan or Alberta, and despite a growth rate that has lagged behind the other two provinces, its manufacturing sector remains substantially larger (see Table 6).

TABLE 6

INDUSTRY SHARES OF GROSS DOMESTIC PRODUCT,
CANADA AND WESTERN PROVINCES, 1986

Industry	Manitoba	Saskatchewan	Alberta	B.C.	Canada
		(% share based on values in $1981)			
Resources					
Agriculture	6.7	20.4	4.8	1.4	3.3
Other Primary	2.8	10.7	25.1	7.6	6.2
Utilities	3.4	2.9	2.5	3.1	3.2
Manufacturing	11.4	4.4	6.7	13.5	18.6
Construction	6.6	7.2	8.0	6.6	6.7
Total Goods Producing	31.0	45.6	47.1	32.2	38.0
Transport, Communication	12.4	11.3	9.1	12.7	8.0
Trade	12.5	10.3	9.6	11.1	11.6
Finance Insurance and Real Estate	16.9	12.0	13.7	16.4	15.5
CBP Service	20.0	15.8	14.8	21.1	20.3
Public Administration and Defense	7.2	5.1	5.7	6.5	6.6
Total Service Producing	69.0	54.4	52.9	67.8	61.9
Total	100.0	100.0	100.0	100.0	100.0

Note: Totals may not add due to rounding.
Source: Conference Board of Canada, Winter 1987.

Manitoba has essentially a branch-plant and branch-office economy. Decisions are made and profits declared outside of the province. Ontario-based firms employ nearly as many Manitobans as do locally owned firms (80,000 compared to 97,000). No other province is so closely linked to Ontario (see Table 7). Over 50 percent of Manitoba's jobs are located in Canadian and foreign firms based outside the province. No other province is so dependent on enterprises with out-of-province ownership (see Table 8).

TABLE 7
PERCENTAGE OF EMPLOYMENT ACCOUNTED FOR BY
ONTARIO-BASED FIRMS BY PROVINCE, 1975

Province	%
Newfoundland	27
Prince Edward Island	NA
Nova Scotia	36
New Brunswick	33
Quebec	29
Manitoba	41
Saskatchewan	31
Alberta	31
British Columbia	26

Source: Statistics Canada, *Employment by Domestic and Foreign Controlled Enterprises in Canada: A Provincial Analysis*, 1975, Cat.: 13-57A.

The average size of Manitoba firms is especially small. Next to Prince Edward Island, Manitoba is the province most dependent on small-sized firms for employment. The largest one thousand employers account for only 43 percent of Manitoba workers employed in firms with twenty or more workers, compared to 75 percent in Ontario (where the largest one hundred employers account for 51 percent of the work force), 56 percent in British Columbia and 50 percent or more in Saskatchewan and Alberta.[37]

TABLE 8
PERCENTAGE OF EMPLOYMENT BY PROVINCE AND OWNERSHIP LOCATION, 1975

Province of Employment	Active Wholly in Province	Active Mainly in Province	Active Mainly in Other Provinces
Newfoundland	47	18	39
Prince Edward Island	NA	NA	NA
Nova Scotia	41	15	44
New Brunswick	36	16	48
Quebec	42	28	30
Ontario	39	54	7
Manitoba	32	17	51
Saskatchewan	33	25	43
Alberta	35	22	43
British Columbia	45	20	35
Canada (average)	40	36	24

Source: Statistics Canada, *Employment by Domestic and Foreign Controlled Enterprises in Canada: A Provincial Analysis*, 1975, Cat.: 13-57A.

Manitoba businesses have little impact on the rest of the country. Manitoba membership in the *Financial Post 500* consists of seventeen businesses, only twelve of which are provincially based, and these include three Crown corporations and three cooperatives.[38] Ranked by sales, the leading Manitoba industrial firm, Federal Industries, placed fifty-ninth in 1987 with sales of $1.6 billion. None of Canada's fifty most profitable companies is based in Manitoba. No Manitoba-based companies are among the top ten enterprises in any of the energy, forestry, transportation, communications, food and beverage, automotive products, real estate or construction industries. Two of the ten leading merchandizing companies — Hudson's Bay and Canada Safeway — list Winnipeg as their national headquarters, but they are merely subsidiary operations. The same holds for Manitoba's single entry in the mining sector, Hudson Bay Mining and Smelting. Only in the grain industry does Manitoba have a leading position, with the head offices of three of the ten companies (two of them cooperatives) located in Winnipeg.

The picture that emerges is of a diversified but slow-moving economy, comprised mainly of locally owned, small- and medium-sized enterprises, with most larger enterprises being branch-plant, branch-office subsidiaries of Ontario and United States corporations. Since Winnipeg lost its role as linchpin of a booming prairie economy based on wheat, Manitoba has not found a niche for itself in the national or international economy. Massive hydroelectric development, the major economic thrust for the past twenty-five years, has few of the linkages required to spark permanent industrial investments. Manitoba's vulnerability is being exposed as corporations respond to the global restructuring. Absentee owners are phasing down or closing out their Manitoba operations in traditional, smokestack industries. While some new, high-tech, information-based companies have started up in Manitoba, they are not numerous enough to offset this trend.

Agriculture

The most dramatic trend in Manitoba's economy has been the erosion of agriculture's dominant position. At its height seventy years ago, farming accounted for 40 percent of all gainfully employed Manitobans and 60 percent of goods production. By 1985 farming accounted for 9 percent of employment and 21 percent of goods production. The number of farms has declined by over 50 percent — from 58,000 in 1941 to 27,000 in 1986 (see Table 9, and Chapter 10) — and industries linked to agriculture have been adversely affected (see Chapter 11).

TABLE 9
NUMBER OF FARMS IN MANITOBA, 1901-1986
(Thousands)

Year	Number
1901	32
1911	44
1921	53
1931	54
1941	58
1951	52
1961	43
1971	35
1981	29
1986	27

Source: Statistics Canada, *Census of Canada*, various years.

Farmers are increasingly forced to seek part-time and seasonal employment, which may be part of the cause for the rural relocation of food processing and implement manufacturers. Farmers, desperate for off-farm income, constitute a pool of flexible, hard-working labour with no trade union background.[39]

Manufacturing

In the early 1950s manufacturing production surpassed agriculture; by the late 1960s it also surpassed agriculture in numbers employed. This represents a dramatic reversal in the relative positions of Manitoba's two largest sectors. In 1920, agriculture's share of the value-added of all goods producing sectors was twice that of manufacturing; by 1984 manufacturing's share was twice that of agriculture. Agricultural employment was 4.3 times that of manufacturing in 1920; in 1984 manufacturing employment was nearly 1.5 times that of agriculture.[40]

Since the late 1950s both the composition and markets of manufactured products have shifted. Until fairly recently most manufacturing complemented the agricultural sector, or provided light consumer goods for the provincial market. From the late 1950s, however, with an increased weight of industrial goods — electrical products, machinery, metal fabricating and transportation equipment — manufacturing has been oriented somewhat more to external markets (see Table 10). In 1979, Manitoba exported 56 percent of its manufacturing output, compared to 48 percent in 1974. The most important destination was Ontario, followed by Alberta and Saskatchewan; international destinations accounted for only 11 percent of manufacturing sales, a significant fact given the FTA.

TABLE 10

DESTINATION OF MANITOBA'S MANUFACTURING OUTPUT
BY PROVINCE, 1974, 1979

Destination	Manufacturing Output			
	1974		1979	
	Sales ($000)	%	Sales ($000)	%
Newfoundland	3,205	.16	19,494	.52
Prince Edward Island	1,273	.06	7,019	.19
Nova Scotia	23,407	1.14	36,818	.99
New Brunswick	16,509	.80	24,905	.67
Quebec	120,662	5.86	265,423	7.13
Ontario	263,697	12.91	512,005	13.76
Manitoba	1,076,144	52.23	1,623,345	43.61
Saskatchewan	125,925	6.12	299,035	8.03
Alberta	137,480	6.68	334,923	9.00
British Columbia	73,745	3.58	187,848	5.05
Yukon/Northwest Territories	5,392	.26	3,678	.10
Outside Canada	209,914	10.20	407,595	10.95

Source: Statistics Canada, *Destination of Shipments of Manufacturers*, Cat.: 530 (1974 and 1979).

During the 1970s, Manitoba's manufacturing sector performed better than all sectors of the provincial economy.[41] As Table 11 shows, it is still far more important than is manufacturing in the other prairie provinces, even though they have enjoyed a faster rate of growth. But the degree of diversification is about the same for all three provinces, and significantly less than in Ontario and Québec.

TABLE 11
RELATIVE IMPORTANCE OF MANUFACTURING,
MANITOBA, SASKATCHEWAN, ALBERTA, 1980

	% of Employment	% of Gross Provincial Product
Manitoba	9.4	14.0
Saskatchewan	3.6	6.2
Alberta	5.5	9.6

Source: N.E. Cameron, J.M. Dean, and W.S. Good, *The Manufacturing Sector in Manitoba* (Ottawa: Economic Council of Canada, 1984).

Manitoba manufacturing is dominated by small firms, much more so than in Canada as a whole. Firms employing twenty-five people or less account for 20 percent of all Manitoba's manufacturing employment, compared to 14 percent in all of Canada, and for 36 percent of sales, compared to 14 percent in all of Canada. Nor has there been any increase in the relative importance of giant manufacturing firms in Manitoba. In 1980 only eight firms in all industries employed more than five hundred people; only four employed more than one thousand.[42]

Manufacturing employment nearly doubled between 1921 and 1941 (from 19,000 to 34,000), and doubled again between 1941 and 1981 (from 34,000 to 68,000).[43] But this performance falls far short of manufacturing growth in the rest of Canada. And Canada's record is the poorest in the industrialized West. Furthermore, while Manitoba's manufacturing advanced rapidly during the 1970s, it lost its momentum and fell back badly after the 1981 recession; it has yet to show signs of recovery. Between 1961 and 1981 manufacturing employment jumped from 55,000 to 66,000, or 20 percent — just short of the national average. But by 1987 Manitoba employment had fallen back to 57,000, about the same as in the mid-1960s, while national employment remained nearly constant. In 1966, manufacturing's share of total provincial employment stood at 15.9 percent, compared to 24.4 percent in Canada. The gap had narrowed significantly by 1981, but widened again by 1986 (see Table 12).

TABLE 12
RELATIVE IMPORTANCE OF MANUFACTURING,
MANITOBA AND CANADA, 1966, 1981, 1986
(Manufacturing Employment as a Percentage of Total Employment)

	Manitoba %	Canada %	Manitoba/Canada %
1966	15.9	24.4	65.2
1981	14.7	19.3	76.2
1986	11.6	17.3	67.1

Source: Statistics Canada, *The Labour Force*, Cat.: 71-001.

In Manitoba, real investment in manufacturing rose sharply until 1970, showing wide fluctuation thereafter with a slightly downward general trend, while real investment in Canadian manufacturing doubled between 1961 and the recession of 1974, and rose by another one-third between 1977 and the 1981 recession. The 1981 recession featured a sizeable drop in investment (33 percent in all of Canada, 41 percent in Manitoba) and a very slow revival. But by 1987 Canadian investment had nearly recaptured 1980-81 levels, whereas the recovery in Manitoba has been more anemic.[44]

The reason for Manitoba's vulnerability to the economic crisis requires further investigation, but it is consistent with the observation that the hinterland acts as a buffer for the heartland against the volatility of demand. During boom periods the hinterland picks up a proportionate share of increased demand, but during periods of recession or stagnation, reduced demand falls heavily upon it. Similarly, during periods of restructuring, hinterland areas may feel the brunt of industry rationalization and consolidation. Industries subject to this so-called "cushion effect" are those oriented to national and international markets rather than regional markets, and those that mainly comprise branch plants whose owners can readily redirect orders to heartland plants.

Northern Resource Development

Until the 1960s, northern resource development was nearly dormant. Since then, mining and hydroelectric power have become important sectors in the Manitoba economy. Mining's share of goods production rose from 3.3 percent in 1960 to 16.2 percent in 1970, declining slightly to 14.8 percent in 1980. Electrical power, gas and water utilities rose from 5.8 percent in 1970 to 12.3 percent in 1980. Because both sectors are so capital intensive, however, neither contributed substantially to employment. For example, only 1,300 new mining jobs were created between 1961 and 1981,[45] while most mining equipment was imported, and most of the profits exported. Utilities, being mainly publicly owned, have made a larger contribution to the provincial economy.

The economic crisis featured a disastrous drop in metal prices, and struck mining even more severely than manufacturing. Mining employment fell from 6,900 in 1981 to 3,900 in 1986, less than the number employed in 1961.[46] Even full recovery will not bring back all of these lost jobs. Massive hydroelectric developments in the 1980s will maintain that sector's contribution to total output, but when the construction phase is completed, it will have added very few direct jobs.

Finance and Distribution

Although once the financial, warehouse and wholesale centre for the prairie region, Manitoba's position in these sectors has eroded, particularly since the 1960s (see Tables 13 and 14). While employment in these sectors has continued to grow, it has lagged behind growth elsewhere in Canada.

Services

As a distinct sector, services is a statistical convenience, lumping together several unrelated activities whose only common feature is that they are non-goods producing. For example, it includes education, health and welfare — public sector activities financed primarily from tax revenues. In 1987, these areas alone employed over 83,000 Manitobans — more than manufacturing, mining and utilities combined. But it also includes firms providing services directly to other businesses — such as accounting, trucking, consulting and advertising — as well as personal services such as taxi cabs and haircuts, and services to the general public which include communications, entertainment, hotels and restaurants. The 74,000 jobs provided by these firms in 1987 exceeded the numbers occupied in both agriculture and manufacturing.[47]

TABLE 13

RELATIVE IMPORTANCE OF FINANCE AND DISTRIBUTION,
MANITOBA AND CANADA, 1951-1981
(Wholesale Trade)

	Manitoba		Canada		Manitoba/ Canada
	Employment 000	% of Total Employment	Employment 000	% of Total Employment	
1951	15	5.1	195	3.7	1.38
1961	20	5.9	290	4.5	1.31
1971	20	4.9	349	4.1	1.20
1981	26	5.2	559	4.7	1.11

Source: Statistics Canada, *Census of Canada*, various years.

While the service, transportation, distribution, finance, real estate and insurance sectors do not produce goods, it is mistaken to think of them as entirely detached from the goods-producing industries. It is true that the goods-producing sectors of all modern economies employ a declining proportion of the paid labour force. In Manitoba, only one-third of today's work force actually produces goods, the rest produce "services." But the commercial sector would dwindle to little or nothing without goods production. For example, at least one-third of Manitoba's large transportation sector depends on moving manufacturing input or output. Similarly, most high technology in the province comprises services. Without a growing manufacturing base, professionals in such fields as design, computer programming and process engineering would migrate, removing skilled people upon which new manufacturing depends. To a disturbing degree, this has already happened. Social services would also dwindle since they are paid for mainly from the taxes generated from private-sector employment. It is not surprising, then, that the slow-down in manufacturing and agricultural production since 1981 has been accompanied by a parallel slow-down in the growth of service employment.

TABLE 14

RELATIVE IMPORTANCE OF FINANCE AND DISTRIBUTION,
MANITOBA AND CANADA, 1951-1981
(Finance, Insurance and Real Estate)

	Manitoba		Canada		Manitoba/ Canada
	Employment 000	% of Total Employment	Employment 000	% of Total Employment	
1951	9	3.0	144	2.7	1.11
1961	12	3.6	229	3.5	1.02
1971	16	3.8	358	4.2	0.90
1981	25	5.0	636	5.3	0.94

Source: Statistics Canada, *Census of Canada*, various years.

Conclusion

The evidence suggests that Manitoba's economy is fragile, and that its historically diversified character, from which its relative economic stability has previously derived, is being gradually eroded. This can be seen most clearly in agriculture and mining, and especially in manufacturing. The process is related, at least in part, to the fact that Manitoba's is a peripheral economy, a hinterland, particularly of Ontario, with a disproportionate number of small branch plants and offices. Manitoba's economy is structurally weak, and the structure is gradually eroding.

The province's relative decline, which began some seventy years ago, is likely to be accelerated as a consequence of the global restructuring of capital and the FTA with the United States. This bodes ill for Manitoba's future — the province could suffer the same fate in the twenty-first century as did Atlantic Canada in this century.

Provincial governments in the postwar period have not been able to reverse Manitoba's long-term decline. This is not to say that the policies of provincial governments have been unimportant. The Pawley government, for example, stabilized the decline and protected the social net, unlike the disastrous Lyon government which accelerated the decline and savaged social programs.

However, the global restructuring of capital may so adversely affect our fragile peripheral economy that the primarily defensive strategy of the cautious and pragmatic NDP may no longer be the most "realistic" course of action. A more active role for government, and/or a different form of politics, may be needed if serious economic and social decline is to be prevented. Whether social democracy, particularly as practiced by the province's liberal NDP, can rise to this challenge remains to be seen. What the evidence strongly suggests is that more of the same is no longer enough.

NOTES

1. M.C. Urquhart and K. Buckley, eds., *Historical Statistics of Canada*, 2nd ed. (Cambridge: Cambridge University Press, 1983), 91-103.

2. H. Chorney, "The Political Economy of Provincial Economic Development Policy: A Case Study of Manitoba" (Master's thesis, University of Manitoba, 1970).

3. D.J. Snidal, "A Financial History of Manitoba from 1950 to 1965" (Master's thesis, University of Manitoba, 1967), 58.

4. Census of Canada, 1961, Catalogue 94-747, "Employed Labour Force by Industry, Age and Sex."

5. Ibid., Catalogue 94-551, "Occupation and Industry Trends (SL-1)."

6. Snidal, "Financial History," 70.

7. Chorney, "Political Economy," 41.

8. Ibid.

9. Manitoba, *Manitoba Budget and Economic Review* (Winnipeg: Department of Finance, 1961).

10. Manitoba, *Manitoba Budget and Economic Review* (Winnipeg: Department of Finance, 1960).

11. Canada, Dominion Bureau of Statistics, Catalogue 68-208, "Provincial Government Finance," 1957 and 1968.

12. Manitoba, *Legislative Assembly Debates and Proceedings* (Spring 1963).

13. The Honourable Gurney Evans, quoted in Harold Chorney, "Manitoba Development Fund: The N.D.P. Meets Big Business in Manitoba," *Canadian Dimension* 6, no. 7 (February-March 1970): 21.

14. Ibid.

15. Manitoba Development Fund, "Annual Reports."

16. Chorney, "Manitoba Development Fund."

17. Chorney, "Political Economy," 55.

18. Statistics Canada, Catalogue 61-206, "Private and Public Investment in Canada," 1958 to 1968.

19. Statistics Canada, *Canada Year Book*, 1951, 1969.

20. Snidal, "Financial History," 158.

21. James A. McAllister, *The Government of Edward Schreyer: Democratic Socialism in Manitoba* (Kingston and Montréal: McGill-Queen's University Press, 1984).

22. Ibid.

23. *Winnipeg Tribune*, 5 July 1969.

24. McAllister, *Government of Edward Schreyer*, 141.

25. James O'Conner, *The Fiscal Crisis of the State* (New York: St. Martin's Press, 1973), 9.

26. Calculated from Manitoba, Department of Finance, "Public Accounts of the Province of Manitoba."

27. Manitoba, *Manitoba Budget Address* (Winnipeg: Department of Finance, 1977).

28. Statistics Canada, *Private and Public Investment in Canada*, 1969-1977.

29. Manitoba, *Manitoba Budget Address* (Winnipeg: Department of Finance, 1978), Appendix.

31. Clarence Barber, *On the Form and Presentation of the Government of Manitoba's Budget* (Winnipeg: Department of Finance, 1983).

32. Manitoba, *Manitoba Budget Address* (Winnipeg: Department of Finance, 1980), Appendix.

33. Frances Russell, "Lyon Government's Record Wasn't Very Impressive," *Winnipeg Free Press*, 6 April 1988.

34. Ibid.

35. Manitoba, *Public Accounts of the Province of Manitoba*, 1988.

36. Manitoba, *Manitoba Budget Address* (Winnipeg: Department of Finance, 1987).

37. Statistics Canada, Catalogue 13-574, "Employment by Domestic and Foreign Controlled Enterprises in Canada: A Provincial Analysis," 1975.

38. *Financial Post 500*, 1988.

39. Jim Silver, "Packing It In," *Canadian Dimension* 21, no. 3 (1987): 16.

40. Statistics Canada, "Employment by Domestic and Foreign Controlled Enterprises."

41. N.E. Cameron, J.M. Dean and W.S. Good, *The Manufacturing Sector in Manitoba* (Ottawa: Economic Council of Canada, 1984).

42. Statistics Canada, "Employment by Domestic and Foreign Controlled Enterprises."

43. Census of Canada, 1981, Catalogue 94-747, "Employed Labour Force by Industry, Age and Sex."

44. G. Mason and L. Mercer, "Survey of Canadian Manufacturing, 1985," *Western Economic Review* (Summer 1986).

45. Census of Canada, 1981, "Employed Labour Force by Industry, Age and Sex."

46. Statistics Canada, Catalogue 71-001, "The Labour Force."

47. Ibid.

SECTION TWO

The Métis in Manitoba:
Dispossession, Dispersal and Marginalization

Manitoba entered Confederation in 1870 as a Métis province. Twenty years later, it was no longer so. The original inhabitants of Red River had been largely dispossessed, and many had dispersed to relocate in scattered Métis villages further west. Their dispossession and dispersal were a part of the process of primitive accumulation, by which the Prairies were forcibly transformed from a pre-capitalist to a capitalist mode of production. The result was the marginalization of the Métis.

The process of primitive accumulation involves, in part, the separation of pre-capitalist producers from their means of production, in order that capital accumulation can occur:

> So long . . . as the worker can accumulate for himself — and this he can do so long as he remains in possession of his means of production — capital accumulation and the capitalist mode of production are impossible.[1]

Thus the Métis were separated from the land to serve the interests of eastern capital. This process of separation from the means of production is seldom peaceful. In Manitoba it was effected not only by military force, but also by government and private lawlessness, dishonesty, violence and racial bigotry. The negative consequences are with us today, as can be seen in the chapters by Reinart, Falconer, Hull and Loxley.

Don Bailey examines in detail the process of primitive accumulation referred to earlier by Phillips. Bailey argues that the role of racism is especially important in explaining the dispossession of the Red River Métis, since their dispossession was not necessary for the emergence of capitalism. The Métis, he argues, could well have been incorporated into the emerging mode of production. That they were not was a function of the irrationality of racism and religious bigotry rather than the needs of the new mode of production.

To the importance of racism as an explanatory variable, St.-Onge adds the role of class differentiation. In an earlier article she has described how differing rates of dispossession and dispersal in the Métis village of Pointe-à-Grouette (now Ste. Agathe) depended on the class position of particular Métis families.[2] Here she examines the origins and social structure of the Métis village of Saint-Laurent, to which some of the Red River Métis fled after 1870. Their dispossession forced them to eke out a precarious existence on the margins of the new, more powerful mode of production. But in describing the historical development of the marginalized Métis village of Saint-

Laurent, St.-Onge is able to identify the emergence of sharp social and economic differentiation, and the beginnings of a class structure.

In this and other work, St.-Onge has place herself among the small but important minority of writers on Métis history who do not orient their work around the concept of "nation." Elsewhere she has observed that:

> Writing on the history of the metis in the last century has been characterized by a nationalist approach. The majority of historians in the field today still concern themselves with the questions of when and how a "people" came into being.[3]

She questions the nationalist paradigm on the grounds that "the nationalist approach has difficulty dealing with the complex *internal* structures, tensions, and conflicts found among the metis populations."[4] Furthermore, many of the Métis who have been able to move into the *petite bourgeoisie* have become assimilated, and no longer think of themselves, nor are they identified, as Métis. St.-Onge's approach to the study of Saint-Laurent enables us to see this more complex reality of Manitoba's marginalized Métis.

The two chapters which follow reveal a part of the underside of the opening of the west and Manitoba's entry into Confederation. And they document the continued marginalization of many of the descendants of the original inhabitants of the province. The political, social and economic life of Manitoba still bears the birthmark of the dispossession and dispersal of the Métis and other Native people which accompanied its entry into Confederation. It is part of the daily, but largely silent, experience of a minority, punctuated both by the occasional flare-ups of racial hatred and the ongoing struggles of the original inhabitants of Manitoba.

NOTES

1. Karl Marx, *Capital, Volume I* (Harmondsworth: Penguin, 1976), 933.
2. Nicole St.-Onge, "The Dissolution of a Metis Community: Pointe-à-Grouette, 1860-1885," *Studies in Political Economy* 18 (Autumn 1985): 149-72.
3. Nicole St.-Onge, " 'Nationalist Perspectives': A Review Essay," *Manitoba History* 14 (Autumn 1987): 37.
4. Ibid., 39.

The Métis Province and Its Social Tensions 3

Donald A. Bailey

Manitoba and British Columbia have so far been the only provinces to join Confederation with Euro-Canadian residents not in firm control of their respective government and economy. In both provinces, racial tensions accompanied the triumph of Euro-Canadian predominance, as the Métis of Manitoba and the Asians and Indians of British Columbia lost the economic opportunities they had begun to establish.[1] In Manitoba, however, the actual significance of events was further obscured by the blending of racial tensions with bicultural rivalries transported from central Canada. Until very recently, the linguistic and religious tensions of Manitoba's history have been studied apart from the problem of Métis land claims. Yet only by studying them together can we hope to understand the origins of the economic and social marginalization of Manitoba's Métis throughout the twentieth century.

The most settled region of Rupert's Land formed a very small province in 1870. This province of Manitoba was not predominantly inhabited by peoples of purely European descent. The census taken that first summer sought to exclude persons who did not spend at least a portion of the year in some manner of settled occupancy, but who merely travelled in and out of the new province, however frequently. Even so, the census yielded a population of 558 Amerindians, 1,565 whites, and 9,840 persons whose descent derived from both the other peoples.[2] Manitoba thus attained political recognition as an overwhelmingly Métis province. After only a decade, and within the same boundaries, Manitoba's population had increased more than fivefold, to 65,954, while the combined Indian and Métis population had actually declined, to 6,767. By 1901, while the 1882 boundary extension had virtually quadrupled the territory, the Indian and Métis population had only doubled, to 16,277 persons, but the province's total population had reached 255,211. The proportion of those recognizing partially or wholly Amerindian origins now stood at a mere 6.4 percent.[3] What had happened? The early history of Manitoba must be judged as disastrous for the province's founding people, and this disaster bears investigation.

In this interpretation, I shall be using the word "Métis" to indicate an ethnic group whose dynamic history has evaded all hard-and-fast definitions except those of popular usage.[4] Those included in the group share the following characteristics: original descent from a union of normally a western European father and an Amerindian mother; ancestral participation in one or more aspects of the fur trade; and self-consciousness of a shared community, culture, and economic activity that led to several political demands in the mid-nineteenth century. Since no satisfactory English word or euphemism emerged from the experiences shaping Métis ethnicity, I shall follow the recent practice of including Anglo-Protestants with the Franco-Catholics who first enjoyed unrivalled use of the word. The exclusions from the group are equally important, however, for not every child of the fur trade assumed this new nationality.

Innumerable individuals managed to assimilate completely into the white or Indian communities, most of whom lost all Métis associations in a process that need not have been conscious or difficult. Therefore, no census returns based on racial, linguistic or religious expectations will reveal the full potential of Métis identification, although the census tracts do roughly chart those willing to be recognized as Métis at any given time.

Generalizations are always hazardous, but today's Métis realities were crystallized by certain broadly recognizable trends in nineteenth-century Canadian attitudes and behaviour. Among the Anglo-Celtic Protestants of Ontario, whether they remained in central Canada or moved to the west, hostility towards anyone of French and/or Roman Catholic background tended to exist. This prejudice was sometimes hidden by yet another, shared by significant numbers of Euro-Canadians irrespective of language or religion: namely, a contemptuous misunderstanding of Indian culture and of the Métis culture that they barely distinguished from it. The dynamics of western Canada were thus immensely complicated, because neither the Euro-Canadian nor the Métis communities knew which of their cultural attachments was the more meaningful for their present or future well-being. During the crucial early years, conflicting loyalties perhaps bore down hardest on the French Canadians and English Métis, while appearing easier for the French Métis and even more so for English Canadians. The irresolution of the French Canadians contributed significantly to their own loss of status when their natural Métis allies suffered the loss of their lands. All these cultural factors obscured the economic developments of the period.

Before the close of the nineteenth century, the Canadian west had lost control of its own economy, the French and Roman Catholics had lost the political means of protecting their culture, and the Métis had been stripped of a crucial means (land) for their successful transition from one largely independent variety of economic activity to another. The historical fate of Manitoba has been to have its local developments interpreted too often from the perspective of national themes, when the uniqueness of the province's origins is its most significant feature. What features distinguished the Red River Settlement as it approached Confederation?

The Métis Before the Insurrection
Cultural Affiliations with Euro-Canadians

The statistical data, oddly enough, are better for the cultural than for the economic features. In 1870 the French Métis comprised 48 percent of the population, the English Métis, 34 percent — a total of over 82 percent. This racial-cultural feature distinguished Manitoba from other provinces, and was a crucial component of many Canadians' attitudes towards the Métis province. Many observers had doubted the propriety of the HBC's jurisdiction over the Red River Settlement and thought little of what that settlement called government.[5] Canadians tended to think of Manitoba as culturally primitive, an attitude shared both by many of the clergy who appealed for various kinds of support from the east, and by many of the 819 whites present in 1870 who had not been born in the colony. It was probably less prevalent among the 747 native-born whites (the descendants of the Selkirk settlers and other early arrivals). Easterners initially greeted the insurrection of 1869-70 and the Provisional Government at Fort Garry, like the earlier one at Portage-la-Prairie, more with derision than acknowledgment.[6] However, the seriousness of the situation and the clamour of the eastern press meant that Sir John A. Macdonald's government had to react. Macdonald preferred an early, nonmilitary conclusion to the impasse, and thus entered the negotiations that led to the Manitoba Act of 1870.

While Ontario and Québec newspapers were initially agreed in describing the Red River society as primitive, riotous, and in need of chastisement, the Ontario press found other offensive characteristics in the rebellion. In doing so, it changed the opinion being expressed in Québec papers.[7] The population that was soon to receive provincial autonomy was 52 percent Roman Catholic and just under 48 percent Protestant (6,247 and 5,716 persons, respectively).[8] The 1870 census did not distinguish the inhabitants' preferred languages, but traditional opinion estimates that slightly over half the population was by preference French-speaking.[9] Ontario papers interpreted Louis Riel's inspiration and support to be entirely French and Catholic, and Protestant opinion was quick to discern the machinations of some Roman Catholic clergy behind the insurrection. The Québec press immediately took offense at this characterization of the event, and began to defend its religious and linguistic brethren at Red River. Thus, both in its origins and in its historical representation, Manitoba reproduced the bicultural features of Confederation and continued these eastern tensions.

To do so, however, immediately and subsequently obscured the diverse cultural reality of those origins. Manitoba was indeed almost evenly Franco-Catholic and Anglo-Celtic-Protestant, but these divergent features were superficial in comparison with the more profound aspects of Métis ethnicity, which in fact lent a pervasive, if not uniform, commonality to more than four-fifths of the original Manitobans.

European culture was by no means deeply rooted in Rupert's Land. Whites had been on the coast of Hudson Bay since the 1670s, and in the southern river valleys since the 1730s. The origins of the Métis in the area date from these arrivals, but literacy in French and English, as well as instruction in the Christian faith, followed slowly. The first schools and churches in the region date from the arrival of Abbé Joseph Provencher in 1818, with English-Protestant institutions following within half a decade.[10] Despite the dedication and diligence of the clergy and teachers of the era, though no doubt partly because of their narrow cultural assumptions, European acculturation was little more than a veneer in 1870, even if we notice the few, usually male, children who had been sent to Britain, Ontario, or Québec for their education. That just over one-half of the 1,565 white inhabitants in 1870 had been born in the Canadas, Britain or elsewhere cannot have much affected the colony's culture as a whole. The Métis were recorded as loyal adherents of respective Christian faiths, but they were also independently minded.[11] Both the economics and the culture of their lives had stronger features than the noteworthy parallels with central Canadian society.

Socio-Economic Origins

The hunters and gatherers of the Prairies and woodlands readily found advantages in exchanging their surplus furs and foodstuffs for guns and other equipment of European or Canadian manufacture. For about two centuries, the people of the plains controlled their own cultural and economic life, making only those concessions which they thought beneficial to themselves.[12]

Changes nonetheless occurred, at first gradually, but later much too quickly for easy adjustment. The diminishing supply of buffalo shifted migration and settlement patterns, and initiated frictions between peoples who previously had been able to choose whether to cooperate with or ignore each other. The white trading posts and settlements had opened new opportunities for gainful labour in transporting materials and supplying agricultural products.[13] The independent spirit of the Métis found satisfaction and advantage in pursuing one or more aspects of the fur trade, in construction and transportation within or between settlements, in cultivation of the soil and exploitation of woodlands, lakes and streams, or in various combinations of these alternatives. Whites were occasionally attracted to the freedom of the plains, while increasing numbers of Métis settled more or less permanently into sedentary options, at least for part of each year.

Naturally, divisions of labour and variations in economic advantages emerged from the intersections of this variety of activity. Although whites were predominantly involved in the mercantile, professional, or agricultural occupations, Métis were also participating in the ownership and management of mercantile operations, the religious calling, or settled agriculture. The English Métis sometimes saw themselves as more ''progressive'' in their ways (meaning more settled and capitalistic), but in everything they did — cultivation of the soil, the fur trade, or labour services around the settlements — parallels with the French Métis remained more striking than their divergences. In the decade between 1838 and 1849, the gap between the two Métis groups narrowed dramatically. The proportion of English Métis who cultivated ten or more acres rose from 17.7 percent to 28.2 percent; the French Métis's proportion jumped from 2.3 percent to 20.7 percent.[14] Widespread trilingualism and frequent intermarriage softened the cultural distinctions imported from European heritages, while the economic activities of the region either created social differences of equal importance to those of language and religion or secured a social bond that was in fact the most important cultural feature of the region.[15] Talk of the new, Métis ''nation'' during these decades is eloquent testimony to this phenomenon.

While eastern ambitions and attitudes intruded into Rupert's Land, the economic and cultural autonomy of the region survived even the stresses accompanying the transfer of title from the HBC to the Dominion of Canada, and those leading through the insurrection to the creation of the province of Manitoba — at least for almost a decade. When that autonomy collapsed, the Métis province was no more.

Canadian national historiography has traditionally focussed on the perishing throughout the Prairies of the nascent Franco-Catholic culture derived from Euro-Canadian origins, and has treated as of peripheral interest the simultaneous weakening of Métis society in its economic and everyday activities. Here, I seek to emphasize the ties between these separately regarded phenomena. They both fell victim to the same

Ontario drive for western hegemony. But the cultural tensions separating Ontario from Québec served as an ideological cloak for Ontario's economic victory over the west.

Seen from the east, the Prairies were either an inhospitable and probably worthless burden or an exploitable promise of Eden.[16] Seen from within the west, but with the eyes of those easterners who had come to seek their fortune, the Prairies offered great opportunities, but only if the culture and institutions of their birthlands could be imposed there. Both French Canadians and Anglo-Celts tended to share such views of the plains and the native-born plainspeople, even while they retained the intercultural rivalries of the Canadas as a sort of counterpoint to the remarkably cooperative society functioning at Red River. Eastern-educated Métis, such as James Ross, son of historian Alexander Ross, suffered the tensions of indecision between the "superior" culture from which they thought the west would benefit and the plains culture whose possessors they did not want to see victimized.[17] During the crisis of 1869-70, James Ross was to vacillate between Louis Riel and those Canadians who opposed his provisional government.

In 1835, the HBC had restructured the Council of Assiniboia to provide a more immediate governance in the region. The council soon had both French- and English-speaking members; it came to publish laws and announcements in both European languages, to hire officials who severally or together could serve the society in both languages, and to provide financial subsidies to both Protestant and Catholic schools in equal portions.[18] But it lacked the coercive power to enforce its authority, and the structured institutions to win the respect of newcomers. The contrasting economic tensions of disappearing buffalo herds and the heady speculation familiar to many frontier communities aggravated political uncertainties. The future of Rupert's Land appeared to be tied to the Confederation discussions in the east, but no one was certain how, or when. Among the English-speaking "Canadians" and Métis in the Red River Settlement and its near neighbours, tensions led to several petitions for improved government that were ignored by the HBC and in the east.[19] There were short-lived "provisional governments" instigated by Protestant Canadians and Métis at Headingly and St. James in May 1863, and then at Portage-la-Prairie in January 1868. These anglophone groups were thus in no position to object to Riel's impatience or illegality, but they misunderstood his goals and resented their own loss of the initiative.

Issues and Resolution: 1869-1870

So many questions were in dispute. Would the local inhabitants have any influence in the transfer of their territory to Canada? Would they become a colony of the dominion government, or be allowed to continue their present proto-autonomy, and if so, in what form? Would their current occupancy of particular land be confirmed, or did the arrival of eastern surveyors foretell, as the Métis feared, the loss of lands lacking registered title? Would the institutions and personnel of government continue to serve the settlement in both French and English, or were the self-proclaimed precursors of Canadian civilization going to realize their tactless aspirations for the re-creation of Ontario society in the west? The question of safeguarding the settlement's confessional schools appears to have been overlooked until the return of Bishop Alexandre Taché from Rome, via Ottawa, at the end of the winter.[20]

What Riel thus sought and obtained from Macdonald's government amounted to guarantees for the cultural survival of a Métis province within the Dominion of Canada. This was a dynamic society, one already undergoing profound changes in its economic and cultural life. Settled agriculture, mercantile prosperity, the further penetration of Euro-Canadian culture: these developments were well underway and understood to be so by Riel.[21] But he hoped to secure control over that development for those native to the region. In this, he was soon to be disappointed.

The significance of the cultural guarantees in the Manitoba Act are easily missed, because they are not presented in one grouped series of articles.[22] Articles 9 through 13 provided for an upper house, styled the Legislative Council and appointed by the lieutenant governor. Article 16 required that the twenty-four electoral districts for the Legislative Assembly have "due regard . . . to existing Local Divisions and population." Articles 22 and 23 provided, respectively, for the protection of local practices with respect to confessional schools and for legislative and judicial language rights for both French and English. Articles 31 and 32 provided, respectively, for land to be settled on the children of "half-breed residents" and for the security of titles to land already possessed by residents of the colony.

The integrity and autonomy of the Métis culture require that these articles be read together. By 1890, every one of them had been abrogated, legislatively overridden or circumvented, or judicially undermined. Métis culture, as an influential presence in the new province, had been overwhelmed on all fronts, including (in 1885) the military. The Métis province had been transformed into an outpost of Ontario — economically, politically and to a large extent even culturally. This social revolution had tragic results that continue to this day. The majority of prairie Métis became economically marginalized and culturally disoriented. On the periodic occasions when claims are revived for one or more of the rights originally promised for the province's founders, the troubled conscience of the dominant culture has reacted, despite some ambiguities, with an often passionate irrationality.

Promise and Disillusionment: 1870-1900
The Question of Métis Land Claims

Land was the basic right: it potentially connected cultural rights to economic and political power. But in the 1870-90 period very few Métis realized the importance of what Euro-Canadians meant by ownership, while those who did encountered a myriad of obstacles to registering their claims. Métis tardiness in appreciating the importance of title to particular land plots was originally due to the abundance of land, and social attitudes emphasized its commonality. Not land, but the resources on it; not possession, but usufruct, were what had traditionally mattered to plains people.[23] Only gradually had they begun to adapt to sedentary, possessive behaviour and attitudes.

By the mid-nineteenth century, the disappearance of the buffalo on the eastern Prairies and the concentration of mercantile life in the Red River and Assiniboine River valleys encouraged a system of land holding known to similar cultures elsewhere. A narrow strip of land along one of the rivers would be settled by a family. The strip ran back from the river into the open prairie, and it might also cross the river in order to stake a claim to the woodlands on which a part of the family economy depended, or to the higher ground on which the family's shelter might more securely be built. Social communities developed up and down the river, and families could retain their cohesion by expanding close to the parental holding.[24]

In socioeconomic terms, such landholdings sustained diverse forms of life. Sedentary activities ranged from trade and transportation sheltered in hasty or substantial buildings, to livestock raising and extensive agriculture. The Anglo-Protestant Métis in particular paralleled French and British Euro-Canadians in devoting energies to these proto-capitalist activities. In 1867, for instance, Métis farmers alone harvested 15,000 bushels of grain; the usual potato crop could reach 12,000 bushels.[25] Beside these wealthier exploiters of the land there lived — at least during certain seasons — the wage labourers of commerce and transport, the small and sometimes larger independent carters of goods along routes joining the Red River Colony to St. Paul, Minnesota, and to the fur-trade outposts further west. Others might leave behind even less evidence of seasonal occupancy, as their often insubstantial shelters were abandoned for the fur and buffalo hunt that occupied the summer months. However temporary the stay along the river, modest exploitation of its resources occurred, usually including the cultivation of a few acres of land. A mile or two inland, the natural hays provided fodder for horses and other livestock owned by the riverside dwellers.

In legal terms, these diverse landholdings might have been purchased from the HBC and registered in the manner deemed conventional by the cultures of eastern Canada. The HBC had also frequently ceded, or come to recognize, less formal claims to land that had long been settled and exploited by current or former employees and others. These claims appeared better established than those resting on merely "peaceable possession . . . in those parts of the province in which the Indian title has not been extinguished." But even this occupancy was protected in Article 32.4 of the Manitoba Act. The lieutenant governor was authorized to regularize these different forms of entitlement to land (Article 32.5), but the initial efforts of the first holders of this office were frustrated, even overruled.

D. Bruce Sealey, Douglas N. Sprague, Philippe R. Mailhot, and Gerhard Ens have produced works thoroughly demonstrating the despoliation of Métis lands and the government lawlessness that accompanied it.[26] In brief, acts of both ignorance and acquisitiveness were committed by legislators, administrators, and judges, at both the provincial and federal levels. A census was taken three times in five years. Surveyors deliberately overlooked or failed to notice the scattered and hastily constructed buildings and markers that gave evidence of merely seasonal occupancy. Municipal road allowances were carved out of even well-cultivated tracts of land, often at inconvenient trajectories. And filings for formal registration were more often than not refused, challenged, or postponed. The riot of delays, cancelled registrations, and new beginnings made it all the more discouraging for Métis claimants and all the easier for newcomers and speculators to register claims to what confusion married to collusion regarded as unoccupied lands.

The deterioration continued when scrip was introduced as an alternative to registration of specific claims. Scrip was good either for land yet to be determined or for whatever money could be obtained by selling its potential.[27] Undervaluing the title to a tangible tract of land, hard up for ready cash, or demoralized by the constant obstacles and other signs of persecution, many Métis exchanged their scrip for paltry sums of money, and left forever the province they had founded.[28]

Even more confusion and spoliation accompanied the disposal of lands promised to Métis children. Article 31 of the Manitoba Act was actually a brilliant response to a subtle problem. Despite the two-century claim of the HBC, the western lands were still arguably the actual possession of Indian tribes, with whom the Dominion of Canada had yet to negotiate. From one or more ancestors, the Métis shared in such Indian claims, yet they were now a people apart. "Towards the extinguishment of the Indian Title," 1.4 million acres within the new province were set aside for "the children of the half-breed heads of families." The apportionment of these lands required more than the indecisive series of census-taking. For instance, what generation and what gender determined the status of family head? At what age might children be said to be legally possessed of their estate? In the interests of local equity, should the descendants of the Selkirk Settlers, although not mentioned in the act, have had a similar legacy established for them? Much mischief could be derived from these problems. In addition, there was the intrinsic challenge of assigning lands to children in the vicinity of their parents' habitation, as deemed important in their culture. Since even the hay fields two miles back from the riverside strip and the claim on the opposite shore were under challenge, family continuity was made even more difficult.

The Failure of Politics

Could a Métis province established on democratic principles not have better protected the interests of its majority? Even if significant responsibility for the despoliation of Métis land claims can be placed on federal misunderstandings and complicity, the provincial government might better have controlled its own fate.

In fact, for the first half-decade it managed to do just that. Lieutenants Governor Adams G. Archibald (1870-72) and Alexander Morris (1872-77) cooperated with a conscientious legislature in the passage of the Half-breed Land Protection Act, 1873, section 1 of the Courts of Queen's Bench Act, 1874 (which introduced into Manitoba the legal protections for infants' estates enjoyed in England), and the Infant Estates Act, 1878. These acts attempted to protect Métis claims to their pre-Confederation occupancy and their children's rights not to have their land disposed of before they came of age.[29]

Unfortunately, these legislative efforts were undermined by less conscientious judges (federal appointees originally from the east). The sons and grandson of Chief

Justice Edmund Burke Wood were employed in legal, real estate and land registry offices, out of which they cooperated with the family head and their friends in extensive duplicity where transfers of Métis land claims were concerned. Even the presence on the Bench of Judge Joseph Dubuc, and the 1881 hearings that investigated such legal and judicial irregularities, were unable to halt the rout of Métis landholdings,[30] in which, it must be admitted, Métis naivety and greed occasionally played a role.

The Legislative Assembly itself suffered some internal weaknesses. Métis members of the Legislative Assembly (MLA)never formed a majority there, although their people comprised over 80 percent of the population. In the first three elections, however, nine or more Métis were elected, and this no doubt accounts for some of the sympathetic legislation just described. With two "Old Settlers" and three to six French Canadians in each of these legislatures, pre-Confederation attitudes easily prevailed.[31] Nonetheless, the early cabinets contained no French Métis until the 1875 appointment of Charles Nolin. Both English and French Métis were inclined or easily persuaded to concede such demanding responsibilities to easterners or Manitobans of purely Euro-Canadian descent.

Taché and George-Etienne Cartier convinced French-Canadian professionals to leave Québec and to lend their skills to the new province.[32] Lawyers such as Joseph Dubuc, Marc A. Girard, and Joseph Royal immediately were elected to the legislature or appointed to the Court of Queen's Bench in Manitoba, and they went on to become senators or lieutenants governor there or in the North-West Territories. Although loyal to the language and religion of French Canada and sympathetic initially to the fortunes of the Métis in Manitoba, these men had more paternal than fraternal attitudes towards their putative cultural allies. They were too ready to trust Anglo-Protestant and federal assurances, to counsel patience, and to rationalize delays.[33] The worst of the French-Canadian newcomers of course saw opportunities for personal fortunes in the prevailing land speculation, and saw no reason for only Anglo-Protestants to enjoy the benefits.

Gradually, French Métis became mistrustful of their professional leaders, including members of the clergy, while English Métis appear often to have entered the process of assimilation into the expanding Canadian population. Tensions were thereby aggravated in several directions simultaneously. Bishop Taché's failure to secure the pardons promised to Louis Riel and Ambroise Lepine hurt his credibility, even though he had worked closely with Lieutenant Governor Archibald in charting the early course of the province. With the increasing departures of the Métis from the province, Taché and some of his priests participated in the purchase of their land and scrip.

It is difficult to judge how much Taché expected to assist some Métis out of the misfortune of others, but his motives were certainly not personal advantage. He devoted the land to the settling of French-Canadian arrivals from Québec and, after 1874, New England; that is, to the establishment of contiguous French-Catholic communities.[34] Métis suspicions, however, were not entirely reassured through such an exchange in ownership. Such suspicions developed both *between* the two races sharing one language and religion and *within* the common Métis culture, along with the distinctions between the two languages and the two religions. Superimposed on these were the cultural suspicions of central Canada, which at Red River after 1870 aggravated any intracultural cleavages that differences in economic attitudes and opportunities already foreshadowed.

The Clash of Cultures

The imposition of intra-Canadian rivalries into the Red River region had preceded the 1869-70 crisis and, indeed, helped to precipitate it. For at least a decade before Confederation, recent arrivals from Ontario had revealed their general contempt for those native to the colony, especially if they were Franco-Catholic Métis. Dr. John Christian Schultz personified many of their worst qualities, though he spoke for many others through his ownership (1864-66) of *The Nor' Wester*. He combined personal ambition with unscrupulous business practices, showed his dislike for the HBC and contempt for the Métis, and argued vociferously for union with Canada.[35] Meanwhile, a popular clergyman at Headingly, The Reverend G.O. Corbett, used the local press to denounce Roman Catholicism in the early 1860s, again not being unique in his sentiments. The prejudiced intemperance of Thomas Scott, which precipitated his execution by the Riel government in March 1870, is well known. All these examples led to Métis suspicions about the union with Canada, to the extent that Riel's intentions were immediately misinterpreted in the autumn of 1869. While he sought to safeguard Métis interests through a union with Canada on negotiated terms, local observers anticipated that the French Métis-initiated uprising was motivated to prevent union.[36]

It is no doubt accurate to balance the solid achievements of Riel's local diplomacy (which soon broadened the base of his support), statesmanlike constitution, and peaceful transition of power against the ill-effects of the Scott execution. But would history have unfolded differently without the shibboleth of Scott? The Ontario press denounced the language, religion and culture behind the insurrection months before the Scott episode, and the Anglo-Protestants of both Canadas who volunteered for the Wolseley expedition did not need Scott's memory to motivate them, however much passion it aggravated. Colonel Garnet Wolseley returned east before the winter began in 1870, once assured of the peaceableness of the colony, but the troops he left behind acted out their contempt, especially of the Métis. They were harassed, intimidated, assaulted and even in individual cases murdered with impunity, while their own misdemeanors were harshly dealt with.[37] The Métis soon avoided entering the new capital of Winnipeg, which did not render any easier the registration of their land titles.

The verbal and press assaults on the French language and Catholic schools that accompanied the physical harassment of the Métis contributed after mid-decade to the demographic and economic transformations of the young province. Since the majority of Métis were by this time as seriously engaged in agrarian and other quasi-sedentary occupations as the white settlers, they remained patiently on their lands awaiting the conclusion of the process of distributing land and securing titles.[38] With the sleight of hand that reduced the number of section 31 claimants among the Métis by perhaps 40 percent, substituted (on grounds of "equity") Old Selkirk Settler claimants to free lands, and issued scrip in compensation to the dispossessed, the federal government was at last ready to begin the final registration of titles in 1875, after a new census.[39] The definition of "occupancy" and the manner of officially establishing it favoured white settlers and speculators over Métis settlers and their children, not only in the recognition of claims but in the size of grants allowed if recognized at all.[40] The Métis desertion of the province, in favour of the North Saskatchewan River valley and other Canadian and American sites to the west, only became significant after 1875, but once begun, it moved quickly.[41]

Population Shifts and the Transformation From Homeland to Hinterland

Significantly, yet largely coincidently, the influx of those who replaced them only began about the same date. The 1,200 men in Wolseley's Expeditionary Force were promised 160 acres each if they remained in the west,[42] and other emigrants from Ontario immediately joined them, while Taché and Cartier were trying to encourage Québec emigrants to journey west. But the first bulge in population occurred after 1873-75, when Icelanders, Mennonites, and New-England French Canadians began to augment the stream of settlers from Ontario, Britain and the United States. At the end of the decade, the Anglo-Celtic population comprised 58 percent, the German-speaking population (overwhelmingly of Russian Mennonite origin) just over 13 percent, those claiming French ancestry had fallen to just over 15 percent, and the Métis and Indian together comprised 10.3 percent. In religious terms, this population shift revealed an 1881 Roman Catholic population of only 18.6 percent.[43] These ethnic and religious trends, respectively rising for some and falling for others, continued during the 1880s.

In contrast, the economic pattern did not much change during the first decade. Although settlers from Ontario participated in the prosperity and speculation, the accruing benefits remained largely in the province. Commerce by steamship or wagon-cart continued to use the American railways reaching into Minnesota, and its profits were enjoyed by wholesalers like A.G.B. Bannatyne and J.H. Ashdown, whose goods were purchased, in roughly equal portions, in Britain, the United States, and eastern Canada. These men and other wealthy Manitobans also won their way against eastern interests in maintaining control of the local handling of the sale of western grain. Their entrepreneurship enticed the CPR route away from the more rational Selkirk bridgehead to a Winnipeg site in 1881. Although the major benefits of prairie growth hereafter increased for the CPR and other eastern interests, the local magnates continued to prosper, sharing with eastern capitalists in the monitoring of the western economy, and dominating their local society and its politics.[44]

In the words of Gerald Friesen, the 1880s saw the completion of Manitoba's transformation from "homeland to hinterland."[45] But in fact two transformations overlapped. The overall determination of the prairie economy passed from local initiatives, whether natural or human in origin, to eastern initiatives. Proto-capitalist activities, without much changing their local objective description, increasingly became the instruments at the periphery of the mature capitalism taking shape in central

Canada. This process was no doubt inevitable, and was of course at the heart of Ontario's interest in the west. But did this larger transformation *require* the local transformation, which deprived the Métis of their wealth and influence and which made Anglo-Celtic Protestants the agents *cum* beneficiaries of the expansion of eastern capitalism?

The local transformation assisted Ontario's ambitions at the expense of potentially equivalent ambitions in Québec, but we may ask whether the destruction of Franco-Catholic Métis culture was necessary for Ontario's rapid hegemony.[46] Métis agriculture resembled Selkirk Settler agriculture in 1870, and even exceeded it in the number of acres under cultivation. Furthermore, the Métis tenure centred on the fork of the Red and Assiniboine Rivers. It could have been bypassed, had that really been necessary, if the railway had crossed the river at Selkirk. The dominance that eastern capitalism sought and gained over the western economy could well have been exercised over Métis farmers and merchants, and did not require their dispossession. It was the particular competitiveness of Ontario capital *vis-à-vis* that of Québec, and the particular arrogance of Anglo-Canadian Protestantism, joined to Euro-Canadian assumptions of cultural superiority, that saw virtue or advantage in that dispossession. The cultural revolution in Manitoba between 1870 and 1890 was indirectly effected in the interests of mature, metropolitan capitalism; it was directly effected by a constellation of diverse cultural prejudices.[47]

The Assault on Cultural Institutions

In the first half of the 1870s there was the same general respectfulness in cultural matters that we have already noticed in the matter of land distribution and titles. The Public Schools Act of 1871 translated into statute the dual confessional traditions of education established in the colony decades before Confederation. A series of acts between 1873 and 1876 provided for official bilingualism in petitions for the incorporation of municipalities to be published in the *Manitoba Gazette*, in the proclamation of elections and establishment of voters' lists, in the publication of bylaws and official notices in municipalities where the francophone population was large enough to so warrant, and in the panelling of juries whenever a trial in French was requested. Even as late as 1885, when the collegiate departments were established for secondary schools, the legislature's objectives included "laying the foundations of a thorough education in the English and French language and literature."[48]

The respect for the province's origins, however, was already beginning to crumble. One of the first efforts of the members of Wolseley's Expeditionary Force had been to establish an Orange Lodge in Winnipeg, soon to be reproduced across the southern half of the province, wherever Presbyterian and Methodist settlers from Ontario set down roots. More than one of these settlements displaced the Métis occupation of the same land, with only the diplomacy of Louis Riel and A.G. Archibald preventing bloodshed. Significantly, the stream along which one of the dispossessed settlements was located, the present site of Carman, was renamed the Boyne.

The shifting demographic patterns of the province provided a pragmatic and financial, althouth inexcusable, rationale for the assault on biculturalism. As early as the autumn of 1876, the Protestant section of the board of education followed the Winnipeg School Board and the Manitoba Teachers' Association in calling for a single system of nonsectarian education and the use of English textbooks only. The same year, sections 9 through 13 of the Manitoba Act were altered or abrogated through the abolition of the Legislative Council, whose resemblance to that of Québec had been intended to safeguard the interests of the province's minority. By the terms of the British North America Act (1871) this alteration was almost certainly unconstitutional.[49]

A series of thwarted political coups made 1879 the watershed of two sociocultural eras. Although Premier Robert Davis had included one Métis from each of the Euro-Canadian backgrounds in his 1875 Cabinet (Nolin and Norquay), Métis discontent continued to grow. A challenge to his own reelection in 1878 increased Charles Nolin's irritation with the French element from Québec. While Premier John Norquay and his French-Canadian lieutenant, Joseph Royal, were in Ottawa for the virtually annual negotiations with the federal government, Nolin decided to attempt a coup. Royal easily reknit the francophone party upon his return, but then tried to use the discontent to engineer Norquay's resignation from his new premiership. Norquay in turn easily defeated Royal's efforts, but only with the temporary ejection of all French influences in the government. The cabinet became exclusively anglophone and a bill to demote French from its official status as a language of record passed the legislature, but was reversed by Lieutenant Governor Joseph Cauchon (the first and only francophone in that office in Manitoba).

An important by-product of these failed coups was a new election at the end of the year, based on a redistribution of constituencies that otherwise would not have taken effect until 1882.[50] The new legislature contained only four Métis, in contrast to the previous house's nine, and even the number of Old Settler MLAs was reduced from two to one. Between 1879 and 1881, three acts removed the protection enacted earlier for the land claims of Métis children and retroactively legitimized the many dubious land sales of the previous decade.[51] John Norquay survived as premier until late 1887 and attempted to soften the effects of the shift in power relationships within the province. But he was merely a symbol of the old order, while the reality had already changed.

The 1880s witnessed increased expression of Anglo-Protestant frustration with institutions and regulations serving the Franco-Catholic population. A pamphlet calling for the exclusion of French "from our legislature, from our courts, from our statutes, and from our public schools" was widely distributed in the province and its sentiments were echoed in the press and legislature.[52] D'Alton McCarthy's famous speech at Portage-la-Prairie in August 1889 may well have directly provoked the following year's Official Language Act, but the undermining of the minority's school rights which accompanied the act had already been planned by Joseph Martin and the new premier, Thomas Greenway.[53] The language and education acts of 1890 removed the last vestiges of constitutional protection for Manitoba's founding people. French did persist in schools located in Franco-Manitoban areas, as well as in aspects of Manitoban culture, press and politics throughout the twentieth century, but it achieved all these results as a private, not official, language of Manitoba. At least one annual speech in the legislature and the exiguous delivery of provincial government services in French failed to compensate for the political and demographic destruction of Franco-Catholic Métis preeminence in the province whose foundations that culture had built.

A Search for Explanations

Several important aspects of this revolution have been only insufficiently emphasized, and rarely together. First, the onslaught of Anglo-Protestant and Eastern European settlers was probably in the cards and would have made inevitable the reduction of the Franco-Catholic, perhaps even Métis, elements to a minority. Pragmatic considerations about financing parallel records and institutions and assimilating large numbers of immigrants to Canadian culture would certainly have followed. Second, had this growth been merely natural, rather than accompanied by so much cultural arrogance and intolerance, not to mention governmental lawlessness, the province's original foundations would have survived intact, supported by a vigorous minority, who in turn would have been more generously reinforced by Franco-Catholic immigration from whatever source. Secure lands and settled agriculture might well have forestalled both the significant Métis exodus after 1875, with all its disruptions to mortality and fertility rates, and the assimilationist pressures towards those who remained. Third, the constitutional guarantees for the minority would have sounded more credible from a significant, rather than what was soon an almost negligible, minority. Nothing would have prevented Anglo-Protestant polemics, but a minority sustaining itself at something between 20 percent and 35 percent (which I do not think is an unreasonable postulation) might well have weathered occasional political storms.[54] A majority's intolerance or sense of economy is likely to be less obstinate and less disruptive of social harmony than the acrimony generated by an unjustly treated minority continually seeking the modest restoration of rights. Fourth, divisions within the Franco-Catholic ranks must not be ignored, for they played their role in weakening the minority's resistence. In an article on the relationship between Métis and French Canadians during the early decades, Robert Painchaud asserts that the lack of rapport has been enveloped in a virtual conspiracy of silence, and Antoine Lussier has followed Painchaud in studying this important question up to the present.[55]

Euro-Canadian attitudes toward the Métis varied enormously, from a full sense of comradeship, such as that shared between former schoolmates Joseph Dubuc and Louis Riel, to an utter contempt of cultural primitiveness, such as opinions expressed at Red River in *The Nor'wester* or in Toronto by the editors of the *Globe*. On balance, however, the more sympathetic Euro-Canadians still presumed a responsibility for the cultural "improvement" of their Métis or Indian neighbours, a presumption which the latter increasingly came to resent. Again, on balance, Anglo-Protestant Métis were a little more successful in making the cultural transition than were the Franco-Catholic Métis. This contrast was initially only slight, if discernible at all, but it was augmented during the 1870s by the contrasting fortunes of French, with those of Anglo-Celtic, Euro-Canadians. Psychologically and culturally, it can only have made a significant difference whether one's Métis group shared an association with the rapidly ascending or with the rapidly descending Euro-Canadian group. In the 1870-74 period the French Métis decreased by 24 percent, but the English Métis by only 12 percent, within the original boundaries of Manitoba.[56] Furthermore, we must emphasize that intragroup frictions tend to appear more threatening within a defeated or deprived alliance than within a triumphant one. Exhortations to unity appear more necessary even as they actually aggravate divisiveness. The same pluralism which enriches and even strengthens a dominant culture is too often perceived as endangering the besieged one.

As early as the 1874 general election, some francophone constituencies were contested between French-Canadian and Métis candidates. Taché and Dubuc were being pressured from both English and French colleagues to discontinue their association with Riel, and were suspected by Métis sources of not obtaining Riel's pardon and the registration of land titles as quickly as promised.[57] Taché's purchase of Métis scrip, which he used to secure contiguous settlement for new arrivals from Québec and New England, did not enhance his credibility among the Métis who remained. The Nolin-Royal-Norquay affair in 1879 publicized rifts already deepening.

The abrogation of Franco-Catholic cultural rights in 1890 appears to have injected new sources of disaffection between the groups. While the French Canadians sought an alliance with Anglo-Celtic Catholics and Anglicans in defence of confessional schools, the Métis tended to place greater value on language rights. In the court challenges involving the latter in 1892, 1909, and 1916 the litigatants were French-Canadian versus French-Métis individuals. In 1892, Mr. Pellant charged that Mr. Hébert, being semiliterate, was ineligible for municipal office, while in 1916 the civil suit between J.P. Dumas, a short-term, Métis MLA, and Mr. Barribault initiated a rift within the French community.[58] Whereas *l'Association d'Education Française du Manitoba* was trying to prevent the termination of the Laurier-Greenway Compromise of 1896, which had permitted second-language instruction in the schools, it adopted a position of strict neutrality in Mr. Dumas's implied challenge to the 1890 Official Language Act. While private French Canadians tried, successfully, to have Dumas withdraw his suit altogether, *l' Union Nationale Métis* had been prepared to support him.

To trace the story through the twentieth century would require a second study, but various pieces of evidence indicate at least some *malaise* in relations between the Métis and the Euro-French members of the Franco-Manitoban community. Some of the friction is of course veiled by divisions between social classes, but it is equally arguable that racial antagonisms lay behind the lack of economic opportunity. Today, the francophone community reveals differing attitudes towards the advantages of French immersion and *français* programs: some Métis see speaking French as only one more obstacle to economic opportunity, while the Euro-French "treat them as savages regardless" of what language they speak.[59] Even within the church, criticism of Métis features on a new statue of the Virgin, unveiled in St. Boniface Cathedral, suggest that all is not well within the francophone community.[60]

Towards a Conclusion

As regards the socioeconomic fortunes of those recognizing themselves as Métis, Jean Lagassé's government study in 1958 revealed that only 25 percent of the Métis then employed were working in mainstream industrial or commercial enterprises; 10 percent were farming, though usually on plots insufficient to sustain a family without additional activity; 15 percent were engaged in lumber and pulp operations; the same proportion in seasonal work, such as gathering furs, fish, wild rice, seneca root, and berries; and the remaining 35 percent were casual labourers.[61] These figures do not include the number of unemployed Métis, but in themselves they indicate a rural and even marginal existence significantly different from that of the general population (see Chapter 4). The Métis's pre-Confederation reputation for hard work has disappeared, and the 1870 potential for building on early habits of settled agriculture and commerce has not been realized.

But suddenly we find ourselves caught up in a circular argument that returns us to an opening question: who *are* the Métis? Are they only those who are recognized as such by themselves, their neighbours, and census-takers? What are the analytical consequences of admitting that the majority of Métis are not identified as Métis at all, that they may be fully assimilated into Euro-Canadian society, where they appear to be ranged amongst most of the latter's socioeconomic classes? No one knows the extent of this possibility, yet to ignore it implies a haste to render the Métis identity equivalent to economic marginalization.

The Métis are not alone in suffering economic misfortune, nor are they utterly missing from the ranks of those enjoying economic success. In addition, cultural catastrophe has not been unique to the Métis and Manitoban experience. In all such cases, some members of the suffering communities accept their fates passively, while others find themselves able to surmount the difficulties. The story we have outlined in this study explains the conditions in which many Métis find themselves, but it only partly explains what determined where any individual Métis is today.Here, we are returned to the larger circle. If the smaller circle connects recognized Métis to conditions of poverty and "half-breed" people in poverty back to those recognized as Métis, what may need explanation is why the "successful" Métis escape classification. The explanation must have something to do with the demoting of Métis ethnicity from a position of respect and influence, a development which drives some Métis to eschew their heritage, while it disadvantages those who choose to affirm it. In this circumstance is one more parallel with the circumstance of Euro-French Canadians. In both cases, an officially Canadian culture and people have been dispossessed in their own house. The psychological trauma thereby enduced is more severe than that of mere conquest (indeed suffered in both cases) or of conventional immigration from a foreign land.

While assimilation into the dominant culture remains an option (if visible distinguishing features do not meet racial prejudices), the nagging question persists, why should a "founding people" *have to* assimilate to anyone else's culture in their own land? A people transfixed by the *mentalité* captured in that question is not generally receptive toward historical adaptations connected to technological and other "progress," for such progress is perceived as contaminated through its associations with the dominant culture. The cultural neutrality of technology, if it exists, is masked by the ethnic culture of those most actively seizing its opportunities.

In conclusion, the origins and the tragedy of the Métis province are not subject to simple ethno-cultural explanations. A series of intermingled polarities created the new Métis nation in the early nineteenth century: French-English, Catholic-Protestant, Ojibwa (Chippewa)-Cree, and two competing fur-trading companies. Out of this mixture emerged a new people, speaking many of their heritage languages while developing at least two of their own: Michif and Bungi. The polarities of agriculture and hunting, sedentary and nomadic ways of life, possessive individualism and primitive communism complicated the fusion in its socioeconomic aspects. But the fusion had begun vigorously, and at Red River was achieving a maturity of economic self-sufficiency within a complex society. The "new nation" was conscious of itself and wished political control over its own destiny. The Red River Insurrection of 1869-70 wrestled that official autonomy, within provincial limitations, from the Canadian authorities and fancied it was secured by constitutional protections. It was a false promise.[62]

Culturally, the internal cohesion of Métis ethnicity was divided by external ties to two Euro-Canadian cultures still warring within the bosom of their new confederation. Economically, Manitoba was soon overwhelmed by the forces of Canadian capitalism, wielded by Anglo-Protestants from Ontario in an age when cultural bigotry was less trammelled by empirical considerations or virtues of tolerance than at other times. Politically, the Canadian state and its agents were prepared, not only to countenance unconstitutional machinations, but actively to initiate them — through rationalizations that blended Euro-British cultural arrogance with the interests of liberal capitalism. These various forces worked together in such a way that French Métis appear to have suffered more than English Métis, as French-Catholic Canadians lost the political influence that an officially recognized culture normally has in its possession. The Franco-Manitobans were and are not exclusively Métis; Métis Manitobans were and are approximately only half French and Catholic; but through language, schools, land claims, and even an upper legislative chamber, their fortunes were interconnected in the provisions of a constitution that did not survive a single generation under the onslaught of Anglo-Protestant capitalism from Ontario. The troubled conscience of twentieth-century Manitoba was thoroughly earned. Exorcising such a conscience at this late date may not be possible, but the official recognition of land claims, language rights, and confessional schools should be the obvious minimum for a restored harmony in the Métis province of Manitoba.

NOTES

The author gratefully acknowledges the contributions of Jennifer Brown, Gerald Friesen, Derek Cook, and Jim Silver to the accuracy, perspectives and lucidity of this interpretation, through their critical reading of earlier drafts, while he frees them of any responsibility for his occasional persistence against their advice.

1. See Doug Daniels, "Canada," in Jay A. Sigler, ed., *International Handbook on Race and Race Relations* (New York: Greenwood Press, 1987), 47. If the Meech Lake Accord wins

acceptance, no new provinces are likely to share in this distinction with Manitoba and British Columbia.

2. For the ethnic and religious census of Manitoba in 1870, see James A. Jackson, *The Centennial History of Manitoba* (Toronto: McClelland and Stewart, 1970), 113, to suggest only one source. D. Bruce Sealey writes, "The census included only those Indians who lived in a reasonably permanent community for at least a portion of the year. The figures thus exclude Indians who lived a completely nomadic life and wandered back and forth across the boundaries of the province." He infers, further, that perhaps as many as 2,000 Métis were excluded for the same reason. D. Bruce Sealey, "Statutory Land Rights of the Manitoba Métis," in Antoine S. Lussier and D. Bruce Sealey, eds., *The Other Natives: The/Les Métis*, vol. 2, *1885-1978* (Winnipeg: Manitoba Métis Federation Press/Editions Bois-Brulés, 1978), 6-7.

3. *The Canada Year Book 1905*, see "Population," Table 1, "Sex, Conjugal State, Birthplace, Race and Religion," 5. The percentages in the text are calculated from the figures in this table. The *Year Book*'s Table 1 has been checked against the Census of Canada publications of 1881 and 1901. The latter's figure for 1881 (62,260) appears to be in error.

4. This definitional paragraph owes a great deal to the first three papers, by Dickason, Peterson and Foster, composing Part I, "Métis Origins: Discovery and Interpretation," in Jacqueline Peterson and Jennifer S.H. Brown, eds., *The New Peoples: Being and Becoming Métis in North America* (Winnipeg: The University of Manitoba Press, 1985), 19-91. The third component, self-consciousness, was facilitated by specific historical events, such as the fall of New France and the establishment of the Selkirk Colony in 1812, that need not be discussed here. But see Ron G. Bourgeault for the fruitful suggestion that class consciousness was also a central component in Métis ethnic-consciousness. Ron G. Bourgeault, "The Indian, the Métis and the Fur Trade: Class, Sexism and Racism in the Transition from 'Communism' to Capitalism," *Studies in Political Economy* 12 (Fall 1983): 45-80.

5. A Canadian delegation in London told the colonial minister, in February 1865, "'It would appear that nothing deserving the name of 'Government' exists in the populated portion of the territory known as the 'Red River Settlement'." Arthur S. Morton, *A History of The Canadian West to 1970-71*, 2nd edition (Toronto: University of Toronto Press, 1973), 862.

6. Ibid. See also Frits Pannekoek, "Some Comments on the Social Origins of the Riel Protest of 1869," in Antoine S. Lussier, ed., *Louis Riel & the Métis: Riel Mini-Conference Papers* (Winnipeg: Pemmican Publications, 1979), 67-68. Since this article is more accessible in Lussier's anthology, it is cited here, but the publisher lost Pannekoek's footnotes, and readers seeking them need to go to an earlier publication of the article, in *Historical and Scientific Society of Manitoba* series 3, no. 34 (1977-78): 39-48. Doug Owram shows that eastern expansionists had widely believed the residents of Red River to desire annexation, so that they were much surprised by an insurrection that appeared to be opposed to that development. Doug Owram, *Promise of Eden: The Canadian Expansionist Movement and the Idea of the West, 1856-1900* (Toronto: University of Toronto Press, 1980), 81.

7. For the statements in this paragraph concerning attitudes in the eastern press, see Arthur Silver, "French Quebec and the Métis Question, 1869-1885," in Carl Berger and Ramsay Cook, eds., *The West and the Nation: Essays in Honour of W.L. Morton* (Toronto: McClelland and Stewart, 1976), 91-113.

8. Jackson, *The Centennial History*, 113.

9. The Métis were normally bilingual, if not multilingual: French or English (often both), together with Cree, and/or the nascent Métis languages, such as Michif or Bungi. The discernible sophistication of at least Michif lends credence to the existence of a Métis "nation." See John C. Crawford, "What is Michif? Language in the Métis Tradition," in Peterson and Brown, *The New Peoples*, 237, passim.

10. The most accessible, comprehensive and succinct discussion of these developments is by George F.G. Stanley, "French and English in Western Canada," in Mason Wade, ed.,

Canadian Dualism/La Dualité Canadienne: Studies of French-English Relations/Essais sur les relations entre Canadiens français et Canadiens anglais (Toronto and Québec: University of Toronto Press/Les Presses de l'Université Laval, 1960), 311-25.

11. Pannekoek, "Some Comments," 74. Verne Dusenberry submits as an indication of Métis religious devotion that "they seldom embarked upon a hunt without having a priest accompany them." Unfortunately, the statement lacks time and place specificity. Verne Dusenberry, "Waiting for a Day That Never Comes: The Dispossessed Métis of Montana," in Peterson and Brown, *The New Peoples*, 122. An ironic effect of the conversion of the Métis working for the HBC was their demands in the 1840s to have Sunday as a day of rest. Bourgeault, "The Indian, the Métis and the Fur Trade," 69.

12. Irene M. Spry, "The Tragedy of the Loss of the Commons in Western Canada," in Ian A.L. Getty and Antoine S. Lussier, eds., *As Long as the Sun Shines and Water Flows; A Reader in Canadian Native Studies* (Vancouver: University of British Columbia Press, 1983), 203-28; Irene M. Spry, "The Transition from a Nomadic to a Settled Economy in Western Canada, 1856-96," in *Proceedings and Transactions of the Royal Society of Canada*, 4th ser., vol. 6 (June 1968), 187-201; and Gerald Friesen, *The Canadian Prairies: A History* (Toronto: University of Toronto Press, 1984), chapters 5-7.

13. Lionel Dorge points out that the production of pemmican, virtually monopolized by the Métis, was the first and for a long time the major "industry west of the Great Lakes." Lionel Dorge, "The Metis and Canadian Councillors of Assiniboia," *The Beaver* (Summer 1974): 12-13. See also Frits Pannekoek, "The Fur Trade and Western Canadian Society, 1670-1870," CHA Historical Booklet No. 43 (Ottawa, 1987), 19. Pannekoek states that 100,000 pounds of pemmican were needed by the HBC in 1840, and perhaps 200,000 pounds in 1870.

14. Friesen, *The Canadian Prairies*, 91-119; Pannekoek, "Some Comments" and "The Fur Trade." Although several scholars have mentioned the slightly more "modern" activities of the Anglo-Protestant Métis than of their Franco-Catholic counterparts, one of the few to present concrete evidence for this has been W. Leland Clark, "The Place of the Métis Within the Agricultural Economy of the Red River During the 1840s and the 1850s," *The Canadian Journal of Native Studies* 3, no. 1 (1983): 69-84. The percentages cited in my text are in Clark, "The Place of the Métis," 72.

15. Describing the intercultural relations within the Métis community — as found in both work and play, occasional marriages, and even interdenominational church attendance — Irene Spry is unable to accept Pannekoek's view that religious differences deeply divided the settlement. Irene M. Spry, "The Métis and Mixed-bloods of Rupert's Land," in Peterson and Brown, *The New Peoples*, 96-118. Compare to Pannekoek, "Some Comments," 65-75; also, "The Rev. Griffiths Owen Corbett and the Red River Civil War of 1869-70," *Canadian Historical Review* 57, no. 2 (June 1976): 133-49.

16. Owram, *Promise of Eden*, passim.

17. Sylvia Van Kirk, " 'What if Mamma is an Indian?': The Cultural Ambivalence of the Alexander Ross Family," in Peterson and Brown, *The New Peoples*, 207-17.

18. Stanley, "French and English," 320-21; Cornelius J. Jaenen, "The History of French in Manitoba: Local Initiative or External Imposition?" *Language and Society* 13 (Spring 1984): 5-6.

19. The petitions of 1843, 1845, and 1851 are described in Dorge, "The Métis," 14, 17. See also Pannekoek, "Some Comments," 66-68.

20. W.L. Morton, ed., *Manitoba: The Birth of a Province* (Winnipeg: Manitoba Records Society Publications, 1965; 1984), xvii.

21. Marcel Giraud, *The Métis in the Canadian West*, vol. 2, George Woodcock, trans., (Edmonton: University of Alberta Press, 1986), 370.

22. The Manitoba Act, 1870, is reprinted in Morton, *Manitoba*, as Appendix II, 251-59.

23. See Irene Spry, in Getty and Lussier, *As Long As the Sun Shines*, 203-28: also Thomas Flanagan, "Louis Riel and Aboriginal Rights," in ibid., 248-52 and passim.

24. Giraud, *The Métis in the Canadian West*, 380-85; G. Herman Sprenger, "The Métis Nation: Buffalo Hunting vs. Agriculture in the Red River Settlement (circa 1810-1870)," in Lussier and Sealey, *The Other Natives, vol. 1, 1700-1885*, 115-30.

25. Pannekoek, "Some Comments," 71.

26. D. Bruce Sealey, *Statutory Land Rights of the Manitoba Métis* (Winnipeg: Manitoba Métis Federation Press, 1975); D. Bruce Sealey, "Statutory Land Rights of the Manitoba Métis," in Lussier and Sealey, *The Other Natives*, vol. 2, 1-30; D.N. Sprague, "The Manitoba Land Question, 1870-1882," *Journal of Canadian Studies* 15, no. 3 (Fall 1980): 74-84; D.N. Sprague, "Government Lawlessness in the Administration of Manitoba Land Claims, 1870-1887," *Manitoba Law Journal* 10, no. 4 (1980): 415-41; D.N. Sprague and P.R. Mailhot, "Persistent Settlers: The Dispersal and Resettlement of the Red River Métis, 1870-85," *Canadian Ethnic Studies* 17, no. 2 (1985): 1-30; and Gerhard Ens, "Métis Lands in Manitoba," *Manitoba History* 5 (Spring 1983): 2-11.

27. I speak here of land scrip, which was meant to be exchanged for land, and which was tightly tied to the registered owner; nonetheless, it was exchanged or sold to others and became an important object of speculation. There was also money scrip, which could more easily serve as a means of exchange. This ease was especially true in the case of the Métis, whose scrip was treated as personal property, whereas scrip issued to descendants of the Selkirk Settlers or to members of the Wolseley expedition was treated as real estate. David Boisvert and Keith Turnbull, "Who Are the Métis?" *Studies in Political Economy* 18 (Autumn 1985): 126, 129-31. See also Sealey, in Lussier and Sealey, *The Other Natives*, vol. 2, 18, 22.

28. Sprague and Mailhot calculated that only 10 percent of the "half-breeds" enrolled on the 1870 census were absent from the 1875 census, yet just over 53 percent of these original settlers were not recorded as occupying their lands by the surveyors of 1871-73. "By 1883, more than 70 per cent of the Métis and more than 50 per cent of the native English had seen the land they occupied in 1870 patented to others." While most of the patents were registered in 1876-77, not a single patent to a Métis was recorded before 1877, two-thirds of them being after 1878. It should come as no surprise, then, that comparisons of communities in the Saskatchewan River valley in 1885 with those in the Red River valley of 1870 revealed that more than 80 percent of the persons resettled at the one were not native to the region, while more than 80 percent of those who had come from Manitoba were "legally" landless when they left. Sprague and Mailhot, "Persistent Settlers," 7.

29. For a close examination of developments from the perspective of local Manitoba initiatives, see Ens, "Métis Lands in Manitoba," 2-11. This article is equally valuable concerning the fate of claims originally ascribed to Métis children.

30. Ibid., 9-10.

31. Ibid., 6, Figure 1.

32. Friesen, *The Canadian Prairies*, 200; Jackson, *The Centennial History*, 112.

33. Giraud, *The Métis*, 375-80; Gerald Friesen, "Homeland to Hinterland: Political Transition in Manitoba, 1870 to 1879," *Historical Papers: Saskatoon 1979* (Canadian Historical Association Meetings), 33-47; Robert Painchaud, "Les Rapports entre les Métis et les Canadiens-français au Manitoba, 1870-1884," in Lussier and Sealey, *The Other Natives*, vol. 2, 53-74.

34. Giraud, *The Métis*, 390-92; Philippe R. Mailhot, "Ritchot's Resistance: Abbé Noël Joseph Ritchot and the Creation and Transformation of Manitoba" (Ph.D. dissertation, University of Manitoba, 1986), chapter 9. I am grateful to Gerald Friesen for directing my attention to this dissertation.

35. Later, as lieutenant governor of Manitoba (1888-95), Schultz was to question the constitutional propriety of Premier Greenway's legislation against the minority's language and school rights, but during the 1860s no one would have thought him capable of such sensitivity.

36. Jackson, *The Centennial History*, 83-84; Pannekoek, "Some Comments," 67-75.

37. Friesen, *The Canadian Prairies*, 195-96; Jackson, *The Centennial History*, 111; Giraud, *The Métis*, 376-77.

38. "In 1875, the vast majority of Métis people were farmers . . . [and] in the older parishes were cultivating their land as extensively as the original white settlers. . . . " Sprague goes on to say, "As late as 1875, nine tenths of the 1870 population had not yet moved. They remained on their river-lot farms patiently awaiting the patents which section 32 so clearly promised." Sprague, "The Manitoba Land Question," 79-80. See, however, Mailhot, "Ritchot's Resistance," 225-42. While Mailhot confirms Sprague's assertions, he also describes Abbé Ritchot's entrepreneurial energies in attempting both to resettle Métis from less to more favourable lands and to settle immediately after the Manitoba Act as many previously unsettled Métis and Franco-Catholic newcomers as possible.

39. Sprague, "Government Lawlessness," 418. One effect of the eleven amendments made to sections 31 and 32 of the Manitoba Act between 1873 and 1884 was to reduce the number of persons eligible for allotments from about 10,000 to just under 6,000. Sprague and Mailhot, "Persistent Settlers," 78; and Sealey, "Statutory Land Rights," 15-19.

40. Sections 31 and 32 spoke of different kinds of land claimants, and their fates were not alike. Sprague writes, "Métis recognized settlers received about half as much as the whites, regardless of the number of acres they cultivated." The federal government's discrimination against the winterers (i.e., buffalo hunters who occupied Red River lots only in the winter, sowed in the spring, and returned in the fall to harvest the otherwise untended crop) was even more severe; an 1875 amendment to section 32 had the effect of denying patents to approximately 1,200 families. Thus, for example, in the Rat River district, "Ninety-five percent of the acres at stake were . . . held back as Dominion Lands, saved to be taken up later by newcomers." Sprague, "The Manitoba Land Question," 80-82.

41. Naturally, there were both indigenous and Red River Métis settlements further west dating well before 1870. While such migration would not have ceased simply because of the creation of Manitoba and its constitutional protections, my point is that the unconstitutional events after 1870 dramatically augmented and hastened the exodus.

42. Sprague, "The Manitoba Land Question," 75.

43. *The Canada Year Book 1905*. Obviously, it cannot easily be known how the "French" and the "Métis" identified/distinguished themselves in these census data, but their combined totals nonetheless indicate a catastrophic loss of preeminence.

44. Friesen, *The Canadian Prairies*, 205-9.

45. Friesen, "Homeland to Hinterland," 33-47.

46. For a different emphasis, see Doug Daniels's arguments that the requirements of monopoly capitalism (that theories derived from political economy) better explain which groups suffer oppression in Canada, and when, than do racial theories referring to visible minorities. Daniels, "Canada," 47-48.

47. For a discussion of the peculiar flavour of Anglo-Protestant prejudices when transplanted to the west, see J.E. Rea, "The Roots of Prairie Society," in David P. Gagan, ed., *Prairie Perspectives; Papers of the Western Canadian Studies Conference* (Toronto: Holt, Rinehart and Winston, 1970), 46-55.

48. Jaenen, "The History of French in Manitoba," 8; Jackson, *The Centennial History*, 114.

49. Jaenen, "The History of French in Manitoba," 10; Jackson, *The Centennial History*, 138. The British North America Act, 1871, virtually entrenched the Manitoba Act, 1870, in the Canadian constitution, for it forbade the Canadian Parliament to modify the latter in any way and implied that even the provincial legislature's authority to amend it was limited to "the qualification of electors and members of the Legislative Assembly and laws respecting elections in the said province." Sprague argues that many of the eleven laws modifying Manitoba's sections 31 and 32 passed between 1873 and 1884 were thereby actually unconstitutional, and I suggest that the abolition of the Legislative Council should have been subject to the same restriction. Sprague, "Government Lawlessness," 415-19.

50. Friesen, "Homeland to Hinterland," 41-46; Jaenen, "The History of French in Manitoba," 10-11.

51. Ens, "Métis Lands in Manitoba," 6 (Figure 1), 8.

52. Jaenen, "The History of French in Manitoba," 9.

53. Friesen, *The Canadian Prairies*, 215-17; J.R. Miller, "D'Alton McCarthy, Equal Rights, and the Origins of the Manitoba School Question," *Canadian Historical Review* 54, no. 5 (December 1973): 369-92.

54. After reminding us that the Métis population in 1941 of only 8,692 compares badly with the 1870 figure of 9,830, Jean Lagassé estimates that a "natural increase" would have produced a population of over 55,000 without further mixed marriages, while such marriages might have lifted the total to 100,000-200,000. Jean Lagassé, "The Métis in Manitoba," in Lussier and Sealey, *The Other Natives*, vol. 2, 113. Another forty-five years would of course have further augmented that number today, while analogous increases for the Euro-Québec, Franco-Catholic population would yield a combined total easily sufficient to justify the continuation, on demographic grounds alone, of minority-rights protection in the provincial constitution. We cannot be sure that something like these numbers do not, in fact, exist, in the form of Métis now fully assimilated who deny a part of their ancestry. But their ethno-cultural disappearance remains a significant event.

55. Robert Painchaud, "Les Rapports," 53-74; Antoine S. Lussier, "The French-speaking Mixed Bloods' Relations with the French-Canadians in Manitoba since 1900," a paper delivered at, among other occasions, The Métis and the Constitution Conference, University of Manitoba (17 October 1985).

56. Lagassé, "The Métis in Manitoba," 113.

57. Painchaud, "Les Rapports," 66-68; Giraud, *The Métis*, 378-79, 390-91.

58. Joseph Eliot Magnet, "Court Ordered Bilingualism," *Revue Générale du Droit* 12 (1981): 241; Lussier, "The French-Speaking Mixed Bloods' Relations," 3-4.

59. Lussier, "The French-Speaking Mixed Bloods' Relations," 9-10.

60. Ibid., 11-13.

61. Lagassé, "The Métis in Manitoba," 117.

62. Between the writing and publishing of this chapter, I have received the well-researched, book-length study by D.N. Sprague, *Canada and the Métis, 1869-1885* (Waterloo: Wilfrid Laurier University Press, 1988). None of its conclusions change those already presented, with large help from Professor Sprague's scholarly articles, in this chapter.

Even more significant is the belated publication of the paper by Gerhard Ens, "Dispossession or Adaptation: Migration and Persistence of the Red River Métis, 1835-1890," *Historical Papers: Windsor 1988* (Canadian Historical Association Meetings), 120-44. While agreeing with Sprague's arguments concerning racial intolerance and not denying other unsavory reasons for the emigration of the Métis from Manitoba, Ens stresses the continuation of pre-1870 economic reasons and dates the periods of greatest exodus to 1872-75 and 1880-82. Although I would now present some details of my interpretation a little differently, I see Ens and Sprague as more complementary in a still evolving research area, than contrasting, and I would not modify my general thesis.

Race, Class and Marginality in an Interlake Settlement: 1850-1950

4

Nicole St.-Onge

It is the curious fate of people who have experienced the expansion of imperialism to be considered inherently incapable of progress and development.[1] The "backwardness" of Canadian Natives, for example, is often explained in terms of their inability to think beyond their group affiliations, and to break through walls of "unprogressive" customs and traditions, due to some "racial" shortcoming.[2] Researchers falling back on racial explanations for uneven socioeconomic situations thus avoid any analysis of how society has developed and how it functions.

For many Métis in western Canada, racism is a fact of life, even though, as Lagassé points out, most Métis would escape identification if they were affluent and resided in predominantly white communities. Many European nationals have coarse black hair, high cheek bones, dark skin pigmentation and deep brown eyes — all traits used in describing the Métis.[3] In fact, instances of Manitoba's Métis "passing" for whites after socioeconomic improvements are well documented. For example, in a 1947 letter to the Father Provincial, the Oblate missionary for Abbeville, Manitoba comments:

> Population catholique [est de] 164 personnes dont plusieurs ont l'humeur vagabonde. Dans 7 familles métisses on parle encore sauteux. *Les 40 ou 50 métis bien évolué devraient figuré sous la rustique "Canadien Français"* ce qui ferait c.f. = 108, métis peu évolué = 50, Ang., ind., etc. = 6.[4] (emphasis added)

When asked to define "halfbreeds," people evoke physical characteristics. The indicators are general life style, living conditions, work performed, language spoken and clothes worn. Dipankar Gupta's comment on the dominant society's perception of French Canadians holds true for the Métis: "Racism is the most comprehensive ideological weapon of domination and ... it does not always obey the protocol of color."[5]

This chapter examines how, since the 1850s, capitalist development in Manitoba's interlake area, and the interpretation of this region's history, have been heavily influenced by a western racist ideology. This ideology, coupled to the other politico-socioeconomic dynamics of capitalism, led to the development and maintenance of "racially" distinct marginal communities. Racism alone, however, was used to explain the existence of these communities in terms of a perceived racial difference that affected the residents' culture, world view and work habits. The specific community examined is a Métis settlement on the southern shores of Lake Manitoba.

The Mirage of Race: The Scientific Bases for a Theory of Human Races

What is meant by concepts such as "race" and "racism," and what should their position be in a materialist, analytical framework? Should "race," "racism" and the closely related and currently more popular, polite and nebulous term "ethnicity" be seen as *fundamental variables*, having a reality independent of our awareness of them? Or should they be seen as *objects of critical analysis*? Should ethnicity, race and racism be analytical tools in studies of society, or should the key questions be how and why they have come to give an apparent (but erroneous) sense to the phenomenal world?

Robert Miles points out that physical characteristics are still used to categorize people, without regard to other traits that set them apart.[6] Certain phenotypical variations are interpreted using the word "race," but the word is used in a diffuse way,[7] without regard to a formal or scientific definition. It is simply part of everyday discourse, and is assumed (wrongly) to have a scientific basis referring to discrete categories of people separated by their physical characteristics. Social significance is attributed to these "categories" to justify or generate different patterns of behaviour.[8] Rebuttals of racial theories by geneticists and biologists have not "trickled down" from scientific discourse, and therefore have not negated the belief in races, and the existence of a racist world view within the Western world's popular culture and ideology.

Miles's explanation for the persistence of these folk concepts is based on a fundamental distinction made by Marx between *phenomenal* form and *essential* relations.[9] The "phenomenal form" is the way in which the phenomena of the external, social world are perceived and represented in human experience, while "essential relations" refers to the real conditions of existence of the phenomenal forms. For example, the differing experiences of the indigenous population to the advance and development of capital in what was called British North America have been ascribed to racial differences.[10] But such analysis fails to examine the impact of imperialism, how it varies at the core and periphery, and what is experienced by populations differently situated within capitalist relations of production. As Miles points out:

> We must not unquestioningly incorporate in a scientific analysis the categories of description and analysis used in everyday discourse because, in so far as that discourse is uncritical and confines itself to the direct experience and appearance of the social world, then there is the possibility of creating a false and misleading explanation.[11]

Since "race" has no biological reality but is a social construct, authors basing their analysis on the assumption of the existence of "races" confuse the phenomenal form, in which economic and political conflicts appear, with the underlying *structural* characteristics of these social formations.[12]

Miles argues that race and racism cannot be traced directly to the development of capitalism, since there is a great delay between the rise of capitalism as a mode of production, and the development of an ideology seeing "coloureds" as inferior beings. It is also difficult to label it a "child of imperialism" since such an explanatory framework would have difficulty dealing with the development of racism within Europe, *vis-à-vis* the Irish or the Jews, for example.[13] Nevertheless, by the second half of the nineteenth century, racism had become a central element in the world view of large segments of the bourgeoisie and was influencing the thinking of elements within the working class. Racism began to have real material effects. It became what Marx termed a "material force," influencing and being influenced by the conditions of production. In this context, that is, capitalist expansion imbued with a racist ideology, the Métis settlement of Saint-Laurent developed.

Saint-Laurent du Manitoba

In the Red River Settlement (1821-70), as in many British colonies, basic social divisions, including the division of labour, were understood to be the product of racial or ethnic, not class, divisions. This "racial" perception, and the resulting fragmentation of labouring groups, was the result of a deliberate policy by HBC officials, and not merely the product of racist assumptions, or the straightforward dictates of a mercantilist economy. As Ron Bourgeault notes in relation to the possibility of "home guard" Indians being involved in wage labour around the fur trade post:

> Any change in productive relations such as allowing Indians access to wage labour jobs around the posts, was forbidden, since such change would contribute to the breakdown of the peasantry. Together with an already highly developed ideology of racism among the colonizers which served to justify the nature of this exploitation, this division enhanced subjective racial ideas of differences among the European labourers around the posts. The difference was also maintained economically between the two divisions of labour, primarily through the tariff or the rate at which labour was exchanged or sold for goods. The tariff was much higher for the primary producer than for the wage worker.[14]

Cultural differences were emphasized, defined as racial, and presented as having a direct bearing on the labouring potential of individuals. The English, Orkneymen, French Canadians, Franco-Roman Catholic Métis, Anglo-Protestant "halfbreeds," and finally the "full-blooded" Natives, were seen as occupying distinct socioeconomic positions as a result of their "race." To what extent this was internalized by the actors involved is difficult to assess. Irene Spry has argued that class governed social interaction and blurred (some) of the racial distinctions in Red River to an extent greater than previously thought.[15] However, it is clear from existing archival material that the authorities' perception of racial divisions affected the economic roles of individuals.

Between 1760 and 1821 there emerged a need for a source of wage labour located within the territory. Indians, or more accurately those engaged in the primary task of producing furs for exchange, could not be recruited in large numbers since this would threaten the very existence of the fur trade. Thus fur trade officials turned to the "mixed-blood" children of European or Canadian workers and local women who had not been absorbed culturally and economically into the "Indian class." Out of the curious combination of the demands of mercantilism for a local wage labour pool, and a preexisting racist ideology, a new "biological" category imbued with specific social and economic characteristics crystallized:

> For reasons of class and race [they] were no longer to be considered as Indians and were not allowed to become English; they were, as their colonizers called them, "Half-Breeds" (or the French equivalent, "Métis").[16]

With the merger of the HBC and the North West Company in 1821, many in this evolving racial category could not be employed full-time in wage-labour occupations. The streamlining of the fur trade labour force, coupled with improved technology (the York boats), resulted in a rapid rise in the unemployed or underemployed Métis population of the Red River.[17] This surplus population specialized in the production of commodities indirectly tied to the fur economy. A fluid Métis underclass of bison hunters, fishermen and salt makers emerged. They tried to diversify out of their precarious existence but met with only limited success. They were opposed by HBC officials who were suspicious of any perceived threat to their labour and "plain provision" reserves.

Only in the 1850s and 1860s did significant class differences within the Métis population occur. An elite composed of small traders and farmers emerged, but their primary loyalties became (or remained?) class, not racial, ones: they remained largely passive during the events of 1869-70.[18] The supporters of Riel framed their demands for socioeconomic improvement and security in racial and nationalistic terms, but motivation came from their membership in an oppressed and increasingly marginalized class.

By the late 1820s, semipermanent settlers were emerging in the Saint-Laurent, Duck Bay and Oak Point areas where fishing could be carried out.[19] These areas also became rallying points in spring and autumn for Métis involved in the production of salt on the shores of Lake Manitoba. Settlers combined such activities with some buffalo hunting. These lakeshore settlements were a direct result of market demands for certain staples. They were never self-sufficient.

By 1858 there were ten families (two from North Dakota) living in Saint-Laurent. Their involvement in the hunt and the exploitation of the more northerly salt springs forced the Métis into a seminomadic existence, but they consistently returned to what was by then an Oblate mission area where good fishing grounds existed.[20] There is no archival documentation to suggest that much agricultural activity occurred in Saint-Laurent prior to the early 1860s. Farming was barely a viable occupation (in terms of both output and market demands) in the heart of the colony, let alone in the interlake hinterland.[21]

Race, Class and Missionaries' Perceptions: Saint-Laurent, 1850-1900

Oblate missionaries imbued with a racist ideology perpetuated the process of racialization of Red River society, while emphasizing further distinctions along religious and linguistic lines. Missionary letters are filled with interpretations of existing economic situations using a racist world view. These letters advocate specific actions that very much take the concept of race into account. For example, during the worst of the 1867-68 famine,[22] the Saint-Laurent Oblate, Father Simonet, apparently unaware of the effects of starvation, attributed the Métis lack of interest in doing *corvée* work for the mission to their laziness and inherently indolent character. The resident priest for the parish of Sainte-Claire, assessing the economic prospects for his parish, argued that even though the local Métis were reasonably well off:

> Quant aux métis qui composent en grande partie ma paroisse, à part de respectable,
> de jouisseurs ... la chose capitale pour l'avenir de Sainte-Claire est de *remplacer*
> *en grande partie les métis par des familles canadiennes-française, autrement nous*
> *aurons le même resultat qu' à Saint-Laurent.*[23] (emphasis added)

In other words, poverty, marginalization and even cultural traditions were the result of
the biologically inherited and unchangeable predisposition of the Métis, and were
unrelated to the structural constraints of a peripheral staple-producing economy.
Solutions advanced were posited in terms of altering the genetic composition of the
local population rather than in terms of addressing economic problems.

Whatever the merits of the ecclesiastical assessment of Métis character, these
underclasses of labourers (HBC hired hands) and staple producers experienced severe
material hardship and social dislocation between 1865 and 1875 with the decline of the
fur trade centred on the Red River, the decimation of the bison herds, and the transfer
of power from the HBC to the Canadian government. For Saint-Laurent, documented
hardships begin with the famine of 1867-68. The statistical summary produced by the
Executive Relief Committee indicates that seventeen out of thirty-six households (47
percent) were in need of immediate relief, even though most included able-bodied
men.[24] Even among the "non-indigent" families only one or two reported possessing
enough potatoes and cattle to carry them through the winter. In the 1860s the vast
majority of these people still counted on fishing and bison hunting to feed their families
and produce an exchangeable commodity. Neither of these staples were in plentiful
supply in the late 1860s.

It is therefore not surprising that the starving segment of the population took action:

> In March 1870, during the Riel Rebellion, the [Saint-Laurent and Oak Point]
> Half-Breeds took possession of the HBC post at Oak Point and killed 8 or 10 head of
> cattle, distributed the beef among themselves as well as some dry goods taken from
> the store.[25]

They treated the clerk in charge kindly, "furnishing him with fresh meat and staples."
Seemingly as an afterthought, the chronicler (writing in 1895) comments that Father
Camper was very much displeased with his charges.

This foray, however, brought only fleeting relief to the desperate families. Commenting on the months following the March trading post takeover, Brother Mulvihill
states:

> After March [came a] time of hunger. There was no flour to be found just dried
> jackfish. A métis, François Bonneau, was suffering from extreme want and poverty.
> He once had been a buffalo hunter. [Bonneau tells the chronicler] "I have eaten
> nothing in the last 3 days save and except 'des petites poires qui me donnent la
> chiche [*sic*], mon corps est toujours lache et je suis bien faible.' " Bonneau had been
> one of the bravest [hunters] on the plain.[26]

Nevertheless, the Métis stayed in Saint-Laurent, slowing giving up their bison hunting
and salt making activities for lack of a product or market,[27] and making the transition to

commercial fishing coupled with either dairy farming, trapping, harvesting of wild produce, occasional winter freighting on the lakes and, after World War I, farm labour.[28] Dairy farming became a viable alternative for some of the Saint-Laurent families because, unlike other areas of the province,[29] several of them were successful at securing letters patent for their land. Of twenty-four lots surveyed, fourteen were at least partially patented in the name of the original claimants. But by no means all of these fourteen Métis patentees had sufficient capital, expertise or market outlets to bring the land into production. Also the number of families residing in Saint-Laurent had increased from twenty in 1866 to 130 in 1893, most of whom were presumably without title to the land they occupied.

After 1870 the writer of the Saint-Laurent *codex historicus*, in a curiously dichotomous manner of thinking, criticized the Métis for their lack of responsibility towards land ownership, while in the next text he acknowledged their crippling poverty, which would impede any attempt at successfully bringing their land into production and would make the selling of scrip or sections of land for hard cash a frequent necessity. Commenting on the land speculators who were operating in the area, Brother Mulvihill states:

> Few if any of the Half-Breeds availed themselves of this good occasion to procure and secure additional property, no, but they sold their script [*sic*] to speculators or land grabbers for whatever they could get for it. This script was sold for 35 cents on the dollars . . . [also] The Half-Breeds of this parish as well as other parishes not only sold their script but also the 240 acre lot which each obtained . . . not one of them owns a 240 acre lot just now in 1895 at least in this parish.[30]

Yet in the same text Brother Mulvihill expresses deep concern over how the lakeshore inhabitants can make a living. In the spring of 1867 he anxiously notes that black flour is selling for between seven and ten dollars for a one-hundred-pound sack.[31] In an entry made in 1875, Mulvihill comments that "the Fathers did not at all expect such crowds of people at the retreat, especially as the poor people *have to subsist from day to day* (emphasis added) by the chase [and therefore were skirting famine by suspending such activities for many days].[32] Despite this pragmatic realization of the constraints under which the Métis lived, the overall tone is one of condemnation. In 1877 Father Lacombe wrote to the Father Superior:

> La population de Saint-Laurent est composée presque exclusivement de métis qui habitent les bords du lac. Ils se sont bâti des maisons aux environs de la mission et cultivent chacun un petit morceau de terre. Anciens chasseurs de la forêt, ils gardent encore leurs vieilles habitudes et passent plusieurs semaines à poursuivre le gibier.[33]

But even at this early date the Oblate chronicles betray the existence of emerging class divisions in the settlement. While still making deprecating racial remarks about the Métis, they noted that Saint-Laurent was fragmenting along occupational lines: "il y en a cependant un certain nombre qui ne s'éloignent jamais de la mission et qui vivent du produit de leur jardin et de la pêche."[34] Like the priest of Abbeville, the Oblates maintained a racist paradigm in the face of social change by "whitening" those of their charges who became economically successful and no longer fit the stereotype. For example, when describing an exceptionally hard-working woman, Brother Mulvihill commented: "It may be added that Mrs. (Cecile Larivière) McLeod had been both tall and strong and good-looking and resembled a French-Canadian rather than a half-breed."[35] By the 1900s the Oblates' lack of esteem for their Métis charges translated itself into an active campaign to recruit French-Canadian and Breton farming families for settlement in Saint-Laurent.[36] It was hoped that by bringing in new blood the parish would become a prosperous agrarian settlement.

The Métis perceptions of these laymen and clerical officials, along with those of their French-Canadian and Breton *protégés*, have been perpetuated and presented as truth in the literature published by ethnologists and historians. Giraud's lengthy, scathing condemnation of this class of people sums up twentieth-century attitudes towards this race:

> Il est logique que cette état de décomposition se traduise par l'isolement d'une grande partie de la société métisse dans les provinces de l'Ouest. *On ne saurait attendre d'éléments réduits à ce degré de déchéance qu'ils obtiennent, du moins en nombre appréciable, un droit d'accès à la société blanche,* ou bien, lorsque les unions s'accomplissent, elles risquent fort de se faire entrer éléments de même niveau, et de demeurer sans profit pour les métis. L'isolement se manifeste déjà dans les groupes que nous avons observés autour des lacs Winnipeg et Manitoba, dont la décadence est pourtant moins prononcée. *A Saint-Laurent, Français et Canadien s'unissent dans un égal mépris du groupe de couleur. Leur hostilité s'y exprime en paroles malveillantes, presque haineuses, surtout de la part des familles françaises récemment introduites par les Pères Oblats*: la conduite de celle-ci, faite de travail et d'abnégation, ne saurait s'harmoniser avec les habitudes de vie des métis. Les Canadiens n'adoptent pas une attitude plus conciliante, bien qu'ils n'atteignent pas au niveau de ces manifiques familles du "vieux pays." Sans doute quelques unions sont inévitables ... Et il existe, nous l'avons vu, parmi les métis, des familles assez évoluées pour ne pas encourir sans injustice, l'hostilité systématique des Blancs. Mais les alliances qui s'opèrent entre les uns et les autres sont mal vues de ces derniers. Non seulement, elles ne dissipent points leurs préventions, mais elles paraissent les aggraver. C'est précisément des Canadiens dont les familles comptent une ou plusieurs unions de cette nature qu'émanent les critiques les plus sévères, comme *s'ils éprouvent une vive humiliation d'avoir à admettre parmi eux des représentants de ce groupe inférieur.*[37] (emphasis added)

Saint-Laurent du Manitoba, 1900-1945

If one rejects the biological explanation for the second-class citizen status of the Saint-Laurent Métis (or, more accurately, the labelling of the poorer section of the population as Métis), other avenues must be explored. What were the underlying relations, coalescing between 1900 and 1945, that produced such antagonistic social groups, whose very existence was justified and reinforced by racist ideology? Through written archival material and with the help of oral history, the impact of the Western concept of race and of capitalist expansion in the interlake area on the development of a "racially distinct marginal community" can be assessed.

In 1900 Saint-Laurent was still experiencing the rapid capitalist penetration that had already resulted in socioeconomic fragmentation during the closing years of the preceding century. The village's economic development, essentially based on the production of staples, strongly resembled communities on the more northerly shores of the lake,[38] with which it still had familial and business ties (as in the previous century with salt production).[39] The village was linked to an international economy through its production of pelts and fish but, unlike the northern settlements, it was also tied to the provincial economy through the selling of dairy cream to Winnipeg.[40] This provincial connection was crucial in the rise of clear, socioeconomic differences in Saint-Laurent.

The Saint-Laurent farming segment was largely composed of recently arrived French immigrants but it also included a few families of Métis descent which had successfully "passed" into it during the interwar period. They, unlike the families more fully tied to an international economy by their greater dependence on fishing and trapping for income, were always reasonably assured of a fairly steady market for their products between 1870 and 1950. On the average, Manitoba farmers in 1936 had an overall net income of $303.12, a drop of 62 percent from 1926, but still not nearly as great a downward trend as that experienced by other primary producers.[41]

Between 1900 and 1945, most residents of Saint-Laurent fished commercially to some degree. The arrival of the railway in the early 1900s tied producers to international markets, especially Chicago.[42] This was a mixed blessing since, by pushing up demand and production, it threatened to further deplete fish stocks. As early as 1890, the Department of Indian Affairs had noted that

> the lower portion of Lake Winnipeg and portions of Lake Manitoba have ceased to be good fishing grounds after having been operated upon by large fishing establishments for a comparatively short period of time.[43]

This comment also reveals the direct competition that individual fishermen faced from large companies. Independent fishermen in Saint-Laurent had difficulty absorbing the loss of property and lives which occurred frequently through storms and treacherous ice conditions.[44] As one respondent noted, a person could live on independent fishing, but he had never heard of anyone getting rich by it.[45]

The problems plaguing small family fishing outfits between 1900 and 1945 were similar, in an exacerbated form, to those faced by farmers. Hundreds of competing petty commodity producers sold to a handful of companies which often cooperated with each other and expatriated most of the profits out of the region. As the Rothney-Watson report noted:

> Only four frozen fish companies [largely controlled by American capital] operated in Manitoba and by the 1930s they were cooperating to reduce competition. The individual producers were largely helpless in advocating for better prices and efforts at organization largely failed [due to] difficulties of sustaining collective mass solidarity within the confines of a capitalist market . . . [and] no permanent

and mutual group spirit emerges from an organization based on motives of diversity, individualism and self-interest.[46]

Intensified competition during favourable market periods, and cyclical slumps in prices due to an unstable international economy, meant a precarious existence for those of the Saint-Laurent fishermen who were heavily dependent on bought food staples. An example of fluctuating prices is the abrupt 1914-15 slump in demand. By early February prices fell by 50 percent; by the end of the month buyers had stopped purchasing.[47] This spelled disaster for fishermen who had gone in debt to get onto the ice. But by 1920-21, the prices were the highest in living memory,[48] and most fishermen were able to make a profit, making the continuing reluctance of Métis villagers to pay church dues a mystery to the religious authorities. This prosperity was not to last. By the 1930s, price had once again plummeted:

> Market conditions have changed considerably in the last few years and what was once an extensive and favourable market cannot now absorb present production at any price and indeed can only take care of a fraction of the whole production at any price which will net the fishermen even a small profit.[49]

Fishermen were faced with widespread seasonal debts (getting outfitted, credit during a bad year, unexpected low prices) that often left little room for capital accumulation.[50] Moreover, though prices tended to rise, there is little evidence that fishermen's buying power increased at the same pace. Statistics illustrating the return to fishermen compared to market prices (1931 to 1956) indicate that the prices received by the fish companies had risen much more rapidly. Profits did not trickle down to primary producers.[51] For some of the more common species of fish, such as whitefish, prices based on sale to first buyer were to remain at a static low for decades.[52]

In Saint-Laurent fishermen never really formed a distinct socioeconomic (or racial) grouping. Farmers, hunters and gatherers, and trappers all participated in the winter fishing industry. What distinguished the participants from each other was the importance of fishing in the family budget, the scale on which it was undertaken, and the other staple-producing activities linked to it. The so-called ''white'' families — families who had attained a certain degree of material well being and social acceptability — were combining fishing with dairy farming.[53] The revenues derived from these activities must have been considerable since church authorities in 1905 expected them to pay the greatest amount of tithes per year ($10.00), while poor families were only expected to contribute $2.00. Only thirty-five families out of a total of nearly two hundred were considered well-to-do by the Oblates.[54]

These farmer-fishermen sometimes put up to two hundred nets under the ice and their outfits were comprised of at least one team of horses (later bombardiers) and some hired hands. If the season was good they were able to clear a substantial profit and reinvest it in other economic activities.[55] If the catch or the market was poor they could count on income from cream or hay sales to recoup their losses, at least partially honour their debts, and pay their hired hands. Produce from their gardens and cattle herds lessened their dependence on merchants. Though there were differences in herd size, number of fish nets put out, degree of land and capital controlled, and level of help (financial or other) received from religious authorities,[56] all could weather several bad fishing seasons without being beggared.

At the other end of the socioeconomic scale were the Fort Rouge residents,[57] most of whom were also engaged in fishing. Fort Rouge was an impoverished fringe area of Saint-Laurent, separated by the railway tracks from the main mission area and containing at most perhaps one hundred households. Several Métis villages had such small communities on their outskirts. These seem to have been given distinct names to emphasize their separateness.[58] Respondents defined Fort Rouge as being somehow more traditional. The fishing-farming respondents considered them closer in appearance and custom to the Indians. Most still spoke Cree or Saulteaux to each other, and the older women still wore the black shawl and smoked corn pipes in the 1940s.[59] Though the origins of Fort Rouge are nebulous, indications are that it was populated at least partly by descendants of the families listed as indigent in the 1867-68 famine, and also by families which had come to the settlement in the 1880s and 1890s, when hunting and trapping no longer generated sufficient revenue. By this time, very little free land would have remained in the parish.

Well-to-do residents thought of Fort Rouge as a tough place, had few social contacts with its inhabitants, and denied having any relatives there.[60] In the eyes of the clergy, these Métis had serious problems when it came to religious or moral obligations and duties.[61] Oblates would deplore their ''savage mentality,'' their reluctance to obey directives given at the pulpit, and their tight-fistedness when it came to paying church dues.[62] At the turn of the century the resident priest was already complaining:

> Il y a toujours qui se plaignent. Ils [the Métis] peuvent tout depenser pour satisfaire leur vanité, leur orgueil, leurs passions, leurs désirs déréglés, pour les plaisirs, pour la boisson, etc. . . . et ils n'ont que des murmures et des plaintes à faire entendre quand on leur demande quelque chose pour le Bon Dieu![63]

In defence, these impoverished villagers would point to the Oblates' prize-winning dairy herd, large land holdings and stone buildings, and ask why they should pay tithes. Outside funds had established the church's presence in Saint-Laurent and therefore the Oblates should look elsewhere for money.[64]

What really distinguished Fort Rouge people from other villagers was the chronic serious poverty that often resulted in hunger.[65] These Métis did not own land, did not have the money to build up a dairy farm, could not (because of their subsistence activities) plant large gardens and were, interestingly enough, even more sensitive to the vagaries of an international economy than their more established neighbours.[66] Interviews indicate that these people worked quite hard but that the very activities that were open to them almost assured them a life of poverty.[67] In winter many ice fished, but on a small scale. They fished with the help of dogs and sleighs on the edge of the lake, and rarely put out more than twenty or twenty-five nets. What was left after family (and dog) needs were met was sold to the fish companies. However, since prices were usually quite low, returns tended to depend on quantities harvested. Presumably in a good year some money could be made since these fishermen had little overhead cost.[68] But a series of bad years could be disastrous, and as Lagasse points out, alternative sources of income came into direct conflict with home gardening, which would have lessened their dependence for foodstuffs on often unscrupulous merchants.

Besides fishing, the Fort Rouge underclass engaged in trapping, berry picking, seneca root digging and frog harvesting, coupled with some form of seasonal wage labour.[69] Other villagers also participated from time to time in such activities but viewed them as sources of supplementary income to be undertaken when time permitted.[70] For the Fort Rouge underclass, revenues generated by these occupations were crucial to their material well being. A decline in the supply of any one of them could easily spell material hardship for these people. The precariousness of their livelihood was further exacerbated by the prices for these goods, which fluctuated wildly, and the same events which adversely affected fishing often had an impact on them. For example, in 1914-15 Inspector Jackson wrote:

> The price of fur has been very low this season — muskrats about 10 cents each, and to show what a drug [sic] in the market furs are one reliable Indian informed me that he took some muskrat skins into the HBC's store and they refused to buy at any price.[71]

Rothney and Watson also report a large slump in the demand for furs during the early years of the Depression.[72] Both these dates coincide with a downward trend in fish prices, and the income generated by berry picking or seneca root harvesting could not be increased sufficiently to compensate for loss of revenues in other sectors.[73] These were also periods when, trying to weather the "down" years, the fishermen-farmers with large outfits would be cutting back on their labour needs. Marginal people, neither fully staple producers nor fully wage labourers, suffered the most when an economic slump, usually affecting both spheres, occurred.

Conclusion

From the data presented it can be concluded that, in Manitoba, an impoverished underclass was created and reproduced between 1850 and 1945. One need not resort to race for the explanation. The lack of access to land, the lack of capital, and (in Saint-Laurent) the lack of clerical support marginalized many of these old settlers and led them into a cycle of "debt-peonage" to the merchant representatives of national and international economies. The producers of fish, fur and seneca root, never seemingly able to generate enough revenue to support themselves, were dependent on traders for credit to see them through the year in food and equipment. In this manner, the very means of production were not owned by the Fort Rouge people even when they were not involved in a wage-labour relation.[74] A racist ideology hardened the attitudes of better-off settlers and authorities, and to a point this was a serious handicap. Explanations for their *déchéance* never went beyond perceived racial shortcomings. Consequently, some options and opportunities which were opened to others were out of reach *a priori* for this group.

What is significant about the history of this underclass is that by the 1950s well over 80 percent of the descendants of the eighteenth- and nineteenth-century European and Canadian workers and local Native women did not perceive themselves, and were not perceived by others, as ''half-breeds,''[75] having been fully integrated into the so-called ''white'' society. Any obstacles encountered in their daily lives were not the products of a racist ideology (which they themselves often espoused). When ''half-breeds'' and Métis were defined by society at large, some allusion to Indian ancestry was made and physical characteristics were noted, but in fact these were given social significance only because of the lifestyle led by the individuals. A ''half-breed'' or Métis was poor, unschooled, lived in a shack, engaged in a variety of seasonal employments, was not submissive to authority and was very much a part of the reserve labour force of Manitoba.[76] Once an individual was enmeshed in this cycle of poverty, a theory of racial determinism was invoked. Métis were poor because of inherited characteristics. If a (once defined as) Métis family became prosperous, its white parentage would be emphasized until the day when, at least in the Oblate parishes, it would merge with the French-Canadian element.

The dynamic of capitalism produces an underclass. Many former colonies have a marginalized, staple-producing reserve labour force. Most individuals do not engage in staple production by choice. In Manitoba, when industrial jobs were obtainable there was a distinct tendency to abandon seasonal jobs in favour of employment which produced more predictable returns.[77] In Saint-Laurent, as in most of the interlake region, this underclass became viewed as racially or ethnically distinct because of a series of specific socioeconomic and historical circumstances which affected relations of production and reinforced an emerging racist ideology. Slight phenotypical variations were negatively evaluated, and this evaluation (for the Métis in 20 percent of the cases) reinforced the very real impact of chronic material hardship. It became a part of society's common sense that ''most poor people in the interlake were natives, and that most natives were poor.'' To this day, the authorities, the public, and even the people affected, think in terms of Indian and Métis problems, or of injustices done to Natives, and posit solutions with ethnic boundaries in mind, not realizing that they are buying into an ever-evolving racist paradigm. Such a paradigm displaces critical analysis away from class-based issues and obscures the capitalist process of differentiating society between the haves and have-nots. This process occurs not merely in the sense of capital versus the working class but also of capital versus a marginalized, staple-producing, reserve labour force *subclass*.

NOTES

In this chapter, the author's spelling of ''métis'' has been changed to conform with the publisher's style, ''Métis,'' which is used throughout the rest of the book.

1.   Dipankar Gupta, ''Racism Without Colour: The Catholic Ethic and Ethnicity in Quebec,'' *Race and Class* 25, no. 1 (1983): 23.

2.   Marcel Giraud, *Le Métis Canadien* (St. Boniface: Editions du Blé, 1984).

3.   Jean H. Lagasse, *The People of Indian Ancestry in Manitoba: A Social and Economic History*, vol. 3 (Winnipeg: Department of Agriculture and Immigration, 1959), 5.

4. Oblats de Marie Immaculée (OMI), Archives Deschâtelets (AD), L641, M271, 55, 1947.

5. Gupta, "Racism Without Colour," 24.

6. Robert Miles, *Racism and Migrant Labour* (London: Routledge and Kegan Paul, 1982), 9.

7. Ibid., 7.

8. Ibid., 10.

9. Ibid., 14.

10. Giraud, *Le Métis Canadien.*

11. Miles, *Racism and Migrant Labour*, 32.

12. See Peter W. Ward, *White Canada Forever: Popular Attitudes and Public Policy Toward Orientals in British Columbia* (Montréal and Kingston: McGill-Queen's University Press, 1978), for an interesting example of a book based on the premise that racial differentiation has an inherent impact on social behaviour.

13. Miles, *Racism and Migrant Labour*, 146.

14. Ron Bourgeault, "The Indian, the Métis and the Fur Trade," *Studies in Political Economy* 12 (Fall 1984): 54.

15. Irene M. Spry, "The Métis and Mixed Bloods of Rupert's Land Before 1870," in Jacqueline Peterson and Jennifer S.H. Brown, eds., *The New Peoples: Being and Becoming Métis in North America* (Winnipeg: University of Manitoba Press, 1985), 95-118.

16. Bourgeault, "The Indian, the Métis," 61.

17. Russell G. Rothney, "Mercantile Capital and the Livelihood of Residents of the Hudson Bay Basin: A Marxist Interpretation" (Master's thesis, University of Manitoba, 1975), 62-113.

18. Nicole J.M. St.-Onge, "Dissolution of a Métis Community," *Studies in Political Economy* 18 (Autumn 1985): 149-72.

19. Hudson's Bay Company (HBC), Public Archives of Manitoba (PAM), B235, November-December 1828, Fort Garry Correspondence Book.

20. OMI-AD, L381, M27C, 1858-1895, Historical Notes (Parish of Saint-Laurent).

21. Herman G. Sprenger, "An Analysis of Selected Aspects of Metis Society, 1810-1870" (Master's thesis, University of Manitoba, 1972).

22. PAM, MG2B6, 1868 Statistical Summary, Executive Relief Committee, District of Assiniboia (Parish of Saint-Laurent).

23. OMI-AD, L1074, M27L, 4-17, Parish of San Clara.

24. PAM, MG2B6, 1868 Statistical Summary, Executive Relief Committee, District of Assiniboia (Parish of Saint-Laurent).

25. OMI-AD, L381, M27C, 1858-1895, Historical Notes (Parish of Saint-Laurent).

26. Ibid.

27. According to the tables compiled by Sprague and Frye, only three heads of family in Saint-Laurent had been HBC employees. D.N. Sprague and R.P. Frye, *The Genealogy of the First Métis Nation* (Winnipeg: Pemmican Publications, 1983).

28. PAM, Manitoba Oral History Project (MOHP), 1985, Interviews C385, C383.

29. Nicole St.-Onge, "Métis and Merchant Capital in Red River: The Decline of Pointe-à-Grouette, 1860-1885" (Master's thesis, University of Manitoba, 1983).

30. OMI-AD, L381, M27C, 1858-185, Historical Notes (Parish of Saint-Laurent), 66.

31. Ibid., 7.

32. Ibid., 28.

33. Missions de la Congrégation des Missionaires Oblats de Marie Immaculée (Rome, Maison Générale, 1878), 171-75.

34. Ibid.

35. OMI-AD, L381, M27C, 1858-1895, Historical Notes (Parish of Saint-Laurent), 66.

36. OMI-AD, L111, M27C3, Rapport du Bicaire des Missions de Saint-Boniface 1893, 9; Missions de la Congrégation des Missionaires Oblats de Marie Immaculée (Rome, Maison Générale, 1889), 281; Missions de la Congrégation des Missionaires Oblats de Marie Immaculée (Rome, Maison Générale, 1907), 327-29.

37. Giraud, *Le Métis Canadien*, 1,271-72.

38. Lagasse, *People of Indian Ancestry in Manitoba*.

39. PAM-MOHP, 1984, Interviews C341, C351-2, C349.

40. Ibid., Interview C353.

41. F.H. Leacy, ed., *Historical Statistics of Canada*, 2nd ed. (Ottawa: Statistics Canada, 1983), Section M.

42. Morris Zazlow, *The Opening of the Canadian North* (Toronto: McClelland and Stewart, 1971), 92.

43. Rothney, "Mercantile Capital," 153.

44. PAM-MOHP, 1984-1985, Interviews C349, C382, C385.

45. Ibid., Interview C349.

46. Russ Rothney and Steve Watson, *A Brief Economic History of Northern Manitoba* (Mimeo, 1975), 41.

47. Ibid., 57.

48. OMI-AD, L381, M27R9 (Parish of Saint-Laurent), 58.

49. Rothney and Watson, *Brief Economic History*, 58.

50. Ibid., 46.

51. Lagasse, *People of Indian Ancestry in Manitoba*, 69-70.

52. Leacy, *Historical Statistics*, Section N.

53. PAR-MOHP, 1984, Interview C353.

54. OMI-AD, L381, M27R9 (Parish of Saint-Laurent), 2-4. In this document the poor segment of the population is labelled Métis but the writer is quick to point out that there are "good" Métis families who are fully capable of meeting these higher financial obligations.

55. Ibid.

56. PAM-MOHP, 1984, Interviews C351-2, C356, C360. For a contrasting opinion of the clergy, listen to Interviews C342-C344.

57. This area no longer exists. It would seem many of its families moved to Winnipeg in the 1950s and 1960s.

58. Lagasse, vol. 1, *People of Indian Ancestry in Manitoba*, 72.

59. PAM-MOHP, 1984, Interviews C342-3, C351-2, C357, C363, C364.

60. Ibid., Interview C346 (even though Saint-Laurent inhabitants usually recognize quite distant kin ties).

61. Missions de la Congrégation des Missionaires Oblats de Marie Immaculée (Rome, Maison Générale, 1920), 273.

62. OMI-AD, L381, M27R9.

63. Ibid.

64. Ibid.

65. PAM-MOHP, 1984, Interview C351-2, C364. For an interesting if biased description of Fort Rouge-type inhabitants, see Missions de la Congrégation des Missionaires Oblats de Marie Immaculée (Rome, Maison Générale, 1901), 85-98.

66. Walter Hlady comments in a draft version of volume 3 of Lagasse, *People of Indian Ancestry in Manitoba*, on Métis attitudes toward gardening: "For many the necessity to go out harvesting the seneca root, fishing, cutting pulpwood and taking casual employment, all of which usually meant leaving the home community for extended periods, was a valid reason for not gardening."

67. For the large picture see volumes 1-3 of Lagasse, *People of Indian Ancestry in Manitoba*.

68. For an interesting discussion on fish prices for the Lake Winnipeg fishermen, see PAM-MOHP, 1984-85, Interview C383.

69. Ibid., Interviews C357, C363, C385.

70. Ibid. Listen to Interview C357 describing father's occupations.

71. Rothney and Watson, *Brief Economic History*, 57.

72. Ibid.

73. Lagasse, *People of Indian Ancestry in Manitoba*, 77-86.

74. Rothney and Watson, *Brief Economic History*, 66. For a description of a remarkably similar socioeconomic situation involving non-Native staples producers, see Jim Faris, *Cat Harbour: A Newfoundland Fishing Village* (St. John's: Institute for Social and Economic Research, Memorial University, 1967).

75. Lagasse, vol. 1, *People of Indian Ancestry in Manitoba*, 77.

76. Ibid., vol. 3, chapter 8.

77. Ibid., 52.

SECTION THREE

Class, Gender and Changing Forms of Struggle

Social classes, and class conflict, are a necessary function of capitalist relations of production. An identification of their characteristics requires an empirically detailed historical analysis. That is what the following chapters by Errol Black and Reg Skene attempt to do. The struggles engaged in by women are also best understood through this type of analysis. Üstün Reinart uses the methods of oral history to recreate an exciting, recent period in the long history of women's struggles against oppression. The three chapters in this section are linked through their interrelated focus on class, gender and forms of struggle.

Black argues that the ''character'' of a trade union movement, and the ''vision'' which that movement develops, are functions of the struggles in which it has been engaged, and the manner in which it has waged those struggles. In Manitoba, the mainstream of the labour movement has long been reformist, with the labour Left largely squeezed out. This is the consequence of, among other things, the loss of the Winnipeg General Strike, the Left's identification with the Communist Party of Canada in the 1930s, the anti-Communist hysteria of the Cold War, and the general economic prosperity of the postwar years.

The reformist character of the labour movement has been built by the pursuit of a legislative strategy, the political expression of which became the NDP brand of social democracy. This form of struggle appeared relatively successful until recently, but Black argues that this appearance was a function of good economic times, rather than effective strategy. The strategy adopted by Manitoba's labour movement is not adequate for tough economic times, he argues, and this inadequacy is made more difficult to resolve by the fact that the Left has long since been marginalized. Its absence will be especially felt, given that the recently changing structure of the labour movement — the much higher proportions of public sector unions and women, for example — will likely result in increasingly frequent and more politicized clashes between the state and the ''new'' labour movement over public expenditure cuts. Whether the result will be the emergence of a new and creative militancy remains to be seen.

A central theme of Skene's chapter is the relationship between theatre and social class, and the expression of class conflict at the ideological level. Theatre, like all cultural forms, is not classless. C.P. Walker's early twentieth-century efforts are an example of theatre as a class project.

First, theatre is business. It is a means of accumulating capital through the ''merchandizing of entertainment.'' An interesting example of theatre as business is Skene's exposé of the means by which Walker established a monopoly position in the

Winnipeg theatre business. It throws new light on the "golden era" of Winnipeg theatre, and on Winnipeg citizens' fond memories of the "good old days" of the Walker Theatre.

Second, Walker's theatre project functioned as a means of ideologically legitimizing class rule. In the early twentieth century, Winnipeg's capitalist class existed on the frontier; the veneer of "civilization" was thin; theatre was a means of civilizing. Exposure to "high culture" helped to create the illusion that the capitalist class was more civilized, and thus better, than the tens of thousands of European immigrant workers flooding the city at the time, and helped to legitimize the huge gulf between south-end mansions and north-end ghettos.

Third, Skene's analysis of Walker's theatre project affords a glimpse of the class consciousness of Winnipeg's business elite. Some of the most revealing observations come from the pen of Harriet Walker, herself an activist in the Winnipeg Women's Canadian Club and the Canadian Women's Press Club; the clubroom of the latter was described by Nellie McClung as the place where "the seed germ of [Manitoba's] suffrage association was planted."[1] Harriet Walker refers to Winnipeg's working class as "the phase of life over which polite society discreetly draws the curtain," and adds, ruefully it seems, that it is "a very thin curtain, through which may be seen the dark and fearful shadows on the other side." The business elite's fear of the alien, immigrant working class, and the vast gulf between the classes, is starkly revealed. Mrs. Walker then refers to Ibsen's *Ghosts* by saying that "it is plays like this that set young blood tingling — and old blood too — and arouse the desire 'to see life'." Again we see the fear of the working class, the fear that it might reach beyond its north-end ghettos to ask more of life, to "see life," and in so doing threaten the privileges of the capitalist class.

None of this is expressed in class terms, but in terms of public morality. Morals became the vehicle through which the fear of the working class and the desire to control it was expressed. The "dark and fearful shadows" were too close, too real, and the curtain separating them from the frontier capitalist class too thin, to take risks with a play like *Ghosts*, which dared to suggest that the moral values held by the apparently civilized capitalists were not really very different from the moral values of the working class. After all, Walker's theatre had nothing to do with prying open the hidden secrets of an unjust society, and everything to do with bolstering the self-confidence, and legitimizing the rulers, of that society.

Reinart's chapter picks up the struggles of the women's movement some sixty years after Harriet Walker's observations about the threat posed by Winnipeg's working class. What is especially noteworthy about Reinart's work is that she has recorded the voices of the kinds of activists who make movements work, but whose organizing efforts are usually overlooked by historians. The work of many of the women activists whose struggles spanned the period from Nellie McClung to the Winnipeg Women's Liberation Movement has been ignored. For example, even so important a figure as Beatrice Brigden — a founder of the Manitoba CCF — is mentioned but once in Nelson Wiseman's history of the Manitoba CCF/NDP. As Joan Sangster has recently written:

Brigden's absence from the annals of CCF mythology can also be explained by the fact that her political priorities were grass roots organizing and the construction of a feminist consciousness within the Party. Unfortunately, the latter in particular has not been deemed important by many historians.[2]

It is on just such organization and consciousness-raising that Reinart focusses.

An interesting theme in her study is the practical/theoretical difficulties faced by feminist activists in trying to allocate their time and energies among the frequently mutually incompatible tasks of developing their theoretical sophistication, organizing for political action, and providing needed services to women. As recently as the 1960s and 1970s the absence of institutionalized services to meet women's needs was massive, and is itself a revealing reflection of the priorities of the state and the gender bias of the ruling ideology. This gap had to be filled and the task, with all its practical and financial difficulties, was shouldered by these small bands of feminists on the fringes of Manitoba society. The scale of the task inevitably wore them down, and stole time from the politically essential tasks of organizing for political action and theorizing the nature of women's oppression.

The women described by Reinart are representative of the feminist activists whose struggles to organize and politicize created one of the great social movements of the postwar era. Reinart's description of the Family Law Coalition is an important example of the means by which social change is effected, and throws light on the changes and problems described later by Hofley and Falconer.

Reinart identifies different ''strands'' of the Manitoba's women's movement, and emphasizes their class and cultural dimensions and limitations. The women she describes were, for the most part, well educated, white and middle class. They were not, for the most part, working class or Native, and they did not address themselves to the needs that are specific to such women. Reinart advocates that the women's movement incorporate and meet the needs of working-class and Native women, and in this respect her chapter is linked with those of Black and Falconer. In building upon the dimensions of, but not being limited to, class, gender and culture, an even broader, more effective movement for social change can be built.

NOTES

1. Susan Jackel, ''First Days, Fighting Days: Prairie Presswomen and Suffrage Activism, 1906-1916,'' in Mary Kinnear, ed., *First Days, Fighting Days: Women in Manitoba History* (Regina: Canadian Plains Research Center, 1987), 64.

2. Joan Sangster, ''The Making of a Socialist-Feminist: The Early Career of Beatrice Brigden, 1888-1941,'' *Atlantis* 13, no. 1 (1987): 14.

5

Labour in Manitoba:
A Refuge in Social Democracy

Errol Black

Trade union movements have a core of common characteristics which place them in conflict with capital. First, they spring from, and are a critique of, capitalist institutions. Second, they have, if only implicitly, a program to modify or transform institutions which they seek to advance through collective action. Finally, they have a vision of a different society in which working people have better lives.

Such movements are not, however, always the same. They vary according to place and time because they are shaped by the particular context within which they develop — cultural conditions, the arrangements to regulate the sale of labour power and the exploitation of labour, the ethos of the employing classes — and by the content of the struggles the movement wages to advance and/or defend its interests.

Struggle is the key. It is through the struggles in which workers and trade unions are engaged, the way they wage these struggles, and the outcomes of these struggles, that a movement establishes its vision and acquires a decisive character. Thus the character of a trade union movement can only be determined through an historical, empirically detailed analysis of its struggles.

This chapter attempts to establish the character of the labour movement in Manitoba by focussing on the labour and political organizations which working people struggled to create, and the ways in which the needs and aspirations of working people have been manifested through the activities of such organizations. The analysis examines the roots of the movement and the major developments early in this century, especially the Winnipeg General Strike and the Depression. But the emphasis is on the period since World War II.

The main conclusion is that in the struggles preceding World War II, the reformist current became dominant. The movement's main objective became to secure a place for itself within capitalism, that is, to achieve an accommodation with capital. This strategy reached its culmination in 1969 with the election of the NDP. The latter part of the chapter explores the possibilities for trade union and working-class advances under the Manitoba NDP's brand of social democracy.

The Beginnings

The development of the Manitoba economy was part of the strategy to integrate Canada's western hinterland into the national economy, which sought to populate the region and bring the arable land into production. Capital investment and the spread of wage labour were geared to this objective. Thus, much capital investment in the nineteenth and early twentieth centuries was concentrated in railways, distribution facilities and related manufacturing establishments. Capital, and therefore wage labour, concentrated in Winnipeg; the rest was dispersed in small pockets along the major transportation networks.[1]

In 1901, 70 percent of Manitoba's population was rural.[2] Winnipeg accounted for 60 percent of the urban population and the manufacturing jobs. The only other city of consequence was Brandon, with 7.5 percent of the population and 9 percent of the manufacturing jobs.[3] It was within the context of a political economy dominated by agriculture and a single urban centre, Winnipeg, that the trade union movement emerged and developed.

Craft Unions

From the outset, the movement in Manitoba developed along lines similar to those in Ontario. Until the mid-1890s, most skilled workers came from Ontario. They had experience in the international craft unions based in the United States, and they accepted the unions' limited aims of advancing sectional interests through collective bargaining, and class interests through the activities of trade union centrals.

The legislation governing unions — the Trade Union Act, 1872 — favoured craft workers, and workers with skills in short supply. It severely restricted tactics like strikes, boycotts and picketing, which were used by unions to force employers to concede recognition, and it left employers free to use any tactics they wished to thwart unionization.[4] The first unions formed in Manitoba in the early 1880s were craft unions of printers, metal trades workers, transport workers and carpenters.[5]

The Knights of Labour

In Ontario, the dominance of craft unions was challenged in the 1880s by the Knights of Labour. They penetrated Manitoba in 1883, organizing a local of ten telegraph operators. In place of the particularism and exclusionist policies of the craft, the Knights called for the organization of all workers — irrespective of skill, sex or race — into industrial and regional assemblies. In place of strikes, the Knights stressed education and independent political action. And in place of immediate gains at the bargaining table, they held out the vision of "the gradual replacement of capitalism by workers' producer cooperatives."[6]

By 1887 the Knights had five assemblies, with a combined membership of nearly 1,500.[7] The Knights diminished in influence after the 1880s, due to attacks by employers and craft unions, and the fact that their philosophy was ill-suited to workers' struggles against the brutality of a capitalism bent on subordinating labour to the imperatives of accumulation. However, during their brief tenure in Manitoba, the Knights demonstrated the potential for expanding the scope of reformism through social unionism. This social unionism was manifested in efforts to unionize the unskilled and the marginal; campaigns to help the unemployed and to win legislation beneficial to labour (the Shop Regulation Act, 1888); collaboration with the craft unions to establish a Winnipeg Trades Council; establishment of a tailors cooperative in the aftermath of a failed strike in 1887; and sustained efforts to make the problems and concerns of labour political issues.[8]

Labour Enters The Political Arena

Throughout the 1880s and much of the 1890s the Canadian and Manitoban economies were stagnant. Employers took advantage of depressed labour markets to "starve" striking workers into submission, or replace them — sometimes, as in the 1887 tailors' strike, with workers from central Canada.[9]

Confronted by hostile employers and pro-business governments, workers reconstituted the Winnipeg Trades Council in 1894, and began to consider independent political action. This idea emerged due to the increasing influence of skilled workers from Britain, who were familiar with labour's interventions into British politics. In 1896, workers formed the Winnipeg Labour Party to promote their aims by working through parliamentary institutions. In 1900 the Labour Party recorded its first electoral victory, sending Arthur Puttee, a solid labour man, to the House of Commons.[10]

With the economic revival in the late 1890s — part of a world-wide revival — some obstacles to trade union organization weakened, and the movement made gains. A 1902 federal survey identified forty-six locals in Manitoba. The ten locals outside Winnipeg were railway workers. Winnipeg membership was concentrated amongst railway workers too, but there were also locals of garment workers, theatre employees, street railway workers, teamsters and quarrymen, and two locals in the public sector — letter carriers and civic workers. A majority of the locals were affiliated with the TLC and the Winnipeg Trades Council.[11]

The trade union movement quantified in this survey consisted primarily of skilled, Anglo-Saxon workers who had immigrated to Manitoba from Ontario and Britain.[12] Its cornerstones were the craft unions, most headquartered in the United States, and a politics of labourism and "soft" socialism, as expressed through the Winnipeg Labour Party.

Class Against Class

The expansion in Canada's economy which started in the late 1890s was based largely on a boom in international markets for resources, especially wheat. Manitoba and Winnipeg were major beneficiaries of the accelerated pace of prairie settlement and development. Manitoba's population more than doubled from 1901 to 1916, from 255,211 to 553,860, and the proportion living in urban areas increased from 27.6 to 43.5 percent. Winnipeg's population was 163,000 in 1916, accounting for 68 percent of the province's urban population, up from 60 percent in 1901.[13]

The growth in population resulted largely from immigration, much of it British. But significant numbers also came from Eastern Europe — Russia, Poland and the Ukraine. Some East European immigrants did "bull work" in the construction of new railways. Thousands more were ghettoized in the north ends of Winnipeg and Brandon, relegated to track jobs on the railways and low-paid labouring jobs, often of a casual and seasonal nature.[14]

The boom stimulated manufacturing in Manitoba. From 1900 to 1915, Winnipeg's manufacturing output increased by 453 percent, second only to Vancouver among

Canada's top ten manufacturing centres. The number of establishments increased from 103 to 298, the number of workers from 3,155 to 15,295, and the average number of employees from 30.6 to 51.3.[15]

Skilled Versus Unskilled Workers

For most of the first decade of this century the growth in labour demand created a shortage of skilled workers, making it easier for them to unionize. Conditions facing unskilled workers were much less favourable. Continuing immigration, and the concentration in cities every autumn of unemployed hands brought west for the harvest, ensured that even the meanest employers could obtain all the workers they required.

The differential conditions faced by skilled and unskilled workers were reflected in the pattern of unionization. From 1902 to 1910, locals in Manitoba increased from 46 to 104, in Winnipeg from 36 to 69. Unionization was concentrated in four main groups: the building trades (19), the printing and allied trades (6), the metal, engineering and shipbuilding trades (19), and the railway trades (43). These four accounted for 84 percent of Manitoba locals. Unionization amongst unskilled workers was almost nonexistent, apart from track workers and labourers on the railways, construction labourers, and a few relatively unskilled manual workers in the public sector.[16] By 1912, locals in Manitoba and Winnipeg had increased to 139 and 82, respectively. All but nine of the Manitoba locals were affiliated with international unions based in the United States.[17]

The growth in the number of locals and in memberships was evidently achieved with comparatively little strife, as suggested by the data in Table 15, which indicate that strikes in Manitoba were of short duration relative to strikes in the country as a whole.

TABLE 15

NUMBER OF DISPUTES AND DAYS LOST IN MANITOBA AND CANADA, 1901-1912

Period	Disputes			Days Lost		
	Manitoba	Canada	Manitoba as % of Canada	Manitoba	Canada	Manitoba as % of Canada
1901-05	28	559	5.0	34,340	2,461,999	1.4
1906-10	29	511	5.7	108,695	3,280,524	3.3
1911	8	99	8.1	1,165	2,046,650	*
1912	7	150	4.7	28,450	1,099,208	2.6
1901-12	72	1,319	5.4	172,650	8,888,381	1.9

*Note: Less than 0.1 per cent.
Source: Canada, Department of Labour, *The Labour Gazette* (February 1914): 913-30.

There were disputes with recognition as the central issue: for example, CPR trackmen in 1901; Winnipeg bakers and forty female confectioners in 1902; carpenters and joiners in 1904; street railway workers in 1906; and brewery workers in 1911. There were also disputes in which the legitimacy of the union was the central issue: for example, the bitter confrontations between metal trades workers and Vulcan Iron Works in 1906, and between 116 women garment workers and their employer in 1909.

The majority of disputes, however, involved such things as wages, hours of work and the violation of union rules.[18]

The Two Strata of the Working Class

The patterns in immigration, employment and unionization which characterized the first decade of the century combined to divide the working class into two distinct strata: primarily skilled workers of Anglo-Saxon backgrounds, many of them British-born, in the craft unions; and unskilled immigrant workers from Eastern Europe, concentrated in low-paid, nonunionized manual jobs.[19] The differences in the backgrounds of these workers, and in their objective circumstances, were manifested in profound differences in consciousness which affected not only the way they related to capitalist employers and the state, but also to other workers.

The skilled stratum was the bulwark of craft union traditions and of a politics "which eschewed sophisticated ideological notions in favour of practical, specific legislative proposals."[20] These workers tended also to be chauvinistic and elitist toward unskilled and "alien" workers, a tendency reflected in the campaign by the Winnipeg Trades Council for legislation to protect white women from the designs of oriental employers, and its call for an end to Eastern European immigration in 1914.[21]

Workers in the lower stratum, in contrast, were victimized by the limitations of craft unionism and electoral politics, making them receptive to alternative forms of unionism, and a politics arising from a class analysis of capitalist society. They also recognized the necessity for a solidarity transcending occupational and industrial divisions.

This dichotomy must not be overdrawn: as both Ross McCormack[22] and Doug Smith[23] have pointed out, the situation was more complex. While British workers concentrated in the mainstream, reformist tendency, they also figured prominently in the intellectual develoment and leadership of the alternatives to reformism — a "fuzzy" syndicalism which led to the formation of the OBU in 1919, and revolutionary socialism. The British workers who embraced radical and/or revolutionary socialist ideas seem to have come out of work situations where the conflict was particularly intense, especially the metal trades shops like Vulcan Iron Works and Dominion Bridge, where employers were relentless in their efforts to maintain domination of their workers, and the CPR shops, where the company embarked on a campaign to de-skill the machinist and related trades.[24]

The Emergence of Two Distinct Political Currents

The working class was divided, and this division gave rise to two distinct political currents. The first was the reformist current, which started with the Winnipeg Labour Party in 1896, and extended through the Manitoba Labour Party (1910), the Labour Representation League (1912), and the Dominion Labour Party (1918).[25] The second was the challenging current, which found its initial formal expression in the Manitoba wing of the Socialist Party of Canada (SPC), formed in 1904. The SPC brought together East European immigrants active in the ethnic-based socialist clubs in Winnipeg's north end, and British working-class intellectuals who supported a "revolutionary socialist viewpoint."[26]

But the SPC failed to make significant inroads in Manitoba, for two main reasons. First, it had an ambivalent position on trade unions and their role in the struggle for socialism. Unions were treated, at best, as irrelevant in the revolutionary process, and at worst as an impediment to the development of a revolutionary consciousness. Second, the SPC vacillated on the role of the party in electoral politics and struggles for immediate reforms. The ambivalence on trade unions alienated trade-union activists; the vacillation on reform antagonized core supporters in the East European immigrant community.

A split developed in the SPC in 1909-10 on the question of affiliation to the Second International (it was opposed by the executive). This split was formalized in 1911, with the creation of the Social Democratic Party (SDP) of Canada. The Manitoba wing of the SPC intervened in the 1911 provincial election to secure the defeat of Labour Party candidate Fred Dixon. This serious tactical error contributed to the formation of a branch of the SDP by disaffected members of the SPC.[27]

On general principles and on vision there was little difference between the SPC and SDP.[28] The main advantage of the SDP in Manitoba was that it allowed somewhat more scope than the SPC for its members to adapt their activities to local conditions. One manifestation of this was SDP collaboration with the Labour Party to elect candidates in civic and provincial elections and to agitate for reforms.[29]

The employing classes and the state did not remain passive in the face of the upsurge of working-class support for trade unions and reformist and left-wing politics. In the early years of the century the federal government experimented with legislation designed to prevent strikes and force workers to submit to third-party intervention in the resolution of disputes, a process which culminated in the Industrial Disputes and Investigations Act, 1907. At the same time, armed militia were used to break the strikes of militant workers, as happened in the street railway dispute in 1906, and employers obtained injunctions from the courts to end strikes and stop picketing, as happened at Vulcan Iron Works in 1907 and in a building trades dispute in 1908.[30]

A severe economic slump in 1913 restored the initiative in class relations to employers. Trade unions were weakened by declining memberships and depleted treasuries. Employers exploited this situation to impose cuts in wages, increases in hours and speed-ups in production, and to declare their establishments "open" shops. At the same time, the Manitoba government legislated a reduction in the minimum wage for children and increases in the maximum hours for women.[31]

Conditions shifted again in 1915, with the impetus to business provided by the war and a rapid reduction in unemployment. Trade union organization flourished. New locals were formed amongst workers never before unionized, including telephone operators, retail clerks, and civic office workers. With the deterioration in living and working conditions which accompanied the war, the desire for unionization spread throughout the working class.

The 1919 Winnipeg General Strike

Industrial conflict also intensified. In 1917, there were eighteen strikes in Manitoba, and "more man-days of labour were lost in Winnipeg due to strikes and lockouts than in the previous four years combined."[32] Many ended in defeat for the workers, including a major packing house strike, a strike of the F.W. Woolworth Company, and a strike of the metal trades shops (Vulcan Iron Works, Dominion Bridge, and Manitoba Bridge and Iron Works), which the employers ended by obtaining court injunctions. These losses increased workers' hostility, not just against employers, but also against the state.[33]

The escalation of conflict in Winnipeg was part of a general "revolt" of labour across Canada.[34] In Winnipeg and western Canada, this revolt was also aimed at the limitations of craft unions and the servility of their leaderships. This created an opportunity for the militant and left-wing leadership within the western labour movement to develop a new form of unionism, one which would exploit the rise in the solidarity and militancy of the working class.

In mid-March 1919, a majority of 250 delegates attending a conference of western labour in Calgary approved a radical platform, called for a general strike in June in support of this platform, and recommended an end to affiliation with international organizations and the reorganization of workers along geographical and industrial lines. They also established, as ultimate aims, collective ownership of the means of production, production for use rather than profit, and a workers' state.[35] This was the OBU.

There was much support for the OBU, especially in Manitoba, but its agenda and timetable were overtaken by the events of April and May. In April 1919, the Metal Trades Council (formed in 1918) presented demands to the metal trades shops. The employers refused to recognize the council and on 2 May the workers struck, joining the building trades workers who had downed their tools the day before.[36]

In response to an appeal for support, the council conducted a vote on a general strike, which would have as its objectives a living wage, the right to organize, and the eight-hour day. The vote endorsed strike action by a margin of 11,000 to 500.[37] The strike began on 15 May. Within two days virtually the entire economy of Winnipeg was shut down. Some estimates place the number of workers on strike at 35,000, the majority unorganized.[38] The strike in Winnipeg triggered sympathy strikes in Brandon and across the country.[39]

The Winnipeg strike dragged on for six weeks. Employers and the state were intent on ending it without concessions to strikers. The militia was brought in, a special constabulary replaced the regular police force, and employers organized a Committee of One Thousand to whip up public hysteria against the strike. The leaders of the strike were arrested and imprisoned. The climax came on 21 June when, in response to a peaceful demonstration protesting the arrests of strike leaders, the mayor read the Riot Act. The demonstration went ahead, the police attacked the demonstrators, killing two and wounding as many as thirty, and the city was placed under martial law.[40]

This demonstration of state brutality crushed the spirit of the strike and it was formally ended on 23 June.[41] The working class of Manitoba was defeated. There were no concessions, and in the immediate aftermath of the strike many thousands of workers were victimized — fired, blacklisted, harassed and hounded by police.[42]

It is important to recognize that events in Winnipeg were not isolated, but rather were part of a phenomenon affecting virtually every community in Canada, and every capitalist country in the world.[43] The significance of Winnipeg in the Canadian context is that it was here that solidarity, militancy and opposition to capital and the state were most complete.

Interpreting the 1919 Winnipeg General Strike

The argument has been made that there was no revolutionary threat from the working class in Manitoba, that the strike was about trade union rights and modest demands for improved wages and shorter hours. The point that is missed in this argument is that any general strike, irrespective of the demands that provoke it, threatens established authority and must therefore be crushed. The problem with the Winnipeg General Strike was that it was the wrong weapon in view of the objectives at stake; or to put it another way, the objectives set for the strike were too modest relative to its potential in the hands of a disciplined working class.[44] This point was perceived by the Reverend A.E. Smith, a leader in the Brandon strike, who suggested some years later that the strike failed because:

> There was no working class party with a conscious understanding of this power and what should be done . . . yet objectively here was revealed more clearly than by any other event in Canadian labour history the elemental factors of working class power.[45]

Smith is correct. There was no working class party with this understanding. Leadership of the strike was made up of men involved in and identified with every current in the labour and left-wing politics of Manitoba. These men submerged their differences and collaborated in leading a strike with modest objectives and a single tactic, that of avoiding any action which would ''give the master class the occasion they so much seek: of covering the labour movement with stigma, by accusing us of breaking their sacred law.''[46] They did not anticipate the brutality of the state, and had no response to it when it came.[47]

But the ruling classes understood the show of working-class power and also understood its potential. This is why the general strike had to be crushed — to ensure that there would not be another, by a working class constituted with a conscious understanding of its power and what to do with that power.

The defeat of the working class of Winnipeg (and Manitoba) was simultaneously the triumph of capital. This triumph seemed complete — socialism and mass unionism were weakened, the working class was demoralized, and the general strike was discredited as a tactic for advancing working-class interests. There was, to be sure, a flurry of political activity by labour in response to the victimization of workers and the trials of the strike leaders, but this was a manifestation of the weakened condition of the class, not of its strength.[48]

The Reconstitution of Labour and the Left

After 1919, Manitoba's economy stagnated and unemployment increased from 2.1 percent in 1919 to an average 6.9 percent from 1921 to 1925.[49] Within this context there were two major developments in the labour movement. First, a bitter struggle ensued between the international craft unions and the OBU for the allegiance of workers in Manitoba. Second, the various political organizations on the left wing of the trade union movement consolidated into two main currents, a moderate, reformist Left, represented by the ILP, and a revolutionary Left aligned with the Communist Party of Canada (CPC).

The OBU Versus the Craft Unions

The conflict between the OBU and the craft unions intensified in July and August 1919, when the OBU failed in its bid to gain control of the Winnipeg Trades and Labour Council, and set up a rival OBU Council.[50] In the ensuing struggle over the memberships of existing locals, the OBU found itself up against not only the craft unions, but also hostile governments and hostile employers, some of whom either concluded closed-shop agreements with craft unions, or compelled workers to sign contracts disavowing organizations favouring sympathetic strikes.[51]

Nevertheless, in the months immediately following the strike the OBU made substantial gains. By October 1919, it had 9,000 members in Winnipeg — mainly in the railway shops, the garment industry and the metal trades, but also amongst confectionary workers, teamsters, tailors and some construction trades. In August, 1920, Winnipeg's 900 street railway workers joined. This was the apex.[52] In Canada, the OBU peaked at the end of 1919 with ''a membership of 41,150, organized into 101 local units with eight central labour councils and two district boards.''[53]

The OBU began to disintegrate in the 1920s, for two reasons. First, the economic conditions which prevailed after 1919 undermined the entire trade union movement. From 1919 to 1923 union membership dropped from 20,000 to 10,000. And of the fifteen strikes reported for the 1920-25 period, one-half were broken ''and most of the rest ended in compromises that saw men get their jobs back without union recognition.''[54] Second, the OBU's organizational strategy, especially its emphasis on building itself by capturing the memberships of existing craft unions rather than by organizing the unorganized, was out of joint with the times. After the events in Winnipeg in May and June 1919, workers were on the defensive, struggling to maintain their unions and their standard of living. The conflict between the OBU and the craft unions weakened workers' capacity to defend themselves.

The OBU made a last-ditch attempt to strengthen its position in February 1922 by aligning with the Workers' Party of Canada (WPC) — the public face of the CPC until 1924, when it was disbanded. At the founding convention of the WPC, R.B. Russell, secretary of the OBU, proposed an alliance which would recognize the OBU as the trade union arm of the WPC. This was rejected. The convention opted instead for struggle and agitation within existing trade unions, and opposition to dual unionism and secessionist efforts.[55] This resolution isolated the OBU at the margin of the union movement.

With an improvement in economic conditions in the 1920s, labour's fortunes improved. By the end of the decade union membership was back to the levels of 1919 and 1920.[56] Most of these gains were in the craft unions and were achieved with little resistance. From 1926 to 1930 there were sixteen reported strikes involving 1,451 workers. Only four ended with clear-cut victories for workers. The one exception to the pattern of union activity during this period was in the garment industry, where Communist activists who had been expelled from international unions organized the Industrial Union of Needle Trades Workers. This organization won some important victories in the face of opposition from employers and the state (in the form of police protection for strike breakers).[57]

The Independent Labour Party Versus the Communist Party of Canada

The major struggle for labour in the 1920s was in the political sphere. In the 1920 provincial election, labour and socialist parties ran eighteen candidates. They elected eleven: ten in Winnipeg, including John Queen, George Armstrong and William Ivens, who were still in jail serving out the one-year sentences they had been given for their part in the general strike; and the Reverend A.E. Smith of Brandon, a candidate for the Manitoba branch of the Dominion Labour Party (DLP).[58]

After this election a split developed within the DLP over candidates for civic elections in Winnipeg and resulted in the resignations of Fred Dixon and S.J. Farmer. In December 1920, Dixon, Farmer and J.S. Woodsworth were instrumental in forming the ILP, which brought together reformist trade unionists, parliamentary socialists and progressive Methodists.[59]

The militant and revolutionary elements in the working class — people associated with the SDP, which in 1918 passed a resolution supporting unification with the SPC "on the basis of the Bolsheviki program,"[60] and people radicalized by the events of 1919 — came together with the formation of the CPC in 1921. In Manitoba, support for the CPC came primarily from the East European and Jewish communities in Winnipeg and Brandon, but it also attracted people like H.M. Bartholomew, a labour leader in Brandon,[61] and the Reverend A.E. Smith and his family.[62]

Throughout the 1920s, the ILP concentrated on building electoral support, on the grounds that control of government was a precondition for the establishment of a cooperative commonwealth:

> The conflict of interest between the workers and the capitalist is a struggle for the control of government — the capitalist to retain and the worker to secure it by political struggle. This is the class struggle.[63]

The ILP gained most of its support in Winnipeg and Brandon, but also found support in northern communities such as Flin Flon and Dauphin, and from elements of the farming community in the north. Wiseman estimates that by the early 1930s the party had 800-1,000 members in seventeen branches.[64]

The CPC, in contrast, had a two-pronged approach to promoting working class consciousness: building solidarity and militancy in existing trade unions, and winning the Canadian Labour Party (CLP), which had been established by the TLC in 1917, to the CPC program.[65] The focus of the CPC was clarified in 1925 with the publication of *Steps to Power*, a pamphlet detailing the program of the Trade Union Educational League (TUEL) — a CPC organization.[66] This program called for "industrial unionism, Canadian trade-union autonomy, organization of the unorganized, independent labour political action, nationalization of industry with workers' control."[67] Under this program, the CPC organized workers in a number of important industries, including Winnipeg's garment industry, and in 1926 joined with the Canadian Brotherhood of Railway Employees, the OBU, the Canadian Federation of Labour, and some smaller unions to form the All Canadian Congress of Labour (ACCL) — a nationalist trade union centre opposed to the TLC.[68]

Until the mid-1920s the possibility existed that the reformist and left-wing currents in the Manitoba labour movement would achieve an accommodation. But the divergence between the two currents was accentuated in 1925 when the ILP refused to join forces with the CLP in the federal elections. In the latter 1920s the CPC escalated its attack on the ILP and its leadership, castigating them for their rejection of the CPC's brand of revolutionary socialism.[69]

In 1929, a further break occurred when the CPC replaced the TUEL with the Workers' Unity League (WUL), and abandoned its strategy of working within the existing unions and building the CLP. The WUL was formed to build a revolutionary centre based on "Red" industrial unions, detached from and in opposition to existing trade union organizations — including the ACCL. While the question of its relations with existing trade union organizations was already a matter of debate within the CPC, it seems clear that the decision to form the WUL was the result of a direction from the Red International of Labour Unions to struggle against "capitalism and its agent the social reformist trade union bureaucracy."[70] The result was to bring the CPC into opposition to both the ILP and the mainstream trade union movement, and to isolate the CPC — the organized Left — much as the OBU had been isolated in the early 1920s.

The 1930s

The 1930s were heralded by a worldwide collapse of capitalist investment and production. In Winnipeg, the index number of employment plummeted almost 30 percent from 1929 to 1933,[71] and in 1939 employment was still 15 percent below the 1929 level.[72] Unemployment amongst trade union members jumped from 7.1 percent in 1929 to 20.3 percent in 1933. Not until early 1941 was the rate back to 7.1 percent.[73]

The mass unemployment and mass misery of the 1930s exposed yet again the limitations of international craft unions. Most simply settled in to wait out the crisis. Not a single strike was reported for international craft unions in the printing, construction and metal trades from 1931 to 1939.[74]

The Workers' Unity League

However, other segments of the working class — industrial workers, unskilled and semiskilled workers, and the unemployed — did fight back. There were eighty-eight strikes reported for Manitoba from 1931 to 1939. In the first half of the decade many were initiated by unions organized by or affiliated with the WUL.

A major strike started in June 1934 when miners in Flin Flon, organized by the WUL, struck the Hudson Bay Mining and Smelting Company in response to the firing of union activists. The company refused to bargain on reinstatement for the fired workers, union recognition, a pay hike or safer working conditions, and enlisted the aid of Premier Bracken to break the strike. A company-initiated vote on a return to work held on 30 June resulted in a confrontation between union members and their wives, and those workers who wanted to comply with the company's demand that they vote. This incident provided Bracken with a pretext for arresting the strike leaders, and after a meeting with the antistrike forces in Flin Flon, he pledged government support to end the Communist-led strike. The strike ended on 14 July with the return to work of most workers, and the dismissal of about 150 union militants.[75]

In Winnipeg there were strikes in foundries, scrap metal and waste material yards, box factories, cold storage plants, bakeries, fur factories, bedding and furniture factories.[76] But the key struggles were in the garment industry.

The garment industry posed special problems because it consisted of many small establishments and a dispersed work force. For example, in 1932 there were twenty-four establishments, with an average of thirty-six workers, manufacturing women's clothing.[77] This situation, replicated in most branches of the industry, made it extremely difficult for workers to unionize and win improvements in wages and working conditions. When particular establishments were struck, employers replaced striking workers.

Communist organizers had attempted to overcome this problem in 1928 with the formation of the Industrial Union of Needle Trade Workers. This union was involved in many successful single-establishment strikes in the early 1930s, but in 1934 it lost a major dispute which had brought four hundred cloakmakers into confrontation with eight employers for thirty-one days. Here again police intervention, resulting in the arrest of twenty-four workers on picket lines, helped employers to end the strike without conceding any of the major demands of the workers.[78]

The WUL also played a decisive role in organizing unemployed workers, especially those in federal relief camps and on relief projects operated by the Manitoba and local governments. The WUL organized a number of strikes and extraparliamentary actions by such workers. These efforts culminated in the On-to-Ottawa Trek of 1935. In Manitoba, some one thousand workers were ready to join the trek, but this

> travelling display of the grievances of the single unemployed was halted in Regina on Dominion Day, when RCMP forces and the trekkers clashed in a battle to stop the protesters before they gained too much momentum and before they had a chance to reach . . . Winnipeg.[79]

The impact of the WUL in Manitoba and elsewhere remains a subject of considerable debate.[80] There seems little doubt, however, that WUL activities did much to prevent labour's collapse in Manitoba, by inspiring workers to struggle creatively, by keeping their grievances on the political agenda, and by signalling to governments and employers that efforts to legitimize an economic system that caused such widespread misery were becoming ever more problematic.

In November 1935, however, the CPC again changed its strategy. The WUL was scrapped and CPC activists in the unions were ordered to bring their unions into the TLC. As Norman Penner put it, the CPC

> had come full circle, from ending the secession of the OBU in favour of working within the [TLC], to helping create the ACCL as a Canadian Centre opposed to the [TLC], to setting up the WUL as a "revolutionary trade union centre" opposing both the ACCL and the [TLC], and, to complete the circle, dissolving the WUL to join the [TLC] and opposing the ACCL. . . . [81]

Again, this change in strategy was ordered by the Communist International as part of its campaign to establish united-front opposition to fascism.[82]

The twists and turns in the ideological positions and tactics of the CPC created dissension in the party and undermined its credibility with the working class. With the dissolution of the WUL and the return to the craft unions in 1935, the party's influence and impact in Manitoba diminished.

The Co-operative Commonwealth Federation

While the CPC was moving to the left in the early 1930s, the reformist current was moving right. In 1932, the CCF was established in Calgary by progressive intellectuals, many of them clergymen and leaders of farm, labour and reformist political organizations. However, the CCF was not a labour party. It made no provision for trade unions and workplace struggles in the movement to bring about the cooperative commonwealth. Moreover, with its emphasis on achieving state power through constitutional means, the new party rejected not only revolutionary action, but also any kind of extraparliamentary activity aimed at destabilizing the established order — a stance which immediately placed the party in direct conflict with the CPC and the WUL.[83]

In Alberta and Saskatchewan the CCF had its base amongst farmers and their organizations. By contrast, in Manitoba it became established through an affiliation with the ILP, which resulted in candidates in provincial elections running under a joint label. This relationship ended in 1943 with the dissolution of the ILP.[84]

Lost Opportunity for the Left

The tragedy of the divergence between the reformist and left-wing currents, and the hostility this engendered, is that there was much support for a progressive politics in Manitoba in the 1930s. This was especially evident in Winnipeg where, as Wiseman observes, "the municipal leftist vote consistently exceeded 40 percent."[85] In 1935, Communist and ILP members controlled Winnipeg city council.

In the two Manitoba elections held in the 1930s, the ILP elected five members with 17 percent of the popular vote in 1932, and the combined ILP-CCF ticket elected seven members with 12 percent of the vote in 1936.[86] The latter election also sent Communist candidate James Litterick to the provincial legislature — a first in Canada.[87] There was also support for left-wing parties in federal elections, as shown in Table 16.

TABLE 16

PROPORTION OF VOTES CAST FOR LEFT PARTIES* IN FEDERAL ELECTIONS,
MANITOBA AND CANADA, 1926-1945

Election	Manitoba	Canada
1926	8.7	1.5
1930	10.2	1.3
1935	22.7	9.6
1940	19.4	8.5
1945	36.5	17.8

*Note: Labour parties — from 1935 on the CCF — and Communist Party.
Source: F.H. Leacy, M.C. Urquhart and K.A.H. Buckley, eds., *Historical Statistics of Canada* (Ottawa: Statistics Canada, 1983).

These data suggest that in the absence of conflict between the reformist and left-wing currents, and internal conflict within both, labour might have achieved substantial political gains in the 1930s. As it was, the concrete gains that were made — notably, the creation of a Department of Labour in 1931, the extension of the minimum wage to adult males in 1933, and the Strikes and Lockouts Prevention Act of 1937 — did little more than sustain the idea that it was possible to achieve improvements in the conditions of working people through legislative reform.

The Depression ended with World War II. From 1939 to 1945, employment increased by 46 percent. The unemployment rate for trade union members dropped from 9.6 percent in 1939 to 0.9 percent in 1943, and thousands of workers who had resigned themselves to never working again were pressed into service to meet the imperatives of war production.[88] The conditions created by the war provided the basis for the consolidation both of trade unions and of reformism in Manitoba.

The Consolidation of Reformism

Three major developments affected the Manitoba labour movement during and immediately after the war: the rise of industrial unions through the Congress of Industrial Organizations (CIO) and the CCL; the 1944 adoption by the federal government of legislation which established workers' rights to unionize and bargain, and imposed on employers the obligation to bargain with unions; and the final demise of the CPC as an important factor in labour politics in Manitoba, and the consolidation of the CCF as the party of the reformist ("soft") Left.

The Rise of the Industrial Unions

The CIO's militant drive to organize mass-production industries in the United States, starting in 1935, sparked similar efforts in Ontario. Militant workers, many of whom had been active in the WUL and retained their allegiance to the CPC, adopted the sit-down strike and plant occupation as tactics to win recognition and force industrial employers to the bargaining table. In 1939 the TLC caved into pressure from its American counterpart — the American Federation of Labour (AFL) — and suspended CIO affiliates. This led to the formation in 1940 of the CCL, a new trade union central bringing together the ACCL and CIO affiliates.[89]

During the war, trade union membership in Canada more than doubled, from 362,223 in 1940 to 831,697 in 1946. These gains were concentrated in CCL affiliates. By 1946 the CCL, with 38 percent of union members, rivalled the TLC, with 43 percent, as the dominant trade union central.[90] The national surge in organization was accompanied by an equally dramatic increase in strike action: 1943 saw 401 strikes involving 218,000 workers — the highest levels since 1919. Manufacturing accounted for 55 percent of the strikes, 65 percent of the workers involved, and 75 percent of the time lost due to strike action in 1943.[91]

Manitoba, with an economy still dominated by agriculture and relatively small-scale industry, was on the periphery of these developments. Nevertheless, favourable economic conditions plus the impetus from CIO organizing drives in Ontario affected Manitoba workers. From 1941 to 1946, union locals in Manitoba increased from 214 to 292 and memberships rose from 18,557 to 38,681.[92] Strike activity increased, but as indicated in Table 17 it was of a lesser (statistical) magnitude than in Canada. This was partly because most strikes in Manitoba were small. In 1945, for example, there were eleven, with eight involving thirty or fewer workers. The other three — a strike of foundry workers in Selkirk, and of cold storage plant workers and compositors in Winnipeg — involved fifty, sixty-one and 120 workers respectively. The major exception occurred in the meat-packing plants in St. Boniface and Winnipeg in 1946, where workers were involved in a nationwide strike to secure a common agreement for all packing-house workers employed by the industry's dominant firms.[93]

TABLE 17

STRIKE ACTIVITY IN MANITOBA RELATIVE TO CANADA, 1941-1946

Strike Indicator	Manitoba	As % of Canada
Union members, 1946	38,681	4.6
Number of strikes, 1941-46	39	2.4
Workers involved, 1941-46	2,778	0.4
Man-days lost, 1941-46	31,901	0.4

Source: Canada, Department of Labour, *The Labour Gazette*, various numbers.

There were also increased demands for legislation to establish trade union rights and improve social welfare programs, plus increasing support amongst rank-and-file members for an expanded political role for labour, as reflected in growing support for the CCF in most parts of Canada.

In 1943 the CCF made major gains in the Ontario election, and public opinion polls briefly gave the party top spot at the federal level. In the same year, the CCL passed a resolution to endorse the CCF "as the political arm of labour in Canada, and recommend to all affiliated and chartered unions that they affilate with the CCF."[94] While the TLC adhered to the AFL policy — no explicit endorsation of political parties — its 1943 convention did pass a resolution mildly supportive of the CCF, calling on its affiliates and members "to support candidates who favour the policies of the trade union movement as represented by this Congress."[95]

The CCF in Manitoba experienced the same surge of support. Party membership jumped from 800 in 1942 to 3,300 in 1943, and the party won two provincial by-elections in 1943, electing D.L. Johnson in Brandon and Barry R. Richards in The Pas.[96]

The Twists and Turns of the Communist Party of Canada

CCF gains during the war were partly attributable to the fact that after 1935 there was no left-wing alternative. In 1935 the CPC abandoned its revolutionary rhetoric and tactics and aligned itself with the right wing of the labour movement as part of the Popular Front against fascism. CPC activists and unions became indistinguishable from international craft unions.[97] The Popular Front strategy ended in 1939, when Stalin concluded a nonaggression pact with Hitler. The ensuing war against fascism was denounced by the Communist International and its constituent parties, including the CPC, as an imperialist war. Then in 1941 Hitler invaded the Soviet Union, and the CPC threw its full support behind the war, urging industrial peace and increased productivity and opposing trade union support for the CCF.[98] Finally, in 1944, the CPC called for the collaboration of the CCF, trade unions and progressive farmer groups with the Labour Progressive Party (LLP) (formed in 1943 as the legal face of the CPC, which had been outlawed in 1940) to oust the Liberal government.[99] The frequent changes in the character of CPC intervention in worker's struggles in Canada left it isolated and vulnerable.

At the end of the war and in the immediate postwar period the anti-Communist hysteria which swept North America resulted in the expulsion of Communists from leadership positions in trade unions. The CCL initially resisted this hysteria but in 1948 joined in the purge. A.R. Mosher, president of the CCL, justified such action on the grounds "that Communists are loyal in the first instance to Russia rather than to their own countries,"[100] a proposition supported by referring to the 1935-46 period.

The Consolidation of Reformism in the CCF and the Labour Movement

A similar "purification" took place in Manitoba. In 1945, D.L. Johnson and Barry Richards were suspended from the CCF over relations with the Soviet Union. Johnson was subsequently expelled from the party as a "fellow traveller," sympathetic to collaboration with the LPP. He later joined the CPC and contested his Brandon seat for the LPP in 1949. Richards was readmitted to the CCF in late 1945, but in 1949 he too was expelled, along with Wilbert Doneleyko, CCF MLA for St. Clements, for opposing the anti-Communism of the CCF leadership, and supporting cooperation with the LPP.[101]

The attempt by the Manitoba CCF to distance itself from the CPC was inspired both by a fear that anti-Communist hysteria was undermining the party's electoral base, and by the hostility of the party's leadership to dissent. The expulsions did not help the party electorally. CCF support in Manitoba peaked in 1945 with 35 percent of the popular vote and 10 seats in the legislature. In 1953 the vote dropped to 17 percent, with five seats.[102]

The consolidation of the CCF was paralleled by a consolidation of the labour movement. By 1950, locals in Manitoba had risen to 317 and membership to 57,900. Both the TLC and CCL had labour councils in Brandon and Winnipeg.[103]

Manitoba's relatively low level of strike activity continued after the war. Apart from a strike at the Sherridon mine and the participation of railway and packing-house workers in nationwide industrial actions, there were only twenty-two short-lived strikes in Manitoba between 1946 and 1950, involving only 2,863 workers.[104]

Faced with labour's strength during the war, the federal Liberal government made concessions. The most important was the 1944 Privy Council Order 1003 (PC 1003), which confirmed workers' rights to unionize, to be recognized by employers, and to bargain collectively. But restrictions on strikes and other pressure tactics were retained.[105]

Labour's postwar strength and militancy prevented a retreat from PC 1003. In 1948 its provisions were incorporated in the Industrial Disputes and Investigation Act. Manitoba passed a Labour Relations Act which extended the same rights to workers in the provincial jurisdiction, with the same restrictions: the definition of unfair labour practices for unions; a prohibition of strikes during negotiations and the life of a collective agreement; and the assumption by the state of a paramount right to intervene in disputes. Moreover, the new act failed to outlaw company unions, allowed certification to be challenged by employers in the courts, and excluded provincial public-sector workers from its coverage.[106]

A further, perhaps decisive, factor contributing to the demise of the labour Left was the substantial improvement in workers' postwar material conditions. Rising living standards were attributable to rising real wages, as reflected in Table 18, and an expansion in the social wage through programs such as hospital insurance (1958) and Medicare (1968). These gains supported the view that capitalism could be reformed to meet workers' needs.

TABLE 18

PERCENTAGE INCREASES IN AVERAGE WEEKLY WAGES AND SALARIES
(INDUSTRIAL COMPOSITE) AND THE CONSUMER PRICE INDEX,
MANITOBA, 1946-1975

	Average Weekly Wages and Salaries	Consumer Price Index
1946-50	31.5	34.1
1950-59	60.0	19.1
1959-69	53.5	26.9
1969-75	72.8	43.6

Source: Leacy, Urquhart and Buckley, *Historical Statistics of Canada.*

In summary, with the elimination of the Communists by the early 1950s, the reformist current, based in the TLC and CCL unions and in the CCF, solidified. The new institutional arrangements effected during and immediately after the war, including the industrial relations legislation of 1948, the unemployment insurance program of 1940, and the federal government's commitment to the use of fiscal and monetary policies to maintain "full" employment, prevented the reemergence of a left-wing, socialist alternative. A sustained period of growth and rising living standards which lasted until the late 1960s seemed to legitimize these institutional arrangements — and the virtues of reformist politics.

The Changing Labour Movement: 1945-1969

In the twenty-five years following World War II, the structure of Manitoba's labour movement changed. The extent of this change is suggested by Table 19, which presents selected trends in Manitoba's political economy. These trends had several implications.

TABLE 19

INDICATORS OF MAJOR ECONOMIC AND SOCIAL TRENDS IN MANITOBA, 1951-1981

Indicator	1951	1961	1971	1981
Manitoba population as % of Canadian population	5.5	5.1	4.6	4.2
Per capita income in Manitoba as % of Canadian per capita income	100.9	94.3	94.1	92.6
Farm population in Manitoba as % of total Manitoba population	28.2	18.8	12.8	9.4
Population of Metro Winnipeg as % of total Manitoba population	45.6	51.7	52.9	57.0
Female labour force in Manitoba as % of total Manitoba labour force	22.2	28.1	35.2	41.2
Proportion of Manitoba labour force in:				
Agriculture	24.6	17.2	11.4	8.5
Other Resources	2.3	2.4	2.1	2.0
Manufacturing	14.8	13.6	13.7	14.1
Transportation, Communication Utilities	12.1	11.7	9.8	10.4
Construction	5.3	6.2	5.4	5.3
Trade	17.5	16.8	15.8	17.4
Finance, Insurance and Real Estate	3.0	3.6	3.8	5.1
Community, Business and Personal Services	14.4	18.7	22.8	28.6
Public Administration and Defence	5.5	7.6	8.1	8.7
Gross Manitoba government expenditure as % of personal income	5.7	10.8	16.8	21.3

Sources: Statistics Canada, *Census of Canada*, 1951, 1961, 1971 and 1981; *The Canada Year Book*, various numbers; Canada, Department of Finance, *Economic Review*, 1974 and 1985.

First, relative declines in Manitoba's economy and population increased its dependence on the federal government. Consequently, the Manitoba government's capacity to respond to economic and social problems was constrained by the availability of funds from, and/or influenced by initiatives of, the federal government. The full implications of this dependency would become evident in the 1980s (see Chapter 14).

Second, the relative decline of agriculture forced the provincial government to shift the emphasis of economic development to manufacturing, mining, and especially hydroelectric power. Declining rural populations shifted political power to Winnipeg, and to a lesser extent the north, enabling the election in 1969 of a government ostensibly more sympathetic to labour (see Chapter 2).

Third, the increased proportion of women in the work force brought thousands of new workers into the trade union movement, with which they had had little previous direct experience. Their concerns did not figure prominently in the bargaining agendas of most trade unions. In time, more unions turned to organizing women, and more women looked to organization to deal with workplace inequities.

Fourth, the changing industrial structure of the work force — a declining proportion in agriculture, stagnating proportions in ''old'' industries like manufacturing, mining, construction, trade and transportation, and rising proportions in services, finance and government — made it more heterogeneous.

Finally, the growth in the state sector, and the new arrangements for regulating industrial relations, necessitated that the labour movement gain greater influence over state sector activities.

These new conditions influenced changes in the institutional character of the union movement. The most important of these were: the transformation of industrial unions into craft unions writ large, due to their implicit agreement to deliver industrial peace and stability as a *quid pro quo* for recognition and wage increases;[107] the 1956 merger of the TLC and the CCL to form the Canadian Labour Congress (CLC); the endorsation by the CLC of the NDP (formed in 1961); and the rise of major public sector unions with no ties to international unions based in the United States. The 1956 merger was replicated in Manitoba, with affiliates of the CCL and remnants of the OBU joining the Manitoba Federation of Labour (MFL), formed by TLC affiliates in Manitoba in 1954.

The Emergence of the New Democratic Party

With the formation of the MFL in 1954, a role in the political process became a major issue on labour's agenda. Labour had developed the view that union gains were dependent on the institutional context created by the state, so its postwar efforts focussed on changes in labour legislation, improved conditions in labour markets, and the extension of benefits like health care, pensions and income maintenance.

In 1957 the MFL established ''a political education committee to meet with the CCF and other political parties (except the Communist Party) 'pledged to support the political platform of the MFL.' ''[108] In 1958 the MFL supported the CLC's decision to join in the formation of the NDP.

There was opposition to the new party idea from some trade unionists who had come out of the TLC tradition.[109] They were either placated or defeated, and in 1961 the Manitoba NDP was created with Russell Paulley, a trade unionist, as its first leader.[110]

Public Sector Unions

Public-sector unionization accelerated in Canada in the late 1960s and 1970s. In Manitoba, this took two forms: the growth of the Canadian Union of Public Employees (CUPE), formed by a merger of the National Union of Public Employees and the

National Union of Public Service Employees in Winnipeg in 1963; and the tentative transformation of the Manitoba Government Employees Association (MGEA), which had existed as a sort of weak company union since the war, into an organization which performed more of the functions of, and had more of the rights associated with, traditional trade unions.

CUPE grew steadily, using its base amongst civic workers to organize relatively low-paid workers, many of them women, in hospitals, school divisions, universities, personal care homes, and other parts of the public sector.[111] The MGEA, in contrast, was forced by rank-and-file pressures, and a takeover attempt by CUPE in the early 1970s, to transform itself into a union-like organization. The MGEA established bargaining rights for civil servants in 1965. In 1969, with the NDP in office, the MGEA rejected being brought under the Labour Relations Act and obtaining the right to strike, opting instead for the substitution of arbitration for mediation in settling disputes. In 1973 a ''bad'' arbitration award led to a rank-and-file revolt, resulting in a restructuring of the organization and affiliation with the CLC. The MGEA also altered its position on the strike weapon, but by this time the NDP government had changed its position, so the status quo prevailed.[112]

Within this context, the development of the trade union movement was marked by steady, if unremarkable, growth and a continued low incidence of strikes and other signs of militancy. The main trends for 1957-71 are summarized in Table 20.

TABLE 20
AVERAGE NUMBERS OF TRADE UNION MEMBERS AND STRIKES
IN MANITOBA AS A PERCENTAGE OF CANADA, 1957-1971

Period	Union Members		Strikes		Workers Involved	
	Number	% of Canada	Number	% of Canada	Number	% of Canada
1957-61	59,976	4.2	6	2.3	563	0.6
1962-66	63,192	4.1	9	2.2	2,230	1.3
1967-71	77,536	3.7	7	1.3	1,545	0.6

Source: Canada, Department of Labour, *The Labour Gazette, Labour Organizations in Canada,* and *Strikes and Lockouts in Canada,* various numbers.

Much of the membership gain for 1957-71 was due to a change in the status of federal and provincial government employees, whose organizations were not recognized as trade unions until the late 1960s. Their inclusion added about thirteen thousand members.

Apart from mining, where membership doubled due mainly to the organization of mine workers at INCO in Thompson, there was little membership growth in traditional unionized sectors. In manufacturing, construction, transportation, communications and utilities, membership increased by 13 percent from 1957 to 1970 — from 43,751 to 49,641.[113]

The Brandon Packers Strike

Of the strikes waged during this period, only that by the 103 members of United Packinghouse Local 255 at Brandon Packers in 1960 was of particular significance. It was a bitter, violent dispute, similar in many respects to the Gainer's dispute in Edmonton in 1986. It centered on an attempt by new ownership and management to reduce Brandon workers' wages relative to wages in Winnipeg's Big Three packing houses. When the strike began on 29 February 1960 the company brought in an alternative work force, provoking picket-line confrontations, police intervention, and the sabotage of company property, and resulting in a commission of inquiry headed by Justice G.E. Tritschler. A settlement was reached on 29 August 1960, just before the commission was to begin hearings, because, as was later revealed, the owners feared their criminal activities would be exposed. The inquiry went ahead.

The Tritschler inquiry has been analyzed in detail by the late George F. Mac-Dowell.[114] Tritschler found the dispute attributable to a union conspiracy, and recommended changes to the Labour Relations Act to further constrain union activities. He called for government-supervised strike votes, and the definition of unions as legal entities, the latter because he believed "the need for responsible behaviour will cause a gradual weeding out of irresponsible leadership whose retention would jeopardize the financial position of unions."[115] These recommendations and others were legislated in 1962 and 1963.

The Brandon Packers strike demonstrated that labour "rights" provided by the state were tenuous — sometimes illusory. When unemployment was high, as in 1960, employers would reduce wages and benefits and undermine unions. If workers resisted, the company would be supported by the state: police protection for strikebreakers, government mediation, and commissions of inquiry which would condemn workers and propose legislative changes to weaken unions.[116]

Labour Legislation as the Focal Point of Struggle

In a presentation to the Manitoba government in 1960 the MFL outlined its view on the purposes of a Labour Relations Act:

> Too often it has been taken for granted that the Act was designed only for the purpose of restraining organized labour.
>
> What a Labour Relations Act should do is promote with all the means at its disposal, a mature collective bargaining relationship between employers and unions.[117]

This view was virtually identical to that of provincial governments since 1948. Governments believed unions caused industrial unrest and had to be restrained, and that industrial peace would attract capital to the province. Unions believed existing legislation favoured employers.

With the amendments to the act in 1962 and 1963, the pro-employer bias became obvious. Labour challenged these changes, but because it had accepted the rules of the game — that union-employer relations would be regulated by a Labour Relations Act — the challenge could only request repeal of the amendments.[118]

The government established the Labour Legislation Review Committee in 1964, chaired by H.D. Woods of McGill University. The MFL's 1965 brief to government noted that labour was cooperating with the Woods committee as a means of demonstrating

> to the public and to those who have constantly attacked us, that we are, indeed, responsible members of a democratic society and are anxious and willing to play a significant role in the development and progress of the Province . . . [119]

The Labour Relations Act preoccupied labour throughout the 1960s, but it was not the only matter addressed by the MFL in its ''organize for legislation''[120] strategy. The MFL submitted proposals for Medicare, government-run automobile insurance, legislation to curb pollution and improve health and safety in the work place, human rights legislation, and curtailment of the use of injunctions in labour disputes. Labour concluded from these experiences that to protect against the erosion of its rights and to advance its interests, it must elect a sympathetic government.

The Election of the New Democratic Party

In the mid-1960s the NDP's fortunes in Manitoba improved. In the 1965 federal election its share of the popular vote was 24 percent, up from 16.7 percent in 1963. In the 1968 election it was 25 percent.[121] The provincial party, with a political agenda virtually identical to the MFL, and with modest support from trade unions and unionists — mainly locals of industrial unions in Winnipeg[122] — recorded similar gains, its share of the popular vote rising from a postwar low of 15.2 percent in 1962 to 23 percent in 1966. In 1969, an NDP government was elected in Manitoba with 38.1 percent of the popular vote and 28 of 55 seats.

James A. McAllister's analysis of the 1969 election suggests the NDP had much working-class support:

> support for the Schreyer government was greatest among voters who were non-British, Roman Catholic, and working class. It was weakest among middle-class voters of British origin. But strong support was also manifested among working-class voters, no matter what their ethnic background or religious affiliation.[123]

Wiseman reaches a similar conclusion: ''Part of every constituency won by the NDP had been in the CCF-NDP column at either the federal or provincial level sometime in the past.''[124]

Subsequent elections demonstrated that 1969 was not an aberration. The coalition that elected the NDP in 1969 has prevailed in three of the five elections since 1969 — in 1973, 1981 and 1986.

Labour Under Social Democracy

In its initial term, the NDP government proceeded with most of its platform. Of particular importance were the establishment of a (diluted) state-run automobile insurance program (Autopac) despite much opposition from the private insurance industry, the elimination of health-care premiums, an expansion in public housing, and changes in employment standards legislation and the Labour Relations Act.

Little in the program was innovative. As McAllister states:

> the legislative behaviour of the NDP government was similar to that of Liberal and Conservative governments in office prior to 1969 and not particularly innovative compared to provincial governments elsewhere. . . . The Schreyer government adapted itself to this status rather than attempting to depart radically from previous practice.[125]

Reform of the Labour Relations Act in 1972 was a partial exception. Most of the changes the MFL wanted were included, with some exceptions, most notably the proposed restrictions on "the importation of strike-breakers."[126]

Relations between labour and the government soured during Schreyer's second term, for three main reasons. First, the NDP was exposed as just another government whose vision consisted of little more than perpetuating itself in office. This translated into substituting Schreyer's version of the public good for party policy on all issues that risked controversy and conflict. The result was paralysis. Second, the Schreyer government supported the 1975 federal wage control program. Schreyer had publicly promoted wage controls to contain inflation. An angry MFL disapproved in a brief to the government in December 1976,[127] and appealed to the government "to withdraw... from its agreement with the federal government in the matter of supporting ... controls and the anti-inflation board."[128] The appeal was ignored. Third, in September 1976, a local of the Canadian Association of Industrial, Mechanical and Allied Workers (CAIMAW) struck Griffin Steel in Transcona over wages, fringe benefits and compulsory overtime. In February 1977 Griffin reopened and fired all strikers who failed to return to their jobs, replacing them with strikebreakers. Over the next six weeks there were numerous picket-line clashes and 370 picketers were arrested. The strike was broken in April 1977 when the courts granted an injunction restricting the number of pickets.[129]

CAIMAW, which was not affiliated with the CLC, received little tangible support from the MFL. However, MFL spokesmen did meet with members of the NDP caucus and party executive in April to demand legislative action to restrict the use of strikebreakers. The demand was ignored.

The CAIMAW strike demonstrated that even with the new labour act and labour's "own" government, employers' ability to recruit strikebreakers left unionists vulnerable in confrontations. The dispute also reconfirmed that conflict on the picket line would bring the state into the dispute on the side of employers.

The Lyon Years

In 1977, Manitobans elected a right-wing Tory government headed by Sterling Lyon. It cut public spending and eliminated civil-service jobs, inspiring similar actions by private employers. This was reflected in major strikes involving Safeway workers, brewery and construction workers, and employees of the Manitoba Liquor Control Board. Strike activity in Manitoba in 1978 was among the highest since 1945: 34 strikes, 6,541 workers involved and 292,640 person-days lost.[130]

The MFL called a conference for 5 July 1978 to establish strategy to counter the antilabour offensive. But the MFL *Beacon* called not for the mobilization of labour to take the offensive, but for mobilization in support of labour peace:

> In Manitoba the result is the worst record of lockouts and strikes in our history since 1919. If this current alarming course of crisis and confrontation continues, you, as a worker and all citizens of Manitoba face a bleak future indeed.
>
> The time has come to call a halt to this alarming drift towards chaos.[131]

Settlements were eventually reached in all the major strikes, including Safeway, where the company had reopened most stores with strikebreakers. In 1979, the issue was "right-to-work" laws, endorsed by the Labour Relations Council of the Winnipeg Builder Exchange, the Manitoba Chambers of Commerce and the Union of Manitoba Municipalities. The MFL initiated a campaign to mobilize members against such laws. The campaign included hints from MFL president Dick Martin that any attempt by Lyon to pass "right-to-work" legislation would be opposed, if need be, by a general strike.[132]

At the same time, the MFL was working to get a labour program endorsed by the NDP prior to the next election. NDP conventions passed labour-initiated motions on antiscab and plant closure legislation, and better legislation on technological change.[133]

In April 1981, with an election pending, the NDP's new leader, Howard Pawley, announced that an NDP government would not pass antiscab legislation in its first term of office:

> As a *quid pro quo* to organized labour, Mr. Pawley promised that a NDP government would pass plant-closure legislation and make amendments to the Labour Relations Act which would be of benefit to labour.[134]

The NDP was returned to office in November 1981.

The Pawley Government and Labour Legislation

In 1982, the NDP government passed first-contract legislation. In 1983 it set up the Labour Law Review, coordinated by Marva Smith, which led to changes in legislation in June 1984. These fell far short of what labour had expected and what the government had implicitly promised. There were no measures to deal with plant closures or technological change. Final-offer selection (FOS) arbitration was advanced as an alternative to antiscab legislation — an alternative apparently worked out in consultation with MFL officials, including Dick Martin — but was withdrawn in the face of business opposition.[135] It seems likely the government accepted the arguments of business that any major departure from prevailing labour relations legislation in Canada would dry up investment in Manitoba.

There were minor reforms in the 1984 legislation. When virtually all other jurisdictions in Canada were becoming more coercive toward labour, Manitoba's modest reforms assumed added significance for the MFL. Its 1985 brief commended the government for its efforts:

We are fortunate in the province of Manitoba. We have worked hard, and we have elected a government which believes in promoting the interests of ordinary people — even if it means taking on corporate interests, and even if it means bucking the trends which have been orchestrated in the board rooms of Bay Street and Wall Street.

That is no enviable position for any government to occupy.[136]

This demonstrates the "Catch-22" in the labour movement's "legislative strategy." The crisis conditions of the early 1980s constrained the NDP government's capacity to concede reforms to labour, because such reforms would antagonize business, yet the minor reforms that were conceded were sufficient to sustain labour's belief in the correctness of its strategy. In February 1986, the Pawley government was elected for a second term — mainly, it would seem, because of a belief that an NDP government would hold down unemployment and maintain social-welfare programs.

Labour Under Social Democracy in Manitoba

Union membership in Manitoba increased from 104,000 members in 1971 to 139,000 in 1979, or 33.6 percent. By 1981 membership was 153,000, but dropped in the 1982-83 depression. Currently, membership is about 148,000, 42 percent above the 1971 level, and representing about 37 percent of paid nonagricultural workers.

Union membership in Canada as a whole, however, increased even more: from 1971 to 1977 by 41 percent and from 1971 to 1984 by 63 percent. Membership growth in Manitoba kept pace with Canada only from 1977 to 1981, when the increases were 10.1 and 10.7 percent, respectively.[137] A similar pattern is evident in strike activity since 1971. Table 21 compares strike activity in Manitoba and Canada from 1971 to 1985.

TABLE 21
STRIKE ACTIVITY IN MANITOBA IN RELATION TO
CANADA BY PROVINCIAL PARTY IN POWER, 1971-1985

Strike Activity[1]	NDP 1971-1977[2]	Conservative 1978-1981	NDP 1982-1985
Number of Strikes	20	36	12
As % of Canada	2.3	3.4	1.8
Workers involved	4,692	4,724	1,198
As % of Canada	1.1	1.1	0.4
Man-days lost	86,748	146,208	30,833
As % of Canada	1.3	1.8	0.6

Notes: [1]Averages for the periods identified; [2]Excludes strike data from 1976.
Source: Canada, Department of Labour, *Strikes and Lockouts in Canada*, various issues.

These data suggest that while strike activity was lower in Manitoba than in the rest of Canada, there was a surge during the Lyon years. This surge in strikes, together with a flurry of demonstrations — including civil servants, women, and university faculty and students — and MFL campaigns against "right-to-work" laws and the erosion of Medicare, is supportive of the idea that employers became more hostile to labour and more assertive in their relations with labour during the Conservative interlude.

In terms of general welfare, there is evidence that labour has done better under NDP governments than under the Lyon government. Table 22 shows that unemployment was lower, and average weekly earnings higher, relative to national figures when NDP governments were in office.

TABLE 22
UNEMPLOYED WORKERS AND AVERAGE WEEKLY EARNINGS
IN MANITOBA AS PERCENTAGE OF CANADA, 1971-1985

Period	Unemployed Workers	Average Weekly Earnings (Industrial Composite)
1971-77	3.4	90.9
1978-81	3.5	89.4
1982-85	3.2	91.6

Sources: Statistics Canada, *The Labour Force*, various numbers; and Manitoba Bureau of Statistics, *Manitoba Statistical Review*, various numbers.

Future Prospects

A central theme of this chapter is that the struggles of the 1930s and 1940s resulted in the triumph of reformism in the Manitoba labour movement. Since the war, and especially since the mid-1950s, this reformism has led to efforts by labour to secure and strengthen its position by electing sympathetic governments. This objective was seemingly achieved in 1969 with the election of an NDP government with a political agenda that incorporated many of the reforms sought by labour.

The ''New'' Labour Movement

Since 1969 there has been a remarkable transformation in the character of the labour movement. The labour movement now is much different from that which looked to social democracy to provide it with a refuge.

There is a much higher proportion of women in trade unions, and they constitute a much higher proportion of the memberships of trade unions. Women accounted for about 18 percent of trade union members in 1971, and 42 percent by 1984.[138]

There have been significant shifts in the distribution of trade union members by industry. In 1971, resource industries, manufacturing, transportation, communications and utilities accounted for two-thirds of union members. Currently, the proportion is about 37 percent.[139]

Rising educational levels of the working population, and the shift in the industrial and occupational composition of union membership, has almost certainly raised the average educational level of union members. Data from the 1984 Statistics Canada survey of trade union membership indicate that the proportion of workers unionized rises with the level of education: 0-8 years, 30.3 percent; some secondary/no postsecondary, 31.3 percent; some postsecondary, 28.8 percent; postsecondary certificate or diploma, 44.4 percent; and university degree, 46.7 percent.[140]

Finally, public-sector unions have become numerically predominant in Manitoba. The two main unions are the MGEA and CUPE, which in 1984 had 18,860 and 15,849 members respectively. Among private-sector unions, the United Food and Commercial Workers, which also has members in the public sector, and the United Steelworkers of America top the list with 9,134 and 6,162 members respectively.[141]

Additional details on the 1984 distribution of union members by industry and sex are provided in Table 23. These data reflect the increased importance of women and public-sector workers in the trade union movement, and show that the two are closely related: 86 percent of women union members are concentrated in education, health and welfare, and public administration. These data also show that there are industries where unionization has yet to make headway, particularly in finance, trade and other services, including personal services and eating establishments, all of which have high proportions of women members. This ''new'' labour movement, like the old one, is aligned with the NDP. However, events during the term of office of the second Pawley government made this alignment more problematic.

TABLE 23

TRADE UNION MEMBERSHIP IN MANITOBA BY INDUSTRY AND SEX, 1984

Industry	Paid Workers	Union Members	Union Members as % Paid Workers	Women Union Members	
				Number	As % of All Members
Agriculture	10,697	70	0.6	70	100.0
Forestry	1,833	841	45.9	—	—
Fishing/Trapping	194	101	52.1	—	—
Metal Mines	8,592	2,125	24.7	0	—
Other Mines	1,997	405	20.3	0	—
Manufacturing	58,197	19,624	33.7	4,944	25.2
Construction	18,391	3,351	18.2	154	4.6
Transportation, Communication & Utilities	50,895	33,641	66.2	6,523	19.4
Wholesale Trade	24,502	2,619	10.7	371	14.2
Retail Trade	57,866	5,101	8.8	2,712	53.2
Finance	10,563	217	2.0	0	—
Insurance/ Real Estate	11,544	2,835	24.6	1,409	49.7
Education	34,660	22,734	65.6	12,547	55.2
Health/Welfare	56,233	31,528	56.1	25,076	79.5
Other Service	69,532	4,643	6.7	3,061	65.9
Federal Administration	17,454	11,326	64.9	4,599	40.6
Provincial Administration	17,500	11,497	65.7	4,714	41.0
Local Administration	12,265	6,939	56.6	1,503	21.7
Total	463,066	159,631	34.5	67,685	42.4

Source: Statistics Canada, unpublished data from Survey of Union Membership, December 1984, provided by T. Scott Murray.

Social Democracy in a Time of Economic Crisis

Manitoba experienced a depression in 1982, followed by stagnation. This created an increase in the deficit and in the proportion of current revenues required to service the debt. These problems were exacerbated by a federal government intent on alleviating its own deficit ''problem'' by reducing, in relative terms, transfers to provinces under financing arrangements for established programs — education and health — and equalization arrangements.

At the same time, the federal Conservative government has instituted a policy package designed to rejuvenate the private sector and restore the preeminence of markets. The FTA with the United States, the privatization of government enterprises, and the deregulation of transportation were key elements of this strategy. As well, this strategy was based on an implicit acceptance of a national unemployment rate of about 8 percent, which is deemed necessary to contain unions and maintain discipline in production.[142]

A side effect of federal policies was that provincial governments were forced to institute fiscal restraint. At the same time, provincial governments were reluctant to deviate from existing tax and legislative regimes for fear of frightening off ''scarce'' private-sector capital. The NDP government in Manitoba was no exception. After the election in February 1986, cabinet ministers in key economic portfolios began to stress the need to curb growth in the deficit.

For the labour movement, the objectives in electing a NDP government were relatively modest: legislation to secure trade union rights and strengthen labour in its dealings with private-sector employers; improved labour market conditions, specifically, improved employment standards and minimum wages, and low unemployment; and an expansion of public-sector services of benefit to workers.

Gains were made on some of these items, but they fell short of what labour believed necessary to achieve the refuge it sought under social democracy. A major constraint on labour has always been employers' ability to replace striking workers, especially in periods of high unemployment. In the 1970s, labour identified antiscab legislation as the key reform. During the Conservative interlude it added a second reform to its agenda — improved plant closure legislation.

The two NDP governments under the leadership of Howard Pawley refused to enact such legislation. Nor were there significant changes in labour market conditions. Unemployment remained high, and employment standards and minimum wages tended to be adjusted in line with changes in other jurisdictions. In short, the refuge labour was seeking under social democracy was only partial. The labour leadership argued that things would be worse under any other government, and maintained its efforts to achieve the desired reforms — not by mobilizing workers, but by seeking to make deals with the NDP cabinet.[143] This approach resulted in some ''reforms.'' For example, in 1987 FOS was included in the Labour Relations Act as a method of dispute resolution. But FOS not only fell short of antiscab legislation, it also divided the labour movement.

Fiscal restraint was reflected in a generalized deterioration of working conditions in the public sector, which for many public-sector workers included the conditions under which they provided services to people. This increased friction with the NDP government. The first Pawley government avoided confrontation by trading jobs for wages with the MGEA in 1983.[144] As well, it allowed public-sector employees in Crown corporations and agencies more involvement in decision-making for concessions on wages.[145] Under the second Pawley government, however, there was less scope for such trade-offs and the probability of confrontations increased.

The Manitoba government managed to avoid restraint measures comparable to those imposed in other jurisdictions in 1986 and 1987. Indeed, it went against the current and provided for both significant increases in spending on social-welfare programs and increases in taxes — including taxes which in the short-run, at least, adversely affected profits.[146] By mid-1987, however, the government was under increasing pressure, from both business interests and critics of the increases in income and payroll taxes, to get spending under control and cut the deficit. This pressure was accentuated by the failure of the Limestone Hydro project and other major public-sector projects to generate a sustained improvement in underlying economic conditions. At this juncture, the NDP government was faced with a dilemma. It had accepted the argument that it would have to reduce the deficit, but in doing so it risked alienating its constituency in the labour movement.

There seemed to be two potential lines of development. First, while the limitations of labour's legislative strategy were exposed in the 1980s, it was possible that the absence of a left-wing (socialist) current within the labour movement could produce a solution involving union leadership in a collaborative effort with government to resolve the fiscal crisis at labour's expense. Labour's *quid pro quo* would be concessions benefiting the union leadership, and strengthening its reformist tendencies: appointing union leaders to public-sector jobs, involving them in tripartite bodies to address specific issues, and/or expanding their opportunities to participate in ''charting the course'' for the Manitoba economy. Elements of such a solution were already evident both in the crossovers of personnel between government and the trade unions (for example, Wilf Hudson's move from a job with the government to the leadership of the MFL; John Walsh's move from executive-secretary of the MFL to special assistant to the premier; the recruitment of Gary Doer, MGEA president, to the NDP) and in certain of the policy initiatives of both Pawley governments, in particular the appointment of trade union directors in some Crown corporations, the establishment of the Workplace Innovation Centre in 1986, and the tripartite conferences on the economy organized by the government in 1982 and 1984.[147] This solution was, however, contingent on a quiescent trade union rank and file. The other possibility was that workers would abandon the NDP.

In the event, the issue was decided by an unanticipated election in 1988. A renegade member of the NDP caucus voted against the government in a vote on the 1988 budget — a deficit-reducing budget which, along with increases in automobile insurance rates in the order of 20 percent, antagonized virtually the entire electorate. The defeat on the budget led to the resignation of Howard Pawley, his replacement by Gary Doer, and the 26 April election.

In the election, the NDP was again reduced to third-party status with twelve seats and 20 percent of the popular vote. The MFL and major trade unions campaigned for the

NDP, but to little avail. Poll results published on 16 March 1988 indicated that union members were abandoning the NDP:

> Only 24 percent of union households were willing to give the NDP another chance. However, 38 percent said they would support the Conservatives and 37 percent favored the Liberals.[148]

While it will be some time before the full implications of this development become clear, the one thing that seems certain is that labour in Manitoba for the forseeable future will be confronted with a government hostile (or at least unsympathetic) to its interests. This means, of course, that the movement leadership will be faced with the difficult task of mobilizing the rank and file to defend and advance the interests of working people in Manitoba. Whether a new militancy can emerge, and develop into a creative alternative, depends on the capacity of labour to rediscover the class nature of Manitoba society.

NOTES

The research for this project was supported by a grant from the Manitoba Careerstart Program. I would like to thank Richard Groen for doing much of the legwork for me, Jim Silver and Joe Dolecki for comprehensive and detailed critiques of the first version of this chapter, and Janice Mahoney for getting the manuscript into a form which would allow others to read it.

1. Chapter 1 in this volume.

2. *Census of Canada, 1901* (Ottawa: King's Printer, 1905).

3. Ibid.

4. This point is made by Stuart Marshall Jamieson in *Times of Trouble: Labour Unrest and Industrial Conflict in Canada* (Ottawa: Task Force on Labour Relations, 1968), 69-70.

5. See Doug Smith, *Let Us Rise: An Illustrated History of The Manitoba Labour Movement* (Vancouver: New Star Books, 1985).

6. Richard O. Boyer and Herbert M. Morais, *Labor's Untold Story* (New York: United Electrical, Radio and Machine Workers of America, 1980), 88.

7. Doug Smith, *Let Us Rise*, 16.

8. Ibid., 17. Smith indicates that the Knights were also concerned about the effects of alcohol on working people, supporting temperance organizations and promoting greater control of the liquor trade.

9. Ibid., 16.

10. Ibid., 28. Smith notes that Arthur Puttee got 66 percent of the votes from the working-class voters in Winnipeg's north end.

11. *The Labour Gazette* (Ottawa: Department of Labour, May 1903).

12. Nelson Wiseman makes this point in the introduction to his *Social Democracy in Manitoba: A History of the CCF-NDP* (Winnipeg: University of Manitoba Press, 1983).

13. *Census of Canada, 1916* (Ottawa: King's Printer, 1918).

14. See Doug Smith, *Let Us Rise*, 21-22, for more on this point.

15. *Census of Canada, 1916.*

16. *The Labour Gazette*, various numbers.

17. Ibid.

18. These details on particular disputes are drawn from reports in various numbers of *The Labour Gazette*.

19. Both Smith, *Let Us Rise*, and Wiseman, *Social Democracy*, allude to this division.

20. Wiseman, *Social Democracy*, 7.

21. Ibid., 8.

22. Ross McCormack, *Reformers, Rebels, and Revolutionaries: The Western Canadian Radical Movement, 1899-1919* (Toronto: University of Toronto Press, 1977).

23. Smith, *Let Us Rise*.

24. Ibid.

25. Wiseman, *Social Democracy*.

26. For an extended treatment of the socialist parties and their policies and memberships see Norman Penner, *The Canadian Left: A Critical Analysis* (Scarborough: Prentice-Hall, 1977).

27. See Smith, *Let Us Rise*. According to most accounts the Ukrainian Social Democratic Party in Winnipeg figured prominently in both the SPC and subsequently the SDP. See, for example, William Rodney, *Soldiers of the International: A History of the Communist Party of Canada — 1919-1929* (Toronto: University of Toronto Press, 1968).

28. Penner, *The Canadian Left*, 49-50.

29. Smith, *Let Us Rise*, provides a useful account of this collaboration.

30. In some cases employers were able to defeat striking workers by tapping the labour surplus in the local labour market or by recruiting abroad. This was the fate suffered by 40 female confectionary workers who struck their employer in 1902, of the printers at the Moore Printing Company in 1902, of striking printers at 15 firms in 1906 (who were replaced by 50 printers recruited in Britain), of street railway employees in 1906, and of 116 women in the garment trade who struck in opposition to the open-shop policy of their employer in 1909. These data and the data in the text are drawn from various numbers of *The Labour Gazette*.

31. See Smith, *Let Us Rise*, and Wiseman, *Social Democracy*.

32. David Jay Bercuson, *Confrontation at Winnipeg: Labour, Industrial Relations, and the General Strike* (Montréal: McGill-Queen's University Press, 1974), 57.

33. These issues are discussed in Bercuson, *Confrontation at Winnipeg*.

34. Gregory S. Kealey, "1919: The Canadian Labour Revolt," *Labour/Le Travail* (Spring 1984): 11-44.

35. Charles Lipton, *The Trade Union Movement of Canada, 1827-1959*, 4th ed. (Toronto: NC Press, 1978), 188-89.

36. See ibid., for a concise account of the events leading to these strikes.

37. Smith, *Let Us Rise*, 51.

38. Lipton, *The Trade Union Movement*, 191.

39. The strike in Brandon is dealt with in Tom Mitchell, " . . . 'Next Time It Must be Revolution': Brandon's 1919 Labour Protest," mimeo, 1986.

40. Strikes in other locations were brought to an end using measures that were similar to, if less extreme than, those employed to break the strike in Winnipeg. See Lipton, *The Trade Union Movement*, and Kealey, "1919."

41. For additional references to the Winnipeg General Strike see the bibliography prepared by Craig Heron and Gregory S. Kealey, "Labour Conflict and Working-Class Organization" in Daniel Drache and Wallace Clement, eds., *The New Practical Guide to Canadian Political Economy* (Toronto: Lorimer, 1985), 62-70. Readers should also consult a recent article which documents the significant role played by women in the general strike: Mary Horodyski, "Women and the Winnipeg General Strike of 1919," *Manitoba History* 11 (Spring 1986).

42. See Smith, *Let Us Rise*, for a brief account of what happened after the strike was crushed.

43. Kealey, "1919."

44. The other element involved in Winnipeg is that there were important sectors of the trade union leadership who were sympathetic to the Russian Revolution and talked openly about the possibility of a similar development in Canada. For example, the famous Walker Theatre meeting in Winnipeg on 22 December 1918 ended with three cheers for the Russian Revolution and "deafening cries of 'Long live the Russian Soviet Republic! ... Long live the working class!'" Cited in Ian Angus, *Canadian Bolsheviks: The Early Years of the Communist Party of Canada* (Montréal: Vanguard Publications, 1981), 51. The strike did not have revolutionary objectives, but there seems little doubt that the ruling class recognized the potential for mass action on such a scale to create its own revolutionary dynamic.

45. Cited by Mitchell, "'Next Time.'"

46. This statement was made by the leadership of the Brandon sympathetic strike in its *Strike Bulletin No. 3*, 23 May 1919. Cited by Mitchell, "'Next Time.'"

47. Although, of course, we will never know if the outcome would have been any different, or, indeed, if the strike would have been called in the first place had the working class been constituted in a mass party (or under the leadership of a vanguard party).

48. The point here is that with the defeat of the general strike, the political sphere became the vent for worker hostility to the ruling classes in Manitoba and worker dissatisfaction with conditions they faced in the labour market and in work places.

49. *The Labour Gazette*, various numbers. These data were gathered in a survey of trade unions. Returns were not always complete and with the sorts of fluctuations which took place in union memberships the data submitted were not always reliable.

50. These events are described by David Jay Bercuson in *Fools and Wise Men: The Rise and Fall of the One Big Union* (Toronto: McGraw-Hill Ryerson, 1978).

51. See Smith, *Let Us Rise*.

52. Bercuson, *Fools and Wise Men*.

53. D.C. Masters, *The Winnipeg General Strike* (Toronto: University of Toronto Press, 1973), 141.

54. Smith, *Let Us Rise*, 60.

55. These events are described by Angus, *Canadian Bolsheviks*, Rodney, *Soldiers of the International*, and Ivan Avakumovic, *The Communist Party in Canada: A History* (Toronto: McClelland and Stewart, 1975). Tim Buck gave the following assessment of the OBU in his history of the Communist movement: "The O.B.U. was established by a mass breakaway from the A.F.L unions in 1919. As long as it existed as a general union, it was dependent upon anti-A.F.L. secessionist sentiment. Cultivation of that sentiment was its main activity." Tim Buck, *Thirty Years — 1922-1952: History of the Communist Movement in Canada* (Toronto: Progress Books, 1952), 13-14.

56. The OBU retained 40 to 50 locals and about 24,000 members until the 1930s, but it had little real impact on the labour movement in Canada after 1920, finally disappearing into the CLC in 1956. See Bercuson, *Fools and Wise Men*.

57. Smith, *Let Us Rise*, provides a lively account of the activities in the garment industry during this period.

58. Masters, *The Winnipeg General Strike*.

59. For accounts of the formation of the ILP see Smith, *Let Us Rise*, Masters, *The Winnipeg General Strike*, and Kenneth McNaught, *A Prophet in Politics* (Toronto, University of Toronto Press, 1959).

60. Penner indicates that the Manitoba branch of the SDP "voted in March 1918 in favor of affiliation to the Communist International a year before the International was formed, and two years before the Conditions of Affiliation had been drawn up." Penner, *The Canadian Left*, 78.

61. Avakumovic describes Bartholomew as "one of the greatest socialist orators in the Prairies." Avakumovic, *The Communist Party*, 24.

62. The involvement of the Reverend A.E. Smith and his family in the Communist Party is described in A.E. Smith, *All My Life* (Toronto: Progress Books, 1949). Stewart Smith was the first Canadian student at the Lenin School in Moscow. He subsequently became closely identified with Tim Buck. See Avakumovic, *The Communist Party*, 56-57.

63. Wiseman, *Social Democracy*, 12.

64. Ibid., 11.

65. The TLC initiated formation of the CLP in 1917 as a federation of provincial parties. The DLP was the Manitoba branch of the CLP. Nothing much came of the CLP, until the TLC convention in 1921 when, on the initiative of the Winnipeg branch of the DLP, the CLP was formally constituted as a national party. The SDP branch in Manitoba had considered becoming part of the CLP at its convention in 1918, but rejected the idea. The Anglo-Canadian wing of the party, however, went against the SDP position and was involved in the formation of the DLP in 1918. See Angus, *Canadian Bolsheviks, 21-23*.

66. Penner, *The Canadian Left*, has a detailed discussion of *Steps to Power* and its implications.

67. Ibid., 128.

68. The initiative for the formation of the ACCL came from A.R. Mosher, head of the Canadian Brotherhood of Railway Employees. See Angus, *Canadian Bolsheviks*, 173-74.

69. See Penner, *The Canadian Left*, and Angus, *Canadian Bolsheviks*, for observations on the relationship between the CPC and the ILP in Manitoba.

70. Cited in Angus, *Canadian Bolsheviks*, 278.

71. *The Canada Year Book*, various numbers. The base year for the index was 1926.

72. Ibid.

73. The figures for trade union members are from a series published in *The Labour Gazette*. Smith suggests that the overall unemployment rate may have reached 25 percent in the depths of the Depression. Smith, *Let Us Rise*.

74. This observation is based on a survey of data on strikes published in *The Labour Gazette*.

75. For additional details see Smith, *Let Us Rise*.

76. *The Labour Gazette*, various numbers.

77. *The Canada Year Book*, various numbers.

78. *The Labour Gazette*, various numbers from 1934 and 1935.

79. Bryan D. Palmer, *Working Class Experience: The Rise and Reconstitution of Canadian Labour, 1800-1980* (Toronto: Butterworth, 1983), 211.

80. See Angus, *Canadian Bolsheviks*, 274.

81. Penner, *The Canadian Left*, 138-39.

82. Most explanations of the "failure" of the CPC to have a decisive influence on the character and development of the working class in Canada cite the influence of the Communist International on deciding the politics of the CPC. There is no question that the reversals in policy after 1935 destroyed the credibility of the CPC. The only way in which the CPC could have avoided this fate was to dissociate itself from the Communist International. But, of course, if it had done so, it would then have ceased to be a Communist party in the sense in which such a party was understood in the context of the 1930s.

83. See Palmer, *Working Class Experience*, 211-15.

84. For a discussion of the relationship between the CCF and the ILP in Manitoba see Wiseman, *Social Democracy*. One of the objectives of the CCF was to bring together workers and farmers (direct producers) in a common struggle. The irony in this is that the initiative came at the very time when the agricultural sector of the economy was losing its dominant position in the prairie region.

85. Wiseman, *Social Democracy*, 11.

86. Ibid.

87. Smith, *Let Us Rise*, 93.

88. *The Labour Gazette* and *The Canada Year Book*, various numbers.

89. See Lipton, *The Trade Union Movement*, for an account of these events.

90. *The Labour Gazette*, various numbers.

91. Ibid.

92. Ibid.

93. Ibid.

94. Ibid., (October 1943), 1443.

95. Ibid., (October 1943), 1439.

96. Wiseman, *Social Democracy*.

97. Angus, *Canadian Bolsheviks*.

98. Ibid.

99. Ibid. See also Penner, *The Canadian Left*, for a discussion of these events.

100.*The Labour Gazette* (December 1948), 1354.

101.Wiseman, *Social Democracy*.

102.Ibid.

103.*The Labour Gazette*, various numbers.

104.Ibid.

105.For an interesting discussion of the operation of PC 1003, see H.A. Logan, *State Intervention and Assistance in Collective Bargaining* (Toronto: University of Toronto Press, 1956).

106.Leo Panitch and Donald Swartz provide a useful analysis of the post-war legislation in "Towards Permanent Exceptionalism: Coercion and Consent in Canadian Industrial Relations," *Labour/Le Travail* 13 (Spring 1984).

107.For a discussion of this point see Robert Laxer, *Canada's Unions* (Toronto: Lorimer, 1976).

108.Smith, *Let Us Rise*, 115.

109.In Manitoba there was also opposition to the idea of including organized labour in the "new party" because of a fear that it would become a single-class (workers') party with no appeal to farmers and professionals, as well as a concern that labour influence would move the party to the right. The irony is that the elements in the population that opponents of the new party were concerned about alienating were not only small in numbers or in decline, but were also the most reactionary in the population. See Wiseman, *Social Democracy*, 83-105.

110.Mr. Paulley worked as an upholsterer in the Transcona Shops. He was first elected leader of the CCF in 1960.

111.Laxer, *Canada's Unions*, has an interesting discussion of the rise of CUPE in the Canadian trade union movement.

112.For a brief discussion of this history, see Manitoba Labour-Management Review Committee, *Report — Public Sector Employee-Employer Relations in Manitoba* (July 1974), 99-102.

113.*Union Growth in Canada in the 1960s* (Canada: Department of Labour, 1976).

114.G.F. MacDowell, *The Brandon Packers Strike: A Tragedy of Errors* (Toronto: McClelland and Stewart, 1971).

115.Ibid., 221.

116.One of the points that MacDowell makes is that Tritschler glossed over blatant violations of the Labour Relations Act by the company, such as the discharge of striking workers.

117.Manitoba Federation of Labour (MFL), *Legislative Proposals, 1960*, 4.

118. MFL, *Legislative Proposals, 1963*.

119. MFL, *Legislative Proposals, 1965*, 3.

120. The letterhead of the MFL stationery has the words "Organization for Legislation" as the main caption.

121. F.H. Leacy, ed., *Historical Statistics of Canada*, 2nd ed. (Ottawa: Statistics Canada, 1983).

122. James A. McAllister, *The Government of Edward Schreyer: Democratic Socialism in Manitoba* (Montréal and Toronto: McGill-Queen's University Press, 1984), 111.

123. Ibid., 122-23.

124. Wiseman, *Social Democracy*, 123-24.

125. McAllister, *The Government of Edward Schreyer*, 24-25.

126. Ibid.

127. MFL, *Legislative Proposals, 1976*, 2.

128. Ibid., 5.

129. Errol Black, "The Picket Line: The NDP Takes Sides," *Canadian Dimension* 17, no. 3 (1981).

130. Canada, Department of Labour, *Strikes and Lockouts in Canada*, 1978.

131. MFL, *Beacon* 1, no. 1 (July 1978): 1.

132. For a discussion of the issues involved in this campaign, see *Beacon* 2, no. 1 (February 1979).

133. Opposition to these measures was minimal but Sidney Green, who subsequently left the party, opposed them on the grounds that such legislation would create a situation where labour became dependent on legislation to win its battles and vulnerable to changes in legislation under governments not especially sympathetic to labour. Mr. Green favoured a reduction in constraints on labour and capital in collective bargaining.

134. Errol Black, "In Search of 'Industrial Harmony': The Process of Labour Law Reform in Manitoba," *Relations Industrielles* 40, no. 1 (1984): 143.

135. See ibid., for a complete discussion of this episode in the development of labour law in Manitoba.

136. MFL, *Legislative Proposals, 1985*, 2.

137. The figures for Manitoba are from Manitoba Labour, *Directory of Labour Organizations in Manitoba, 1985*, and Canada Labour, *Directory of Labour Organizations in Canada, 1985*. It should be noted that the Manitoba figures include members of the Manitoba Teachers' Society. In 1984, this organization had 12,265 members.

138. These figures come from ibid., plus unpublished data collected by Statistics Canada in *Survey of Union Membership* (May 1985). I would like to thank T. Scott Murray, Statistics Canada, for providing me with the unpublished data.

139. Ibid.

140. Ibid.

141. Manitoba Labour, *Directory of Labour Organizations, 1985*, 6.

142. The Bank of Canada, for example, has consistently urged caution in attempting to reduce the unemployment rate, on the grounds that its model of the economy demonstrates that inflation would be difficult to control if the unemployment rate drops below 8 percent. See, for example, David Rose, "The N.A.I.R.U. in Canada: Concepts, Determinants and Estimates, a Summary of Technical Report 50," *Bank of Canada Review* (December 1988): 20-26.

143. This is a feature of the labour movement in Manitoba which merits further study.

144. In 1983, MGEA agreed to forego wage increases for job security. The amount involved was $10 million — or about $600 per MGEA member. Gary Doer, then president of the MGEA, in

a subsequent assessment of the deal suggested "there must be a longer-term agreement not only between our organization and the government, but also the labour movement and the business community . . . a general contract that takes the long view." Reported in Dian Cohen and Kristin Shannon, *The Next Canadian Economy* (Montréal: Eden Press, 1984), 173.

145. In 1987, the minister of education in Manitoba, Jerry Storie, suggested that the teachers accept a wage freeze in exchange for participation in the allocation of funds from a special project designed to stimulate innovation and improvements in education. The funds for this special project were to be generated from the savings that would result from the wage freeze — although the amount earmarked for the project was substantially less than the savings that would be generated. The teachers rejected the proposal.

146. The tax increase which has generated the most controversy is the increase in the payroll tax for corporations with payrolls greater than $150,000. Business leaders have argued that this tax discourages both investment and job creation in the province. Again, this is an issue that merits further study.

147. The conferences were designed to enlist the support of both business and labour in dealing with the conditions resulting from the 1982 depression. With the improvement in the economy in 1984 and subsequent years, interest in these exercises in attempting to establish a consensus on fiscal and economic policies seems to have diminished.

148. Maria Bohuslawsky, "Union Members Desert NDP ranks," *Winnipeg Free Press*, 18 March 1989.

6   C.P. Walker and the Business of Theatre: Merchandizing Entertainment in a Continental Context

Reg Skene

In the three decades which followed the completion of the transcontinental railway in 1885, business opportunity in Winnipeg was predominantly a function of greatly expanded east-west trade. Tariff barriers against American goods guaranteed that eastern Canadian manufacturers and suppliers would dominate the lucrative new markets created by the rapid settlement and development of western Canada, and preferential freight rates secured Winnipeg's position as major wholesale distribution centre for eastern goods in the Canadian west.

A marked exception to the east-west trading pattern was the commercial enterprise known at the time as "the show business" (this was before Irving Berlin taught us to drop the definite article and to think of the activity as exempt from comparison with other money-making ventures). Unlike traffic in other goods and services, provision for supplying entertainment to the new market developing in the Canadian west continued to operate along pre-CPR north-south lines, establishing Winnipeg as the northernmost outlet of a continental entertainment system. This pattern ensured that for some time to come, even in periods of economic nationalism, the staple items of the cultural diet of Winnipeg and western Canada would be of American origin, selected and presented under American control.

This chapter undertakes a close study of the theatrical enterprises of C.P. Walker, the American-born entrepreneur who, in the early years of this century, forged Winnipeg's link with the American entertainment industry. Walker dominated Winnipeg theatre business from his arrival in 1897 until the early 1930s, when he was forced out of business by adverse economic conditions and the determined efforts of American movie interests to end live theatre in Canada altogether.

Professional entertainers found their way to Winnipeg with some regularity after 1878, when the rail connection between Winnipeg and St. Paul, Minnesota, was established. Minstrels and touring repertory companies provided diversion and reminded citizens of the frontier community of the more complex social and cultural life many of them had left behind in eastern Canada and the British Isles when they moved west. The most lucrative entertainment market in the early years was, however, the "floating" population of single males that provided much of the labour force in the rapidly growing city and which, cut off from domestic roots, looked to alcohol, prostitution and raucous forms of "variety" entertainment to counter their boredom.

A note in the program issued for the official opening of the Walker Theatre in 1907 looked back on the situation as it existed in the 1880s:

During the years beginning about 1880 and lasting while the "boom" was in progress, Winnipeg supported a number of so-called "Variety Theatres." These were not what one could term "strictly legitimate" theatrical enterprises but were conducted mainly as auxiliaries to the bar-room of the saloons to which they were attached. One of these places was the Pride of the West Saloon, which, it may be remarked, derived most of its pride from the fact that it had a piano in its hall. A miniature vaudeville show was also put on at this place. The old Ontario Bank, located in the Higgins Block, about where the new Bank of Toronto now stands, and the building formerly occupied by the Imperial Dry Goods Co., was also used for variety entertainments. Another music hall of some notoriety was the Opera Comique, conducted by our present townsman Mr. Dan Rogers. This was housed in the old courthouse on Main Street, the site of which is now occupied by the Bijou Theatre. Mr. Rogers was continually in difficulties with the liquor licensing officials, and for a time paid a fine at the police court regularly every morning.[1]

Local entrepreneurs, notable among them ex-building contractors William Seach and Charles Sharp, attempted in the 1880s and 1890s to cultivate a theatrical market distinct from the notorious saloon entertainment. A series of local halls and public buildings were converted to theatres, and dramatic features of general family appeal were booked through agents in St. Paul. In their attempts to cultivate a market for "legitimate theatre," local entrepreneurs had to cope with the traditional antitheatrical prejudice of the Methodist, Presbyterian and Congregationalist clergy, and a persistent impression among Winnipeg's respectable, God-fearing lower-middle class that professional stage entertainment was essentially an adjunct of the saloon and the brothel.

By the end of the 1890s, however, a promising new market for stage entertainment had emerged — Winnipeg's energetic capitalist class, the commercial elite that had come to dominate all aspects of Winnipeg's economic, political and social life. Self-confidently cosmopolitan in outlook, and driven by a determination that Winnipeg should achieve its destiny as the "Chicago of the North," Winnipeg's capitalist class looked to the establishment of cultural institutions which both in structure and content would reflect the values by which they lived and the sense of purpose they shared.

Walker's theatre organization was closely tailored to fit the cultural aims and social values of Winnipeg's commercial elite. It was itself "big business," and therefore worthy of respect. Part of a continental system devoted to the ruthless pursuit of monopolistic control of entertainment, its operation was something a hard-headed businessman could understand, while its risks gave it an air of romance in the eyes of the inveterate gambler who lies just under the surface of the career entrepreneur. It dealt in "high-class entertainment," New York shows and big stars, at once placing Winnipeg on an equal cultural footing with established metropolitan centres like Chicago, and providing the capitalist class itself with "genteel" entertainment so that it could become civilized and separate itself from the crudity of working-class diversions. By raising the level of gentility and cultivation in Winnipeg, it might even provide a means of uplifting the tastes and aspirations of the working class, and help Winnipeg overcome the stigma of being considered an unruly frontier town.

In a very direct sense the Walker theatre operation is an example of the establishment of a cultural institution as a conscious project of a definable economic and social class. As such it provides an opportunity to study the interface of economics and culture at a crucial point in Winnipeg's social history.

The Red River Valley Theatre Circuit

It was Winnipeg's position as northern terminus of the Northern Pacific Railway (NPR) system, making it America's gateway to the "Great Northwest," that brought Fargo theatre manager C.P. Walker to the city in 1897. Walker, in fact, made the move to Winnipeg at the suggestion of NPR president, J.J. Hill,[2] probably with Hill's financial backing, and certainly with a mutually beneficial NPR transportation contract in hand.

In 1888 the Liberal government of Thomas Greenway had invited the NPR to build its own line north to Winnipeg, and to develop its own rail system in western Manitoba to compete directly with the CPR. The opening of an American rail route to the Great Lakes was expected to result in lower freight rates for grain shipments, and to expand north-south trade in other commodities. The lowering of freight rates never occurred since the NPR did not compete aggressively with the CPR, and a tariff wall kept trade in American manufactured goods at a minimum. Nevertheless, on a symbolic level, for a few years the American presence in Winnipeg was palpable and impressive. Throughout the 1890s the NPR's palatial Manitoba Hotel, close to the corner of Portage and Main, was the centre of the social life of Winnipeg's economic elite. But the dream of Winnipeg achieving a new level of prosperity through its rail link with the United States faded rapidly. In 1901 a financial crisis within the NPR brought about the loss of its Manitoba lines. Hugh John Macdonald's Conservative government assumed their control and granted them on generous terms to MacKenzie and Mann, who made them part of their growing rail empire, the Canadian Northern. In the same year a fire destroyed the Manitoba Hotel; it was never replaced. Walker's theatre operation, functioning as it did in an area of commerce where no tariff barrier against American imports existed, was in fact the only important remnant of what once had seemed a plausible scheme for more comprehensive north-south trading ties.

Walker established himself in Winnipeg by taking a long-term lease on a newly renovated theatre on the northwest corner of Notre Dame and Adelaide — the former Bijou, owned by Confederation Life. He named it the Winnipeg Theatre and opened for business in September 1897. This acquisition positioned Walker to take advantage of the new North American touring arrangements, which had been created in 1895 with the formation in New York of the "syndicate" or "theatre trust." Seven powerful members of the American theatrical establishment had combined to manage the North American touring operation. The syndicate was directed by Abe Erlanger, of the Broadway firm of Klaw and Erlanger, and controlled the major theatres in key cities of the United States, as well as the all-important New York productions, plays and actors.[3] Managers affiliated with the syndicate could book an entire season through New York, but to maintain affiliation, one needed a theatrical audience which would support runs long enough to pay transportation and salary costs and still provide substantial profit for both the syndicate and the management of the theatre.

Besides the Winnipeg Theatre, Walker owned or controlled theatres in Fargo, Grand Forks, Grafton and Fergus Falls. While individual theatres in this ''Breadbasket Circuit'' could not support extended runs, collectively they could. Walker's system of cost-splitting made it possible to bring into the Red River Valley attractions that otherwise would never have ventured west of St. Paul.

Walker's competition in Winnipeg was the Grand Opera House, which opened in the spring of 1897. It was the most recent venture of veteran local theatrical entrepreneurs William Seach and Charles Sharp, who were booking attractions through St. Paul. With Walker intercepting all major attractions by booking through New York, the Grand Opera House was in trouble from the start. Walker also handled booking for several small circuits like his own in the American northwest, thus bolstering his negotiating power with Erlanger. He maintained a New York office and spent extended periods there each spring and summer, setting up the season's bookings for his growing theatrical empire.

Cultural Propaganda in a Frontier City

It was the very thinness of the veneer of civilization on this booming frontier city that caused Winnipeg's ruling elite, and the journalists who catered to it, to place an extraordinary value on the cultural institutions reputed to lead to a more genteel existence. This edge of cultural hysteria provided Walker with his main marketing leverage, and he consciously set about creating an extensive propaganda machine which took as its theme the importance of theatre as an instrument in the civilizing process.

A major ally was Charles Handscomb, the drama critic of the *Manitoba Free Press*. Handscomb's prose style was carefully crafted, lucid and ironic — more suited to crusading personal journalism than the limited scope of the drama columns of the *Free Press*. Early in 1898, he launched a weekly newspaper aimed at the same emerging capitalist class to which Walker hoped to appeal. *Town Topics* was a substantial tabloid, published every Saturday on high-quality magazine paper, attractively laid out and printed, and lavishly illustrated with photographs. Special sections within the journal gave complete, detailed coverage to society events, horse shows, musical and dramatic activities, and other developments which affected the life style of Winnipeg's social and economic elite. The front page and an additional page of column space were devoted to social and political commentary of ''The Lounger'' — generally the work of Handscomb himself.

Handscomb's account of the readership of his periodical, published in a 1902 appeal for advertisers, yields interesting insight into his understanding of the nature of the market to which he had access:

> *Town Topics* is never thrown aside. It is kept. Its matter is of interest to the wife and to the daughters, who are concerned in the social life of Winnipeg, the doings of our society people, and the happenings in circles musical and theatrical.

> No Winnipeg home is ashamed to have *Town Topics* come within its doors. As a clean, high-grade journal, it is sought and kept by the ladies who discuss its items and not infrequently contribute to its columns.
>
> There are no waste papers in these two thousand copies. From week to week now it is seldom that a dozen papers remain unsold.
>
> It is a conservative estimate that at least five people read each copy of *Town Topics*. In other words the paper reaches ten thousand readers each week — these readers for the most part, women of culture and means — women who have the money with which to purchase whatever they like.[4]

Handscomb's observations are consistent with Thorstein Veblen's analysis of the function of women as surrogate conspicuous consumers within the capitalist class.[5] In the context of such an analysis, pursuit of cultural refinement by the wives and daughters of successful businessmen would be regarded as one aspect of a comprehensive program of conspicuous waste, aimed at advertising the economic status of the businessmen themselves. Gentility might well be defined as the degree of success achieved in fulfilling such a program.

Walker's press releases provided a great deal of the reading in each issue of *Town Topics*. Whether Walker was a direct investor in the tabloid or simply a major advertiser, *Town Topics* was an important part of his propaganda apparatus, just as his patronage and support must have been crucial to Handscomb's financial solvency.

An even more important ally was Walker's wife. Harriet Walker had been a child actress, a musical comedy star on the New York stage, and a song and comedy sketch writer for Witmark and Sons, the New York publishers. With the establishment of the Red River Valley Circuit, she became press agent for the entire chain. Shortly after its founding, she began to write a regular column of theatrical criticism and commentary for *Town Topics* under the heading of ''The Matinee Girl,'' signed with the pseudonym ''Rosa Sub.'' The column was sharp and racy, the opinions civilized and well informed, the commentary intelligent and often biting.

Walker had journalistic enemies whose implacability counterbalanced the loyalty of his friends. Among them was the architect and journalist, Charles H. Wheeler, who had planned and supervised the Winnipeg Theatre renovation for Confederation Life and who was drama critic of the *Winnipeg Tribune*. Wheeler was short-tempered, vain and intolerant, with a strong pride in what he believed to be his high level of journalistic objectivity.[6] Also increasingly hostile was Wheeler's editor, R.L. Richardson. Richardson was a fiercely independent journalist and politician, who had founded the *Winnipeg Tribune* in 1890 to pursue an editorial policy based entirely on his own political convictions. He was elected as the Liberal member of Parliament (MP) for Lisgar in 1896, but broke with the party in 1900 and successfully ran in that year's election as an independent. However, a petition to unseat was pressed against him in 1901, and he was unseated by the united action of both parties, losing the ensuing by-election in 1902.[7] Richardson was not the kind of man to submit quietly to pressure exerted on the press by the Walker propaganda machine nor, after his political adventure, did he harbor any love for the Liberal Party or its supporters at the *Free Press*, many of whom were Walker's cronies.

Establishing a Monopoly

In September 1898, after a year of losing ground to Walker, William Seach installed at the Grand Opera House a resident company organized by Harold Nelson, a Toronto elocution teacher turned actor. He thus opened the possibility of a locally based, production-oriented, all-Canadian theatre operation as an alternative to Walker's essentially American touring house. Nelson's company had an impressive classical repertoire and enjoyed modest critical success. Judged on cultural content alone, it seemed precisely suited to the civilizing function which theatre was thought to perform in a frontier society. In fact, much of Walker's New York programing seemed light-weight by comparison. But box office figures revealed that Winnipeg theatregoers preferred imported froth in the comfortable surroundings of the Winnipeg Theatre to sincere but modestly mounted performances of worthwhile plays at the humbler Grand Opera House.

In November 1898, Nelson and company left for an ill-fated tour of the Canadian west. They broke up at Indian Head in what is now Saskatchewan in January 1899, as the result of a quarrel between Nelson and his tour manager.[8] Nelson returned to the Grand Opera House in March at the head of a new company consisting of a core of young professionals from Chicago, supplemented by aspiring amateurs from Rat Portage and Winnipeg. Eager to become a North American Coquelin, Nelson persuaded Seach to back him in a lavish production of Rostand's new play, *Cyrano de Bergerac*, currently the rage of Paris but not yet seen in London. It was a dismal failure.

Charles Handscomb was patronizing in the *Free Press* and cutting in *Town Topics*. Harriet Walker was even more forthright:

> Whatever may be said of Mr. Nelson, it cannot, after his production of Rostand's famous play, be truthfully asserted that he lacks nerve. But there are different kinds of nerve, you know. There is one kind we must perforce admire, and there is another kind — oh, well, no matter.[9]

The most astonishing critical response came from Charles Wheeler in the *Tribune*. The usually irascible Wheeler not only overlooked the production's shortcomings but extravagantly praised its every feature:

> Mr. Harold Nelson in the title role never acted better in his life. The part fit his style and peculiar talents like a glove, and it is just here, where his fine intelligence and elocutionary powers have plenty of scope for histrionic display, that his success is so pronounced.[10]

Wheeler's fulsome praise prompted a vigorous response from Mrs. Walker:

How any self-respecting critic could find anything in the performance to commend is beyond me. The company was so wholly inadequate and incompetent as to render the presentation a burlesque of Rostand's beautiful play.[11]

What appears to be an artistic dispute was really the beginning of the final stage of a commercial war between C.P. Walker and the management of the Grand Opera House. Walker's aim was the establishment of a complete theatrical monopoly; at stake for the Grand Opera House was simple survival. Wheeler knew before he wrote the *Cyrano* reviews that Seach's operation was in severe financial difficulty, and that the lavish production of *Cyrano* was a desperate gamble to draw business from the more successful Walker operation. This accounts for both Wheeler's exaggerated praise of the venture and Mrs. Walker's extreme irritation at its pretensions.

The *Cyrano* gamble was a disaster, but the journalistic controversy continued. By the time it was over, Wheeler had accused *Town Topics* of being an "appendix to Manager Walker's theatre program,"[12] and Handscomb had penned one of the most intemperate attacks ever made by one drama critic on another:

> For years the offensively coarse and arrogant critic of the Tribune has been a menace and a hindrance to the progress of music and dramatic art in Winnipeg. Year by year he has become more inflated by the idea of his own importance, until there now seems to be no length to which this over-swollen humbug will not go. Using the power, and taking advantage of the astonishing latitude given him by a newspaper, he has vulgarly attacked ladies and gentlemen who have been so unfortunate as to fall under his displeasure, these attacks being as vile as the English of his writings.[13]

In July 1899 Handscomb sold his interest in *Town Topics* and joined Haverley's Minstrels as tenor balladist, leaving the journal in the hands of management less friendly to Walker. Mrs. Walker's "Matinee Girl" columns ceased; they were not revived until 1901, when Handscomb returned to Winnipeg, resumed his duties as *Free Press* drama critic, and repurchased *Town Topics*.

When, in October 1899, the Grand Opera House booked the first-rate repertory Valentine Stock Company, *Town Topics* and the daily press praised the company's productions as superior to most syndicate shows. The drama critic, identified only as C.T.D., clearly recognized that the Grand Opera House's survival depended entirely on winning the favour of Winnipeg's elite:

> One is driven to think that because the prices at the Grand are lower and the term popular applied to them, that the 400 prefer selfish exclusiveness to legitimate enjoyment. It may be due, however, to the fact that the Grand theatre has always had an unenviable reputation and that now for the first time in its career it is trying to do well, which by the way deserves every encouragement for theatre goers.[14]

The following week C.T.D. reported that the Grand Opera House's bid for the commercial gentry's support was having some effect, for the house was a crowded one, and the audience representative of all that is best in Winnipeg, (even the Lieutenant-Governor being present) and the reception of "The Private Secretary" most enthusiastic.[15]

Walker was furious at this turn of events but his attempts to influence reviews by threatening to withdraw advertising were greeted with scorn. *Town Topics* commented:

> The truth of the matter seems to me to be this: Press notices in the Winnipeg daily papers of performances at the Winnipeg Theatre were absolutely undependable until lately, when a change has evidently come over the spirit of their respective dreams. Notices used to be flattering "ad nauseam" and praise individually and collectively distributed with no discrimination at all. Now things are changing. The Winnipeg Theatre evidently is no longer to be the spoiled darling of the Winnipeg public. It, like other theatres in other places, is to be subjected to criticism, and naturally its management, after a diet of flattery, with difficulty returns to one of healthfulness.[16]

The Valentine Stock Company was unable to make the Grand Opera House solvent. The company was withdrawn by Christmas, and the Grand Opera House ceased to operate as a functioning, legitimate theatre. Its closure gave Walker a monopoly of theatrical entertainment in Winnipeg, establishing for some time to come that theatre business in the city would be defined primarily as the distribution of an imported cultural product, rather than the development of local production facilities.

During the four years that he was able to maintain his total monopoly, Walker made every effort to demonstrate that a single theatre could serve the needs of Winnipeg's cultural elite — could in fact serve them better and more efficiently if not distracted by competition. The syndicate slate of touring New York shows provided the core of Walker's programing, but he tapped every other conceivable source to keep the Winnipeg Theatre fully booked for the entire year. Independent attractions, if not explicitly blacklisted by the New York office, "Uncle Tom" shows, amateur theatricals, locally written musicals, touring concert artists, military bands and symphony orchestras all found their way to the stage of the Winnipeg Theatre. In the off-season, Walker booked every available repertory stock company to play his theatre for one- or two-week runs. Walker produced shows himself and launched them in the theatres of the Red River Valley Circuit. Then he sent them west to play the one-night stand theatres between Winnipeg and Vancouver for which he handled the booking. At one point two of his companies were touring the west — the Harold Nelson Company with a classical repertoire, and another company doing light comedy.

Walker's prosperity was the envy of other Winnipeg businessmen who would have liked to get into the entertainment business, but the exclusiveness of his New York connection and the economic advantage derived from control of a circuit of theatres made his monopoly virtually unassailable. In the winter of 1901, there were persistent rumors that MacKenzie and Mann intended to establish a hotel-theatre complex in Winnipeg. The idea never materialized, presumably because of the difficulty in finding a source of touring shows without the support of a developed circuit like Walker's.[17]

The Fire Safety Controversy

In the opening years of the new century, trouble loomed for syndicate boss Abe Erlanger. Leading American actresses Minnie Maddern Fiske and Henrietta Crossman were defying syndicate attempts to freeze them out of the touring system,[18] New York producer David Belasco was in open revolt and suing Klaw and Erlanger,[19] and the Shubert Brothers, managers of the highly successful Belle of New York, had begun to acquire theatres throughout the United States in order to establish a rival booking agency. A significant antisyndicate sentiment was making itself felt among the general public and in the editorial columns of a growing number of major newspapers. When the Iroquois Theatre in Chicago burned on 30 December 1903, killing 602 people, both newspapers and the public were quick to blame the tragedy on the greed of the syndicate.

C.P. Walker recognized the danger that a strong public reaction to the Iroquois Theatre disaster held for his operation. On 1 January 1904 the *Free Press* published an interview with Walker in which he attempted to particularize the Chicago situation and to assure the public that there was little chance that a similar fire could occur in Winnipeg.[20] It was not a convincing argument, since Walker's old, wood-frame, second-storey theatre appeared to be inherently less safe than the newly constructed Iroquois Theatre.

Meanwhile, a campaign against the theatre syndicate began in American newspapers, and R.L. Richardson, editor of the *Winnipeg Tribune*, immediately launched a campaign to have the Winnipeg Theatre declared unsafe and Walker's theatre license withdrawn. On 25 January Walker used the columns of the *Free Press* to outline the story of his relations with the *Tribune*. He recounted how the newspaper had tried to pressure him into renewing his advertising, and how, when he refused, he had been told to "look for war now." He also quoted laudatory comments which the *Tribune* had made in the past regarding the Winnipeg Theatre facilities and the "architectural miracle" which Charles Wheeler had accomplished in designing it.[21]

The *Tribune*'s response was immediate. Neither Walker's account of his business relations with the newspaper nor his quotations from past *Tribune* editorials were relevant:

> Mr. Walker's advertising or Mr. Walker's passes are neither here nor there; the question is the safety of the Winnipeg Theatre. Quotations from the *Tribune* of some years ago on the architectural beauty of the interior have nothing to do with the case. The question is the public safety.[22]

Charles Wheeler's position in this controversy was uncomfortable. As an architect, he had been responsible for the defects in the Winnipeg Theatre which his newspaper was now using to pursue the quarrel with Walker. As Richardson increased the pressure on Walker, there seemed no other course for Wheeler but silence. Handscomb, however, was not about to let Wheeler escape so easily. In an article in *Town Topics* Handscomb spoke of Wheeler as though he were dead — the implication being that only the dead could remain so silent in a controversy in which personal honour was at stake.[23]

Political pressure applied on Walker's behalf to all levels of government saved his license, but it was obvious that he could no longer assume universal public approval of his theatre monopoly, nor of his syndicate connection. Even his monopoly on first-rate touring shows would not be safe once the Shubert brothers began their raid on syndicate preserves in earnest.

Vaudeville and the New Mass Market

By 1904, major population changes had radically altered the entertainment market in North America and brought into being a new branch of the show business. The population of Winnipeg, for instance, grew from 42,534 to 67,262 between 1900 and 1904. The total increase in the first decade of the century would be almost one hundred thousand.[24] This remarkable growth was largely the result of European immigration and it represented a potential mass market for low-cost entertainment which was not dependent on a shared literary or theatrical tradition, and which did not require a high degree of literacy for its comprehension and enjoyment. It is no accident that vaudeville — with its acrobats, jugglers, animal acts, dialect comedians, and skits about verbal misunderstandings — exploded onto the scene.

By 1904 plans were far advanced for the opening in Winnipeg of outlets for the major vaudeville chains operating in the midwest. An Orpheum contract in hand, Messrs. Kobold and Kyle announced in August 1904 that they would build a vaudeville house, the Dominion. Some time after the opening of the Dominion, Messrs. Nash and Burrows, holders of a Sullivan-Considine franchise, opened a small vaudeville house known as the Unique. This in turn was followed by the more elaborate Bijou.

The *Ghosts* Controversy

Alan Artibise has commented that Winnipeg's commercial class, unlike that in many other North American cities, did not have to push aside an older and established social elite in order to assume control of civic affairs:

> Winnipeg's commercial class did not have to push anyone out because of the circumstances surrounding the city's foundation; Winnipeg was established by businessmen, for business purposes, and businessmen were its first and natural leaders. In fact, between 1874 and 1914, Winnipeg's commercial and social elites were indistinguishable; membership in one group was almost always accompanied by membership in the other group.[25]

This had interesting consequences when the elite group set about establishing an acceptable cultural framework within which to function. The members of Winnipeg's dominant class were by and large tradesmen turned capitalist, who were faced with the challenge of dealing simultaneously with "new money" and "new culture."

In the first generation, this brought an even sharper division of responsibility along sexual lines than might be found among the elite of more established societies. Within Winnipeg's dominant commercial class, men generally devoted themselves to acquisition, while women focussed on cultural pursuits and the mastery of acceptably elaborate social protocol. A natural consequence of such a division of responsibility was that women were more exposed to elements of contemporary culture than their male counterparts. Not only did they come into contact with a wider range of intellectual influences, but they also had greater opportunity to develop a sophisticated detachment in their judgement of psychological, social and aesthetic issues than their pragmatic, money-oriented husbands.

In a theatre audience, Harriet Walker found the male-female difference both palpable and striking:

> An audience is frequently more interesting than a play, and I have found that in every public audience a woman is vastly quicker witted, keener of repartee, readier to catch fine subtle points, than a man — frankly any man.

> I have observed that if a thinly veiled pungent remark is made it is the woman that grasps it even before it is fully uttered, while the man calmly waits for it to percolate through his denser understanding.

> By intuition, perhaps, occasionally by education, a woman is more appreciative and sensitive to the good and bad in human endeavour than the opposite sex. She is also more enthusiastic, kinder, gentler, vastly more sympathetic. She is moved by her emotions rather than her intellect, and enjoys, when she does enjoy, with a delightful intensity.[26]

However, it did not escape Mrs. Walker's keen and critical eye that the women of Winnipeg's elite were more often successful in meeting acceptable standards of physical attractiveness than those of simple politeness:

> Women never look so well as in their graceful winter frocks and furs. They make a picture positively captivating to the admirer of health and beauty, and who is there who does not admire wholesome, well-gowned and gracious femininity. Fine manners, however, do not go with fine dress. In fact, we are somewhat vulgar and bizarre in our public doings. When a play, a concert or an opera is nearing the end there is at once a restless movement among the audience. The people seem suddenly crazed with a wild desire to get home to the bosom of their families. Before the last word is spoken, or the last note reached, there is a hurried rise, a rush for the door, and an ungovernable race to reach the outer walks early. We sadly lack the gentle art of repose. We need the principle of fine courtesy which should not thus disconcert the performer or interfere with the pleasure of our fellow auditor.[27]

Such examples of frontier boorishness aside, the crusade to raise the level of urbanity in Winnipeg through the arts did have considerable effect, and it was most evident among the women of the city's elite.

It was inevitable that Harriet Walker's conviction that women were fitted by intuition to be "more appreciative and sensitive to the good and bad in human endeavour than the opposite sex," should come to be held by the most socially and culturally active women of her class. It was also inevitable that the most intellectually gifted among these women should observe that they were as well or better equipped to understand social and political matters than their husbands.

The first result of this was the emergence of a remarkable set of female journalists, not just those who, like Harriet Walker, wrote of cultural and social affairs under a pseudonym, but such journalistic pioneers as Cora Hind (agricultural writer for the *Free Press*) and Francis and Lillian Beynon, whose writings on the issues of the day challenged male dominance of public-affairs reporting. The Winnipeg Branch of the Canadian Women's Press Club, of which Harriet Walker was an energetic member, became an important forum for the discussion of social issues.

The second result of this situation was the campaign for women's suffrage, in which Harriet Walker and other members of the Women's Press Club were deeply involved. This culminated on 28 February 1914 on the Walker Theatre stage, in a blistering satirical mock parliament arranged by Harriet Walker, Nellie McClung, the Beynons and others, in which the Roblin government's rationalization of its resistance to female suffrage was savagely ridiculed.

In the first decade of the century, however, the feminist revolt was still only simmering. Male dominance of the political arena was relatively unchallenged, and the main thrust of civic government policy was directed toward maximizing commercial opportunity for the commercial class, and maintaining a secure and prosperous environment for it.

Social problems arising from the economic exploitation of the city's working class, particularly of the great masses of European immigrants living in squalid and overcrowded conditions in the north end, were handled by withdrawal into a system of virtual economic apartheid. Alan Artibise describes the nature of the situation:

> Sheltered in their lavish homes in Armstrong's Point, Fort Rouge, and Wellington Crescent, and engaged in a social and business life centred around the Manitoba Club, the Board of Trade, and the St. Charles Country Club, the governing elite's callous stance was often the result of ignorance. While some of these people supported social improvement efforts such as foreign mission work, for the most part they gave little serious thought to the problems in their midst. Temperance, direct taxation, the single tax and woman's suffrage were middle-class diversions which overrode the pressing problems of poverty, overcrowding and disease faced by the city's poor.[28]

In a very real sense, the gentility sought by Winnipeg's capitalist class was a means of ignoring the human suffering caused by the economic practices on which its prosperity appeared to depend. If there was an awareness of hordes of foreign-born immigrants living in deplorable conditions, it was to regard them not as people with problems but as being themselves a particularly vexing and dangerous problem. Rather than being seen as victims, they were regarded as inherently inferior culturally and racially (particularly the Jews and the Slavs), and as an infectious source of poverty, disease, vice and violence. It was particularly important to protect respectable women from actual contact or even knowledge of the sordid life such people lived. To mention such matters at all was bad taste; to subject them to public analysis in mixed company would be a major offense against decency.

The assumption that legitimate theatre operations such as Walker's existed for the purpose of affirming the separation of the classes, by establishing an unassailable fortress of high culture and by avoiding serious social analysis, was sharply challenged by the New Drama, some examples of which found their way into regular syndicate programing. The plays of Ibsen, Shaw, Tolstoy and other socially concerned playwrights had become important properties on the cultural commodities market. Leading actresses found Ibsen's strong female roles particularly challenging and were using his plays as acting vehicles in spite of the boldness of the social analysis they contained. A major crisis occurred in Winnipeg cultural circles in March 1904, when the Winnipeg Theatre presented Alberta Gallatin in Ibsen's *Ghosts*.

Advance notices of the play in the "Matinee Girl" column were enthusiastic, as were similar notices Mrs. Walker prepared for the daily press:

> It is a remarkable play in every sense. Its construction is perfect and its theme novel, fearful, fascinating. A woman's heroic yet futile struggle to save her son from the awful moral fate that she fears will be his through inheritance from his lecherous father, is the basis of the play.[29]

Handscomb gave full prominence in both the *Free Press* and *Town Topics* to the laudatory promotional pieces that Mrs. Walker had prepared. Charles Wheeler, on the other hand, had once seen a performance of *The Pillars of Society*, disliked it intensely and determined never to see another Ibsen play. He declined to print the favourable promotional material and refused to attend the production itself.

When Handscomb attended the opening performance and found that the play depended for dramatic effect on an open discussion of venereal disease, he was horrified:

> "Ghosts" is unwholesome, degrading — disgusting. Ibsen is a genius they tell us. Perhaps so. His play is smut — just plain smut. Those of us who were at the Winnipeg Theatre last night were relieved to get to breathe again the pure, wholesome prairies atmosphere ... The audacious daring with which sex questions are discussed in this play has no stage precedent — not even the risque problem plays have gone so far — but the utter depravity of its characters is astounding.[30]

Wheeler, who had not seen the play, was even firmer in his condemnation:

> There is simply nothing to be said about it in a respectable journal, except that it was degrading from the beginning to the end and ought not to be permitted to be produced, if the civic authorities have power to prevent it. As for the theatre management, acting on general principle, they will no doubt only be too pleased to repeat if it is the means of adding a few dollars to the exchequer. For this can have been the only motive for producing a number of very bum shows that have been on the boards this past winter.[31]

Mrs. Walker was perhaps the only one involved in the controversy to understand that masculine recoil from *Ghosts* had more to do with the sexual politics involved in the open discussion of Mrs. Alving's marital problem, and the social panic engendered by the play's analytic approach to questions of moral responsibility, than with with the alleged salaciousness of the text. At any rate, when the talk of ''smut'' actually increased business by bringing out a large male audience seeking pornographic stimulation and smoking-room humour, the irony of the situation was not lost on her:

> On arriving at the theatre, I was surprised and amused to find the audience composed mostly of men — and, be it frankly admitted — with but few exceptions not very intellectual looking men at that!
>
> The opera glass boy did such brisk business that I readily guessed these men expected to see a racy burlesque show. And I laughed up my sleeve when I thought of them sitting through three acts of talk with never so much as a glimpse of a dainty ankle . . .
>
> The critics put ''Ghosts'' on the same low level as such nasty dramatic concoctions as ''The Turtle,'' ''The Conquerors,'' ''Sappho,'' and others where risque dialogue and situations are used to attract and degenerate the public. In all the advertising of such attractions stress is laid on the daring of these certain scenes and in every way the public attention is attracted to them, all with the direct intention of increasing box office receipts. I do not recall a single advance notice of ''Ghosts'' that appeared to bid for such notoriety or patronage of a degenerate public . . .
>
> ''Ghosts'' is not a wildly joyous play! Quite the contrary, it is exceedingly depressing! But it is life! Not the brightest and best of life — but the phase of life over which polite society discreetly draws the curtain! But it is only a curtain, after all. A very thin curtain, through which may be seen the dark and fearful shadows on the other side.[32]

When, later in the month, Blanche Walsh appeared in Tolstoy's *Resurrection*, a play whose heroine was a prostitute, the critical response was similar to that which had been provoked by *Ghosts*, although both Handscomb and Wheeler were more restrained in their criticism. Mrs. Walker took advantage of the occasion to lecture the male critics on the real meaning of morality in art:

> It is unpleasant and even embarrassing to sit through three hours of such plain, unvarnished truth, and the effect is rather depressing, but it must point a strong moral to even the most frivolous young man or woman.
>
> The style of entertainment that is really most damaging to the morale of the community is the very style which is most popular — musical comedy, such as ''The Silver Slipper.'' Do not misunderstand me. I do not mean that the performance contains one lewd word or scene, but there is nothing elevating in it. It is a series of comic songs and sensational dances, the attractiveness of the latter depending in a large measure on the beauty of the performers and the coloring and elaborateness of their lingerie. It is plays like this that set young blood tingling — and old blood, too — and arouse the desire ''to see life.''[33]

It was of course this exposure to ''plain, unvarnished truth'' about social evil — the recognition that neither vice nor disease was confined to the ''lower classes'' and that sexual and economic exploitation by the dominant class was at the root of the problem — that produced the journalistic hysteria over the New Drama, not its alleged pornography. Ibsen's assault on social hypocrisy was bound to be shocking to a community intent on promoting growth and business prosperity at all costs, and on coping with the resultant social dislocation — poverty, overcrowding, illiteracy, disease, prostitution, alcoholism, and violent crime — by a policy of segregation and silence. But as Mrs. Walker stated, the curtain that discreet society draws over this phase of life is ''only a curtain after all.''

Handscomb himself moved to correct the impression that he had attacked *Ghosts* because he thought it sexually stimulating. In a note in *Town Topics* he made it clear that his main objection was that a theatre set up to divert and elevate polite society had no business stripping aside the curtain that made genteel complacency possible:

> ''Ghosts'' is a chiseled schedule of the inner workings of the clinic and those hideous victims who lie on the racks of the medical investigations. It is not for the stage at all. It is a loathsome and fearful parade of knowledge without power to interdict or to allay. It is the gospel of despair, of revolution, of dethroning of tenets and creeds and the narrow church without a vague hint of Calvary. Why? Why? Why? These hideous tableaux, these appalling incisions into the besotted lives and this classical, persistent gnawing revelation without some big, fine, salutary reason? People do not want such conversation, such good argument, such fine distinctions as Ibsen's lavished upon the horrible facts which secretly cripple unfortunates and follow the vicious.[34]

Just how dangerous the reluctance of Winnipeg's governing class to look squarely at public disease and sanitation problems could be, and just how little death respected class lines, was illustrated two years later when Charles Handscomb died of diphtheria at the age of forty.

The Shubert Challenge and the Bernhardt Tour

By 1905 the theatre syndicate appeared to be secure against any challenge the Shuberts and their associates might be capable of mounting. In June, Klaw and Erlanger announced the renewal of contracts with affiliated managers which would give the syndicate effective control of the bookings of 99 percent of the first-class theatres of the United States and Canada until 1 September 1922. This represented access to facilities worth an estimated $100 million.[35]

The long-term contract gave Walker security to proceed with a new, fully modern playhouse. Staging difficulties posed by some of the large-scale spectaculars which Klaw and Erlanger included in their offerings made the new playhouse a necessity. When *Ben Hur* came to Winnipeg in September, with a train load of machinery for a real chariot race, Walker had to stage it at the York Street Auditorium skating rink. The second-storey Winnipeg Theatre stage could not have supported the weight.

The disadvantage of Walker's exclusive syndicate association was revealed the following year when the Shuberts announced they had signed the celebrated Sarah Bernhardt for a North American tour. Walker expected to present Madame Bernhardt at the Winnipeg Theatre, but Erlanger issued an edict forbidding managers under contract to the syndicate to book the Shubert attraction. In Winnipeg, Bernhardt presented *Camille* at the Auditorium, which the Shubert office had booked directly. Mrs. Walker was not impressed:

> The rink was not dried out. The flooring was laid right over the wet mud, and there was no attempt to raise the middle section of the seats — except in matter of price!
>
> This utter disregard for the comfort of the patrons was only one instance of the engagement, in which "circus" methods generally prevailed . . .
>
> I believe Mme. Bernhardt's American tour is under the management of the so-called "Independents" — a few managers who claim that their sole object in life is to benefit the theatre-going public by giving them a higher class of entertainment than they can get through the so-called "Theatre Syndicate." If the Bernhardt performance is an index to the general methods of these "independent" managers, why then the "cruel and oppressive trust" will still continue to corral the pin-money of the *Matinee Girl*.[36]

The Walker Theatre

By the summer of 1906, work on Walker's modern, fireproof theatre was well underway. In July 1905 Walker had purchased 235 feet of frontage on Smith Street, between Notre Dame and Ellice Avenues. The new theatre would be built across the rear eighty feet of three city lots.

Confederation Life sold the Winnipeg Theatre to the Detroit firm of Drew and Campbell for $50,000. The sale was subject to Walker's lease, which guaranteed him possession until 1 September 1906. When his lease on the Winnipeg Theatre expired, Walker moved his operation to the Auditorium Skating Rink until the end of October.

The unofficial opening of the Walker Theatre was 17 December 1906, and the formal opening on 18 February 1907, with the performance of Henry W. Savage's production of Puccini's *Madame Butterfly*. The opening ceremonies were impressive, and when the curtain rose C.P. Walker, Lieutenant Governor Sir Daniel McMillan, Premier Roblin and Mayor Ashdown stepped forward amid hearty applause.

In such a theatre, said the mayor, one could blink one's eyes and imagine oneself in any great city in the world:

> My own thoughts are almost that I could conceive myself in the city of Boston, in some new theatre opened for the first time, or in the city of New York . . . It is the first metropolitan theatre we have in the great northwest. It is a credit alike to the city where it stands, and to the enterprise of the manager, who has brought it about.[37]

To Roblin, the significance of the theatre lay in the civilizing influence it would have on the community within which it stood:

Therefore a magnificent house like this dedicated to the purpose of interpreting the emotions of the heart and soul must be appreciated and is an absolute necessity for a progressive and enterprising people such as those of the city of Winnipeg.[38]

What impressed McMillan was the "enterprise, courage and confidence in the future of our city" which C.P. Walker had demonstrated in carrying the project to its completion:

Many are willing to spend money in business blocks and commercial enterprises but there is only one citizen of Winnipeg, one resident of the province, who would invest a fortune in a theatre, and that citizen's name is C.P. Walker. This great audience — and I never saw a finer — is a testimony to our appreciation of Mr. Walker's enterprise and it is our pledge to him that we will stand by him and support him, that we will do our share to make the Walker theatre famous in the highest theatrical circles.[39]

Walker's remarks were brief, and scarcely audible. The theatre itself was his statement.

The style of the building was Edwardian — grand but not gaudy. The Walker Theatre was of steel-cage construction, and fully fireproof. It was designed so that a hotel and office building complex could be built around it, should Walker be successful in striking an appropriate deal with hotel or business-block interests. The theatre was equipped with the most modern ventilating apparatus available, and it had its own lighting plant with power for two thousand lights. The stage was forty feet deep, eighty feet wide, and seventy feet high, with a proscenium opening of thirty-five feet. The total seating capacity was 1,798. As well as boxes, orchestra and balcony, there was a large gallery where twenty-five cent seats could be provided, even for productions for which box holders paid two dollars.

Walker's inclusion of the twenty-five cent gallery reflected his awareness of the growing mass audience — the working class seeking diversion and entertainment. Like other members of his class, he was well aware that what he thought of as "high-class" drama was by its very nature an elitist diversion. But like a great many of his class who considered themselves liberal and humanitarian, he still entertained the unrealistic hope that the hearts and minds of the poor could be won by cultural means alone, without alleviating their poverty. If the working class could be offered real culture at affordable prices, it might be induced to identify with the cherished aims of the privileged class without insisting on joining it.

There was no doubt that the attractions Walker drew to his new theatre were "high class." In its first three seasons the Walker Theatre featured such American headliners as Lillian Russell and Viola Allen, as well as celebrated stars of the British stage such as Olga Nethersole and Mrs. Patrick Campbell. In March 1909 *Ben Hur* returned to be staged under proper conditions, and was an enormous success.

Wheeling and Dealing in a Continental Context

Walker's Red River Valley Circuit was an important element within the Northwestern Affiliated Theatrical Circuits, a regional organization which controlled all major legitimate theatres in the northwestern United States and Canada. In August

1907 Walker announced the formation, under his leadership, of a similar alliance to control booking for one-night stand theatres in the midwest. Bookings for 360 such theatres in six northwestern states and all of Canada west of Port Arthur were to be controlled by the new combination, with Walker as principal booking agent.

Just at the moment of his greatest triumph, the ground began to shift under Walker's feet. Vaudeville was proving itself better able to satisfy the entertainment needs of the new immigrant working class than the kind of theatre Walker sold. And the social and economic elite which Walker's theatre enterprises were designed to serve was not growing in numbers or in level of confidence, as Winnipeg moved into a slow decline as a financial and distribution centre.

Vaudeville itself had begun to present big stars of the legitimate stage, without the expense of support companies, and without the strain of making a restless audience sit through entire plays. By the time of the opening of the Walker Theatre, both of Winnipeg's major vaudeville houses, the Dominion and the Bijou, were doing brisk business at prices ranging from ten to fifty cents.

Equally threatening was the revival of stock. When Drew and Campbell took over the Winnipeg Theatre, they brought to the city a man with the experience, imagination and good business sense to make the concept of the stock company succeed. W.B. Lawrence had been the manager of the Colonial Theatre in Cleveland, and on his transfer to Winnipeg he brought with him his successful stock company. On 24 September 1906 a mixed program of old favourites and recent Broadway hits was initiated, at prices ranging from fifteen to fifty cents — much below Walker's prices of up to two dollars for special attractions.

In December 1908 a second theatre devoted to high-class stock opened another Grand Opera House. Lawrence's response to the competition was swift. In March 1909 he announced that he had leased both the Grand Opera House and the Dominion Theatre for a ten-year period. Leading players from the former would join the Winnipeg Stock Company, which would continue to produce high-class stock, while a melodrama company would be installed at the Grand Opera House. Under Lawrence's management, the Dominion Theatre would continue its policy of big-time vaudeville, but would switch its contract from the giant Orpheum circuit to William Morris, an independent agent who was challenging the vaudeville monopolists much as the Shuberts were challenging Klaw and Erlanger. Lawrence then announced that he would feature Shubert touring shows, rather than stock, at the Winnipeg Theatre, bringing him into direct competition with Walker's syndicate touring house.

In the meantime, Lawrence's switch to Morris was turning out to be of greater significance that at first appeared. Morris was gearing for a major vaudeville war against Orpheum, and the rumour was that Martin Beck of Orpheum, now without a theatre in Winnipeg, was looking for a local house from which to launch his massive counterattack on Morris, which involved booking the top British variety and music hall artists.

Walker seemed challenged on all sides. His daughter states that a taste for gambling was central to his personality, and that "no poker or faro game ever had so many wild elements of chance as the show business."[40] Charles Handscomb, who knew him well, had remarked that "it's pretty hard to imagine any man or set of men throwing down C.P. Walker — if you know him, I needn't tell you why."[41]

Characteristically, Walker made the boldest move imaginable. He put out the word that the Walker Theatre itself might be available for big-time vaudeville, and he made overtures to Martin Beck to see if Orpheum was interested. Beck was hesitant; he had almost decided to build in Winnipeg instead of entering a contract with an independent manager. But Walker's move was sufficient to convince W.B. Lawrence that the time had come to make a deal with the manager of the Walker Theatre. Walker and Lawrence joined forces, and Martin Beck purchased a lot on Fort Street for a projected Orpheum Theatre.

The deal between Walker and Lawrence was comprehensive. In March 1910 Walker resumed management of the Winnipeg Theatre, and his Klaw and Erlanger touring attractions were routed to this house. The Walker Theatre became the home of Morris's top-line International Vaudeville, while the Dominion Theatre became an outlet for his small-time vaudeville. Lawrence became manager of both the Walker and Dominion theatres. In the autumn of 1910 he installed a new stock company, the Permanent Players, in the Dominion Theatre, with a programing policy identical to that of the old Winnipeg Stock Company. Lawrence continued to manage the vaudeville operation at the Walker Theatre.

An even more dramatic change in Walker's situation was in the offing. In May 1910, Walker announced that he and the other members of the Northwestern Affiliated Theatrical Circuits were leaving the syndicate and establishing an "open door" booking policy — in effect going with the Shuberts. The revolt was short-lived. In November 1910, *Variety* announced that John Cort of Northwestern had made his peace with the syndicate; Cort and his associates, including Walker, would be back within the Klaw and Erlanger fold by 1 January 1911.[42] Shortly afterwards a truce was arranged between the Shuberts and Klaw and Erlanger, and all top attractions became universally available.

In the autumn of 1910, Walker and his partners were dominant in the three major areas of theatrical entertainment — legitimate touring, stock, and big-time vaudeville. However, by midwinter it was evident that Morris's big-time vaudeville operation was in trouble, and that Morris himself was in almost continuous negotiations with Martin Beck of Orpheum for a settlement of the vaudeville war. With construction of Beck's Orpheum Theatre progressing rapidly, Walker knew that time was running out. In early February 1911, he announced that the Walker Theatre would be a legitimate theatre once more. Lawrence and the Permanent Players moved from the Dominion Theatre to the Winnipeg Theatre. The Orpheum Theatre opened on 13 March without "any opposition in vaudeville of the first-class."[43] In April, Sullivan-Considine, another major vaudeville chain, took over the Dominion Theatre and renamed it the Empress.

A Golden Age of Entertainment

The period from September 1911 to the outbreak of World War I was the golden age of live entertainment in Winnipeg. Two major vaudeville houses and several smaller theatres kept Winnipeg supplied with big-time, small-time and "pop" vaudeville acts. Alexander Pantages, in close association with W.B. Lawrence, was moving to pick up the pieces of the shattered Morris vaudeville operation. In 1914 he opened his own vaudeville theatre in Winnipeg, the Pantages.

At the Walker Theatre, one could see two recent New York productions every week throughout most of the year, with occasional weeks of ballet, grand opera and Shakespeare to vary the program. At the Winnipeg Theatre, the Permanent Players presented competent stock versions of recent New York shows, with a change of show every week. The Grand Opera House offered less-recent stock productions, with a slightly less-distinguished cast.

The Orpheum Theatre featured a top-quality vaudeville bill which changed every week. Headliners during a sample two-month period included Lily Langtry, Sarah Bernhardt and Blossom Seeley. Headline acts at the Empress during this period included Karno's English Comedians, featuring Charlie Chaplin; James Corbett telling anecdotes of the ring; and *The Suburban Winner*, a one-act play with a real horse race.

Decline and Collapse of the Touring System

The golden age did not last. Growing transportation expenses and the competition of the movies for stars, theatres and production capital brought about the slow death of the legitimate touring system and, with the advent of talking pictures, of vaudeville. The settlement of the New York Actor's Equity Strike in 1919 raised costs even further, so that by 1920 New York shows reaching Winnipeg had slowed to a trickle. Even by 1913, however, it was clear that a large movement of capital was underway within the American entertainment industry from legitimate touring to motion picture production, distribution and exhibition. Canadian managers of legitimate theatres began to realize that if they were not to become movie-house operators, an alternative source of theatrical attractions would have to be developed. An Anglo-Canadian Booking Office was set up to establish an all-Canadian touring system using British attractions in coast-to-coast tours. The first Anglo-Canadian tour featured Sir John Martin-Harvey in *The Only Way*; he appeared on the stage of the Walker Theatre in February 1914. Further Anglo-Canadian tours were cut short by the outbreak of World War I.

Following the war, with the American road system in a state of almost total collapse, Walker and other managers set up a Canadian touring system along the lines that had been projected in 1913. It was fed largely by British companies, supplemented by whatever American companies remained in the touring business. Companies toured from coast to coast on an all-Canadian route, booked for one or two weeks in major cities, with one- or two-night stopovers in smaller centres. Although an attempt to amalgamate major Canadian theatres under the control of a single corporation, Trans-Canada Theatres Limited, failed in the early 1920s, cooperation between individual theatre managers continued. Walker still had a large hand in the booking for western

Canada. Throughout the 1920s, the play bill at the Walker Theatre was filled in this fashion. Leading British repertory companies were featured, as well as such specialty shows as the annual Dumbells review, and concerts by international entertainers such as Scottish comedian Harry Lauder.

During the late 1920s, Famous Players Canada Limited, a Canadian subsidiary of Paramount Pictures, systematically bought legitimate theatres and independent vaudeville houses as they came on the market. In 1930, with most Canadian theatre real estate concentrated in its hands, Famous Players effectively ended live theatre in Canada by issuing an edict banning all live performances from its theatres in order to protect its investment in talking pictures.

Without a circuit, touring became impossible. Walker attempted to establish a stock company with publicly owned shares, but the venture collapsed in a few months. Now in his late seventies, C.P. Walker found that for him the theatre business had finally come to an end. He died in 1942, as did his wife the following year. The Walker Theatre was sold for taxes to Odeon Theatres Limited and reopened in 1945 as the Odeon, one of Winnipeg's most splendid movie palaces.

Lasting Influence of Walker's Theatre Enterprise

The influence of Walker's theatre enterprise on subsequent theatre movements in Winnipeg has been subtle but deep. Walker thrust the small western Canadian metropolis into the very heart of American show business and kept it there for two decades. Then, during the 1920s, he brought in the best available British classical companies, reestablishing Winnipeg's link with British culture and with the theatrical classics. Both phases of the Walker operation had a crucial influence on subsequent Winnipeg theatrical tastes and on prevailing ideas about the nature and social function of live theatre.

The fact that Walker was a down-to-earth local businessman who was at ease with the powerful financial and theatrical figures of New York and Chicago made a strong impression on Winnipeg. Walker's business acumen, the glamour of his New York and Chicago business contacts, and his proven ability to make money selling both art and entertainment, brought to theatre a respectability in the eyes of the Winnipeg business community that it has never lost. Even today, it seems wrong to Winnipeg citizens that theatre should lose money. The principle of the subsidy is fully accepted, but only if it is seen as a way of keeping ticket prices at an affordable level, not as a way of supporting bad management.

The real defeat that Walker suffered was that of the liberal dream he and his wife shared of a theatre which would at once unify and elevate western Canadian society. The Walker Theatre was designed to be a theatre for all, where the latest New York musicals, Broadway productions of serious plays, Shakespeare, ballet and Grand Opera could be offered in a setting luxurious enough for the carriage trade, but with gallery seats for those who could not afford the usual cost of high culture.

As might have been predicted, the working class in the twentieth century has shown less interest than nineteenth-century liberals had hoped in a "high culture" designed to consolidate the power of a privileged class. Vaudeville, the movies, radio and television have drawn the mass audience, with program content that would not be considered refined as our Victorian and Edwardian predecessors understood the term. And, to a considerable extent, members of the economic elite seeking diversion have stepped down to merge into that mass audience. It has been a process of cultural democratization, the social effect of which has been largely salutary.

But the dream of a majority, mainstream theatre, featuring living actors capable of delighting a wide spectrum of society with both Shakespeare and the frothiest current musical, has not died. It has, in fact, been a major model in shaping our contemporary subsidized theatre institutions. It might be well if we realized that the cultural and class tensions that surface when we attempt to establish artistic policy for those institutions find their roots in our historical experience.

NOTES

1. Walker Theatre program, 18 February 1907.

2. Ruth Harvey, *Curtain Time* (Boston: Houghton Mifflin, 1949), 52.

3. Joseph Csida and June Bundy Csida, *American Entertainment* (New York: Watson Guptill, 1978), 70.

4. *Town Topics*, 4 January 1902.

5. Thorstein Veblen, *Theory of the Leisure Class* (1899; reprint, New York: Macmillan, 1917).

6. Douglas Arrell, "Harold Nelson: The Early Years (c. 1865-1905)," *Theatre History in Canada* 1, no. 1 (Fall 1980): 83-110.

7. *Treherne Times*, 2 February 1906.

8. Arrell, "Harold Nelson," 91.

9. *Town Topics*, 8 April 1899.

10. *Winnipeg Tribune*, 6 April 1899.

11. *Town Topics*, 15 April 1899.

12. *Winnipeg Tribune*, 22 April 1899.

13. *Town Topics*, 29 April 1899.

14. Ibid., 28 October 1899.

15. Ibid., 4 November 1899.

16. Ibid., 18 November 1899.

17. Ibid., 2 March 1901.

18. Ibid, 23 March 1901.

19. Csida and Csida, *American Entertainment*, 138.

20. *Manitoba Free Press*, 1 January 1904.

21. Ibid., 25 January 1904.

22. *Winnipeg Tribune*, 25 January 1904.

23. *Town Topics*, 30 January 1904.

24. Alan F.J. Artibise, *Winnipeg: A Social History of Urban Growth, 1874-1914* (Montréal: McGill-Queen's University Press, 1975), 130-31.

25. Ibid., 25.

26. *Town Topics*, 9 January 1904.

27. Ibid.

28. Artibise, *Winnipeg: An Illustrated History* (Toronto: Lorimer, 1977), 54.

29. *Town Topics*, 27 February 1904.

30. *Manitoba Free Press*, 10 March 1904.

31. *Winnipeg Tribune*, 10 March 1904.

32. *Town Topics*, 19 March 1904.

33. Ibid., 30 April 1904.

34. Ibid., 16 April 1904.

35. *Manitoba Free Press*, 24 June 1905.

36. *Town Topics*, 5 May 1906.

37. *Manitoba Free Press*, 19 February 1907.

38. Ibid.

39. Ibid.

40. Harvey, *Curtain Time*, 49.

41. *Manitoba Free Press*, 17 October 1903.

42. *Variety*, 5 November 1910.

43. Ibid., 8 March 1911.

Three Major Strands in the Women's Movement in Manitoba, 1965-1985

7

Three Major Strands in the Women's Movement in Manitoba, 1965-1985

Üstün Reinart

Much credit is due the women who changed Manitoba's social fabric through their political activities in the women's movement. The women who fought for suffrage around the turn of the century, and who made Manitoba the first Canadian province to give women the vote, were those who started the movement. Theirs was the first wave of feminism. The second wave came in the late 1960s, gathered momentum during the 1970s, and continued into the 1980s. A core group of about fifty feminists in Manitoba invested enormous time and energy, and their efforts changed, to some extent, legislation and public attitudes affecting women's lives. This chapter offers an overview of that second wave.

The information on which this chapter is based comes from three sources. Interviews were conducted with twenty-seven women active in the women's movement during the period under consideration. These interviews were supplemented by a review of the newsletters of the Winnipeg Women's Liberation Movement (WWLM) from 1971 to 1978, and of *Action*, the Manitoba Action Committee on the Status of Women (MACSW) newsletter, from 1976 to 1986.

The methodology used for this chapter has distinct advantages and disadvantages. Because no standardized questionnaire was administered, and because those interviewed did not constitute a random sample of women, no inferences can be drawn about the relative strength of various strands of the movement, about the support the women's movement received among women as a whole, or about the opinions of people other than those interviewed. On the other hand, the elements of this story are told by some of its main actors, and have been verified in group discussions of early drafts of this chapter among some of the participants in the events described. Thus, a number of issues were raised and viewpoints clarified that would typically be missed by more conventional histories. The interview transcripts and other documents on which this account is based were intended to draw together the living participants before they had been dispersed and while their memories were fresh, yet after sufficient time to allow distance and perspective. In this way, this chapter may be helpful as a starting point for more analytical studies which will later be undertaken by others.

The women's movement is an important reminder of the effectiveness of extra-parliamentary politics in putting pressure on public opinion and legislators to effect social and political change. But it also demonstrates the difficulties facing a core group of activists who recognize the urgent need for simultaneous political education, political action and services for women, and who struggle with the dilemma of where to invest their limited energies.

Feminist activists in Manitoba have lived with that dilemma for two decades, two decades of significant achievements and some defeats. Yet the story of the women's movement has not been told. In the centuries-old tradition of the "invisibility" of women's history, studies of the dynamics of the movement, its achievements and its problems are conspicuously absent from most academic and popular publications.

The women's movement in Manitoba was an expression of the women's movement across Canada and the Western world. In Manitoba, however, the most recent upswing took shape under a provincial NDP government. From time to time, feminism in Manitoba has entered into an uneasy alliance with social democracy. Co-option of leaders and groups in the movement has been a constant issue.

The women's movement has been successful in changing the social climate in Manitoba, so that new organizations and government departments have been set up to meet some of the needs of women: the provincial department on daycare; the Family Violence Branch of Community Services; the Pay Equity Commission; the Women's Directorate; the Manitoba Advisory Council on the Status of Women; community health clinics; the Women's Health Clinic; Osborne House; and the Manitoba Committee on Wife Abuse. Many feminist activists now hold key positions in these organizations. It is believed that "we've effected enough change that people can work within the system with integrity."[1]

Feminists now have a choice: to work inside the system to implement feminist policies and services, or to continue to work outside the system to press for action. There are dangers in both choices. It is not always easy to say where effectiveness inside government organizations and government-funded agencies ends, and co-option begins.[2] Inside the system, women can find themselves compromising too much. But those outside the system risk losing access to institutions and bureaucracies which can be tools for change.[3]

During the two decades of its development, the women's movement has had no cohesive political ideology.[4] In general, feminists in Manitoba belonged to one of three political camps: liberal feminists, socialist feminists, and radical feminists. These divisions were common across the continent:

> In British Columbia and in Ontario, the three camps had separated into different women's movements early in the seventies. In Winnipeg, there was a great deal of over-lap between groups. The socialist feminists and radical feminists didn't separate until the late seventies.[5]

Many feminists are proud of the diversity of political and economic views the movement has allowed, seeing it as one of the strengths of the movement.

By and large, the women's movement attracted white women from middle-class backgrounds. The participation of Native and immigrant women remained limited but in the late 1970s and early 1980s a number of organizations representing Native women, immigrant women and women on welfare became active in Winnipeg.[6] Such groups may not define themselves as part of the women's movement, yet they have to be seen in the context of the social and political climate created by popular movements like the women's and Native rights movements.

This chapter will describe the development of the "umbrella" organizations which roughly represented the three feminist camps: the MACSW, which was originally liberal feminist, and soon associated with NDP women representing a left-liberal, social-democratic ideology; the WWLM, which was originally socialist feminist and radical feminist; and the Winnipeg Women's Cultural Education Centre, which attempted to set up a radical feminist group at the Women's Building.

The Beginnings

The 1960s were marked in North America and Western Europe by political unrest. Amidst the rumblings of unrest, women's voices began to be heard, demanding liberation from a system which exploited and oppressed them. Perhaps it was this unrest which resulted in an unprecedented number of royal commissions in Canada—one was the Royal Commission on the Status of Women, which held hearings across the country in the spring of 1967. Some Manitoba women presented individual briefs, and many met for the first time during the hearings in Winnipeg. They also met the Manitoba Volunteer Committee on the Status of Women, which had organized most women's groups in the province to present one joint brief.[7]

Until then, the Manitoba Volunteer Committee, the Women's Institutes, the YWCA, various church groups, the Canadian Congress of Women and the Voice of Women were the women's groups active in the province. All of these, with the exception of the Congress (which had Communist sympathies) and the Voice of Women (which was a peace organization) were traditional, conservative organizations.

The MACSW

The Royal Commission on the Status of Women released its report in September 1970. Four months later, the Manitoba Volunteer Committee voted to establish a new organization, the MACSW. It had a loose hierarchical structure, with a four-member executive committee and twelve active members.[8] Its purpose was to help implement the recommendations of the commission. Many of the women who had presented individual briefs during the hearings became involved with the MACSW. At its inception, it represented liberal feminists.[9]

The majority of the women who founded the MACSW had no quarrel with capitalism. They wanted more rights for women, and for women to share the wealth and power which capitalism yielded to upper- and middle-class men. They believed that reforms could bring women economic, legal and social equality with men, and they believed in the effectiveness of pressure from within the system. Yet the changes they wanted seemed revolutionary: "When you start from nowhere, you have to overcome the suspicions of people who think you hate men . . . and that you're out to destroy families."[10]

The MASCW was run by volunteers, but as Manitoba's most visible women's organization, after 1973 it had access to funds from the Department of the Secretary of State to organize conferences, conduct research and prepare position papers. It concentrated on pressing for legislative changes to improve women's lives.

Soon after the MASCW was established, the Supreme Court ruled in the divorce case of a Saskatchewan woman, Irene Murdoch. The court declared that Murdoch had no right to a share in the farm property which her labour had sustained during a twenty-year marriage. Her story inspired four MACSW women — Jean Carson, June Menzies, Zoë Bud and Muriel Arpen — to develop a skit to inform women of the injustice of existing family laws.

The Balloon Lady

Some of the women who filled the school gymnasium in Brunkild, Manitoba for a meeting of the Women's Institute on 22 November 1973 were scandalized by the presentation of the MACSW women's skit, *The Balloon Lady*: "It was the story of a little lady floating along, supported by a bunch of balloons. Each balloon represented laws or protections women relied on. As each protection was no protection at all, we punctured the balloons one by one. In the end, the balloon lady fell.''[11] One woman in the audience stated: "This really worries me. I'm afraid that we're losing our homes. The children are out on the street . . . because the women are working. I think this is all wrong." Another suggested, "Don't you think, if you appeal to husbands from the angle of protection for their wives and families, not all this silly lib business about no bras . . . , wouldn't they be interested from that point? I know my husband would be.''[12] However, the Brunkild women were disturbed by the issues raised in the skit; issues of ownership of family property and the economic vulnerability of women had never before been discussed publicly in their community.

Over the next two years, the skit was repeated in Manitoba towns on more than one hundred occasions. After each performance, the MACSW women invited questions from the floor and a discussion of the issues followed. The winds of the women's liberation movement were beginning to blow gently through Manitoba towns. As one woman recalled, "We avoided a militant approach. We felt Nellie McClung had been confrontationist. We felt our approach was better.''[13]

While *The Balloon Lady* toured the province, the MACSW was also organizing conferences, preparing position papers on issues like women and politics, the economic position of women in the family, and women in the work force, and was actively lobbying governments and conducting public education and letters-to-legislators campaigns to gain more power for women. Most feminists now acknowledge the MACSW's valuable contribution: "Those women were doing important, courageous work. Their skit was laying the crucial ground work for the most successful coalition of the women's movement which was to come in 1975-76: the Family Law Coalition of Manitoba.''[14]

But in the early 1970s, some socialist feminists thought the MACSW was a "reformist" organization, representing the establishment. Women who wanted to transform society in order to bring about socialism and the liberation of women formed a separate organization, the WWLM, whose beginnings coincided with those of the MACSW.

The WWLM

The political energy generated on university campuses and in political organizations in the United States by the civil rights movement and the opposition to the Vietnam War began to be felt in Canada by the late 1960s. Many young people, including women, were ready for new, radical ideas:

> We were interested in the liberation of women, not in creating rights for women. A lot of women on the left were feeling the connections between left politics and women's politics and wanted to bring them together.[15]

In 1969, the election of an NDP government in Manitoba raised the expectations of socialists in the province. It was to be Manitoba's first experiment with social democracy. The NDP attracted radical new people with high expectations. Even after disillusionment began to set in, energy remained high. Many women associated with the left wing of the NDP channelled that energy into women's politics.[16] Many women who held independent left-wing views were ready for feminism. The WWLM in Winnipeg emerged in that context.

In 1968-69, a group of about twenty women began holding consciousness-raising meetings in Millie Lamb's living room in Winnipeg to discuss socialism and feminism:

> Most of those women were young. Between 19 to 22. I wouldn't even call them political. They were open to left-wing ideas. Many had been involved in the struggle against the Vietnam war. Some came because they were flower children, hippies. That was a radicalizing movement then.[17]

The more they discussed women's oppression, the more they became determined to take the message of the women's movement to the public. But were unsure how. Someone thought of doing street theatre (this was before *The Balloon Lady*), and The Women's Theatre was born. Over the next two decades it was to become an invaluable political and educational tool.[18]

Millie Lamb recalled the period:

> I remember two skits from those early days: "The Shattered Pedestal" and "Votes for Men", a musical. "Votes for Men" was based on the play which Nellie McClung and the suffragists had put on at the Walker theatre in 1914. It was a multi-media performance with songs, dances, slides and skits. We were performing at high schools, shopping malls, labour meetings. I remember a skit about abortion. We had coat hangers and bloody sheets as props. One of our young members was arrested by the security guard at a performance at Polo Park. She was held in the office for a few hours.[19]

By 1971, the group had become the WWLM, and it was publishing a regular newsletter.

At its inception the WWLM represented socialist feminists:

> We were struggling with economic issues from a women's perspective. We were
> also dealing with reproductive and child care issues which no one had accepted as
> Marxist issues.[20]

The women who became involved with the WWLM did not all have a Marxist
perspective and a theoretical base for political analysis. Some had been in the Waffle
movement of the NDP, some (like Millie Lamb) had Communist sympathies, a few
were Trotskyists, and many were politically unaffiliated. Socialist women provided the
political and theoretical backbone of the group, but the WWLM never adopted a clear
Marxist perspective:

> The WWLM was radical, but its radicalism was fuelled more by anger than by
> analysis. Anger against personal relationships which trapped women in positions of
> economic dependence and at the mercy of reproductive roles, anger against the NDP
> and the shortcomings of social democracy, and anger against the US
> administration's actions.[21]

The WWLM was plagued by contradictions and organizational problems from the
outset. It was anxious to define its political direction but it was also trying to expand its
base to include more women, and to educate those who had no background in political
analysis. Its primary purpose was political, yet it hoped to provide necessary services to
women in the areas of pregnancy counselling, abortion referral, crisis counselling, legal
referrals and child care. It immediately began to investigate the possibility of setting up
a day-care centre, and it began to offer abortion counselling at the office of the WWLM:

> There was always a debate about whether we should concentrate on political
> organization, on demonstrations and education. Some of us feared that getting
> caught up in providing services would make us lose sight of the ultimate goal which
> was political. Yet the need for the services was so great that we had the service thing
> built into the group. People who were doing service didn't have time for politics.
> We had the pregnancy information service. We had women doing that. When we
> called a demonstration on the choice issue, those women weren't at the demo. They
> were busy providing the service. There's a need for both, and a small core group of
> people. Where do you put your energies?[22]

The tensions between three different but important goals — political study, political
action, and services to women — continued to pressure the group. To complicate
matters, the WWLM was chronically short of volunteers and money.

In its January 1972 newsletter, the WWLM published a draft policy statement stating
that ''the liberation of women is primarily the task of women, as a separate but integral
part of the movement for human liberation.'' It also stated that the group was not aligned
with any particular party or organization, and that it had no specific philosophy or
theory to which members must adhere. The newsletter also indicated that the WWLM
was determined to resist co-option by rejecting government grants: ''We do not at any

point wish to become dependent upon government funding for our existence: this could easily become a co-opting force."[23]

Finding a suitable organizational structure was difficult. The members wanted a democratic structure which would involve all women in the group. They agreed upon a three-woman coordinating committee which was to set the agenda for business meetings, and remain in contact with the various projects and activities of the group. The committee would be elected by a majority vote of the members on a regular, six-month basis. Other positions in the group (two secretaries, a treasurer, a literature coordinator and a research librarian) would be filled by volunteers.

On average, fifteen to twenty women came to the biweekly meetings,[24] with up to forty women attending emergency meetings. By 1974 the group had a mailing list of 350 members.[25]

In the winter of 1972-73, the WWLM was planning to rent a house to provide the women in the movement with a meeting place, a drop-in centre and an office for the referral services. The June 1973 newsletter announced the opening of "A Woman's Place" at 300 Victor Street.[26] Jean Dunmire described the centre:

> A Woman's Place was an old brown house with asphalt shingling on the outside. It had a brown porch, a stairway to the right. Behind the kitchen, there was a small day care. Children were always running around. The house was always messy. There were never enough people willing to do housework. Always a shortage of volunteers.[27]

Although the group had been opposed to government funding, the opening of "A Woman's Place" had been made possible by an Opportunities For Youth grant from the Department of the Secretary of State. It had been planned to have approximately three women living at the house, and to have space for meetings, a children's play centre, a library, a drop-in centre and a Lesbian Resource Centre, but this proved to be too ambitious. Shortly after the opening of "A Woman's Place," the first stirrings of radical feminism began to appear in Winnipeg.

Radical Feminism in Winnipeg

Radical feminist analysis defines all hierarchical structures and all relationships with men as oppressive to women. Radical feminists (the majority of whom choose a lesbian lifestyle) prefer to avoid men and to form their own cultural and social organizations.

There were undoubtedly small, hidden groups of lesbians in Manitoba before the 1960s, but late in that decade the arrival of new ideas of women's liberation fuelled lesbians' political consciousness and drew them to the women's movement. In Manitoba, they first joined the WWLM. Soon, some emotionally charged debates erupted about the role of the lesbian feminists in the women's movement. Some remained in the socialist feminist camp, but eventually many formed their own organizations.

In the October 1972 WWLM newsletter, Sharon Segal and Marilyn Wolovick referred to a teach-in on women's issues at the University of Manitoba:

> For many of us, they say, one of the most exciting and controversial issues raised was that of radical lesbianism. The concept they raised of devoting ourselves entirely to women (to the exclusion of men) really made good sense in the context of the women's movement. And yet, it's something that many of us found hard to accept personally. Although some of us may not opt for radical lesbianism as our lifestyle, the discussion of it has brought us closer to an understanding of true sisterhood and has revitalized our own commitment to women and the women's movement.[28]

In February 1973, the newsletter announced an educational meeting on women and lesbianism, but the subject brought new tensions to the group. Many heterosexual women were uneasy about the role of lesbian feminists, of whom there were then about ten in the group,[29] in their midst:

> Many women were unsure if it was a lifestyle choice, social deviancy or something connected with feminism. There was a lot of discussion about whether lesbianism should be talked about. Whether it would detract from the cause of Women's Liberation. Whether it would alienate women. Whether it was undesirable for the movement to be identified with lesbian feminists.[30]

> The issue that had to be dealt with was, they'll think we're all lesbians.[31]

Lesbian feminists believed they were in the vanguard of the women's movement and felt the group's ambivalence was a betrayal. In the July 1974 newsletter, an impassioned open letter from an outspoken lesbian feminist brought the debate to a head:

> You, and I refer here to the majority of my straight sisters in the movement, don't want me (us) mucking up your nice little movement. ... You're still back in the dark ages of women's liberation, sucking up for men's (society's) approval, scared to death of the "lavender menace," still promoting the heterosexual ideas which oppress you daily, dismissing lesbianism as an unimportant issue. Worst of all intellectualizing, citing political reasons, doing anything to avoid admitting to yourselves that the simple fact of it is that you cannot deal with the haunting spectre that each of you, too, has the natural capacity for responding to other women.[32]

The letter caused a stir: "It was met with defensiveness, and with genuine concern that we hadn't met their needs." Many women in the group were ready to accept their lesbian sisters and to say "if they want to call us all lesbians — then we are."[33] But the unease remained.

From that point onwards, the WWLM newsletter gave more space to the discussion of lesbian issues and the expression of lesbian viewpoints. The group also established a lesbian discussion group which met every Sunday night. But a year later, another bitter message appeared in the newsletter, expressing the frustration one woman had experienced as a "token lesbian" in the WWLM: "If straight women harass lesbians beyond the point of endurance ... then lesbians will develop their own separatist movement.''[34] The debate had signalled to many lesbian feminists who had been in the closet that the time had arrived to "come out."

The Women's Movement Gains Momentum

In 1975, the feminist art exhibit at the Winnipeg Art Gallery, "Woman as Viewer," marked the celebration of International Women's Year in Manitoba.[35] It was also an expression of the women's movement in full swing in the province.

The arrival of radical feminist singer Heather Bishop in Manitoba in 1976 gave a big boost to feminist culture in the province. Bishop's politics cost her some commercial revenue, but brought political rewards:

> Bishop and her music gave a strong emotional focus to the women's movement. She was the first contact for countless women. Here was this talented artist who was also an outspoken lesbian. She was a source of inspiration — and a very important figure in the movement.[36]

Millie Lamb observed that "by 1975-1976, Women's Lib had become trendy."[37] The MACSW had broadened its base and attracted many women associated with the NDP.[38] With conferences, position papers, public education campaigns and persistent lobbying, the MACSW had successfully raised mainstream awareness about women's issues. Speakers from both the MACSW and the WWLM were frequently invited to speak at various public institutions:

> It was a heady time because the impact of the movement was visible. The responses were quick. We were very noisy — and we were heard. When members of the WWLM wrote letters to the Winnipeg School Division about sexism in schools, the Division hired four people to train teachers on non-sexism.[39]

By 1975, the women's movement in Manitoba had had a significant impact on the services available to women in Manitoba. In July 1971, a group of WWLM women opened the first Winnipeg Birth Control and Abortion Referral Centre. An MACSW subcommittee, the Women's Action Committee on Day Care, had been pressuring the provincial government to establish free, continuous day care in Winnipeg. In 1971 the provincial Department of Health and Social Services set up a day-care subcommittee and gave the first provincial day care subsidy to a day care centre at Monarch Wear.[40] The WWLM was instrumental in establishing a women's studies course at the University of Manitoba in January 1972. In June 1973, an MACSW subcommittee, the Women's Labour Caucus, was formed to organize women around issues affecting them in the work force.[41] In April 1974, a Rape Crisis Centre was established at "Klinic." In June the provincial government announced a $4 million day care program, one-half of which was paid by the federal government, and the first Winnipeg crisis housing project for women in emergency situations (later Osborne House) was established. In 1975 "Woman as Viewer," the first feminist art exhibition in Canada, was staged at the Winnipeg Art Gallery, and two books coauthored by Linda Taylor, Ellen Kruger and

Rose Silversides were distributed to Manitoba Schools.[42] But the most unifying and rewarding work of the women's movement in Manitoba was yet to come — the Coalition on Family Law.

The Coalition on Family Law

The Coalition on Family Law was by far the most successful cooperative effort undertaken by women's groups in Manitoba. It combined pressure from inside the NDP government through the movement's allies, and pressure from the outside through intensive lobbying and demonstrations. As Jean Carson observed, "it was a colossal undertaking. Two years of our lives went into it."[43]

Existing family laws did not recognize the nonfinancial contribution made by women through years of working in the home. If a married couple separated, the woman would not get maintenance payments if the judge found her responsible for the breakdown of the marriage. According to Alice Steinbart, "the family laws were sexist."[44]

The MACSW's early work on family law (*The Balloon Lady* and a conference on women and the law) had publicly raised the issues of the unfairness of family property and family maintenance legislation, and kept it on the agenda. The Provincial Council of Women was pressuring then Attorney General Howard Pawley to review family law, and he established the Law Reform Commission. In 1976 the commission submitted its report, recommending judicial discretion in the division of property, and stating that some married people could opt out of the legislation if they chose. It also recommended maintenace payments based on "fault."

According to Steinbart, "we didn't just want to answer the commission, we wanted to take the initiative and make recommendations."[45] With the MACSW, Women and the Law, the Canadian Congress of Women and the WWLM, women's groups organized a coalition of twenty-five organizations. The early MACSW leaders, Jean Carson and Bernice Sisler, were once more on centre stage. Carson states that the coalition got "a big push from NDP women who had a women's caucus within their party and who had become very active in MACSW."[46]

The groups made separate submissions, all calling for equal ownership of community property by husband and wife, no-fault maintenance, and the establishment of a special agency to collect and enforce maintenance payments to single parents. They also lobbied intensively.

When the legislation was passed in June 1977 it was, according to Steinbart, "the most progressive family law legislation in Canada. It brought instant community of property for the home, and deferred community of property for the other assets. It was a major gain. It scared all the reactionaries."[47]

Sterling Lyon's Conservatives, who won the October 1977 provincial election, planned to repeal the new legislation. The coalition refused to accept this position and once again its members submitted position papers. They lobbied all Conservative MLAs and staged massive demonstrations on the grounds of the Legislative Assembly. The women's movement, and the MACSW in particular, was accused of "belonging" to the NDP. The MACSW responded by stating that "it's a well-founded bias, one that needs no apologies." [48]

When the Conservatives reviewed the legislation, the changes they brought in were less damaging than the women's groups had feared:

> They brought back "separate as to property" with a statement that it should be equally accounted for. [Attorney General Gerald] Mercier believed in "fault" maintenance. We fought and fought. Finally, they brought back limited fault. Mercier even brought in maintenance enforcement procedures. We were the first in Canada to have it provincewide. [49]

This represented a major victory for the women's movement in Manitoba.

The Battle for Reproductive Choice

The WWLM had identified reproductive choice and the availability of safe, legal abortions as a primary issue for women. In 1969, when then Prime Minister Pierre Trudeau visited Winnipeg, the Women's Theatre group participated at a demonstration for choice, wearing black capes and carrying a coffin. In 1971 the group established a pregnancy counselling and abortion referral service in the McIntyre Building. [50]

In 1971, a Toronto-based organization called the Abortion Action Coalition began to organizate in Manitoba around the issue of choice:

> It was a Trotskyist group. They wanted Choice to be the "only" issue the movement should put its energies into. Many women here said "no." The women's movement in Manitoba did not focus all its energy on Choice. We felt it would be a political mistake. [51]

The Canadian Abortion Rights Action League (CARAL) was organized in Toronto to carry the fight for choice across the country, and Ellen Kruger started a Manitoba chapter in Winnipeg. CARAL presented a brief to the Health Services Commission on the need for a pregnancy counselling centre in Manitoba. Such a centre had already been proposed and in 1978 Dr. John Tyson wrote a paper supporting this position. According to Kruger,

> When we heard that, we formed a coalition. Women and the Law and CARAL were instrumental in setting it up. Since about 1974-75, MACSW had been pro-choice. It joined. [52]

The pro-choice activists had hoped to model the new coalition on the Manitoba Coalition on Family Law, but they were unable to attain the same degree of support or success. Between 1979 and 1989 the pro-choice coalition was quiet, but things became more turbulent in 1982, when Dr. Henry Morgentaler arrived to set up an abortion clinic in Winnipeg:

The NDP paid lip service to "choice," but the provincial government wanted nothing to do with Morgentaler's abortion clinic. The feeling was that it wasn't an important issue, that it was a lifestyle issue, that it would go away.[53]

It did not. The Morgentaler clinic was raided twice by police, and its equipment was confiscated. Feminists were infuriated, and in 1984 alone the Coalition for Reproductive Choice raised $130,000 to defend the clinic. This was the largest amount ever raised by a left-wing organization in Manitoba. Approximately $80,000 of the total came from NDP members, who were furious with the government's actions.[54]

The NDP government was faced with such strong pressure that it could no longer ignore the choice issue. To appease the disillusioned feminists among its supporters, the government increased abortion services in hospitals. According to Linda Taylor,

Aside from Quebec and B.C., we're the third best in the country in the provision of abortion services. In Winnipeg, any woman who wants an abortion can get one. It's still difficult for Northern and rural women.[55]

The relationship between the NDP and each of the two broad-based coalitions of the women's movement — the Family Law Coalition and the Coalition for Reproductive Choice — demonstrates both the strengths and the weaknesses of having a political movement that is in an uneasy alliance with social democracy. During the fight for changes in family law, the "inside track" to party members and cabinet ministers proved useful, and NDP members who were sympathetic to women's issues joined the coalition's lobbying efforts. However, the alliance with the NDP became a negative factor during the 1984 battle over Morgentaler's clinic. Although many feminists in the party were angry with the government and disappointed with its refusal to accredit the clinic, some were sympathetic to the difficult position in which then Community Services Minister Muriel Smith found herself. The anger unleashed against Smith and the government was tempered by that sympathy.

The End of the WWLM

In the late 1970s, lacking both money and volunteers, the WWLM began to lose momentum. In 1974, "A Woman's Place" moved to a larger house on Walnut Street but was also plagued by a lack of volunteers. Some of the women who had been active in the group had jobs, and no longer had the time or the energy to do service work. The WWLM began to dissolve:

No one said this is the end of the WWLM, but the core group of women were no longer interested in maintaining it. It was time for us to regroup. We actually closed the house.[56]

About a dozen socialist feminists who had been in the WWLM formed the Socialist Women's Collective in 1975 in order to study political theory.[57] They organized a left-wing contingent in the wage-and-price controls demonstration of that year, and later were the mainstay of the Coalition for Reproductive Choice. They also began work on a paper which was a feminist critique of Marxism.

In 1975, the radical feminists in the WWLM founded their own organization, the Winnipeg Lesbian Society (WLS). The WLS had started as an affiliate of the WWLM, meeting at ''A Woman's Place'' and organizing joint social events. However,

> there was great nervousness on the part of both groups about organizing joint functions. We did hold some joint socials. We acknowledged publicly on the posters that this event was organized by gay and straight women together. But straight women were still nervous about whether they'd be identified as lesbians.[58]

In 1975-76, a new political wave, the Trotskyist Wages for Housework movement, arrived from Toronto and intensified the split between lesbian feminists and socialist feminists in the WWLM. However, as Millie Lamb observed, this group

> argued that society owed women payments for being women and contributing to the GNP [Gross National Product] by doing housework. The majority of the socialist women in the movement rejected the argument, because they felt the road to liberation was a role in the paid work force. We thought it would be a backward step to have cheques going to women to keep them doing housework.[59]

But many lesbians who had nothing to do with Trotskyist politics supported the movement. Having broken their ties with men and mainstream society, they were on the whole poorer than straight women, and less inclined to Marxist analysis.

In 1978, seven women who supported the Wages for Housework movement raised the down payment for an old United Church building on Alexander Avenue and formed the Winnipeg Women's Cultural Education Centre. They named the church ''The Women's Building.''

The Women's Building

From the outset, the collective which bought ''The Women's Building'' was associated with poverty. Socialist politics were discouraged at the centre for fear that lesbians would be reluctant to come. The collective hoped that all women's groups, including the MACSW and the WWLM would be attracted to the facility, but it was more interested in establishing a social and cultural environment than in political action around issues. Nor were men welcomed:

> The lesbians felt threatened that they'd be drowned out in everyone's causes. They wanted women-only space. When the board of the Women's Building tried to take a political position on an issue, there was a lot of tension on whether we should take a stand on issues.[60]

''The Women's Building'' housed an office for Women in Trades, a rape crisis counselling service, a used clothing depot, a bookstore, a women's self-defence group, and, temporarily, an office of the WWLM. The MACSW, however, was not involved:

> We tried to get MACSW located in the building. We lost because they wanted a more accessible area. Also, the Women's Building was fairly run down. There was a general feeling that these middle-class women wanted something more spiffy.[61]

Running "The Women's Building" required a great deal of time, energy and money. Margie Cogill, on the board from 1979 to 1981, described the uphill struggle:

> My experience at that time was that we had no access to funds or anything in the feminist society. There was a perception that the Women's Building and the women who operated it were impoverished and irresponsible. When I was on the board, there was a group of us who had jobs — a bit more established, we paid the bills and worked very hard to do fund-raising. But there was another group, a more radical group which tended to be very poor. Around 1980, we on the board agreed unanimously to recommend that we give the building back to the United Church and pay off our debt. But there was a group of women who couldn't let it go. They were emotionally too attached to it. We stepped out. They took over. But they couldn't pay the heat bills.[62]

The new board was inexperienced, and faced a wide range of problems. The group was denied the zoning for the programs originally planned for the building — a restaurant, coffee-shop and night club — and the building's inaccessibility and lack of adequate parking made it difficult to rent office space. In 1983 "The Women's Building" closed, after having served approximately one hundred women during its four-year existence.

The MACSW in Transition

The MACSW had always had easier access to government funding than other women's groups, but until 1979 this had been only short-term funding. The MACSW could only hire staff on a project basis, for six-month periods. In 1978 the group asked the Secretary of State for funding for a three-year plan, and the request was granted the next year.

In 1980, the MACSW ceased to be run by volunteers. MACSW women were struggling with some of the organizational problems their sisters in the WWLM had experienced in the early 1970s. They wanted to move away from a hierarchical structure, to move from the executive committee towards a democratic collective board, more in keeping with feminist principles. The MACSW had also been changing its politics. It was extending its base, reaching out toward more radical, activist women and to some of the women previously excluded from the movement. It was attempting to establish contact with organizations of women on welfare, Native women, rural women and lesbian feminists.

In 1978, the MACSW voiced its support for Native women in their struggle to change Section 12(1)(b) of the Indian Act, which caused them to lose their status when they married non-status men. In April 1978 the MACSW newsletter identified the issues of immigrant women workers as a subject to be studied. In January 1980, the Brandon office of the MACSW hired an Outreach worker to organize rural women, and in 1982 MACSW meetings began to be held outside of Winnipeg. By the autumn of 1982, the newly formed Manitoba Anti-Poverty Organization asked for an MACSW member to sit on its board. In January 1984, a lesbian support group was started through the MACSW. By then, lesbian feminists comprised approximately one-third of the thirty-member board.[63]

The MACSW had conducted research into the prostitution problem for the Fraser Committee, and in 1984 this led to the development of Prostitutes and Other Women for Equal Rights (POWER). POWER was instrumental in opening a drop-in centre to provide services to prostitutes.

After the WWLM disappeared and "The Women's Building" closed, the MACSW became the umbrella organization coordinating various women's groups. It had escaped the poverty and shortage of resources which had plagued the other groups, partly because it had access to government funding.

Conclusion

In two decades, the women's movement has significantly changed the social, political and personal landscape for many women across North America. In Manitoba, a dominant issue has been whether, and under what circumstances, to work with a relatively receptive social democratic government and legislative system. The decision to do so, and the weaving together of activism with the political establishment, may have convinced younger women that the major battles have already been fought and won.

There does not appear to be a new generation of feminists waiting to join the women's movement in Manitoba. The MACSW's Youth Coordinator, Maureen Smith, says that most female students she has met no longer feel sexism is an issue: "They're interested in 'making it', not in making waves."[64] The women who do join the movement tend to be students in women's studies courses. Women's centres on university campuses combine lesbian feminist and punk anarchist, with very little socialist feminist politics (the only organization of young socialist feminist women in Winnipeg at the time of this writing was the three-member Bread and Roses Collective).

The women's movement may appear moribund in Winnipeg, but it is only now beginning to gain momentum in some rural areas and in northern communities. Furthermore, the new vitality and strength of Native women's organizations — Original Women's Network and Indigenous Women's Collective — reflect some of the new directions the movement is taking in Manitoba.

The MACSW now has five meetings annually, two of which are held outside Winnipeg. One-half of the members of the collective represent women outside Winnipeg.[65] In Thompson, an MACSW chapter started in 1986, and women in remote northern communities are working to organize a northern women's network to address their own issues, such as health care, housing, clean water and racism.

Mobilizing young women is one of the challenges facing the Manitoba women's movement in the 1990s. Addressing the issues of working-class and coloured women is another. Although the province has a large Native and immigrant population with urgent issues, the mainstream women's movement has not been able to address their problems. Instead, coloured women choose to form their own organizations and fight their own battles, partly because they fear racism and associate the women's movement with white, middle-classs women,[66] and partly because their concerns are closely linked to broader issues such as Native self-determination and access to economic resources.

The women's movement seems to be on the threshold of a new phase in trying to deal with new issues. Although a sound base has been built by the generation of women interviewed for this chapter, it is impossible to tell how a new generation of Manitoba women will meet the new challenges they now face.

NOTES

1. Ellen Kruger, interview with author.

2. June Menzies was among the founders of the Manitoba Action Committee on the Status of Women. In 1977, she became the vice-chairperson of the Federal Anti-Inflation Board, pressing for the rollback of negotiated wage settlements at the Health Sciences Centre where the majority of the employees were women, and where increases were an attempt to bring about pay equity (see *Action*, June-July 1977). Muriel Smith, a former minister of community services in the Pawley government, chaired the MACSW in 1975. In 1984, as a cabinet minister, she faced a group of pro-choice demonstrators. She was cast in the role of government apologist at a time when the provincial government refused to accredit Dr. Morgenthaler's clinic.

3. From a discussion with Linda Taylor, Ellen Kruger, Sari Tudiver, Susan White and Millie Lamb, 5 January 1987.

4. Some feminists will say that feminism is a cohesive ideology. However, it is important to note the different definitions of feminism, and different philosophies on political and economic issues.

5. Susan White and Millie Lamb, interview with author.

6. These include such organizations as the Native Women's Transition Centre, the Coalition on Native Child Welfare (which played an important role in the regionalization of child welfare services in Manitoba, leading to the establishment of Ma Mawi Wichi Itata family resource centre), the Congress of Black Women, the Winnipeg Council of Self-Help (which in 1982 became the Manitoba Anti-Poverty Organization), the Original Women's Network, the Indigenous Women's Collective, and others.

7. It was Thelma Forbes, then provincial Conservative minister of urban development, who approached Dr. Nan Murphy, then chairperson of the Manitoba Volunteer Committee, and suggested Murphy organize the women in the province to prepare a major brief to the royal commission. Murphy and June Menzies (then vice-president of the Volunteer Committee) spearheaded the efforty. They held a series of meetings in rural Manitoba in cooperation with the Manitoba Women's Institute and various church groups and broke new ground by raising the issue of the status of women in Manitoba.

8. June Menzies was president, Win Loewen was vice-president, Jean Carson was secretary and Donalda Merton was treasurer.

9. Millie Lamb, who was at the meeting at which the MACSW was formed (January 1971), remembers that some of the women were opposed to the word ''action'' in the group's title, fearing it would sound militant. Two years later, *Action* became the name of the bimonthly MACSW newsletter.

10. Joan Carson, interview with author.

11. Ibid.

12. Transcript of the skit and the discussion which followed at the Brunkild meeting was supplied by Jean Carson.

13. Nan Murphy, interview with author.

14. Ellen Kruger, interview with author.

15. Linda Taylor, interview with author.

16. Whether or not women's energies are well used in involvement with the NDP, the contradictions and limitations of social democracy have remained significant issues for many of the women who were in that group.

17. Millie Lamb, interview with author.

18. The Nellie McClung Theatre Group is still flourishing, giving almost fifty public performances in 1985. Millie Lamb, interview with author.

19. Ibid.

20. Ellen Kruger, interview with author. Kruger was among the women who met in Lamb's living room. She remained in the group until it was dissolved and now heads the Coalition for Reproductive Choice.

21. Ibid.

22. Ibid.

23. *Action* (January 1972).

24. Ellen Kruger, Linda Taylor, Jean Dunmire, interviews with author.

25. *Action* (June 1974).

26. Ibid., (June 1973).

27. Jean Dunmire, interview with author.

28. *Action* (October 1972), 2.

29. Jean Dunmire, interview with author.

30. Ibid.

31. Ellen Kruger, interview with author.

32. Sue White, in *Action* (July 1974).

33. Ellen Kruger, interview with author.

34. *Action* (July 1975).

35. Two feminists, Sharon Corne and Marion Yeo, fought hard against difficult odds to stage "Woman as Viewer" at the Gallery. The Women's Committee of the Gallery had already organized a show containing images of women, created by men. Feminists wanted to show images created by women.

36. Bishop was instrumental in setting up the first pre-trades course for women at the Red River Community College in 1976.

37. Millie Lamb, interview with author.

38. *Action* (1971).

39. Linda Taylor, interview with author.

40. *Action* (1971).

41. The Women's Labour Caucus did research on working conditions, women's wages and sexism in various work places. It also began to work with immigrant women in the garment industry (Millie Lamb, interview with author). During the 1970s, there was an increase in the number of women in trade unions in Manitoba, and significant developments in the area of women and labour. Unfortunately, a full consideration of women and labour is outside the scope of this study.

42. *Confronting the Stereotypes: Handbook on Bias*, researched and written by Women for Non-Sexist Education, under the sponsorship of the Manitoba Human Rights Commission and the Department of Education, 1977.

43. Jean Carson, interview with author.

44. Alice Steinbart, interview with author.

45. Ibid.

46. Jean Carson, interview with author.

47. Alice Steinbart, interview with author.

48. *Action* (October 1978).

49. Alice Steinbart, interview with author.

50. Later, the pregnancy information service was moved to Klinic on Broadway. In 1981, it developed into the Women's Health Clinic, the only women's health clinic in Canada. Today it has a staff of fifteen, and a yearly budget of $250,000.

51. Ellen Kruger, interview with author.

52. Ibid.

53. Linda Taylor, interview with author.

54. Ibid.

55. Ibid.

56. Ellen Kruger, interview with author.

57. The Socialist Women's Collective included lesbian socialists. Some women in the collective formed a women's literature group which still meets.

58. Ellen Kruger, interview with author.

59. Millie Lamb, interview with author.

60. Brigitte Sutherland, interview with author.

61. Ibid.

62. Margie Cogill, interview with author.

63. Ibid.

64. Maureen Smith, interview with author.

65. Margie Cogill and Lydia Giles, interviews with author.

66. Louise Champagne, interview with author.

SECTION FOUR

The Dynamics of Household Formation and Changing Forms of Struggle

That progressive change is largely attributable to various forms of political struggle is a central theme of this book. The family, and matters related thereto, are important focal points for various forms of struggle — personal, economic, ideological and political. The structure of, work arrangements within, and ideology related to the family or household contribute to the oppression of women, and are crucial factors in the broader understanding of political economy. The chapters in this section are empirically detailed studies of aspects of the family or household in Manitoba. John Hofley describes and considers some implications of the dramatically changing structure of Manitoban and Canadian households. Patrick Falconer describes and analyzes various aspects of a particular family structure: female-headed, single-parent, urban Native families.

The concept of "the family" is not a given. Michele Barrett has observed that the family "does not exist other than as an ideological construct, since the structure of the household, definition and meaning of kinship, and the ideology of 'the family' itself, have all varied enormously in different types of society."[1] Hofley demonstrates that the structure of the family has varied enormously within Canadian and Manitoban society in recent decades. He situates these changes in the context of the dynamics of economic change: the economy affects the structure of the family; the changing structure of the family has a reciprocal impact upon the economy. Such relationships are complex and multidimensional, and care must be taken not simply to reduce the conceptualization of the family to changes in the economic sphere. But whatever the complexity the family, and its interrelationship with economic change and political struggles, cannot be abstracted from the study of political economy.

"Family" is an emotionally and ideologically laden concept. Its ideological character and its importance in political struggles have been made clear by the great resurgence of the women's movement in the 1960s and 1970s, and more recently by the ideological use of "the family" by the Right, and by neoconservative governments like those of Ronald Reagan and Margaret Thatcher. The Right has seen the importance to people's belief systems of their immediate household arrangements and their daily tasks of living, and have shaped their ideology accordingly. The Right's call for a return to the patriarchal, two-parent family and its "traditional" values has struck an ideological chord in times of rapid socioeconomic change.

But this concept of family is a simplistic and ideological construct. Hofley examines the concept of the family, making obvious its complexity and its centrality to the study of political economy. It follows from his analysis that the Left has not placed household arrangements and the daily tasks of life sufficiently at the centre of its politics, but for the most part has seen politics and the family as separate issues. It is important to confront the simplistic stereotypes of the Right, and to analyze the problems of real family structures, and then build from such analyses both policy solutions and political movements. Patrick Falconer's chapter attempts to do just that.

Falconer looks at a particularly important example of the changing household forms described by Hofley — the female-headed, single-parent, urban Native family — in the context of Native migration to prairie cities. Urban migration and associated problems are best understood in the kind of context provided earlier in this volume by Phillips, Bailey and St.-Onge. The precondition of the opening of the Canadian west was the dispossession of the original Native inhabitants. Forced onto reserves characterized by underdevelopment, or in many cases no development, Natives were marginalized and impoverished. Their subsequent migration to prairie urban centres is fraught with difficulties whose origins must be traced to the violence and racial bigotry associated with the "clearing of the commons."

What Falconer finds is that the most common form of urban Native household is headed by a young, female single parent, that a very high proportion of these households are living in poverty, and that this family structure may be a mechanism through which Native disadvantage is perpetuated. These characteristics combine to make the unique needs of female-headed, single-parent, urban Native families particularly urgent.

Falconer offers the outlines of a practical research and policy agenda in response to these needs. He recommends initiatives which would address the abject poverty of urban Native single mothers, and the intergenerational impact of this poverty, as well as the overrepresentation of Native single mothers in urban areas. Most importantly, he stresses the centrality of the political struggle waged by Natives, and particularly Native women, if gains are to be made in seeking solutions to the problems.

What Falconer concludes is that single-parent, female-headed, urban Native families have been, for the most part, excluded from the male-dominated Native movement. While Native leaders have begun to place an increased emphasis on Native family issues — especially child welfare — the emphasis has been on Native political control of service delivery and on repatriation of Native children to Native communities. The concrete needs of real Native families tend to be secondary for most Native leaders, and the ideology and politics of the existing patriarchal family is not seriously questioned. Ironically, as Reinart argued earlier, the women's movement has also largely ignored Native women and their concerns. What follows from Falconer and Reinart is that both the Native movement and the women's movement need to bring the real needs of Native women to the fore.

NOTES

1.   Michele Barrett, *Women's Oppression Today* (London: Verso, 1980), 199.

The Long Revolution in Canadian Families   8

John R. Hofley

We are in the midst of a long revolution in how families are formed, who makes up families, how family members see themselves and one another and, most importantly, the ways in which men and women relate. It is very difficult to know exactly where we are in time: are we at the start, somewhere in the middle, or towards the end of this revolution? This chapter suggests that the revolution began with the Industrial Revolution and the rise of capitalism. Since both capitalism and industrialization continue to change, it is impossible to know whether the 1980s represent an apex or not.[1]

"Political economy" is the term used in this book to describe and understand a province such as Manitoba. Almost all studies from a political-economy perspective neglect families and households in their analysis. This is a serious omission. The changes in the nature of Manitoba's economy and the types of households in which its citizens live are dialectical, that is, they have an impact upon one another. The state cannot ignore this relationship, nor can those of us who examine social phenomena from a socialist or social democractic perspective.

These changes are important to understand because they will produce consequences that are still unclear, yet will require policy decisions in the near future. For example, Falconer's chapter, "The Overlooked of the Neglected: Native Single Mothers in Major Cities on the Prairies," demonstrates that Native single-parent families are four times as prevalent as non-Native urban families. His account of the reasons for the prevalence of this type of family arrangement is rooted in a political economy perspective in which "the single-parent family is a primary mechanism through which Native disadvantage is perpetuated in urban areas." The policy suggestions he makes about housing, income, welfare, jobs, nutrition and schooling flow from an explicit recognition of the economic and demographic conditions of urban Natives.

The basic premise of this chapter is that the economic system of a society constrains and shapes production and reproduction, and in the process modifies family organization. This relationship between the economic system and families is not a simple, unidirectional one. Families do not simply react passively to economic changes. For example, the existence of different types of families often exerts pressures on corporations to provide benefits such as maternity leave, flexible work hours, day care and pension reforms. In addition, different types of families consume goods and services in dissimilar ways, hence the production of certain goods and services has to be altered. Also, capital accumulation through the tax system may be affected by changes in families, such as having fewer children, combining children and a job, or obtaining a divorce. In a real sense, the family is also the institution which mediates between the system and individuals.[2] The only other institution in our society with which the family shares this mediating function is the school.

The above sets of forces operate largely at a macro level, but their consequences affect our everyday lives. It is one thing to recognize, for example, that approximately 56 percent of married women work for wages outside of the home; it is quite another thing for a wife, husband and their children to adjust their daily schedules, their hopes and expectations about their roles for one another, and their division of labour concerning housework. Yet this adjustment must be made. It is often made with considerable stress, pain and anger. It is well to remind ourselves that changes create opportunities and difficulties. It is inside the household that such changes will be wrought.

When we use a word such as "family," it is almost impossible to avoid powerful images, positive as well as negative. Much of the current debate about feminism, reproductive choice, sexual orientation, pay equity, family law and family violence is ideological. Groups such as Pro-Choice or REAL Women, as well as persons who are part of the New Right or Moral Majority, argue about these issues from the premise that the heterosexual nuclear family is a "natural" form. This same premise permeated the 1986 Throne Speech from the Progressive Conservative government in Ottawa. The speech had a number of references to the "family," all of which carried positive connotations. Yet we are now acutely aware that many very negative things occur in families, including child abuse, spousal abuse and incest. Why do we ignore the negative?

The primary reason is that much of the vocabulary surrounding the family is ideological. An ideology about the family is socially constructed and usually serves to reinforce a particular set of economic, demographic and class interests. An ideology is based on what we are told to think about the family, not on a sound knowledge of either history or the present.

An ideology that starts with a premise that the natural family is heterosexual and nuclear prevents a person, group or government from exploring the historical forces that have shaped families in the past and continue to shape them today. Neither Reinart's earlier chapter nor Falconer's chapter that follows begin with this ideological premise. Rather, they explore the historical conditions that gave rise to various streams of feminist activity in Manitoba, and the rise of a type of family among urban Natives that is neither the extended family found in preliterate Native societies, nor the nuclear family found in many urban non-Native peoples.

Falconer's analysis of the urban Native family reveals that the ideological notion of the family as an homogeneous entity is false. Variations in family types do not signify "abnormality." Rather, they demonstrate that just as the heterosexual, nuclear family arose in response to the forces of capitalism and industrialization, single-parent families among urban Natives arose in response to the economic, racial and sexual conditions of Canadian Natives on reserves and in prairie cities.

We carry in our heads and hearts many assumptions about family life. Children and parents do not necessarily see their own family in similar ways. Outsiders to a given family may think they see and know what is going on inside that family, but we know that is often not true. For example, we are often surprised when a friend's marriage breaks up or that a neighbour is found guilty of abuse or assault. Men/husbands/fathers tend to see the family in which they are involved quite differently than do women/wives/mothers. In *Women's Work*, Ann Oakley remarked that "the institutionalization of the housewife role as the primary role for all women means that an expansion of their world outside the home is retarded by the metaphor, and the reality, of the world looked at through the window over the kitchen sink."[3] I might add that males often see the family through the window by their desk, in the workshop or the factory. For women, the family is the engine of their lives; for men, it is the caboose. We must all examine our own assumptions, for they will influence not only our daily lives, but the way in which we will reflect upon the changes in families over time.

We have witnessed between 1941 and the present a number of dramatic transformations that have affected families: World War II, the rise of massive retail trade and financial institutions, a sexual revolution that has virtually destroyed the "double standard," a feminist movement that has struggled for the right to equality, a sharp decline in the number of children born, and a rapid increase since 1968 in the number of separations and divorces. The most critical transformation since World War II has been in the nature of capitalism and its labour force demands.

The Labour Force

By World War II, the vast majority of Canadians who had jobs worked for a wage. This wage was earned outside the household and the members of the household depended on it. The nineteenth century had seen a steady decline in the number of married women who contributed directly, through wage labour, to the economy of the household. While wage labour made the man and his family vulnerable to changing economic conditions and often severe unemployment, it placed the female in an even more precarious position. She was dependent on the male for her living and she became more and more isolated from society by remaining in a home or apartment. As work came to be seen as an activity associated with a wage, housework became devalued. It was given lip service in our ideology about families, but little else. There were women, such as the suffragettes, who struggled against these developments, but it was not until the 1960s that these struggles by and for women became powerful.

The feminist movement became strong largely because of the changes in the nature of capitalism begun between 1941 and 1961. During this period Canada's economy moved from one that was based largely on the primary and industrial sectors (employing mostly males) to an economy dominated by the financial, retail and service sectors (employing mostly females). These changes allowed married women to enter the labour force in significant numbers, albeit at wages considerably below those of men. The inequality in the market place reinforced the inequalities in the household; women became conscious of patriarchy (male dominance). These changes in the nature of capitalism and in labour force participation rates of married women have led to changes in educational attainments of women, marriage/divorce/separation rates, and in the variety of household types presently found in Canada, all of which have then reinforced the changes in the nature of capitalism.

TABLE 24

DISTRIBUTION OF LABOUR FORCE, BY SECTOR AND SEX, CANADA, 1941-1981

	1941		1951		1961		1971		1981*	
	M	F	M	F	M	F	M	F	M	F
Primary[1]	39.1	2.5	19.4	3.1	17.8	5.1	11.3	4.7	9.5	3.6
Industrial[2]	29.3	22.4	35.0	25.0	35.3	17.8	36.1	16.6	34.0	18.6
Transportation[3]	7.4	2.4	8.7	4.3	8.3	3.7	7.8	3.2	11.5	3.9
Trade & Service[4]	19.7	60.3	22.0	54.6	26.8	58.1	30.0	56.8	37.9	67.9
Education & Government 1941-71; Government only 1981	4.4	12.5	7.9	13.1	11.7	15.4	14.8	18.6	7.1	6.0
Total	3,322,521	827,914	4,072,366	1,146,232	4,568,034	1,698,828	5,286,070	2,659,970	7,229,000	5,000,000

*Notes: The categories were changed in 1976 hence it is difficult to make comparisons between 1981 and previous years; e.g. education no longer separate, after 1976; [1]Includes agriculture, forestry, fishing and trapping, coal mining and other mining; [2]Includes foods and beverages, leather and rubber, textiles clothing, wood products, metals, chemicals, electricity and gas, and construction; [3]Includes railways and transportation; [4]Includes retail and wholesale trade, finance, services, food and lodging, personal and recreational.

Source: Statistics Canada, *Historical Estimates*, Cat.: 71-529.

In 1941, about 40 percent of Canadians were working in primary industries such as agriculture, fishing, mining and lumber (see Table 24). By 1951 this proportion dropped dramatically to 20 percent. By 1968, only ten percent were employed in this sector of the economy. In 1941, 60 percent of Canadians worked in either the primary or industrial sectors. By 1961 this had dropped to 45 percent, and by 1981 to 35 percent. Table 25 documents these shifts between 1931 and 1971.

TABLE 25

LABOUR FORCE CHANGES IN CANADA BY GENDER, 1931-1971
(Thousands)

	Men			Women		
	1931	1971	% Change	1931	1971	% Change
Managerial	211	594	182	11	86	709
Professional-technical	125	602	382	118	475	304
Commercial Proletariat[1]	450	1,171	160	390	1,627	317
Resource Proletariat[2]	142	140	-1	—	—	—
Industrial Proletariat[3]	1,035	1,911	85	105	289	176
Transport/Communications	187	392	110	16	40	148
Agriculture	1,094	400	-63	24	100	318
Not classified	—	439	—	—	664	—
Total	3,244	5,649	74	664	2,960	346

Notes: [1]Commercial proletariat includes clerical, commercial, financial, sales, and service; [2]Resource proletariat includes fishing, hunting and trapping, logging, mining, and quarrying; [3]Industrial proletariat includes manufacturing, mechanical, construction, and labourers.

Source: Wallace Clement, "Canada's Social Structure: Capital, Labour and the State, 1930-1980," in Michael S. Cross and Gregory S. Kealey, eds., *Modern Canada, 1930-1980's*, (Toronto: McClelland and Stewart, 1984), 85.

In addition to these important changes in the nature of our capitalist economy, there was a massive movement of women into the paid labour force. In 1941, about 20 percent of women were working for pay (see Table 26). By 1986, over 50 percent of all Canadian women over fifteen years of age were in the labour force. The same pattern was found in Manitoba. Both nationally and provincially, the proportion of males in the labour force declined between 1941 and 1986 by about 7 percent.

TABLE 26

LABOUR FORCE PARTICIPATION RATES BY SEX,
FOR CANADA AND MANITOBA, 1941-1981

Year	Canada		Manitoba	
	Female	Male	Female	Male
1941*	20.7	85.8	19.3	85.4
1951	24.1	83.8	24.2	82.6
1961	29.5	77.7	31.5	78.1
1971	39.2	75.7	41.7	77.2
1981	51.7	78.4	52.2	78.2
1986	55.3	77.3	56.5	77.9

*Note: Before 1951, the "Gainfully Occupied" concept was used rather than the "Labour Force" concept.
Source: Statistics Canada, *The Labour Force*, Cat.: 71-001, 1986, Table 6.

In both Manitoba and Canada, the patterns are almost identical (see Table 27). There has been a slight decline in the proportions of single men and women in the labour force, due most likely to the increasing numbers of such persons attending postsecondary institutions. There are fewer married men in the labour force (a decline of 8 percent from 1951 to 1986), but for married women the increase is revolutionary. In 1951, about ten percent of married women worked outside the home; by 1986 more than 50 percent did.

TABLE 27

LABOUR FORCE PARTICIPATION RATES BY SEX AND MARITAL STATUS,
FOR CANADA AND MANITOBA, 1951-1986

Year	Canada				Manitoba			
	Single		Married		Single		Married	
	M	F	M	F	M	F	M	F
1951	76.6	58.4	90.0	11.2	76.9	60.2	88.0	11.9
1961	63.5	54.9	86.9	22.1	66.3	55.0	86.1	25.5
1971	63.5	53.5	84.4	37.0	67.3	55.6	84.6	40.4
1981	69.5	53.5	83.4	50.6	70.8	52.3	82.2	52.2
1986	71.5	54.5	80.5	55.7	73.4	56.2	80.3	56.7

Source: Statistics Canada, *The Labour Force*, Cat.: 71-001, 1986, Table 6.

In the past it was generally assumed that married women who were employed were either without children, or had children who were all in school. Table 28 indicates that since 1975 more and more married women with children under five years of age are in the labour force. Thus in 1975, 40 percent of married women with children between three and five years of age worked outside of the home. By 1986 this figure had increased to 60 percent. As the children get older the proportion of married women working increases to almost 70 percent.

TABLE 28

LABOUR FORCE PARTICIPATION OF WOMEN BY AGE
OF YOUNGEST CHILD, 1975-1986

Age of Youngest Child	1975 (%)	1981 (%)	1983 (%)	1986 (%)
< 3 years	31.2	44.5	48.9	54.3
3-5 years	40.0	52.4	55.6	60.0
6-15 years	48.2	61.1	62.0	69.3

Source: Statistics Canada, *The Labour Force*, Cat.: 71-001, 1986.

These vast changes in the labour force participation of married women with children have given rise to the day-care movement. Advocates of day care argued before the Cooke Commission that Canada's day-care system is in a state of crisis. On 30 March 1987, the government of Canada released its recommendations on day care. It basically ignored the majority of the briefs presented to the Cooke Commission about the need for more facilities and day-care spaces, advocating instead a system of tax credits so that parents could choose their own method of day care. Very few funds were designated for the provision of new spaces. As more and more women with children remain in the labour force, there will be continuing pressure placed on governments to provide more spaces. Table 29 documents that, even for preschoolers, only a small percentage is cared for in institutional settings. This may or may not be a ''bad'' thing. However, there is considerable evidence that the demand for more day-care facilities and spaces will not diminish.

TABLE 29

KINDS OF CARE FOR PRESCHOOL-AGE CHILDREN, 1981

Kind of Care	% of Working Couples	% of Single Parents
Nursery School or Kindergarten	37*	32*
Day Care Centre	13	36
Cared for in Own Home	33	37
Cared for in Another Private Home	52	33

*Note: Percentages do not add up because some children are cared for in two different ways.
Source: Statistics Canada, *Labour Force Survey Research Paper, No. 31*, 71-X512, October 1982.

There has been a remarkable increase in licensed day-care centres in Manitoba. For example, in 1974 there were thirty such centres and by 1982 there were three hundred.[4] However, the demand far exceeds the supply. A 1984 report for the Social Planning Council of Winnipeg found that only 40 percent of day-care users were utilizing licensed day-care centres.[5]

For a number of women in the labour force, the choice to remain at home with their children is not a real choice. They may be single parents, women whose husbands' income is not sufficient to support the family, or widows with no other source of income. The Canadian Council on Social Development has estimated that approximately 70 percent of women feel they must work outside the home. The estimate is the same for the United States.[6] For example, in husband/wife families where the wife is employed full-time she provides 40 percent of total income, while wives who work part-time provide 23 percent of total income.[7] These are major contributions.

For some, the choice may be real in terms of their economic situation, but they may feel that they do not want to remain at home. More and more women are attending universities and community colleges (see Table 30). In 1986, among women with college degrees, 79 percent were in the labour force. For those with high school, 56 percent were in the labour force. Only 25 percent of women with less than a grade eight education were in the labour force.[8] Women with postsecondary training are likely to be highly motivated individuals who are well aware of the economic costs to them if they do not pursue their careers or jobs after marriage.[9] These conditions will serve to encourage them, regardless of young children, to remain in the labour force or to minimize their time out of it.[10]

TABLE 30
FEMALE UNIVERSITY ENROLMENTS, 1970-1983

Year	Undergraduate Female as % of Total	Graduate Female as % of Total
1970-71	38.6	22.8
1975-76	46.2	29.5
1980-81	51.5	37.2
1982-83	52.1	39.5

Source: Statistics Canada, *Education in Canada*, Cat.: 81-229.

The present rate of separation and divorce also encourages women to remain in the labour force. Divorce often has drastic negative effects on women's standard of living. It is difficult to know exactly what the effect of divorce is on women's earnings because the category "single parent" or "female head" used by Statistics Canada includes women who are separated, widowed and never married. However, in 1983, 49 percent of all female single parents had incomes below the poverty line (21 percent of male single parents did), and by 1985 this had increased to 60 percent. Median incomes of female heads of families were approximately one-half of those families with male heads. Both marriage and divorce laws encourage each spouse to be as financially independent as possible. For example, the Family Maintenance Act stresses that "both parents are equally responsible for the financial support of their children," and that spouses "have a duty to financially support and maintain each other while living together." It also gives each spouse the legal right to all financial information. If one spouse does not provide this information, the other can obtain a court order and the spouse who withheld the information can be fined up to $5,000. Under the Divorce Act, upon separation, "each spouse must try to become self supporting and financially independent of the other."[11] Thus, a woman who remains outside the labour force for a lengthy period and then becomes divorced is encouraged to find work; this may be very difficult.

These changes in capitalism's labour force needs have had and will continue to have major consequences for Canadian families. One effect is that the vast majority of Canadians no longer see marriage, particularly for a lifetime, as automatic.

Marriages and Divorces

There has been a remarkable decline in the rate of marriage since the late 1960s. We are now below the rates found during the Depression. It is difficult to know exactly why this is occurring, but in part it is happening because the age of first marriage is rising. In 1985, one-half of all grooms married when they were over 25.6 years of age; for brides, one-half were over 23.7 years of age (see Table 31).

TABLE 31

MARRIAGE RATES AND AVERAGE AGE AT FIRST MARRIAGE, 1970-1985

	Marriage Rates*	Median Age	
		Brides	Grooms
1970	8.8	21.4	23.5
1975	8.7	21.5	23.6
1980	8.0	22.3	24.3
1985	7.3	23.7	25.6

*Note: Marriages per 1000 population.
Source: Statistics Canada, *Marriages and Divorces, Vital Statistics*, Cat.: 84-205.

Another factor is the number of common-law unions taking place in Canada, and an increase in cohabitation. Unfortunately, we do not have good historical data on such unions. However, in 1984 Statistics Canada published a Family History Survey which attempts to determine the incidence of cohabitation. They found that about 15.6 percent of males and 17.3 percent of females had cohabited at least once. A little less than one-half marry their commonlaw partner.

TABLE 32

DIVORCE RATES: SELECTED YEARS, 1921-1985

Year	Number	Crude Divorce Rate*
1921	558	6.4
1931	700	6.8
1941	2,462	21.4
1951	5,270	37.6
1961	6,563	36.0
1968	11,343	54.8
1969	26,093	124.2
1973	36,704	166.1
1976	54,207	235.8
1982	70,436	285.9
1983	68,567	275.5
1985	61,980	244.4

*Note: Crude Divorce Rate — Divorces granted per 100,000 population.
Sources: Statistics Canada, *Perspective Canada II*, 1977; *Marriages and Divorces*, Cat.: 84-205.

A third factor may be the incidence of divorce. Divorce rates increased enormously after the changes in legislation in 1968.[12] The rise in rates seems to have peaked in 1982, and we now see a decline in both the number of divorced persons and in the rate of divorce (see Table 32). The presence of children is not as strong a deterrent to divorce as it once was thought to be (see Table 33).

TABLE 33

DIVORCES BY NUMBER OF DEPENDENT CHILDREN, CANADA, 1969-1985

Number of Children	1969 Number	%	1982 Number	%	1985 Number	%
0	12,061	54.9	33,388	47.4	30,076	48.5
1	4,101	18.7	16,235	23.0	13,719	22.1
2	3,124	14.2	15,033	21.3	13,548	21.9
3	1,586	7.2	4,467	6.3	3,732	6.0
4	659	3.0	1,019	1.4	715	1.2
5+	453	2.0	294	0.4	190	0.3
Total	21,964	100.0	70,436	99.8	61,980	100.0

Source: Statistics Canada, *Marriages and Divorces*, Cat.: 84-205.

Over 50 percent of divorces granted in 1985 resulted in the creation of single-parent families. One of the major changes in families over the past twenty years is the increase in the number of single-parent families, and the decline in the number of such families produced by death (see Table 34). In 1971, 59 percent of single-parent families occurred due to the death of a spouse. In 1981 this had declined to 33 percent. Among single-parent families in 1981, 83 percent were headed by women. Many of these families are poor. In 1983, single-parent families headed by women constituted 9 percent of all families and 30 percent of all low-income families. Female heads of single-parent families earn about 55 percent of what male heads of such families earn. Thus women often take on a double burden upon divorce — the children and a low income.

TABLE 34

SINGLE-PARENT FAMILIES IN CANADA BY MARITAL STATUS, 1971-1981

Marital Status	1971 No. of Families	%	1981 No. of Families	%
Separated	61,295	16.0	221,342	31.0
Widowed	222,625	59.0	235,622	33.0
Divorced	57,880	15.0	185,641	26.0
Single	36,945	10.0	71,400	10.0
Total	378,745	100.0	714,005	100.0

Source: Statistics Canada, *Lone Parent Families*, 1984.

Despite the existence of advocacy groups such as "Fathers for Joint Custody," custody tends to be awarded to the woman. In 1970, in cases where husbands petitioned for the divorce, they received custody of the children in 40.2 percent of the cases; in 1985, this had *declined* to 32.4 percent (see Table 35). More and more, custody is being awarded to neither parent; of all children under eighteen in Canada in 1985, about 12 percent lived with neither parent.

TABLE 35

CHILDREN INVOLVED IN DIVORCES BY PARTY TO WHOM
CUSTODY WAS GRANTED, 1971-1985.

Petitioner and Person to Whom Custody Granted	1970	1976	1981	1985
Wife				
To wife	89.2	89.8	87.8	83.3
To husband	4.2	6.1	7.2	7.2
To other[1]	6.7	4.1	5.0	9.4
Total # of cases[2]	11,773	22,505	25,791	38,556
Husband				
To husband	40.2	38.2	37.4	32.4
To wife	40.5	50.8	52.9	49.8
To other[1]	19.2	11.0	9.7	17.8
Total # of cases[2]	5,211	11,709	17,824	17,780
Total				
To wife	74.2	78.9	77.9	72.8
To husband	15.2	15.0	15.8	15.2
To other[1]	10.5	6.1	6.3	12.1
Total # of cases[2]	16,984	42,203	62,434	56,336

Notes: [1]To other person or agency or no award of custody; [2]Cases include each child involved
in a divorce, not just total divorces.

Source: Statistics Canada, *Marriages and Divorces, Vital Statistics,* Cat.: 84-205.

These separation and divorce rates may create new types of families or households, often called "reconstituted families." The majority of divorced persons (estimated at 75 percent) eventually remarry. Among new marriages, about 15 percent involve a divorced person. In 1985, 52 percent of divorced women remarried men who were divorced; 48 percent of divorced men remarried women who were divorced.

Remarriages are not new. In the sixteenth to nineteenth centuries they were common. What makes these contemporary families quite different from anything we have had in the past is that they are due to divorce, not death. It is one thing to adjust to the death of a father or mother. It is quite another to adjust to the physical absence of a parent, interact with him or her on a sporadic basis, and then adjust to a second father or mother. We know very little about the impact of divorce upon family members, and even less about reconstituted families. What studies have been done do not show consistent patterns. We cannot say with any confidence that children and/or adults are positively or negatively affected by divorce and remarriage. However, it is clear that we have thousands of persons living in household arrangements that are quite different from the ideological norm of husband, wife and children.

As mentioned earlier, changing ideas about our sexuality and our sexual identity form an important part of the long revolution in families. These encompass the decline of the double standard in sexual behaviour, the growing consciousness of homosexuality and lesbianism, the feminist movement, the fight for reproductive control, including the abortion controversy, and the remarkable decline in fertility. These issues are not unique to the late twentieth century, but the manner in which they have coalesced is new. I would like to focus on just three aspects of these developments: fertility, childlessness and abortion.[13]

Fertility, Childlessness and Abortion

The decline in marriage rates, the increase in single-parent families, the large number of separations and divorces, and the changes in labour force participation of married women have affected the size of Canadian families (see Table 36). The average size of both households and families has declined remarkably since 1921. Family size has dropped by one person, that is, families are 25 percent smaller in 1981 than in 1921. Household size is smaller than family size because since 1971 the number of persons living alone in apartments or houses has increased significantly.

TABLE 36

SIZE OF HOUSEHOLD, FAMILY AND NUMBER OF CHILDREN, CANADA

Year	Average Size of Household	Average Size of Family	Average Number of Children
1921	4.63	4.38	2.32
1941	4.25	3.9	1.9
1961	3.9	3.9	1.9
1971	3.5	3.7	1.8
1981	2.9	3.3	1.4

Source: *Canada Year Book*, 1961, 1971, and 1980-81. Table 4.27.

The total number of live births has remained relatively constant since 1971 (362,187 births in 1971 and 367,227 in 1985), but fertility rates have declined for every age category, with the size of decline smallest among women aged 25-34. Table 37 shows some evidence to support the popular argument that older women are having children more often than in the past. The fertility rate for women aged 35-39 has increased from 19.4 in 1981 to 21.8 in 1985.

TABLE 37

LIVE BIRTHS AND AGE SPECIFIC FERTILITY RATES BY
AGE OF MOTHER,[1] 1971-1985

	Live Births by Age Group of Mother							
	15-19	20-24	25-29	30-34	35-39	40-44	45-49	All Ages
1971	40,188	124,310	108,824	48,778	20,370	5,728	373	362,187
1976	37,402	114,924	125,930	51,616	13,569	2,664	179	359,987
1981	29,062	110,552	135,598	67,681	15,331	2,080	113	371,346
1985	22,090	98,272	143,836	79,121	21,048	2,317	82	367,227

	Age Specific Fertility Rates[2] by Age Group of Mother							
	15-19	20-24	25-29	30-34	35-39	40-44	45-49	All Ages
1971	40.1	134.4	142.0	77.3	33.6	9.4	6.0	67.7
1976	33.4	110.3	129.9	65.6	21.1	4.3	3.0	60.3
1981	26.4	96.7	126.9	68.0	19.4	3.2	.2	56.7
1985	23.7	85.3	125.3	74.6	21.8	3.0	.1	55.1

Notes: [1]Live births by age of mother and age specific fertility rates do not include births in Newfoundland. Total live births do include births in Newfoundland; [2]Represents the number of live births born to women in each age group per 1,000 women in that age group.

Source: Statistics Canada, *Vital Statistics*, Cat.: 84-202, 84-204, 84-205.

Earlier we saw that Canadian women are marrying later and therefore we expect to find them having children at a later age. Table 38 supports this view. However, when we compare the age at first and second birth to median age of marriage (Table 31) we find that married women in the 1970s and 1980s are still having children relatively soon after marriage.

TABLE 38
MEDIAN AGE OF MOTHERS GIVING BIRTH TO
FIRST OR SECOND CHILD, 1971-1985*

	Median Age at First Birth	Median Age at Second Birth
1971	22.8	25.3
1972	23.1	25.6
1973	23.2	25.8
1974	23.4	26.1
1975	23.5	26.2
1976	23.6	26.3
1977	23.6	26.5
1978	24.0	26.6
1979	24.2	26.7
1980	24.3	26.9
1981	24.5	27.0
1982	24.6	27.1
1985	25.4	27.6

*Note: Excluding Newfoundland.
Source: Statistics Canada, *Vital Statistics*, Cat.: 84-001 and 84-204.

One reason for the decline in fertility is the increasing number of females who marry and remain childless (see Table 39). In 1981, 17 percent of women who had ever been married were childless. The percentage of women remaining childless has increased in each age category.

TABLE 39
EVER MARRIED WOMEN WHO ARE CHILDLESS, BY AGE GROUP, 1971, 1981

	1971		1981	
	Ever Married Childless Women	As a % of All Ever Married Women in that Age Group	Ever Married Childless Women	As a % of All Ever Married Women in that Age Group
15-19	38,665	49.7	48,175	64.9
20-24	224,545	42.0	309,140	54.0
25-29	137,320	20.7	261,835	30.0
30-34	54,885	9.4	129,955	14.2
35-39	42,445	7.4	70,010	9.3
40-44	47,105	8.2	45,625	7.3
45 and over	364,880	13.4	363,805	10.9
Total	909,850	15.8	1,228,550	17.2

Sources: Statistics Canada, *Census of Canada, 1971*, Cat.: 92-718; *Census of Canada, 1981, Population, Nuptiality and Fertility*, Cat.: 92-906.

The number of therapeutic abortions is also affecting the overall rate of fertility (see Table 40). The majority of abortions since 1976 have been performed on women under twenty-four years of age (60.3 percent in 1976 and 57.1 percent in 1984). Table 41 shows that having an abortion is by no means a decision taken only by single women.

Another important change concerning abortions is that in 1975, 8.6 percent of women having an abortion had had one previously; in 1984 this figure had risen to 19.6 percent.

TABLE 40

PERCENTAGE DISTRIBUTION OF THERAPEUTIC ABORTIONS, 1975-1984, BY AGE

Age Group	1976	1980	1982	1984
20	30.7	29.7	26.8	23.6
20-24	29.6	31.8	32.8	33.5
25-29	19.8	19.6	20.4	21.3
30-34	10.9	11.6	12.2	12.7
35-39	6.1	5.3	5.9	6.9
40+	2.9	2.0	1.9	2.0
N=	54,097	65,243	65,812	61,822

Source: Statistics Canada, *Therapeutic Abortions*, Cat.: 82-211.

With the appearance of the birth control pill in Canada in 1961, and with greater accessibility to therapeutic abortions, it was thought that the number of births to unmarried women would decline. However the rate of births to unmarried women has increased from 17.48 in 1961 to 23.89 in 1982 (see Table 42). A similar pattern has emerged for women under nineteen. Here the increase went from 12.42 births/1000 women in 1961 to 17.31 in 1982. A large majority of these women keep their children, thus creating another type of family or household, that of a single, never-married female and her child. Such households are created by the sexual revolution as well as the movement in law to emphasize the individual rights of a female to keep her child regardless of marital status. We do not have good data on these households but it seems reasonable to assume that many are and will remain poor. Their existence has already caused the state to alter some of its policies on welfare and education. For example, in Winnipeg all single-parent heads of households may qualify for welfare and they are *not* required to seek work. In other jurisdictions, this is not the case. In education, the provincial government, through its student loan policy, encourages such women to return to school. Support in the form of loans and bursaries is available for high school and postsecondary education. A number of groups in Winnipeg (YWCA, Salvation Army, Roman Catholic and United Churches) offer shelter, counselling and educational opportunities for pregnant, single, never-married women. This illustrates, once again, the close relationship between changes in families and the development of new social policies by the state.

TABLE 41

THERAPEUTIC ABORTIONS, 1984, BY AGE AND MARITAL STATUS

Age	% Single
20	96.7
20-29	69.2
30-39	28.4
40+	14.7

Source: Statistics Canada, *Therapeutic Abortions*, Cat.: 82-211.

Tables 36-42 have demonstrated that the last two decades have witnessed major changes in the fertility patterns of Canadian women. Technological changes in reproductive control mean that children no longer automatically follow a marriage, that sexuality and sexual orientation can be separated from fertility, and that becoming pregnant does not lead necessarily to a wedding.

TABLE 42

BIRTHS TO UNMARRIED WOMEN, CANADA, 1951-1985

Year	Number of Births		Fertility Rate/ 1000 Unmarried Women	
	All Ages	15-19	All Ages	15-19
1951	13,931	4,548	13.46	9.67
1961	19,581	7,731	17.48	12.42
1971	31,177	14,074	19.46	15.05
1981	45,501	17,354	22.41	16.38
1982	56,286	18,045	23.89	17.31
1985	59,604	15,698	not available	

Source: Statistics Canada, *Vital Statistics*, Cat.: 84-204.

There are many lifestyle options open to men and women today. In a real sense we can no longer talk about the family as if it were an homogeneous entity. What constitutes a family? Are two homosexuals cohabiting a marriage? If they adopt a child, are they a family? Rather than talking about families, we should speak about households. Canadians in the 1980s live in a variety of household arrangements (see Table 43). It is interesting to note that in 1981 only 42 percent of households fit the stereotype of a nuclear family, a decline of 5.4 percent since 1976. More persons are living alone (20.3 percent in 1981). The category "wife/husband with no children" consists of two types of situation, and unfortunately the data do not permit us to distinguish them clearly. Thus, included in the 23.2 percent of 1981 households which had no children are couples who are childless and couples who have had children who no longer live with them. Almost 10 percent of households are now single-parents.

TABLE 43

PRIVATE HOUSEHOLDS BY TYPE, CANADA, 1976, 1981

(Numbers in parentheses are in thousands)

Household Type	1976	1981
Single	16.6%	20.3%
	(1203.9)	(1681.1)
Two or More Unrelated	4.5%	4.5%
	(327.6)	(368.9)
Wife/Husband with Children	47.4%	42.0%
	(3442.2)	(3482.9)
Wife/Husband with no Children	23.8%	23.2%
	(1726.4)	(1921.0)
Single Parent	7.7%	7.7%
	(559.3)	(639.8)
Total Households	100.0%	100.0%
	(7261.4)	(8281.5)

Source: Statistics Canada, *Private Households*, 1976, 1981, Cat.: 92-904.

The variety of household arrangements extant in Canada today can best be seen in Figure 1. While every permutation and combination is not exhausted here (for example, a lesbian household in which there are either biological, or adopted or foster children), we can see clearly the heterogeneity of living arrangements.

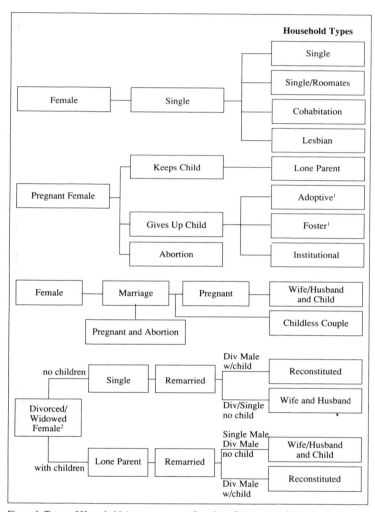

Figure 1. Types of Household Arrangements, as Seen from Perspective of Female

Notes: [1]These households, of course, may contain own biological children as well as foster and/or adopted children. [2]There is one important difference here, that if there are children, the divorced female and her children may have to interact with the father.

This chapter has shown that such heterogeneity results from the complex changes in our society which began long ago, and which fused in the 1970s and 1980s. As long as there is no significant shift in the nature of the capitalistic labour market, I cannot envisage any sudden change in the above patterns. The changes in household arrangements are found across Canada, with very little variation from province to province.

Manitoba does not exist in a vacuum, and some of its decisions cannot be made without consulting Ottawa (see Chapter 14). However, in such fields as human-rights legislation, welfare and education, the province can and should create policies that serve to meet the needs of all types of households, not just of those that fit the ideological norm of a heterosexual nuclear family.

It is true that Manitoba has taken some tentative steps to develop policies that are sensitive to changes in families. For example, Manitoba was the first province to institute a mandatory system of guaranteeing maintenance payments after separation or divorce, reducing the number of defaulted payments from 85 percent to 15 percent. This, however, does not address the more urgent need to guarantee that separated/divorced spouses and children have a decent standard of living or at least one that is consistent with the standard of living of the noncustodial spouse.

Another example of the state attempting to deal with these new realities occurred in June 1987, when the government submitted new human rights legislation that would guarantee protection against discrimination on the grounds of sexual orientation. While progressive, it leaves many questions unanswered. Does this mean that homosexuals/ lesbians should have the right to adopt children? What should a socialist position be on such a delicate issue? Do we have sufficient research on this topic that would help us arrive at a decision?

Falconer's chapter underscores the importance of developing social policies that deal with *real* families, not families that fit a preconceived ideological construct. A political economy approach to social analysis must place the heterogeneity of Canadian families in the forefront. Families experience our society in different ways. We cannot continue to develop policies that ignore these differences.

Members of families bring these different experiences to bear on social legislation. Reinart's chapter indicated that women see families differently than men. Through individual and collective effort many Manitoba women fought to change family law legislation. The changes in 1977 and 1978 testify to their success. The struggle over reproductive choice continues.

Both Falconer and Reinart also demonstrate that the foregoing analysis of the long revolution in Canadian families needs further elaboration by including class, race and gender. A political-economy perspective cannot continue to ignore the importance of family structures and their relationship to such factors. Much work remains to be done.

NOTES

1. See, for example, Michael Anderson, *Approaches to the History of the Western Family 1500-1914* (London: Macmillan, 1980); Barbara Ehrenreich and Deirdre English, *For Her Own Good: 150 Years of the Experts' Advice to Women* (Garden City: Anchor, 1979); Jean-Louis Flandrin, *Families in Former Times* (New York: Cambridge University Press, 1979); Michael Katz, *The People of Hamilton, Canada West: Family and Class in a Mid-Nineteenth Century City* (Cambridge: Harvard University Press, 1975); Joan Kelly, *Women, History and Theory* (Chicago: University of Chicago Press, 1984); Peter Laslett, *Household and Family in Past Time* (London: Cambridge University Press, 1972); Joy

Parr, ed., *Childhood and Family in Canadian History* (Toronto: McClelland and Stewart, 1982); Edward Shorter, *The Making of the Modern Family* (New York: Basic Books, 1975); Lawrence Stone, *The Family, Sex and Marriage in England, 1500-1800* (London: Weidenfeld and Nicolson, 1977); and Eli Zaretsky, *Capitalism, the Family and Personal Life* (New York: Harper and Row, 1976).

2. See Kelly, *Women, History and Theory.*

3. Ann Oakley, *Women's Work* (New York: Pantheon, 1974), 59.

4. Manitoba, *Consultative Paper on Day Care Standards for Manitoba* (Winnipeg: Minister of Community Services and Corrections, 1982).

5. *Child Care Needs and Realities in Winnipeg — 1984* (Winnipeg: Social Planning Council of Winnipeg, 1984).

6. For the United States, see *Time*, 23 June 1987, 46.

7. K. Cooke, *Report of the Task Force on Child Care* (Ottawa: Supply and Services Canada, 1986).

8. Statistics Canada, Catalogue # 71-001, May 1986.

9. The professions, such as medicine, law, pharmacy, dentistry, university teachers and engineers, have been basically male for a long time. However, in recent years the number of females entering and graduating from professional schools has increased. For example, in 1971, 10 percent of doctors were female; in 1981, 17 percent were. In law, 5 percent in 1971 and 15 percent in 1981 were female. Currently, our law and medical schools have female enrollments between 35-50 percent. As these women move through the system, the figures just cited will increase significantly.

10. The increase of women in certain jobs and careers may also affect the nature of these jobs in the future. For example, women are more willing to job-share, and may be less willing to put in the long hours often associated with careers in the professions.

11. Manitoba, *Family Law in Manitoba* (Winnipeg: Attorney General's Department, 1985).

12. It is too soon to tell if changes made in the Divorce Law on 1 January 1986 will have a similar impact. The basic change was in the reduction of the waiting period from three years to one year for a divorce on grounds of separation.

13. On some of these other issues see, for example, Pat and Hugh Armstrong, *The Double Ghetto*, 2nd ed. (Toronto: McClelland and Stewart, 1985); Michele Barrett and Mary McIntosh, *The Anti-Social Family* (London: Verso, 1982); Mary Daly, *Gyn/Ecology* (Boston: Beacon, 1978); Michel Foucault, *The History of Sexuality* (New York: Vintage Books, 1980); and Adrienne Rich, *On Lies, Secrets and Silences* (New York: W.W. Norton and Co., 1979).

9

The Overlooked of the Neglected:
Native Single Mothers in Major Cities on the Prairies

Patrick Falconer

Native migration to prairie cities had proceeded at a phenomenal rate over the last forty years. While reliable records have not been kept, estimates suggest that Winnipeg's Native population has grown fifty-fold between 1951 and 1981. Such a major demographic shift would seem to offer researchers rich ground for investigation. Given the limited educational qualifications and the resource-based employment background of a once predominantly rural population, Native migration to prairie cities would also seem to demand major public policy and programing initiatives.

Neither the research opportunities nor the policy demands have been enthusiastically embraced. Urban Native policy is not well developed at any of the three levels of government, and there is an almost complete absence of Native-specific programs operating in prairie cities. Indeed, government has chosen not to recognize urban Natives as a special client group.[1]

The academic community, a major contributor to public awareness and the policy development process, has fared only modestly better. Scant attention has been afforded Native urbanization, and the research which has been undertaken is problematic. First, published research offers little in the way of consensus: few researchers have explicitly sought to test previous findings, or to extend the elements of theory latent in the literature. Second, research has offered classifications of urban Natives which are of academic interest, but are not amenable to the development of concrete policy responses.[2]

The purpose of this chapter is to advance a research and policy agenda that appears long overdue, an agenda that addresses a distinctive feature of the urban Native community: the nature of its family composition. As a subject area, the relationship between urbanization and the Native family is poorly understood, and conflicting observations are found in the limited number of family-centred studies now available. Some researchers not only argue that the traditional role of the family among Natives differs from industrialized societal norms, but also that this role has been steadfastly maintained through the process of urbanization.[3] However, alternative evidence, suggesting limited Native success in preserving extended family relationships, has been presented in a recent series of studies published by the Institute of Urban Studies (IUS).[4] Their results indicate that most urban Native families are headed by single parents, and that Native single-parent families experience severe economic hardships relative to the rest of the urban Native community.

This study presents a descriptive analysis of urban Native families based on the 1981 Census of Canada. The findings support the thrust of the IUS research. Furthermore, as the census data provide the first opportunity to compare the circumstances of urban

Native single-parent families to those of other families throughout the prairie provinces, the study contributes a number of original findings.

First, the structure of Native households changes dramatically over geography with a number of significant patterns relating to urban proximity. Most notably, Native single-parent families are heavily concentrated in major cities. Further, major cities are also the location where Native single-parent families have the youngest age structure, are the most likely to live in poverty, and are most likely to be headed by women. In this regard, when reference is made to urban Native single-parents, we are concerned almost exclusively with single mothers.

Second, these patterns are largely specific to Native single-parent families, being much less evident in the case of their non-Native counterparts, and being uncharacteristic of two-parent families in general. Finally, the findings of this study, combined with the results of a recent study on Native education,[5] suggest that the single-parent family may be a primary mechanism through which Native disadvantage is perpetuated in urban areas.

Consequently, the study is at once both critical of, and pertinent to, urban Native research and policy development. The studies published through the IUS are singular among recent literature examining urban Native conditions in recognizing the numeric prominence of single-parent families and the strong relationship between household type and socioeconomic status. Most earlier studies failed to recognize these phenomena, and the government reports and discussion papers which followed did not incorporate household-based, socioeconomic analysis within their scope. While the former lack of recognition is lamentable, the continuing neglect raises serious questions as to the ability, or perhaps desire, of government to respond to new insights in urban Native circumstances. Government, however, is not alone in failing to respond, as it appears that most Native organizations — national, regional and urban-based — have not competently represented the interests of their single-parent constituents.

The findings of this study, buttressed by those of the IUS publications, also have significant theoretical and policy implications. On the theoretical front, the results raise more questions than they answer. To what extent does the migration of Native single mothers contribute to their predominance in urban areas? To what extent is it the result of either births out-of-wedlock or marital conflicts which take place in urban areas? What socioeconomic and cultural factors underlie these phenomena? How do single mothers relate to their extended families as well as the larger Native social and political community? What are the implications of the urban single-mother phenomenon for the analysis of Native acculturation? What are its implications for the study of the family in contemporary Native culture? These are but a few of the major issues raised by this study that will demand concerted attention in future research.

On a policy front, it is essential to recognize that the demographic characteristics of urban Natives do not parallel those of rural Natives. Moreover, many of the problems facing these two subpopulations are decidedly different in nature. Where limited economic opportunity continues to confront rural Natives, the breadth, depth and intergenerational influence of the disadvantage experienced by Native families headed by single mothers makes addressing their needs the foremost demand in urban Native policy development. Not only are policy and programming initiatives for this group urgently required, they are also entirely plausible.

But, as government has shown little interest in committing resources to urban Natives in the past, there is little reason to expect that the availability of new information alone, provocative though it may be, will displace bureaucratic and political indifference. The urban Native community, activists and progressive organizations can and should play significant roles in responding to the plight of urban Native single mothers, as urban Native women increasingly recognize the need to develop and mobilize their own political power.

A Critical Survey of Past Research

In the limited literature on Native urbanization, specific attention is infrequently given to the role of the family. In that which does, few works cover enough ground to yield results that are more than suggestive, and the results are often conflictual. A critical survey of these works will be valuable, however, in providing a context for the findings of the present study, and indicating the significance of the research agenda which remains to be addressed.

Research on migration is something of an exception to the above, as the influence of the family has often been noted, albeit not rigorously explored. The most common concern has been to establish the motives of migrants, and a general pattern has emerged from such efforts: the primary reasons for relocation are employment and family related.[6] While the former motive appears relatively straightforward, considering the limited wage-labour opportunities present in rural areas of Native settlement, the latter remains ambiguous, as it suggests both positive (to accompany a spouse) and negative (to escape family difficulties) factors. Little effort, however, has been invested in resolving this ambiguity.

Another related concern has been an examination of the demographic characteristics of recent migrants. Clatworthy found that the largest proportion of Native families migrating to Winnipeg was headed by single parents.[7] No rationale was advanced to explain this pattern, but Ryan has suggested that one contributing factor is the low priority afforded young Indian single mothers in the provision of scarce resources on reserves.[8] Thus they are forced to migrate for economic survival.

Migration has also been studied through attempts to identify traits that differentiate migrants who remain in urban centres from those whose residence is temporary. Graves and Arsdale found "stayers" had stronger economic goals than "leavers."[9] Chadwick and White, on the other hand, found acceptance of "white" culture and intermarriage with non-Natives to be the best indicators of long-term residency.[10] Weppner, in a third study, found that success in obtaining employment differentiated "stayers" from "leavers," and that married Natives were generally more attractive to prospective employers.[11]

The dynamics of urban Native marriage have also received attention. Garbarino argues that marital difficulties often arise out of different expectations brought to intimate relationships by urban-bred women and reserve-raised men.[12] Such women are said to expect companionship in marriage, while reserve men are said to see a wife in purely functional terms: as a domestic convenience or a sexual partner. Guillemin presents a similar if distinct perspective by suggesting that urban Native women see marriage as an opportunity to gain a respectable public identity useful in dealing with the social service bureaucracy, while Native men view it as a trap to be avoided.[13] The men's attitudes are said to be consistent with the traditional primacy of their relationship to the band and, as such, temporary cohabitation resulting in offspring is respected through extensive economic and child-rearing support provided by maternal relatives.

Research efforts have also explored the socioeconomic role of the urban Native family. Three competing perspectives have been advanced. The first suggests that the extended family is a cultural tradition of primary and positive influence in urban areas. From this view, the extended family is seen to cushion the shock of urban relocation, and to serve as a collective source of financial and emotional security.[14] Dosman, on the other hand, argues that close kinship relationships characterize only the urban Native poor for whom tradition now limits nuclear family stability: "members of the extended family are not inhibited about crashing, unconcerned about the enormous pressure on the home economy."[15] He contrasts this with the small class of upwardly mobile urban Natives for whom the extended family occupies a decidedly secondary role.

A third perspective, with a structural orientation, has emerged through the work of IUS researchers. Peters argues that urban Native family arrangements have been profoundly influenced by systemic economic forces.[16] She views the family as an adaptive coping mechanism, with single parenthood being encouraged by social assistance schemes that discriminate against two-parent families coupled with the marginal employment opportunities available to urban Native men.

A final area of research that has received attention pertains to the prevalence of different Native household arrangements in urban areas. Stanbury found the incidence of births to unmarried urban Native women to be half that of their reserve counterparts.[17] Siggner, in contrast, found illegitimate births to be more frequent among urban Native women, and that the gap was widening.[18] He suggested that an explanation for this disparity might be the influence of the discriminatory clause in the Indian Act which deprived a Native woman and her offspring of legal status if she married a non-Native man (the clause in question was amended in 1985). As such, Native women with non-Indian partners would find it advantageous to remain unmarried.

Clatworthy, and Clatworthy and Hull, offer the most detailed research to date.[19] They found that single-parent families were the most frequent urban Native household type, and that single parents were at least four times as common among the urban Native population as among urban non-Natives. Moreover, this high incidence was common to both the status Indian and the Métis and non-status Indian populations, a finding that brings the validity of Siggner's hypothesis into serious doubt.

As this brief survey suggests, the role of the family in Native urbanization has received infrequent and spotty attention. Among the demographic research, early studies suggest a relative paucity of Native single-parent families off-reserve, while more recent studies have found this household type to be the most prevalent. Some of the differences in findings can be explained by the distinct tribal and geographic focusses of the research, as well as by period-specific urban Native conditions. However, methodological inconsistencies appear to have played a major role.

Among the more interpretive works, conflicting assumptions appear to have had a significant influence. Three distinct assumption sets can be suggested. The first is a culturally static position that assumes traditional Native values and practices persist unaltered in urban areas. The second perspective reflects assumptions characteristic of "culture of poverty" theory, and submits that initial disadvantage in the affluent urban milieu has distorted these traditions which now act to reinforce Native poverty. The last perspective has a political-economy orientation which views Native domestic arrangements as rational coping responses to institutional pressures and the lack of economic opportunity.

Each of these approaches rests on limited and conflicting research. A partial test of the validity of the competing perspectives is offered by a return to demographic inquiry, as a central ambiguity in the debate involves the household composition of the urban Native population relative to both rural Natives and non-Natives generally.

Methodological Issues

The Prairies have the largest regional share of Canada's Native population, and five major cities with large and expanding Native communities. Consequently, much of the previous urban-based research has been done in this region, ensuring the relevance of this study to a large share of the literature.

The study is based exclusively on Indian and Northern Affairs Canada (INAC) customized data based on the 1981 Census of Canada. Definitions of some of the variables included will prove helpful. First, three populations are used: Registered Indians; Métis and non-status Indians (hereafter referred to as "other-Natives"); and non-Natives.

Second, three types of family-related variables are included. One variable differentiates between families with one parent, and those with two parents, of any marital status, living with one or more unmarried children. Two-parent families without children have thereby been excluded. A second variable refers to an individual's position with the family (single mother, single father, wife, husband). In this case, the data do not allow husbands or wives in families with children to be differentiated from those in families without children. A final variable refers to the age of the oldest child in a family, with three age ranges (1-5, 6-17, and 18+). These age groups are in keeping with recent work in life cycle and family development stages, and will be respectively referred to as "young," "mature" and "older" families.

Third, a central concept is urban proximity. This concept implies both a geographic and a social dimension. In other words, we are talking about, on the one hand, the physical distance from a major urban centre and, on the other, about the level of interaction with mainstream socioeconomic institutions. Six different geographic settings have been developed as measures to operationalize the concept of urban proximity. Three of the settings refer to types of reserve, and conform to INAC classifications (remote, special access and on Crown land — referred to as "remote"; rural; and urban).[20] These reserve types are generally indicative of the geographic dimension. The next three geographic settings correspond to off-reserve areas by population and will be referred to as rural (rural and less than 5,000), small city (5,000-99,999), and major city (100,000+). These are more indicative of the social dimension of the concept.[21]

Fourth, poverty is a concept used throughout the study. This refers to total family incomes relative to the 1981 Statistics Canada "low income cut-off points," based on geography and family size.

Finally, two broad issues of reliability pertain to the data. First, although the 1981 census is said to be an improvement over its predecessors, there is reason to believe the undercoverage of the Native population continues.[22] Second, the limitations of census data in explanatory research should be recognized. As cross-sectional data, causal conclusions rely on observations made only at one point in time. The inherent problems involved are especially true for the study of Native conditions, as changes in the definitions of Native ethnicity from earlier censuses do not allow for longitudinal analysis. Hence, the data base used is most appropriate for exploratory and descriptive research; conclusive explanation must await the availability of longer-term evidence. Subsequent census data should permit some cross-sectional time series analysis to be done, enabling refinement of our understanding of change processes.

Patterns of Native Family Characteristics Over Geography

The results of the comparative analysis of the 1981 census data will be presented in two sections. The first concentrates on the demographic characteristics of household distribution, the relative frequency of single-parent families, the ratio of single mothers to single fathers, and the stage of maturation of families. Descriptive in intent, this emphasis will establish the context for the socioeconomic analysis presented in the second section. This second component of the study includes an examination of income-adequacy and educational qualifications as well as labour force indicators and possible intergenerational dynamics.

Demographic Patterns

As this study focusses on families containing children, it is important to review the frequency of such households at the outset. Figure 2 presents the percentage distribution of families with children for both subgroups of the Native population and the non-Native population by geographic setting.

Families with children comprise a substantial majority of Native households throughout the Prairies. In contrast, families with children comprise only about one-half of all non-Native households. Distributional variation exists for each of the populations. However, these are generally rather minor. Notably, among each population, families with children are least common in major cities. Among urban Natives, nonetheless, families with children still comprise a large majority.

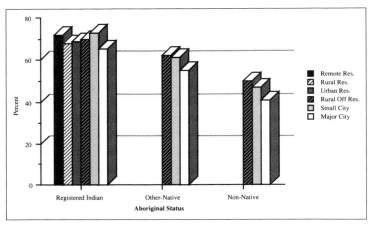

Figure 2. Families with Children as a Percentage of All Households by Aboriginal Status and Urban Proximity, Prairie Provinces, 1981

Source: INAC Customized Data Based on the *Census of Canada, 1981*.

When households containing children are broken down by parental status, as in Figure 3, more significant differences appear. Most evident is the consistently and significantly larger proportion of Native families led by single parents. Where geographic comparison is allowed for, Native single-parent families are roughly twice as common as non-Native.

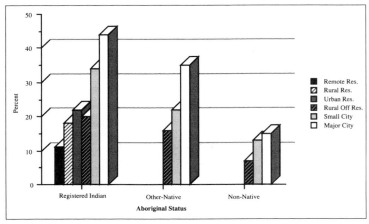

Figure 3. Single-Parent Families as a Percentage of All Families with Children by Aboriginal Status and Urban Proximity, Prairie Provinces, 1981

Source: INAC Customized Data Based on the *Census of Canada, 1981*.

The frequency of single-parent families among all three populations increases with urban proximity. However, this pattern is greatly magnified for the Native subgroups. Among registered Indians, the proportion of single-parent families doubles from remote reserve to urban reserve setting, and doubles again from urban reserve and rural off-reserve settings to major cities. This trend also exists for other-Natives, while it is much less marked, but still significant, for non-Natives.

The actual percentage increases of single-parent families among the three populations provide even greater contrast. Whereas Native single parents are about 10 percent more common than non-Native single parents in rural areas, they are roughly 25 percent more common in major cities. In short, although the frequency of single-parent families increases with urban proximity for all three populations, this relationship is significantly more pronounced for the Native subgroups.

Another pattern associated with urban proximity relates to the ratio of single mothers to single fathers. Figure 4 presents this ratio for each population by geography. Here again, the pattern is much more marked for Natives. Among registered Indians, single mothers outnumber single fathers by roughly three to one on reserves. While no registered Indian single fathers were counted in rural off-reserve settings,[23] this population's single mothers outnumber single fathers by about twelve to one in major cities. Among other-Natives, single mothers outnumber single fathers by four to one in rural settings, eight to one in small cities, and fourteen to one in major cities. In contrast, non-Native single mothers outnumber non-Native single fathers roughly three to one in rural settings, a ratio that increases to only five to one in small and major cities.

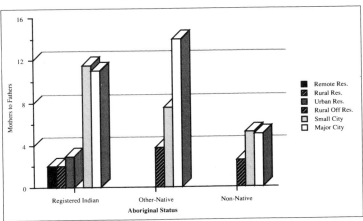

Figure 4. Ratio of Single Mothers to Single Fathers* by Aboriginal Status and Urban Proximity, Prairie Provinces, 1981
*Note: No Registered Indian single fathers were counted as residing in rural off reserve
          settings. As such, a ratio can not be calculated.
Source: INAC Customized Data Based on the *Census of Canada, 1981.*

As the ratio of single mothers to single fathers appears to be related to urban proximity, so too is the age structure of single-parent families (patterns concerning family age structure are described in the text only). Among registered Indians, one in every two single-parent families on remote reserves contains an adult child. This proportion of older single-parent families decreases dramatically with urban proximity: in major cities older families comprise less than one in every five registered Indian single-parent families.

A similar trend also describes the age structure of other-Native single-parent families. In the case of this Native subgroup, older single-parent families are twice as common in rural settings as in major cities.

Variation is also evident in the age structure of non-Native single-parent families as well as the two-parent families of each of the three populations. However, regular patterns are not associated with urban proximity.

Due to the Native single-family specificity of the pattern, dissimilarities between the age structures of Native and non-Native single-parent families are greatest in major cities. Native single-parent families in major cities are considerably younger than non-Native single-parent families. Young single-parent families (oldest child aged 0-5) are twice as common among Natives as among non-Natives. In contrast, older families are roughly three times more common among non-Natives than among Natives.

The age structure of Native single parents in major cities is also much younger than their non-Native counterparts. Figure 5 presents the percentages of single mothers in major cities who are young (aged 15-24) and elderly (65+) among the three populations. Young women comprise more than 20 percent of Native single mothers, and are more than twice as common among Native as non-Native single mothers. In contrast, elderly women are five times more common among non-Natives than Natives.

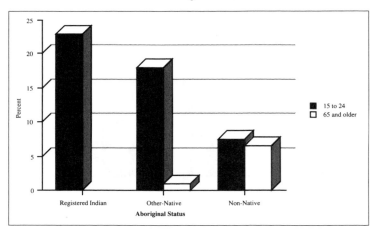

Figure 5. Youth and Elderly as a Percentage of Single Mothers by Aboriginal Status, Major Cities in the Prairie Provinces, 1981

Source: INAC Customized Data Based on the *Census of Canada, 1981*.

To summarize, the analysis of family demographics reveals three very significant patterns that are either exclusive to, or greatly accentuated for, Native single parents. One pertains to the incidence of single-parent families. The second relates to the ratio of single mothers to single fathers. The third concerns the age structure of families and single parents. In each case, these patterns are closely related to degree of urban proximity. In major urban areas, Native single parents are the most heavily over-represented, are almost exclusively headed by women, and tend to be in the earliest stages of family development.

These patterns provide a provocative context for the socioeconomic analysis which follows: the demographic characteristics of urban Native single-parent families are significantly different from both their rural Native counterparts, and urban non-Native single parents. If the limitations confronting single parents in mainstream society (poverty, lack of education, lack of opportunity) also confront Native single-parent families, then they describe the situation of nearly one-half of all Natives heading families in major cities. Moreover, if youth, gender and minority group status reinforce these limitations, then urban Native single mothers are especially vulnerable. The patterns also suggest the need for types of explanatory models which are yet to be adequately developed in the academic literature on Native urbanization. A brief discussion of such theoretical issues will be taken up in the conclusion.

Socioeconomic Patterns

As will be recalled, the literature on Native urbanization suggests that one of the primary motives behind decisions to migrate is to seek improved employment oppor-tunities. The patterns presented in this section suggest that while urban Native two-parent families do indeed enjoy greater fortune, the economic situation of Native single-parent families is worse in major cities than in rural settings. Such evidence is shown in Figure 6, which presents the incidence of poverty by family type and geographic setting.

Income inadequacy characterizes the situation of most registered Indian families on-reserve, where the incidence of poverty for single-parent families is only slightly greater than for two-parent families. Poverty, however, becomes significantly less common for registered Indian two-parent families off-reserve, while it becomes significantly *more* frequent for registered Indian single-parent families, peaking in major cities. Similar patterns also hold for other-Natives. Two-parent families are only slightly less likely than single-parent families to be poor in rural areas, but thereafter their fortunes diverge. As a result, Native single-parent families are roughly twice as likely to be poor as Native two-parent families in major urban centres.

Among non-Native single- and two-parent families, the incidence of poverty is lowest in major cities. In comparative terms, poverty affects more than twice the proportion of Native as opposed to non-Native single-parent families in this setting. In still greater contrast, urban Native single-parent families are roughly nine times more likely to be poor than urban non-Native two-parent families.

One demographic feature of urban Native single-parent families that may partially explain their extremely high incidence of poverty is the young age structure of these households. Figure 7 presents the incidence of poverty among single-parent families in major cities by age group of oldest child. Although the stage of family development appears to explain the incidence of poverty among non-Native single-parent families, it is far less applicable to Natives. While the incidence of poverty drops significantly between young and mature families and again between mature and older non-Native single-parent families, the incidence for Native single-parent families decreases much less substantially.

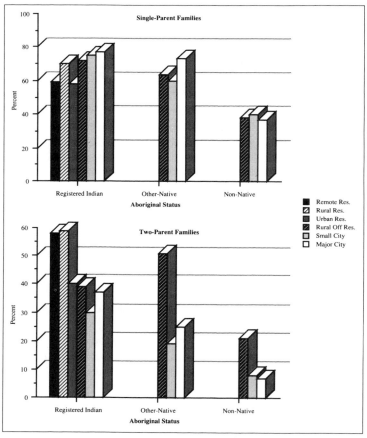

Figure 6. Incidence of Poverty* Among Families with Children by Aboriginal Status and Urban Proximity, Prairie Provinces, 1981

*Note: Poverty is defined as total family income at or below the 1981 Statistics Canada low income cut-off points based on geography and family size.

Source: INAC Customized Data Based on the *Census of Canada, 1981.*

Another factor which might be advanced to explain the high incidence of poverty is welfare dependency. While such a measure was not included in the census variables, labour force indicators were. Figure 8 shows the employment rate of single mothers in major cities. Native single mothers have a much lower employment rate than non-

Native single mothers, even when age is taken into account. Young Native single mothers are nearly three times less likely to be employed than young non-Native single mothers. Among older single mothers, Natives are about one-half as likely to be employed as non-Natives. In percentage terms, the gap between the employment rate actually increases somewhat with age.

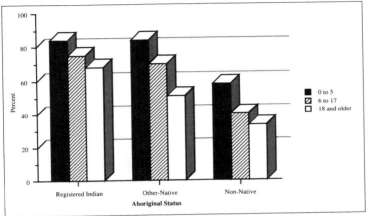

Figure 7. Incidence of Poverty Among Single-Parent Families by Age Group of Oldest Child and Aboriginal Status, Major Cities in the Prairie Provinces, 1981
Source: INAC Customized Data Based on the *Census of Canada, 1981.*

A final socioeconomic indicator that merits attention is level of education attained. Figure 9 presents the percentage of spouses and single parents who have less than a Grade 11 standing, by sex and geography (only national data were available and, as such, they are only indicative of the prairie-specific situation). It is evident that educational attainment increases with urban proximity, but that Native educational attainment remains significantly lower than non-Native attainment even in urban areas. Moreover, the relatively higher level of educational attainment among Native single mothers in urban areas contrasts with their increased incidence of poverty (Figure 6).

In brief, Native single-parent families are most likely to live in conditions of poverty when they reside in major cities, and their incidence of poverty in this setting is only marginally affected by the age of their families. Native single mothers are also unlikely to be employed in major cities, and their rate of employment is not greatly affected by age. Finally, their alarmingly high incidence of poverty and infrequency of employment in major cities are not correlated with lower educational qualifications relative to Native single mothers elsewhere. As in the results of the demographic analysis, most of these patterns appear specific to Native single parents, especially single mothers.

These characteristics of Native single-mothers in major urban centres take on a special significance when considered in the context of Hull's examination of the relationship between family circumstances, Native ethnicity, and levels of education acquired by children.[24] Hull found that the effects of parents' socioeconomic status on children's educational attainment appear to be much more pronounced among Natives than non-Natives. Figure 10 presents the results of this part of his research. The measure of socioeconomic status used is based on the Blishen/McRoberts Index that ranks all occupations by educational requirements and income. As the figure indicates, children in Native families with parents who are not in the experienced labour force appear to have less than a 40 percent probability of completing high school. The importance of this is evident, as Hull found educational attainment to be positively correlated with income levels, and a high-school education to be one of the strongest predictors of employment (his study did not include single parenthood as a variable).

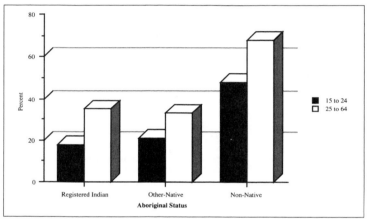

Figure 8. Rate of Employment of Single Mothers by Age Group and Aboriginal Status, Major Cities in the Prairie Provinces, 1981

Source: INAC Customized Data Based on the *Census of Canada, 1981*.

Hull's work must be considered tentatively, as it is based on national cross-sectional data. Further, he only presents a Native versus non-Native comparison. However, his results suggest the existence of a relationship which has particular significance when viewed alongside the patterns identified by this study. As will be recalled, while the incidence of both poverty and unemployment are generalized among Native families on-reserve and in rural areas, they are much more single-parent family specific in major cities. Moreover, Native single-parent families are most heavily overrepresented in these cities. Hence, while the intergenerational influence identified in Hull's work is characteristic of both types of Native families in reserve and rural locales, it is concentrated among Native single-parent families in major cities. This strongly suggest that the Native single-parent families, because of the extremity of their situation, are central mechanisms through which urban disadvantage is perpetuated. In short, the hardships confronting urban Native single parents (almost exclusively single mothers) are not only of immediate severity, but of long-term import for the future of the whole urban Native community. As such, the pivotal significance of addressing the plight of Native single mothers cannot be overemphasized.

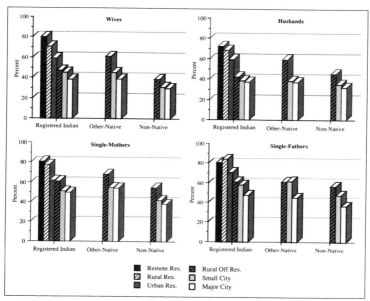

Figure 9. Educational Attainment Among Spouses and Single Parents by Sex, Aboriginal Status and Urban Proximity, Canada,* 1981 (Percentage with less than Grade 11)

*Note: Based on national and not prairie-specific data.

Source: INAC Customized Data Based on the *Census of Canada, 1981*.

Implications for Action and Research

The broad conclusion of this study is that the circumstances of urban Native single mothers parallel neither those of rural/reserve Native single parents, nor those of urban non-Native single mothers. In the case of the former comparison, Native single mothers and their families not only make up a significantly greater share of the Native population in urban areas, but they are also much younger, and more likely to be living in poverty than their rural/reserve counterparts. Moreover, urban Native single mothers appear unable to convert their superior educational attainment into relatively greater labour market success, as other urban Natives have.

Nor are the circumstances of urban Native single mothers consistent with those of urban non-Native single mothers. First, Native single mothers have a considerably younger age structure, as do their families. Second, they outnumber single fathers by a far greater margin, and their families compose almost one-half of all their population's families with children, compared to one in five among non-Native families. Third, they are at least twice as likely to live in poverty, and the likelihood is less affected by the age of the families. Finally, they are at least twice as likely not to be employed as non-Native single mothers, with a percentage gap between the two groups that increases with age.

In short, Native single mothers are a distinct segment of the urban population facing extreme levels of hardship. Yet the causal factors underlying their situation are not as unique as the severity of their position. Rather, theirs is a worst-case manifestation of the failings of our economic, social and political institutions. Thus, any comprehensive approach to addressing their circumstances must be built upon a critical assessment of systemic inadequacies. But, as the will to do so appears distant, recommendations must be tempered by realistic expectation. This tension between structural criticism and political pragmatism will grow more palpable as the discussion progresses. Nevertheless, a research and policy agenda that is compatible with social democratic goals is possible, and necessary.

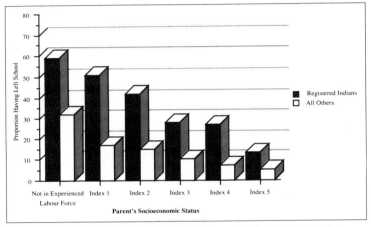

Figure 10. Children Aged 20 to 24 Living with Their Parents Having Left School with Less than Grade 11 Attainment by Aboriginal Status and Parents' Socioeconomic Status,* Canada, 1981

*Note: Parents' socioeconomic status is based on the Blishen-McRoberts index of occupations and refers to the father or single parent; Quintile "0" refers to those parents who had not worked since January 1, 1980 as of Census Day June, 1981.

Source: J. Hull, *An Overview of the Educational Characteristics of Registered Indians in Canada* (Ottawa, Indian and Northern Affairs Canada, Economic Development Branch, 1987), 57.

Four types of initiative are required in light of the patterns that have been identified: one which addresses the lack of political clout of urban Native single mothers; one which confronts the dynamics underlying their frequency in major cities; one which addresses the abject poverty in which they live; and one which responds to the intergenerational impact of this poverty.

The first of these is a pivotal concern. Having been without political voice, the needs of urban Native single mothers have been neglected even by organizations which profess to represent them as part of a larger membership. The rural Native political movement is largely male and elite dominated, and past conflict over women's issues indicates that single-mother dependence on their leadership would be misplaced. Urban Native political organizations, for the most part, are also male and elite dominated, but they are also poorly funded and enjoy little political influence or grassroots community support.[25] Even worse, a recent federal task force on Native women and economic development heard presentations by Native women's groups in major prairie cities, but the plight of single mothers was not brought to its attention.[26] Furthermore, the women's movement has not incorporated Native women's issues within its scope of concern (see Chapter 7).

The issue, then, is if urban Native single mothers can, and should, organize themselves. This is a strategic question that must be resolved by urban Native single mothers themselves, and the recent emergence of small but progressive urban-based Native women's groups suggests that many Native women see few other alternatives. This will be a continuing struggle, as the mobilization of politically and economically disadvantaged women who are dispersed throughout large metropolitan areas is a long-term proposition.[27]

However, the struggle of Native single mothers cannot be staged successfully in isolation. As the following will suggest, many of the substantive matters facing urban Native single mothers will require that emerging urban Native women's groups establish cooperative relations with non-Native women's groups, and mainstream Native organizations, as well as government agencies. Activists, at least initially, can assist by raising the awareness of the needs of Native single mothers in their own organizations. Pressure can also be brought to bear on governments which, to date, have refused to provide core funding to urban Native women's groups.

The academic community can be of assistance in the second area of initiative, confronting the dynamics underlying the overrepresentation of Native single mothers in urban areas. The review of previous research has suggested a number of explanations for the phenomenon which, in turn, suggests the priorization of different types of responses. One of these explanations argues that the discriminatory clause in the old Indian Act encouraged a registered Indian woman, who wished to become the partner of a non-Native man, to migrate and establish a common-law relationship to maintain her legal status and that of her children. The findings of this study, based on data in which common-law relationships are defined as spousal families, revealed the overrepresentation of single mothers in major cities to be a feature common to both registered Indian and other-Native populations. This implies that this explanation has limited explanatory power and, further, that the 1985 revisions to the Indian Act will likely have a marginal effect on the frequency of urban single motherhood for the registered Indian population affected.

The second explanation suggests that the frequency of Native single-mother headed families in urban areas is due to entrenched problems in rural and reserve areas. Two subexplanations have been advanced. One argues that young single mothers are discriminated against in the allocation of resources on reserves. This will require further research to substantiate, including the study of resource allocation patterns in other-Native rural areas. The second subexplanation suggests that violence is directed towards, and/or social stigma is attached to being, a Native single mother in reserve/rural areas. This thesis is not documented in the literature, but it is often raised in discussion, and suggests that the skewed geographic representation of Native single mothers is a symptom of the breakdown of the extended family traditions. Such would hardly be surprising given the degeneration of the Native subsistence economy since pre-contact times — surely there must be a limit to the resilience of pre-capitalist traditions.

If research supports either of these explanations, then much of the onus for response lies with rural Native groups. This may often be problematic. However, it does emphasize the importance of both the continued development of rural-based Native women's organizations, and of urban Native single mothers taking their struggle beyond city boundaries. Moreover, both subexplanations suggest the practical value of designing and operating urban-based programing to assist in the relocation of Native single mothers when reserve/rural conditions are intolerable. Needless to say, a recognition that the scarcity of resources leads to the type of competition where the least powerful become the most oppressed, implies the need for governmental resolve to significantly augment existing levels of funding for reserve and rural Native communities generally.

A third explanatory approach suggests that a large share of the overrepresentation of Native single mothers can be accounted for by social dynamics which are specific to major cities, and which encourage short-term sexual relationships, a high frequency of marital disputes, and/or a high rate of illegitimate births. The responses demanded in this case are the development and expansion of Native-controlled social service agencies mandated not only to provide extensive preventative services and family crisis intervention, but also outreach sex education programs and subsidized contraceptive supplies.

The final explanation is structural, and is largely premised on the combined influence of the general Native disadvantage in the urban labour market, and social assistance programs that discriminate against two-parent families. The explanation appears promising. However, it requires research that compares both the policies and actual delivery of municipal and provincial welfare programs in different geographic settings, as well as a greater regard for the positive role welfare plays in assisting women to escape economic dependence on unsatisfactory marital relationships. If the explanation is upheld by research, then the present welfare policies — which make the provision of assistance to two-parent families conditional on in-person registration on a monthly basis to prove eligibility (and to encourage job search activities) and, in most municipalities, which provide benefits significantly less than those provided to similar-sized single-parent families — must be strongly condemned.[28] Such a welfare approach is seriously flawed when government chooses not to ensure employment for all required to seek it, and must be considered racist when Native job opportunities are so marginal due to a lack of government commitment to Native education in the first place.

It is likely that each of the above partially explains the overrepresentation of Native single mothers in major cities. However, further research is clearly required to more fully understand the underlying cause, and thereby priorize Native and activist efforts.

The third area of initiative needed, one that addresses the abject poverty experienced by Native single-mother families, will require unprecedented responses from government. Previous IUS research has strongly suggested that urban Native single-mother poverty is rooted in welfare dependency (Clatworthy found that 92 percent of Native single-parent families in Winnipeg were dependent on social assistance payments).[29] The major-city specific employment rates presented in this study support this conclusion, and indicate such dependency is much more typical among families headed by single mothers than single fathers. The levels of benefits provided by social assistance to single mothers, therefore, are of direct relevance. Such allowances are intended to provide only for the basic necessities of life. Budget maximums are calculated on the basis of food, clothing, shelter and the most rudimentary personal needs and household supplies. While "special needs" monies can be provided, this is only on the condition of the specific approval of welfare staff, who do not normally allow for expenses related to leisure, recreational or ordinary social and development needs. As a recent Manitoba task force has concluded, "the result is clear. Social assistance budgets ... do not allow for the purchase of goods and services necessary to enter or remain in the regular stream of community life."[30] Both Manitoba and Saskatchewan also offer income support programs for low-income families with children, but in both cases if welfare clients apply for assistance, the benefits are simply deducted from welfare allowances.

Welfare dependency should not be unexpected, as labour force participation for urban Native single mothers is difficult, given their limited educational qualifications, their youth, and especially the triple discriminatory impediments of being a woman, a Native and a single parent. In regards to the latter, society does not recognize the value of a parent's nonformal labour in the home. As the Advisory Council on the Status of Women observed:

> Unlike other economically productive work in the economy, the work of mothers in caring for dependent children is unpaid. Society accepts her unpaid labour as a mandatory grant and rewards it only with minimum support in crisis circumstances.

This situation led the council to advance the following principle:

> Persons engaged in child/dependent care have a right to full independent economic security because they have earned it even though they are not permanently attached to the paid labour force or their attachment is interrupted.[31]

The neglect of this advocated right, and the subsistence orientation of welfare benefits, have an especially deleterious impact on urban Native single mothers. A recent Calgary-based study found that children were the focal point of the lives of Native women and all other interests were subordinated to the task of mothering.[32] Sadly, such devotion to children is an economic liability in our society. Equally unfortunate, provincial governments appear unwilling to substantially increase the level of benefits provided to welfare dependent parents, or to seriously consider acting on feminist recommendations to recognize the productive work of parenting.

Program initiatives designed to assist Native single mothers in entering the full-time labour force are an alternative approach to addressing their poverty. The demands on such a program would be significant. First, the barriers standing in the way of full-time employment are formidable. Second, full-time employment does not necessarily offer an escape from income inadequacy: young working families make up almost one-half of Canada's young family units in poverty. Minimum wage rates are simply inadequate to support a family. Indeed, no single-parent family with more than one child can escape poverty on the earnings of a full-time minimum wage job, and the larger the family, the larger the poverty gap.[33] With welfare benefits at least indexed to family size, and with Native families being generally larger than those of non-Natives, the inadequacies of minimum wage rates present a systemic barrier to full-time labour force participation.

The key to the design of an effective employment program, then, must not only be to assist Native single mothers in acquiring jobs, but also to ensure that such employment is significantly above the lower rungs of the segmented job market. Studies on the efficacy of American programs aimed at welfare-dependent single mothers suggest that individually tailored programs, including academic upgrading, competency-based training, counselling, and extensive linkages with social service agencies will be essential.[34] The governments of the prairie provinces all have some form of existing programing that partially meets these criteria, but they are modest, and none are targetted specifically at Native single mothers.[35]

An interesting model worthy of consideration is a pilot project coordinated by the United States Department of Housing and Urban Development, designed exclusively for welfare-dependent single mothers.[36] The project integrates the resources of all three levels of government, including local low-cost housing authorities and private-sector entities, to develop and implement client-specific programs to enable single mothers to make the transition from welfare dependency to self-sufficiency. Such an approach appears to hold promise, but would require unprecedented levels of intergovernmental cooperation and private-sector involement, as well as major resource investments and long-term commitment. Strong and extended political pressure will be needed to encourage government to coordinate this type of programing.

The final area where initiative is required pertains to the impact of the abject poverty experienced by urban Native single mothers on the educational attainment of their children. Direct government intervention to combat this is made difficult by the lack of guides for policy development. Evaluations of American child nutrition programs in poverty areas have found dramatic health gains for those participating (a valuable objective in itself), but the impact on student performance appears to have been minimal.[37] Research on the impact of Native-run schools is not conclusive. However, studies indicate that increased parental involvement in a child's education is a major factor in the level of schooling attained, whether in Native-run or in public schools.[38] Unfortunately, programs which encourage greater community involvement in schools have often been the first programs to be cut back or terminated by restraint-minded school divisions.

Perhaps the most salient challenges posed by the intergenerational influence identified by Hull involve the broad implications it has for future research, the political development of the urban Native community, and the design of affirmative action programs by government. On the research front, the indication of the enduring impact of poverty among Natives suggests that the "culture of poverty" approach to explaining continuing economic disadvantage requires careful consideration in conjunction with the more structural approaches generally supported by this study. As Hull's work is based on cross-sectional data, time-series analysis will be required to verify his findings. Such analysis should be a priority in future research efforts.

The identification of the intergenerational influence of Native poverty also speaks to the Native community as a whole. The failures of the "Black power" movement in the United States are germane in this regard. The past twenty years have witnessed the fragmentation of urban Black America into an underclass that remains concentrated in ghetto areas, and a middle class that has become geographically and ideologically removed from struggles of ghetto residents. The clearest line between the two groups is family structure, with Black single-mother families representing an ever-larger share of the American poor, while the gap between the incomes of Black two-parent families and white families continues to narrow.[39] In short, the self-help movement has helped those most able to help themselves, while affirmative-action programing, established by government in the face of political pressure, has benefited a select few. A replication of this failure can be anticipated if the elite domination of urban Native political organizations is allowed to continue. The successful mobilization of urban Native single mothers will play a central role in both the democratization of urban Native political development, and the development of an action agenda that promises to represent the interests of those in greatest need.

The intergenerational influence of Native poverty also has clear implications for the acceptability of government policy initiatives. The federal government predilection for entrepreneurialism may create a handful of Native millionaires, but its major accomplishment will be in the continued fragmentation of a potentially united urban Native political front. Affirmative-action hiring initiatives in the public sector raise the same spectre of divisiveness. Those Natives already educationally advantaged will not only become upwardly mobile, but most will probably move to the middle-class neighbourhoods more appropriate to their incomes. This will leave the urban Native underclass to fend for itself, while supporting the twin illusions of government commitment to the disadvantaged, and the supposed ability of any poor individual to overcome the contradictions of class and race. New government policy initiatives must not beguile either the urban Native community or sympathetic activists. Rather, policy measures must be critically analyzed from the point of view of the community as a collective, pressure being brought to bear on government to confront the systemic and social barriers that impede equality not only between Natives and the dominant society, but also among Natives themselves.

NOTES

Although they are in no way responsible for the views expressed in this chapter, I wish to acknowledge the generous support and encouragement given by a number of individuals. Stewart Clatworthy and Ken McVicar both played major roles in the design of the study. The general encouragement of Paul Thomas, John Loxley, Jay Kaufman and David Walker has also been deeply appreciated. My thanks are also extended to the many people who commented on drafts of the chapter and to the editors of this volume for valuable advice. Finally, I wish to thank my wife, Valerie Unwin, for her loving support.

1. The federal and provincial governments have been disputing their respective responsibility for off-reserve registered Indians for more than twenty years. A national study in 1966 advised the federal government that one of the ways to effectively reduce its responsibility for Natives was to pursue "a vigorous policy of out-migration" from reserves. Canada, *A Survey of Contemporary Indians* (Ottawa: Indian Affairs Branch, 1966), 251. While a policy was never actively undertaken (the federal government found that marginal investment in economic development on reserves combined with a high Native birth rate achieved the same end for less cost), the advice was noted. By 1977, a Department of Indian Affairs and Northern Development (DIAND) discussion paper stated "if [Natives] wish to receive federal services [they] must put up with lowered personal opportunity [on reserve]; if [Indians] want increased opportunity, [they] must put up with lowered sustaining goods and services [off reserve]." Canada, *Fundamental Concerns Regarding Indian Local Government* (Ottawa: DIAND, 1977), 45. The provinces have not been willing to assume the special responsibility for off-reserve Natives shirked by the federal government. Indeed, the provinces continue to bill the federal government for the cost of welfare benefits they deliver to urban Natives who have not been self-supporting off-reserve for at least twelve months.

2. M. Nagler, *Indians in the City* (Ottawa: Saint Paul's University, 1970) has categorized urban Natives into six groups, while J. Frideres, *Native People in Canada* (Scarborough: Prentice-Hall, 1983) advanced four, and E. Dosman, *Indians: The Urban Dilemma* (Toronto: McClelland and Stewart, 1972) suggested three. The latter, for example, uses the groupings of "welfare," "anomic," and "affluent" to categorize Natives of diverse family backgrounds and socioeconomic circumstances.

3. For example, see J.G. Redhorse, "Family Structure and Value Orientation in American Indians," *Social Casework* (1980): 462-67.

4. S.J. Clatworthy, *The Demographic Composition and Economic Circumstances of Winnipeg's Native Population* (Winnipeg: Institute of Urban Studies, 1980); S.J. Clatworthy and J.P. Gunn, *Economic Circumstances of Native People in Selected Metropolitan Centres in Western Canada* (Winnipeg: Institute of Urban Studies, 1981); S.J. Clatworthy and J. Hull, *Native Economic Conditions in Regina and Saskatoon* (Winnipeg: Institute of Urban Studies, 1983); and E. Peters, *Native Households in Winnipeg* (Winnipeg: Institute of Urban Studies, 1984).

5. J. Hull, *An Overview of the Educational Characteristics of Registered Indians* (Ottawa: DIAND, forthcoming).

6. For examples of these efforts, see Clatworthy, *Demographic Composition*; Clatworthy and Hull, *Native Economic Conditions*; Nagler, *Indians in the City*; T. Denton, "Migration from a Canadian Indian Reserve," *Journal of Canadian Studies* 7 (1972): 54-62; J. Kerri, " 'Push' and 'Pull' Factors: Reasons for Migration as a Factor in Amerindian Urban Adjustment," *Human Organization* 35 (1976): 215-20.

7. Clatworthy, *Demographic Composition*.

8. J. Ryan, *Wall of Words* (Toronto: PMA Books, 1975).

9. T.D. Graves and M.V. Arsdale, "Values, Expectations and Relocation: The Navajo Migrants to Denver," *Human Organization* 25 (1966): 300-307.

10. B.A. Chadwick and L.C. White, "Correlates of Length of Urban Residence Among Spokane Indians," *Phylon* 32 (1973): 17-21.

11. R.S. Weppner, "Socio-economic Barriers to Assimilation of Navajo Migrants," *Human Organization* 31 (1972): 303-14.

12. M.S. Garbarino, "Life in the City: Chicago," in Jack O. Waddell and Michael O. Watson, eds., *The American Indian in Urban Society* (Boston: Little, Brown and Co., 1971), 168-205.

13. Jeanne Guillemin, *Urban Renegades: The Cultural Strategy of American Indians* (New York: Columbia University Press, 1975).

14. Redhorse, "Family Structure."

15. Dosman, *Indians*.

16. E. Peters, "Native Households in Winnipeg: Strategies of Co-residence and Financial Support" (Master's thesis, Queen's University, 1981) (published in summary form by the Institute of Urban Studies in 1984).

17. W.T. Stanbury, *Success and Failure: Indians in Urban Society* (Vancouver: University of British Columbia Press, 1975).

18. A.J. Siggner, "A Socio-Demographic Profile of Indians in Canada," in J. Rick Ponting and Roger Gibbons, eds., *Out of Irrelevance: A Socio-Political Introduction to Indian Affairs in Canada* (Toronto: Butterworth, 1980)

19. Clatworthy, *Demographic Composition*; Clatworthy and Hull, *Native Economic Conditions*.

20. INAC reserve categories are defined as: remote, special access and/or Crown land (more than 350 miles from urban centres, not accessible by year-round road and on federal or provincial Crown land); rural (50-350 miles from urban centres by year-round road); urban (less than 50 miles by year-round road access).

21. These typologies are not without inconsistency. First, the small number of other-Natives and non-Natives living on-reserve and their skewed distribution threaten reliability. To avoid possible misrepresentations, only the registered Indian population will be included in reserve-based analysis. Second, while the geographic settings within the separate on- and off-reserve areas reflect a specific progression of urban proximity, the relationship of settings between is not as clear cut. Unfortunately, further refinement is not possible.

22. J. Hull, "1981 Census Coverage of the Native Population in Manitoba and Saskatchewan" (mimeo), for example, found the census population counts to be roughly 20 percent lower than recent survey work on northern Manitoba reserves. Specific to urban areas, Clatworthy and Hull, *Native Economic Conditions* estimated Regina's Native population to be 12,000, while the census figures are near 6,000. Alberta, *Demographic Characteristics of Natives in Edmonton* (Edmonton: Native Counselling Services of Alberta and Natives Affairs Secretariat, 1985) also found the proportion of Native single parents to be considerably higher than reported in census data.

23. Statistics Canada suppresses census data with counts below 25. As such, the population of registered Indian single fathers appears to range between 0 and 24.

24. Hull, *Overview*.

25. This assessment is supported by the results of a survey of Calgary Natives who were asked to identify the leader of their community. The most frequent response was "no one" (33 percent), followed by "no response" (17 percent), and "the Mayor" (8 percent). See Calgary, *Native Needs Assessment* (Calgary: Social Services Department, March 1984), Table 27.

26. See Canada, *Native Women and Economic Development Task Force Report* (Winnipeg: NEDAB, 1985).

27. Few of those single mothers dependent on welfare would even be able to afford telephones, which are not provided for in welfare benefits. Thus, even basic communication between Native single mothers is problematic.

28. A 1983 Manitoba task force on welfare found that 48 percent of the province's municipalities (municipalities are responsible for providing welfare benefits to most two-parent families, the provincial government for single-parent families) paid less than 60 percent of the provincial rate. Of those, 45 percent paid less than 40 percent of the provincial rate. See Manitoba, *Report of the Manitoba Task Force on Social Assistance* (Winnipeg: Department of Community Services and Corrections, 1983).

29. Clatworthy, *Demographic Composition.*

30. Manitoba, *Report*, 48-49. Unfortunately, the task force assumed that provincial benefits were adequate to meet the basic needs of recipients. There is strong reason to believe that this assumption is correct.

31. Advisory Council on the Status of Women, *One-Parent Family: ACSW Principles and Recommendations* (Ottawa: n.p., January 1977), 1, 3.

32. M.L. Meadows, "Adaptation to Urban Life by Native Canadian Women" (Master's thesis, University of Calgary, 1981).

33. National Council of Welfare, *The Working Poor* (Ottawa: n.p., 1981), 121, 126.

34. See, for example, J. Ballou, "Work Incentive Policies: An Evaluation of Their Effects on Welfare Women's Choice," *Journal of Sociology and Social Welfare* 4, no. 6 (1976): 850-63; M.L. Chadwin et al., "Reforming Welfare: Lessons From the WIN Experience," *Public Administration Review* (May/June 1981): 372-80.

35. It is also important to note that few Native single mothers make use of such programing. This appears to be a function of both inadequate attempts at outreach and the general cultural inappropriateness of the services offered.

36. United States, *Project Self-Sufficiency: Guidebook* (Washington: Department of Housing and Urban Development, n.d.).

37. M.B. Sanger, *Welfare of the Poor* (New York: Academic Press, 1979).

38. Hull, *Overview*, 5-6.

39. For an interesting analysis of the challenges presently facing urban Blacks, see Nicholas Lemann, "The Origins of the Underclass," *The Atlantic Monthly* 257, no. 6 (1986): 31-55, and *The Atlantic Monthly* 258, no. 1 (1986): 54-68.

SECTION FIVE

Uneven Development, Economic Dislocation and Joblessness

Macroeconomic indicators suggest that Manitoba's economy has performed relatively well during recent years, but these data are potentially deceiving. They obscure as much as they reveal.

As is always the case with capitalism, economic growth is uneven. Ghorayshi describes the uneven development of agriculture in Manitoba and its consequences. While some farms get larger, and account for a growing percentage of farm sales and assets, smaller farms are increasingly squeezed by rising costs of inputs and unreliable sales prices. Those of the smaller farms that survive are increasingly reliant upon family — and especially wives' — labour, and upon off-farm employment and government transfers of various kinds. Many do not survive, as evidenced by the continuing decline in the number of farms, the high turnover of farm operators, and the growing exodus of farmers from the land. Hull adds to this picture by showing that, despite relatively low rates of unemployment, joblessness continues to be a serious problem in Manitoba, especially for those who live in the north or in Winnipeg's inner city, or who are poorly educated, young, Native or female. Silver shows that plant closures and related job loss are a serious problem in Manitoba, and impose a heavy price on the individuals and communities that are its victims. And Ghorayshi describes the uneven development of Manitoba's clothing industry, where large, highly capitalized and technologically advanced plants stand side by side with the small labour-intensive subcontractors which provide the industry with some of its flexibility. Despite the many changes in this industry, it continues to be reliant upon the labour of relatively poorly paid immigrant women, and to be vulnerable to the rapidly changing forces of the increasingly liberalized world market within which it is situated.

These four chapters taken together suggest, as did Gonick, that Manitoba's economy may not be as robust as the macroeconomic indicators might lead us to believe. This is especially so if we allow for the fact that Manitoba's relative economic health is at least partly attributable to the very substantial, but short-lived, public expenditures on Manitoba Hydro's massive Limestone generating station, and Winnipeg's North Portage Development project.

That capitalism develops unevenly, and has uneven consequences, is a theme already encountered in this volume. For example, Phillips, and especially Bailey and St.-Onge, have shown how the great wheat and railway boom of the late nineteenth and early twentieth centuries had as its precondition the dispossession and marginalization of the original Native and Métis inhabitants of the region. Some of the consequences are described in this section by Hull, and elsewhere in this volume by Falconer and Loxley.

In the economy as a whole the result has been domination by huge, multibranch corporations, a characteristic of which is extreme capital mobility. These corporations have no allegiance to community, or even to nation — only to profit maximization. Their ability to move huge sums of capital from place to place in search of maximum profits makes them a socially destabilizing force. This tendency of capital to destructive disinvestment has been aggravated in recent decades by dramatic shifts in the international division of labour, and rapid changes in technological development, which have contributed — along with the "oil crisis" of the early 1970s, and the severe economic recession of the early 1980s — to a much more rapid rate of restructuring of capital, and a much greater rate of social and economic dislocation, with all its related costs. Manitoba is a small player on the periphery of this worldwide process, and is much more likely to be the victim than the beneficiary of this restructuring, while within Manitoba, as Hull and Ghorayshi in particular have shown, it is the weak and the marginal who bear the brunt of the cost.

The response of Manitoba's NDP government revealed the limits of provincial social democracy, and the particular timidity of the Manitoba NDP. Silver, for example, shows how the fear of capital mobility and the pressure of the business lobby combined to prevent the NDP government from putting in place a plant closure strategy. The problem is aggravated by the relationship of organized labour to the NDP, the effect of which is, as Black showed earlier, and Silver shows in this section, to demobilize the labour movement and dramatically reduce its political effectiveness. The consequence has been that the kind of government intervention and political mobilization which is needed to build protection against the increasingly destructive forces of the market is rarely found in Manitoba. The initiatives that are taken are modest, and result in little more than to make Manitoba's NDP governments slightly better, more humane managers of capitalism than their Conservative rivals. The result benefits Manitobans relative to what might otherwise be their fate, but shortchanges them relative to what is possible — even given the real constraints of social democracy at the provincial level.

The Nature and Impact of Capitalist Development in Manitoba Farming

Parvin Ghorayshi

Capitalist development in Manitoba farming has had many important effects. While the number of farms and the farm population has steadily declined since World War II, the remaining farmers have intensified their market relations and integrated into the larger capitalist economy. Despite these changes in Manitoba, as elsewhere in Canada and other industrialized countries,[1] family farm enterprises have survived and remain the backbone of farming. These capitalized family farms are dependent on capitalist markets, but are not completely dissolved by the surrounding capital.

However, the advance of capitalistic relations has greatly increased the polarization and differentiation to be found among these capitalized family farms. This has resulted in greater social and economic diversity among farmers, at the same time as farmers are becoming a small minority within rural Manitoba. Not only have the rural areas lost their agrarian character, but the farming community has become increasingly heterogeneous and divided. The purpose of this chapter is to describe the changing characteristics of Manitoba farms, with a particular emphasis on the stresses being placed on smaller family farms and the many implications for farm families and rural communities in this province.

The Farm and Rural Population

In 1881, 83.5 percent of Manitoba's population was rural. This proportion has since declined steadily except during the Depression, when it went up slightly from 54.9 percent in 1931 to 55.9 percent in 1941.[2] After World War II, emigration to the urban areas resumed at an accelerated rate, and rural Manitobans quickly became the minority. By 1951, 43.4 percent of Manitoba's population was rural, a proportion which reached 27.8 percent in 1986. Although essentially urban, when compared to many other provinces a significant proportion of Manitobans still live in rural areas. However, as in other provinces, only a minority of rural people are now farmers.

The continuous decline in the rural population was accompanied by an even more rapid decrease in the farm population. In 1931, 66 percent of the rural population belonged to the farm community. By 1961, this number had dropped to 51 percent, while by 1981 a minority of rural people (32.6 percent) were living on farms.

Although after 1961 rural Manitoba lost its predominantly agrarian character, Manitoba as a whole had ceased to be an agrarian province well before the Depression. In 1931, only 36.6 percent of Manitobans lived on farms; this figure dropped to 9.6 percent by 1981. Also, living on a farm does not necessarily imply that a person is engaged in farming (we will elaborate on this when discussing off-farm work and off-farm income).

The decline in the rural and farm population reflects the changing nature of Manitoba's economy. There has been a continuous decrease in the proportion of the work force in agriculture, from 24.6 percent in 1951 to 8.5 percent in 1981.[3] Agriculture has lost its relative importance, and the emphasis of economic development has shifted to other sectors.

The decline in the rural and farm population is in line with the decrease in the number of farms, from 58,024 in 1941, to 52,383 in 1951, 34,981 in 1971, and 27,336 in 1986. At the same time, farm families and farm households have grown smaller. In 1951, the average number of persons per farm household was 4.2, and the average number of children per rural family was 2.1. By 1981, the average number of persons per farm family was 3.7, with 1.8 children at home.[4] Farm children increasingly sought employment outside farming.

While Manitoba's agriculture-based economy reached its apex in the 1930s, since World War II there has been a growing population loss and a declining agricultural influence. The reduction in farm numbers, agricultural labour force, and farm and rural population have all shifted political power away from rural areas. In addition, the transformation of farming itself has made the shrinking farm community more heterogeneous and divided, both economically and politically. If agrarianism could be used to describe early farmers' collective outlook, in the 1980s farmers have become a shrinking minority with diversified interests and no single ideological position.

Integration Into the Capitalist Market Economy

Farm numbers are down, but the scale of agricultural production is much expanded. Total dollar value of agricultural sales increased from $181.7 million in 1947 to over $2 billion in 1986.[5] The average farm worker tripled productivity between 1947 and 1965, and the trend continued in the 1970s and to a lesser extent in the 1980s.[6] The cause of the increase in productivity has been the expansion in the scale of production, market relations, specialization, technological advance and a growing substitution of capital investment for labour.

The traditional mixed, self-sufficient farmers who grew wheat for their bread, and raised chickens for eggs and hogs for bacon, were gradually transformed into agricultural specialists. This new breed of farmers became poultry producers, cattle ranchers or wheat farmers who increasingly concentrated on one type of production. By 1986, 59.5 percent of Manitoba farms[7] were typed as wheat and small grain production, 18.5 percent were cattle farms and the rest were dairy, mixed farms, specialty, hay or poultry enterprises.

The specialization of farming was accompanied by intensification of market relations. Farmers steadily expanded their scale of commodity production and integrated into the market economy. For instance, in 1951, only 4.6 percent of farms (240) in Manitoba had over $20,000 of agricultural sales. The size of agricultural commodity production was small in 1951, but expanded as time went on. In 1986, 2.2 percent of farms (600) had over $250,000 annual sales, and 4,660 farms were in the $100,000-$249,999 sales category.[8]

Expansion in the scale of operation has necessitated an exceptionally high increase in capital investment. Average value of farm assets went up from $5,800 in 1941 to $349,524 in 1986.[9] By 1986, total value of land and buildings, machinery, livestock and poultry on Manitoba farms was as high as $9.5 billion. Farming has been transformed from petty production to capital-intensive enterprise.

If Manitoba farmers could be termed ''independent'' commodity producers in the early twentieth century (see Chapter 1), the above figures show that today's farmers are highly dependent on various levels of the capitalist economy. They are surrounded by capitalist markets and depend on market transactions for the survival and prosperity of their farms and families. They are commodity producers who mainly practice capitalistic farming; few hire enough labour to be classified as a capitalist unit.[10]

A growing proportion of farm investment is accounted for by machinery and non-machine technology. Technological innovations have radically transformed agricultural production. The first step was the introduction of farm machinery: steel plows, reapers, combines and stationary steam engines. The second major phase was the development of flexible, maneuverable traction: the internal combustion engine, the differential and the pneumatic tire. The third stage of development was the introduction of chemical technology: artificial fertilizers, pesticides and herbicides. Farmers' expenditure on machinery has gone up over thirty-seven times since 1941. As well, expenditure on chemical technology soared in the 1950s and began to spiral in the 1970s and 1980s. By 1986, the expenditure on fertilizers and pesticides reached over $313.1 million.[11] In the 1990s, major technological change is expected to come from the application of the computer to farming. It is thought that computers will become commonplace on farms; as a managerial tool they will change the style of operation.[12]

Apart from the impact of expanding mechanization on farm input costs, we have to consider its effects on the physical well-being of farm people. Studies have revealed acute effects, in the form of accidents and damage to health. Both are increasing in absolute terms and in proportion to the farm population.[13] The chronic impact includes hearing damage; ailments caused by exposure to chemicals, heat, cold, wind and dust; and physiological effects due to vibration.[14] Unfortunately, few studies have been made of the wider impact of farm technology.

It is important to note here that the reality of farming and rural life today does not match the popular nostalgic and romantic image of rural living as ''simple, pure; slower paced, free from pressure and surrounded by pastoral serenity.''[15] Today's rural life seldom matches this picture, and many scholars suggest that it rarely ever did.[16]

It must be emphasized that the transformation of farming in Manitoba, as elsewhere in Canada, has been fostered by various state policies. The agricultural sector has been subject to increasing regulation and bureaucratic intervention. The involvement of the federal and provincial governments in agriculture has taken many forms: financing farms, developing new production technologies, facilitating the marketing of farm products and the commercialization of agriculture, and providing educational services to the farm population.

The Cost Spiral, Uncertain Income and Farm Finance

A direct consequence of capital-intensive farming has been a steady reliance on a variety of inputs which led to a rise in expenditures. The cost of goods which farmers needed to continue operation climbed annually. The 1970s and 1980s were years of irreversible increases in input costs. Between 1971 and 1987, input costs on Manitoba farms rose by 330.7 percent.[17] Farm operating expenditure and depreciation costs rose from $252.6 million in 1969 to $1.6 billion in 1986.[18] This continuous increase in input costs was accompanied by unpredictable and uncertain farm income.

Figure 11 provides evidence of the financial insecurity that Manitoba farmers encounter. Farm net income declined from $117.8 million in 1969 to $88.7 million in 1970, it went up and peaked at $370.4 million in 1973 and fell again to $319.2 million in 1974. Soaring grain prices explain the explosion of farm income in the mid-1970s. However, the economic uncertainties of the late 1970s and 1980s hit farmers very hard. Farm net income declined drastically from $349.3 million in 1978 to $47.4 million in 1980, the lowest since 1941. It rose to $419.7 million in 1981, but fell again to $83 million in 1983. The major jump came in 1985, when income increased to $656.9 million, but it fell the next year to $465.5 million.[19] Figure 11 shows that not only do farmers face unstable income, but that their farm income lags far behind their soaring input costs.

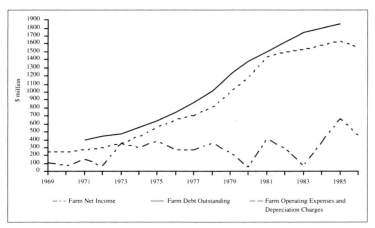

Figure 11. Farm Debt Outstanding, Farm Operating Expenses and Depreciation Charges, and Farm Net Income, 1969-1986.

Source: Canada, Minister of Supply and Services, *Agriculture Economic Statistics* (Ottawa: Minister of Supply and Services, Income and Prices Section, 1987).

Farmers' problems were compounded by the decrease in farm equity values. Falling land values, a decline which began in the early 1980s, have cost farmers billions of dollars in equity, and this continues to be a real drain on the wealth and viability of farms. The current value of land and buildings on Manitoba farms fell from $7.8 billion in 1981 to $5.6 billion in 1986.[20] The impact of uncertain farm income, together with the steady rise in farm expenses and falling land values, has been devastating. It has made forward planning and investment almost impossible, and has resulted in reliance on borrowed capital and off-farm sources of income.

The financing of the dramatic capitalization of agriculture came mostly from outside sources.[21] Thus came the explosion in debt. Higher borrowing is one of the ways that farmers have tried to satisfy the increasing capital needs of modern farming. Farmers' savings and earnings have been completely inadequate to finance their farms and to stay competitive.[22] Manitoba farmers, like their counterparts elsewhere in Canada, borrowed for unexpected purchases and downturns, for paying their debts as well as for raising their level of capital investment. Farm debt outstanding for the declining number of farms climbed from $414.9 million in 1971 to $1.9 billion in 1985,[23] an increase of 355 percent. As a result, debt financing has become an important cost factor. Interest rates reached over 20 percent in 1980, and in real terms remained high throughout the 1980s. Interest now forms a significant part of farm operating expenditures: in 1984 it totalled $183.4 million.[24]

Credit extended to farmers, although on the rise, has not satisfied their financial needs. Many farmers have had to supplement their income with off-farm work in order to keep their farms going. While Manitoba farmers have traditionally worked off the farm to increase their income,[25] by 1986, 35.5 percent of farm operators worked off the farm, up from 30.9 percent in 1971. The trend has been towards full-time (228 days and more) off-farm work and there are indications that this pattern will continue. From 1971 to 1986, the proportion of farm operators with full-time off-farm work climbed from 7.1 percent to 10.8 percent.[26] The overwhelming majority of the operators who reported off-farm work are involved in nonagricultural activities.[27] In Manitoba, farmers complement their income by working in construction, transportation and communication, and occupations related to agriculture, manufacturing and the service sector. By 1981, 22.3 percent of operators indicated that nonfarm activities were their main occupation, up from 19 percent in 1971.[28]

By 1981, of 24,840 farm families,[29] 48.3 percent relied on farming as their major source of income, while for 39.7 percent nonfarm employment was the major source of income.[30] Moreover, nonemployment sources of income such as investment income, government transfers, retirement and pension payments are also important to farm families. The stark evidence is that, on average, nonfarm income is far greater than the average farm income for operators reporting positive farm income.[31] There is a clear trend for farmers to supplement their farm receipts with off-farm income. As Jensen has shown, the capital generated by off-farm work could be substantial.[32] For many farmers off-farm work and income are pivotal to their survival. Each year, a large number of farmers approach the status of the proletariat as they rely mainly on wage-work to support themselves.

Farm Decline, Concentration and Differentiation

Economic problems, the cost-price squeeze and income insecurity have driven many farmers off the land. Despite adopting various defensive measures, many could not survive the competition. It is important to mention that many more farmers have gone out of farming than the census data lead us to believe. Match data, presented in Table 44, allow us to trace the mobility experiences of farmers at each census point. We can determine, for instance, whether a farmer in 1971 continued to farm or left farming in 1976 or in 1981. Likewise, we can have information on the entry dates of each individual farm operator. Between 1966 and 1981 over 31,000 farm operators left farming and over 21,000 entered farming. Of all farm operators in 1981, 19.2 percent had entered farming since 1976, while 27.5 percent of farmers in 1976 went out of farming by 1981.[33] These figures tell a story of an occupation with a very high turnover rate. The popular belief that farming is an occupation for life, in which the family keeps the farm and passes it on to the next generation, is becoming an increasingly inaccurate picture of farming in Manitoba. The rapidly decreasing number of farms and the high rate of exiting from and entering into farming indicate that many households do not remain in production over their entire life cycle.[34] An increasing number of farms stay in production for a short period of time.

TABLE 44

MOVEMENT OF FARM OPERATORS INTO AND OUT OF FARMING, MANITOBA, 1966-1981

	Exitors		Entrants	
	Number	%	Number	%
1966-1971	11,115	28.0	6,350	16.0
1971-1976	11,455	32.8	8,565	25.5
1976-1981	8,810	27.5	6,170	19.2
Total	31,380	—	21,085	—

Source: Statistics Canada, *Match Data*, drawn from *Census of Canada, 1966, 1971, 1976, 1981,* *Agriculture Manitoba.*

Farmers are prone to go out of production and to change their scale of production. Table 45 uses 1971 constant dollars, and shows that the number of small-scale farms declined by 56.5 percent between 1971 and 1981, while medium- and large-scale farms increased by 38.9 percent and 176.9 percent respectively. The tendency is towards large-scale farming, and the indications are that this pattern will continue. By 1986, small-scale farms accounted for 21.6 percent of all farms, and medium and large farms for 35.3 percent and 43.1 percent respectively.[35] Many farmers, especially those with small holdings, could not withstand the cost-price squeeze and the financial insecurity. Those who stayed in farming, as we have seen, increased their scale of agricultural production and intensified their market relations. Fewer farms produce more for the market and control larger assets. Total agricultural sales went up by almost five times between 1971 and 1976, from $337.6 million to over $2 billion. Total farm assets climbed from $2.1 billion to over $9 billion during the same period.[36]

The expanding sales and assets have become concentrated in fewer hands. The clear message of Table 46 is the growing polarization and differentiation among farms. Medium and large farms control most of the farm sales and assets. By 1981, large farms accounting for only 5.7 percent of total farms, made 36.1 percent of agricultural sales and held 22.1 percent of assets. This process of concentration intensified by 1986, such that 912 farms, with annual sales of $100,000 or more, accounted for 65.4 percent of total farm sales. Small farms accounted for 21.6 percent of farms, but only 1.2 percent of agricultural sales in 1986. We are left with a situation where the top one-third of farms produces over four-fifths of total products sold by farmers.

TABLE 45

MANITOBA FARMS CLASSIFIED BY SALES GROUP, 1971, 1981
(Constant 1971 Dollars)

| Sales Group | 1971 | | 1981 | | % Change |
	Number	%	Number	%	1971-1981
Small*	24,216	71.8	15,469	52.5	-36.1
Medium	8,870	26.3	12,284	41.7	+38.9
Large	610	1.7	1,689	5.7	+176.9
Total	33,696	100.0	29,442	100.0	-14.4

*Note: Taking 1971 as the base and using annual farm sales to measure the scale of production,
farms are divided into small, medium and large, with total market sales of up to $9,999,
$10,000-$49,999, and $50,000 and more.
Source: Statistics Canada, *Census of Canada, 1971, 1981, Agriculture Manitoba*, drawn from
unpublished data.

The figures on average assets provide further evidence of the growing differentiation among farms. Not only are large farms highly capitalized, but they have managed to accumulate assets at a much faster rate than the smaller farms. By 1981, large farms had on average 8.6 times more assets than small farms — up from 7.2 times in 1971.[37]

TABLE 46

FARM ASSETS, SALES AND OFF-FARM WORK REPORTED BY
SALES GROUP OF FARMS, 1971, 1981
(Constant 1971 Dollars)

| | 1971 | | | | | 1981 | | | | |
Sales Group	Farms %	Sales %	Assets %	Average Assets $	Off-farm Work %	Farms %	Sales %	Assets %	Average Assets $	Off-farm Work %
Small	71.8	29.7	48.6	40,734	34.9	52.5	11.6	23.5	158,551	47.6
Medium	26.3	47.5	42.6	97,645	16.2	41.7	52.3	54.4	462,791	22.9
Large	1.7	22.7	8.8	293,475	11.8	5.7	36.1	22.1	1,369,686	13.1
Total	100.0	100.0	100.0	60,290	30.0	100.0	100.0	100.0	354,967	35.3

Source: Statistics Canada, *Census of Canada, 1971, 1981, Agriculture Manitoba*, drawn from
unpublished data.

Capitalization and the increase in market relations have intensified polarization and division among farms. While large-scale farmers have prospered and accumulated more assets, a growing number of farmers, especially small-scale producers, could not respond to the pressure of the market. These small-scale farmers have become marginalized as their share of agricultural sales declined dramatically. Not surprisingly, they cannot rely solely on farm income for their survival. Off-farm work has become important for farmers. As we have seen (Table 46), it is a way of life for a very large proportion of small farms; one out of six small farm operators works full-time off his or her holdings. Full-time off-farm work is not nearly as significant for medium or large farms. Indications are that the polarized farming community will become even more stratified. For the majority of small farm operators, farming will be only their secondary source of livelihood.

The Family Farm Enterprise

Farming in Manitoba, as elsewhere in Canada, has undergone a rapid process of commercialization, specialization and mechanization.[38] Despite these changes, the family farm enterprise continues to be the predominant form of production. The important fact about farming in Manitoba is that wage relations have not, universally, taken over agricultural production. In 1981, 70 percent of farms did not hire any wage labour (up from 66.9 percent in 1971), while 32.8 percent of farms hired less than one-person year of labour annually, so that by 1981, 99.7 percent of farms in Manitoba were household producers relying heavily on family labour. Only 0.3 percent of farms hired five or more person-years of labour in 1981, and could be properly defined as capitalist.[39]

In spite of difficulties, family farm enterprises have shown remarkable resistence to being completely taken over by capital.[40] It is important to recognize that the survival of the family farm to a large extent relies on the labour of family members, especially women. Without wives' work most family farm enterprises would collapse.[41] With heightened competition and the cost-price squeeze, most farms cannot afford to substitute hired labour for the multidimensional and flexible work of household members.

In order to grasp the importance of household labour in farming, we have to understand the nature of the family farm enterprise. Family farms are both production and consumption units; the family cannot be considered apart from the agricultural enterprise.[42] The farm household is not completely separated from the realm of production. One does not leave the family to go to work. The public/private split which is characteristic of the majority of capitalist production units is not a necessary feature of the family farm.[43] Direct producers are related by family ties: being part of the family brings the expectation and obligation of work in the enterprise. Direct producers are spouses, children and relatives.

In the family enterprise, work relations are also family relations. The logic of production is as much related to the family as to the enterprise. The survival of the enterprise is a *family concern*. When the family farm faces crisis, family members use a number of strategies to reduce the risk. They may cut personal consumption, intensify subsistence, seek off-farm work or do whatever else is needed to retain the enterprise.[44] The work of all household members is essential to the day-to-day operation of the enterprise.

Generally farming is conceived of as a male occupation, and studies of the agricultural labour force have been gender blind.[45] However, the interdependence between the family and the enterprise creates a situation where women become active participants in what is generally assumed to be men's work. Women plant, harvest, build and help to establish the agricultural settlement.[46] In Canada, a growing number of studies have concerned themselves with women's actual farm work. While the estimation of women's participation in direct agricultural production ranges from seventeen to forty hours per week,[47] women's presence in the perceived male occupations in agriculture is on the rise.[48] As well, the increasing need for at least one spouse to have an off-farm occupation has created a corresponding demand for the other spouse to take care of production in his/her absence. It is not uncommon for wives to quit their paid off-farm work in order to satisfy the labour needs of the enterprise. In many cases, wives may take off-farm work to provide money for farming operations and to allow their partners to be full-time farmers.

The nonseparation of family dwelling and work place means that many aspects of domestic work contribute to the maintenance and reproduction of the family enterprise. Subsistence production for family use, preparation of meals for the work crew, and taking care of the hired labour's needs are instances where domestic work and production work coincide. For women on farms, as for most women, basic housework is an integral part of everyday life.[49] Likewise, household members, especially wives, are active in the administrative part of farm work. In general, male operators depend on women for help with bookkeeping, writing letters, filling forms, providing needed information and dealing with bureaucratic agencies.

Finally, the contribution of household members through off-farm sources cannot be ignored. Surprisingly, studies of off-farm work have focussed exclusively on individual farm operators,[50] ignoring the involvement of the spouse and other members of the family. In Canada, Shaw notes that the income generated through family members accounts for an increasing proportion of total family income.[51] Similarly, in 1981, over one-half of the paid work by farm household members was accounted for by the spouse and children.[52] Studies of Manitoba and Saskatchewan farms show that one-third of women work off the farm,[53] the majority in order to purchase household necessities, contribute to the maintenance and operation of the farm, and improve or sustain the family's standard of living.[54]

The complementary nature of family and enterprise should not lead us to idealize the relations of production within family farms. Although household labour is central in these units, farms are not owned or controlled collectively by all those who contribute labour, and property relations do not reflect the collective labour contribution. For the most part, household members find themselves under the authority of one person — the male operator. While it is good for the enterprise as a whole to have access to household labour, it cannot be assumed that it is equally beneficial for individual members of the family. Often there are conflicts between husbands and wives or between other family members. A number of matrimonial property cases are examples of non-egalitarian and conflictual relationships between husbands and wives.[55] Property relations, together with social perceptions, methods of data collection, conceptual and research frameworks, all have contributed to the lack of recognition of the work of household members, especially women.[56]

As we have seen, family farm enterprises remain the backbone of Manitoba farming. Without the active participation of household members in all aspects of farm work, the survival of the enterprise is threatened. Farm operators, together with their family members, in particular their spouses, try to adapt to the needs of modern farming. Many have not survived the competition and have left farming. Of the existing family farm enterprises in production, increasing numbers are fighting for survival. In 1984, it was estimated that 10-15 percent of Manitoba farms were in a financial position which brought their continued operation into question. Overall, 20 percent of farmers were in serious need of financial adjustment.[57] In 1984, sixty-two farms went bankrupt,[58] and the debt situation has worsened since then.

From Agrarianism to Divided and Conflicting Class Interests

Agrarianism has been used to describe farmers' outlook in the late nineteenth and early twentieth centuries.[59] Phillips (see Chapter 1) refers to farmers as an "agrarian class" at a time when agriculture dominated the economy and rural areas were the centre of political and economic power. Farmer-dominated political parties had some spectacular successes, such as the 1922 Manitoba election, which led to a rural-based coalition that governed Manitoba until the late 1950s. However, the decreasing rural and farm population, transformation of the structure of farming, the change in the nature of farming, and the decline in the relative importance of the agricultural sector itself have all brought drastic changes in the outlook of farmers and farm communities. Farm groups, with the occasional exception of the National Farmers Union, lobby for specific change. Their interest is to survive within the existing capitalist system, rather than to attempt broad social transformation. With the development of capitalism in farming and the growth of large-scale production, there is a growing conservatism among some groups of farmers.

The economic polarization among farms has resulted in diverse political and economic interests among farmers. Farmers of the 1980s do not belong to one class and are not represented by a single voice; they have diverse and often conflicting interests. Various farm organizations represent different groups of farmers. As Wilson states,

> During the 1970s, while the umbrella Canadian Federation of Agriculture [CFA]remained the most credible, respected . . . there was a flourishing of commodity groups on the Prairies which spoke for the interests of their members and complained that CFA or its provincial affiliates did not represent their interests. Such groups as the Canadian Cattlemen's Association, The Palliser Wheat Growers Association, and barley, flax and rapeseed growers' groups remained outside CFA.[60]

Similarly, the Task Force on Agriculture observed that farm organizations lack unity and clarity and are unable to send clear messages to government about what farmers want.[61] This lack of unity could well be a reflection of division among farmers; different farmers want different things. As Mitchell's study has shown, we increasingly see conflicts between various groups of farmers.[62] Instead of a cohesive class interest we observe the emergence of varied interests signalling the division of the farmers' class position into various class fractions and social strata. Indications are that growing polarization will intensify this conflictual situation.

The decline in the number of farms and the farm population, the growing financial difficulties, and differentiation within farms have led to numerous additional problems. Market forces have had consequences for farm families, farm characteristics, and communities where they are located. Rural families, like other families, demonstrate rising rates of unemployment, divorce and family violence.[63] Rural depopulation has hit some communities very hard and many rural service centres have had difficulty remaining viable.[64] Rail-line abandonment has fostered loss of business in many communities.[65] As well, with the loss of population, communities have seen a trend towards consolidation of schools into larger buildings, under the control of larger units.[66] Similarly, declining farm numbers and changing farm structure have a major impact on the country elevator system. There has been a reduction in the number of primary country elevators and an industrywide consolidation.[67] The livelihood of small communities which depend on farm business has been threatened and many communities have already died as a result.

The typical pattern of change associated with population decline is that youth leaves, the average age rises, the birth rate falls and income declines. This selective movement of people increases the burden on remaining residents through extra costs and lower levels of services. Rural poverty is a fact, and many rural elderly live in deplorable conditions, while rural families are experiencing stress and mental health problems.[68] At the same time, however, there is economic growth in the larger centres and expansion of production in the larger farms.

Conclusion

Capitalist development in Manitoba farming has entailed a decline in the rural and farm population, the number of farms, and the proportion of the work force in agriculture. The number of farms has decreased, but those remaining have been integrated into the larger capitalist economy. Farmers have specialized, capitalized and have become highly dependent on capitalist markets, but this has not brought the dominance of the capitalist organization of labour in Manitoba farming. In this province, the great majority of farmers rely on their household members to sustain the family enterprise. Without the active participation of household members, in particular women, the survival of these capitalized family farm enterprises would be at risk.

A very important feature of Manitoba farming, as in Canada and other advanced capitalist countries, has been a trend towards the expansion of the scale of production. Integration into the capitalist economy, the cost-price squeeze and income insecurity have driven many farmers off the land. Small farms have experienced the most dramatic drain. Expanding agricultural sales and assets have become concentrated in the hands of large- and medium-sized farms as the trend has been towards a growing polarization and differentiation among farmers. While large farms prosper, small farms become marginalized and must rely on off-farm sources of income. Capitalized family farms have experienced a rapid internal differentiation and the indications are that this pattern will continue.

While political power has shifted from rural to urban areas, farmers themselves have become more divided and their interests more heterogeneous. Increasing inequality among farmers has brought with it greater conflict over diverging interests. Farmers face common problems, but they meet them with different resources springing from different positions in the agrarian class structure. The extent of the conflict among economic and social strata in farming almost precludes a unified approach to solving the problems of agriculture. If Manitoba farmers were ever a single, class-conscious "agrarian class," with all the power that entailed, they are no longer.

NOTES

1. P. Sorokin, C.C. Zimmerman and C.J. Galpin, eds., *A Systematic Sourcebook in Rural Sociology* (New York: Russel and Russel, 1930); A.V. Chayanov, *The Theory of Peasant Economy* (Homewood, Illinois: R.D. Irwin, 1966); H. Newby, ed., *International Perspectives in Rural Sociology* (New York: John Wiley, 1978); G. Djurfeldt, "What Happened to Agrarian Bourgeoisie and Rural Proletariat Under Monopoly Capitalism?," *Acta Sociologia* 24 (1981).

2. Unless otherwise stated, the information in this section comes from Statistics Canada, *Canadian Census, Agriculture Manitoba*.

3. Statistics Canada, *Labour Force Statistics*, Catalogue # 71-201.

4. Statistics Canada, *Canadian Census 1981, Housing and Families*.

5. Canada, *Agriculture Economic Statistics* (Ottawa: Minister of Supply and Services, Income and Prices Section, 1987).

6. L. Auer, *Canadian Agricultural Productivity* (Ottawa: Queen's Printer, 1970); C. Wilson, *A Century of Canadian Grain* (Saskatoon: Western Producer Prairie Books, 1978).

7. Commercial farms with $2,500 or more annual agricultural sales.

8. Statistics Canada, *Canadian Censuses 1951, 1986, Agriculture Manitoba*.

9. Statistics Canada, *Canadian Censuses 1941, 1986, Agriculture Manitoba*.

10. See P. Ghorayshi, "Canadian Agriculture: Capitalist or Petit Bourgeois?," *The Canadian Review of Sociology and Anthropology* 24, no. 3 (1987).

11. Canada, *Agriculture Economic Statistics*.

12. B. Wilson, *Beyond the Harvest: Canadian Grain at the Crossroads* (Saskatoon: Western Producer Prairie Books, 1981).

13. G.F. Donaldson, *Farm Machinery Safety: Physical Welfare Effects of the Man-Machine Interaction on Farms* (Ottawa: Royal Commission on Farm Machinery, 1968).

14. G.F. Donaldson and J.P. McInorney, "Changing Machinery Technology and Agricultural Adjustment," *American Journal of Agricultural Economics* (December 1973).

15. A. Anderson, *Remembering the Farm* (Toronto: Macmillan, 1977); L. Gerin, *Le type économique et social des Canadiens: milieux agricoles de tradition français* (Montréal: Fides, 1948).

16. See D.A. Dillman and D.J. Hobbs, *Rural Society in the U.S.: Issues for the 1980s* (Boulder, Colorado: Westview Press, 1982); B. Jean, ed., *La réalité en question, réalité sociale et théorie sociographique* (Rimouski: Université du Québec à Rimouski, 1985).

17. Statistics Canada, *Farm Input Price Index*, Catalogue # 62-004.

18. Canada, *Agriculture Economic Statistics*.

19. Statistics Canada, *Net Farm Income* (Ottawa: Statistics Canada, 1986).

20. Canada, *Agriculture Economic Statistics*.

21. Several agencies and institutions, including individuals and relatives, extend credit to farmers. When the cash requirement of farming was low, friends, relatives and other individuals known to the farmer provided the majority of the loan. Individuals and relatives have been replaced by federal and provincial institutions, banks, credit unions, and supply, insurance and trust companies. By 1985, provincial and federal institutions accounted for 33.2 percent of total credit advanced to farmers. The rest was in the hands of private institutions.

22. F.L. Tung and W.D. Jones, "Forecasting Farm Credit Requirements for 1981," *Canadian Farm Economics* 17, no. 3 (1979).

23. Canada, *Agriculture Economic Statistics*.

24. Manitoba, *State of Manitoba Agriculture* (Winnipeg: Manitoba Agriculture, Economic Branch, 1985).

25. R. Bollman, *Off-farm Work by Farmers* (Ottawa: Minister of Supply and Services, 1979).

26. Statistics Canada, *Canadian Censuses 1971, 1986, Agriculture Manitoba*.

27. Off-farm work is not equally important for all types of farmers. Rates of participation in off-farm work vary widely by type of farm — from a low of 18.6 percent for dairy farms in 1981, to a high of 45.5 percent for poultry farm operators for the same year. Except for dairy farm operators who report a decrease in off-farm work between 1971 and 1981, operators of all other types of farm report significant increases in off-farm work.

28. Statistics Canada, "Canadian Censuses 1971, 1981 drawn from Agriculture and Population Linkage (Ag-Pop)," (unpublished).

29. These are families with an operator present.

30. Statistics Canada, *Canadian Censuses 1971, 1981*.

31. Ibid.

32. P.D. Jensen, *An Analysis of Off-farm Work in Alberta* (Edmonton: Alberta Agriculture, 1979).

33. Statistics Canada, *Match Data Drawn from Canadian Censuses 1971, 1981, Agriculture*.

34. This is one of the reasons that Friedmann's concept of simple commodity production is not applicable to Canadian, including Manitoban, farming. H. Friedmann, "World Market, State and Family Farm: Social Bases of Household Production in the Era of Wage-labour," *Comparative Studies in Society and History* 20, no. 4 (1978).

35. Statistics Canada, *Canadian Census 1986, Agriculture Manitoba*.

36. Statistics Canada, *Canadian Censuses 1971, 1981, Agriculture Manitoba*.

37. The Farm Credit Corporation's survey of Canadian farms supports this observation. See Farm Credit Corporation, *Farm Survey, 1984* (Ottawa: Farm Credit Corporation, 1985).

38. B. Bernier, "La pénétration du capitalisme dans l'agriculture," in N. Seguin, ed., *Agriculture et colonisation au Québec* (Montréal: Boréal Express, 1980); D. Mitchell, *The Politics of Food* (Toronto: Lorimer, 1975); M. Hedley, "Independent Commodity Production and the Dynamics of Tradition," *The Canadian Review of Sociology and Anthropology* 13, no. 4 (1976).

39. Statistics Canada, *Canadian Censuses 1971, 1981, Agriculture Manitoba*; P. Ghorayshi, "The Identification of Capitalist Farms: Theoretical and Methodological Considerations," *Sociologia Ruralis* 26, no. 2 (1986).

40. M. Winter, "Corporatism and Agriculture in the U.K.: The Case of the Milk Marketing Board," *Sociologica Ruralis* 24, no. 2 (1984); T. Marsden, "Land Ownership and Farm Organization in Capitalist Agriculture," in T. Bradley and P. Lowe, eds., *Locality and Rurality: Economy and Society in Rural Regions* (Norwich: Geo Books, 1984); Ghorayshi, "Canadian Agriculture: Capitalist or Petit Bourgeois?"; S. Whatmore et al., "Towards Agriculture," *Sociologia Ruralis* 27 (1987).

41. See P. Ghorayshi, "The Indispensable Nature of Wives' Work for the Farm Family Enterprise," *The Canadian Review of Sociology and Anthropology* 26, no. 4 (August 1989): 571-95.

42. J.W. Bennett, *Of Time and Enterprise: North American Family Farm Management in the Context of Resource Marginality* (Minneapolis: University of Minnesota Press, 1982); S. Kohl, *Working Together: Women and Family in South-western Saskatchewan* (Toronto: Holt Rinehart and Winston of Canada, 1976).

43. C. Sachs, *The Invisible Farmers* (New Jersey: Rowan and Allanheld, 1983), 72.

44. M. Hedley, "Domestic Commodity Production," in D. Turner and G. Smith, eds., *Challenging Anthropology: A Critical Introduction to Social and Cultural Anthropology* (Toronto: McGraw Hill, Ryerson Limited, 1979), 280.

45. R. Barichello, *A Profile of Human Resources in British Columbia Agriculture* (New Westminister, British Columbia: Department of Agriculture, 1985); R. Rust, "Agriculture Manpower," *Canadian Farm Economics* 10, no. 1 (1975).

46. Sachs, *The Invisible Farmers*, 13; C. Fairbank and S. Sundberg, *Farm Women on the Prairie Frontier* (New York: The Scarecrow Press, 1983).

47. "Farming Partnership: Just Like a Marriage," *Thunder Bay Chronicle Journal* (October 1982); S. Koski, *The Employment Practices of Farm Women* (Saskatoon: National Farmers Union, 1982), 4; Bennett, *Of Time and Enterprise*, 167; Saskatchewan, *Farm Women* (Regina: Saskatchewan Department of Labour, 1976), 3.

48. P. Smith, "Not Enough Hours, Our Accountant Tells Me: Trends in Children's, Women's and Men's Involvement in Canadian Agriculture," *Canadian Journal of Agricultural Economics* 33 (1986): 172.

49. Kohl, *Working Together*, 35; C. Jones and R. Rosenfeld, *American Farm Women: Findings from a National Survey* (Chicago: National Opinion Research Centre, 1981).

50. Bollman, *Off-farm Work*; C. Coughenour, "The Impact of Off-farm Occupation and Industry on the Size and Scale of Part-time Farmers" (paper delivered at the Southern Association of Agricultural Scientists, Hot Springs, Arkansas, February 1980).

51. P. Shaw, *Canadian Farm Population* (Ottawa: Minister of Supply and Services, 1979), 208.

52. Smith, "Not Enough Hours," 187.

53. Koski, *Employment Practices*, 24-25; R. Berry, "Labour Allocation of Farm Women" (paper delivered at the Canadian Rural Studies Association, Winnipeg, Manitoba, 1986).

54. Koski, *Employment Practices*.

55. *Murdoch* v. *Murdoch*, 1975; *Rathwell* v. *Rathwell*, 1978; *Spencer* v. *Spencer*, 1983; *Wildman* v. *Wildman*, 1983.

56. For a detailed discussion of these issues, see Ghorayshi, "Wives' Work."

57. Manitoba, *State of Manitoba Agriculture*, 4.

58. Ibid.

59. Wilson, *Beyond the Harvest*.

60. Ibid.

61. Canada, Report of the Federal Task Force on Agriculture, *Canadian Agriculture in the Seventies* (Ottawa: Queen's Printer, 1969).

62. Mitchell, *The Politics of Food*.

63. Dillman and Hobbs, *Rural Society*.

64. J.A. Brown and H.D. Olson, "A Study of the Growth of Selected Service Centers in Saskatchewan," University of Saskatchewan Research Report 75-03 (1975).

65. *The Community Impact of Rail Line Abandonment, 1975-76* (University of Regina: Sample Survey and Data Bank, 1976).

66. J. Funk, ''The Origin and Development of Consolidated School Districts in Saskatchewan'' (Master's thesis, University of Saskatchewan, 1971).

67. See Wilson, *Beyond the Harvest*.

68. See Dillman and Hobbs, *Rural Society*; J.L. Walker and L.J. Walker, ''The Human Harvest'' (project sponsored by Agriculture Canada, Manitoba Agriculture, with special assistance from Manitoba Education, 1987).

11

Plant Closures in Manitoba, 1976-1986

Jim Silver

Plant closures are a constant and intrinsic feature of capitalism. Their occurrence has been widely publicized since the oil crisis of the early 1970s, and especially since the severe recession of the early 1980s. But there have been relatively few studies of closures in Canada during this period. Most of the research that has been done has taken the form of case studies of closures in central Canada. Few studies have tried to determine the numbers and characteristics of closures during a particular period; fewer still have ventured beyond Canada's industrial heartland. Nor has much research been done to explain governmental responses, or lack thereof, to plant closures. These are serious omissions, since the increasingly rapid rate of restructuring of capital, particularly since the implementation of the Canada-United States Free Trade Agreement, makes likely an even greater frequency of plant closures in the future.

This chapter takes a somewhat different approach than most of the existing Canadian plant closure literature. It attempts to identify and to characterize all the closures of companies employing fifty or more people in Manitoba for the 1976-86 period. It also reviews some of the literature on the adverse effects of plant closures, describes existing plant closure legislation in Manitoba, and explains why provincial policy responses to plant closures in Manitoba have been so inadequate. It concludes by arguing that while provincial governments are severely constrained regarding policy, a meaningful plant closure strategy is nevertheless possible.

Identifying Plant Closures

It is difficult to identify companies that have closed, wholly or partially, or have moved, in the 1976-86 period. The provincial Department of Labour compiles such data, but it is a recent innovation and is incomplete. The Employment Standards Act, 35.1(1) requires that companies report all layoffs of fifty or more employees which occur within a four-week period, but there are many ways to circumvent this provision: some companies regularly report large layoffs, whether such are actually anticipated or not, to protect against any eventuality; the Department of Labour makes no effort to revise these figures, or to determine actual job loss; some companies manage layoffs so as to avoid either or both the four-week provision and the fifty-person limit; there are not enough staff to monitor the provision; there is no penalty for noncompliance, and even when there is compliance, the legislation omits all companies employing less than fifty people, and all layoffs of less than fifty employees. Consequently, neither the provincial nor the federal government has a complete list of closures. Nor is such a list maintained by any nongovernmental organizations.

Therefore, a list of closures was compiled by comparing, year by year, lists of companies employing fifty or more people in the *Manitoba Trade Directory* (*MTD*) and *Scott's Industrial Directory of Western Manufacturers*. These are not the best sources, as the *MTD* is unreliable, and *Scott's* includes only manufacturers. The best sources are the Statistics Canada Business Register Master File, or the Dun and Bradstreet Reference Guide, but the former is available only to government departments, and the latter is prohibitively expensive.

Usually the explanation for the listing of a company in the *MTD* or *Scott's* in one year and not the next is something other than a closure. For example, it may be a corporate merger or change of name. Thus a variety of other sources were used to confirm closures: the Provincial Corporate and Business Names Branch, the Henderson Directory, newspaper files and, most importantly, interviews with company, union and government officials. No single source can be relied upon completely, so companies have been included in the list of closures only upon confirming the details with more than one source.

The resultant list of closures is likely incomplete, and given my method, it is impossible to know the proportion identified. Nevertheless, the list includes most of the cases which meet the criteria of complete or partial closure, or physical relocation, resulting in the loss of fifty or more jobs.

An Analysis of Manitoba's Plant Closures

Plant closures have been a serious problem in Manitoba. The number affecting fifty or more employees in each of the eleven years from 1976 to 1986, and the resultant job loss, is shown in Table 47. These data can be compared (see Table 48) to the Ontario experience, where plant closures have been said to be particularly serious.

TABLE 47
PLANT CLOSURES AND JOB LOSS BY YEAR, 1976-1986

Year	Number of Closures	Number of Jobs Lost
1976	10	2,948
1977	6	660
1978	4	280
1979	5	940
1980	9	1,321
1981	9	787
1982	8	759
1983	9	1,267
1984	13	1,015
1985	9	822
1986	6	392
Total	88*	11,191

*Note: Seven companies are listed twice, usually because partial closures occurred in different years, so that the number of companies involved is 81.

In absolute numbers, closures have been more serious in Ontario than in Manitoba: more plants have closed and more jobs have been lost. But on the basis of jobs lost per ten thousand labour force participants, the experience in Manitoba has been about the same as in Ontario.

Closures in Manitoba — at least of manufacturing firms — may be related to foreign ownership. In 1981 (see Table 49), of all manufacturing employees in Manitoba, 74.5

percent worked for Canadian-owned firms, and 25.4 percent for foreign-owned firms.[1] Thus, if ownership were not a factor, 25.4 percent of job loss in manufacturing would have occurred in foreign-owned firms where, in fact, 41.8 percent of job loss occurred. This may indicate a higher propensity to closure given foreign ownership (see Table 50). Furthermore, 16.4 percent of manufacturing jobs in Manitoba were in American-owned firms, which accounted for 32.3 percent of the jobs lost, suggesting the possibility of an even greater propensity to closure — twice as high — given American ownership.[2] These ratios should be treated with caution, since the closure data apply only to firms employing fifty or more people, while the proportions employed in manufacturing by ownership apply to all manufacturing firms, irrespective of size. A more accurate comparison would require currently unavailable data on the proportions of manufacturing employees employed in Canadian-owned and in foreign-owned firms with fifty or more employees.

TABLE 48

COMPARISON: ONTARIO AND MANITOBA PLANT CLOSURES, 1981-1985

	Ontario						
	Number of Closures			Number of Jobs Lost			Jobs Lost Per 10,000 Labour Force Participants
	Full	Partial	Total	Full	Partial	Total	
1981	49	13	62	5,497	1,400	6,897	15
1982	73	13	86	9,918	1,232	11,150	25
1983	53	9	62	5,558	1,076	6,634	15
1984	47	16	63	5,526	2,341	7,867	18
1985	54	17	71	5,630	2,015	7,645	17
Total			344			40,193	90

	Manitoba		
	Number of Closures	Number of Jobs Lost	Jobs Lost Per 10,000 Labour Force Participants
1981	9	787	16
1982	8	759	15
1983	9	1,267	26
1984	13	1,015	19
1985	9	822	16
Total	48	4,589	94

Source: Ontario, Ministry of Labour, *Annual Reports on Permanent and Indefinite Layoffs in Ontario*, December 31, 1981 to December 31,1985.

The closure data can be further analyzed by reason for closure, as in Table 51. More than one-third of the closures, and jobs lost, were attributable to rationalization. This proportion would rise to more than 40 percent if the relocation of head offices and special functions were treated as cases of rationalization. As used here, rationalization refers to a corporate restructuring involving closure(s) and the physical relocation of production in order to maximize profits. In such cases the closed plant may still be profitable, or capital invested in the plant may have made it profitable, but production is relocated because doing so is *more* profitable than investing in the Manitoba plant. Whether a particular closed plant is still profitable, or potentially profitable, is of course impossible to tell given the accounting practices of multibranch corporations, and the lack of public access to corporations' books.

TABLE 49

CLOSURES AND JOB LOSS IN MANUFACTURING, 1976-1986,
BY OWNERSHIP AS OF 1981

Owned in	Closures	%	Job Loss	%	Average Size of Closure
USA	14	25.5	2,163	32.3	154
Manitoba	23	41.8	2,063	30.8	90
Ontario	10	18.2	1,365	20.4	137
Quebec	4	7.3	470	7.0	118
Britain	3	5.5	413	6.2	138
Holland	1	1.8	228	3.4	228
Total	55	100.1	6,702	100.1	122

In thirty-two of eighty-eight cases, corporations closed their Manitoba plants and shifted production elsewhere: eastern Canada in the case of Christie Brown, Greb, ICG Keeprite and Kimberley Clark; the United States in the case of Harco Electronics, Rayovac and General Aluminum Forgings; and western Canada in the case of AEL Microtel. In the case of F.G. Bradley, GTE Sylvania, and Moser Manufacturing, production was moved to eastern Canada, leaving a warehouse/distribution centre in Manitoba. In each of these cases, production could have been continued in Manitoba, but the calculus of corporate profit and the mobility of capital dictated otherwise.

TABLE 50

CLOSURES AND JOB LOSS IN MANUFACTURING, 1976-1986,
RELATIVE TO PROPORTIONS EMPLOYED IN MANUFACTURING,
BY OWNERSHIP, AS OF 1981

Proportions Employed in Manufacturing by Ownership, 1981		Closures and Job Loss in Manufacturing, 1976-86			
	%	Closures	%	Job Loss	%
Canadian-owned	74.4	37	67.3	3,898	58.2
Foreign-owned	25.4	18	32.7	2,804	41.8
U.S.-owned	16.4	14	25.5	2,163	32.3

Some of these cases are particularly interesting. Kimberley Clark was making a profit,[3] but not as much as could be made by moving into Ontario and Québec facilities modernized with the help of federal and provincial grants.[4] Harco Electronics started in Manitoba, was helped by government grants,[5] and developed so substantial an American market that it moved its headquarters to California, promptly closing the Manitoba plant to supply the Canadian market from the United States. General Aluminum Forgings was issued a stop-work order due to extremely high levels of lead oxide, but chose not to invest the capital needed to control the pollution. Production was shifted to California, despite the company's initial acceptance of Manitoba government grants in return for promises of job creation.

TABLE 51

CLOSURES AND JOB LOSS BY REASON,* 1976-1986

	Closures	%	Job Loss	%
Rationalization	32	36.4	4,067	36.3
Market Shift	3	3.4	1,841	16.5
Receivership	15	17.1	1,341	12.0
Depression/Reduced Demands	13	14.8	1,190	10.6
Agricultural Manufacturing	8	9.1	938	8.4
Bad Management	5	5.7	720	6.4
Exhaustion of Ore Supply	4	4.5	532	4.8
Moved Head Office/Special Function	6	6.8	429	3.8
Urban Redevelopment	1	1.1	68	.6
Government Policy	1	1.1	65	.6
Total	88	100.0	11,191	100.0

*Note: Based on press reports and interviews.

Of the eighty-eight closures, seventeen (19 percent) followed an acquisition or merger. This, too, is part of the process of rationalization, and often has little to do with a plant's ability to survive. Agricultural problems and farmers' reduced purchasing power led to numerous additional closures: agricultural implement manufacturers such as Canadian Cooperative Implements Limited and Walden Industries, and metal manufacturing firms and foundries linked to agricultural production, such as Canadian Rogers Western, Canadian Steel Tank and Metals Industries, Matthews Mechanical Ltd., and Bell Foundry.

The process of rationalization, and agricultural problems, have led especially to manufacturing closures: fifty-five of the eighty-eight closures (62.5 percent), and 6,702 (58.9 percent) of the jobs lost (see Table 52). This is consistent with the reduced numbers employed in manufacturing in Manitoba — from 66,000 in 1981 to 55,000 in 1986, a drop of 16.7 percent. In Ontario the decline for the same period was 1.7 percent, and in Canada as a whole it was 6.0 percent.

TABLE 52

CLOSURES AND JOB LOSS BY SECTOR, 1976-1986

	Closures	% of Total	Jobs Lost	% of Total
Manufacturing*	55	62.5	6,702	59.9
Mining	5	5.7	632	5.6
Transport	1	1.1	65	.6
Trade and Service	24	27.3	3,550	31.7
Financial	3	3.4	242	2.2
Total	88	100.0	11,191	100.0

*Note: Includes *Winnipeg Tribune*.

It may be that Manitoba's economy is becoming increasingly fragile, or even that a process of de-industrialization is underway, though an examination of this question is beyond the scope of this study. If this is in fact the case, a decline in manufacturing plus dramatic shifts in agriculture and the exhaustion of several northern ore bodies could spell future problems for a Manitoba economy always thought to be stable by virtue of its diversified goods-producing capacity, and especially its diversified and relatively strong manufacturing base. This is a question which requires further study.

The closure data can also be analyzed by union (see Table 53). Unionized jobs have been disproportionately affected by closures. While 37.2 percent of Manitoba's paid nonagricultural workers were unionized in 1984, 60 percent of the jobs lost due to closures were unionized. Three unions have lost more than one-quarter of their membership to closures, six others have lost more than one-sixth. Clearly the trade union movement has an interest in demanding that action be taken on plant closures, or in taking such action themselves if the government does not.

TABLE 53

CLOSURES AND JOB LOSS BY UNION, 1976-1986

Union	Closures	Job Loss	1983 Membership*	Job Loss as % of 1983 Membership*
Food and Commercial Workers	10	1,378	9,134	15.1
United Steelworkers of America	12	1,086	6,162	17.6
Amalgamated Clothing and Textile Workers	4	955	2,126	44.9
Graphic Communications International	1	650	—	—
Canadian Association of Industrial, Mechanical & Allied Workers	7	640	2,084	30.7
Retail, Wholesale and Department Store Union	3	425	1,610	26.4
United Auto Workers	2	370	—	—
Canadian Paperworkers Union	2	186	894	20.8
Oil, Chemical and Atomic Workers International	1	176	—	—
United Garment Workers	1	130	—	—
International Brotherhood of Electrical Workers	1	80	—	—
International Association of Machinists and Aerospace Workers	1	78	—	—
Sheet Metal Workers	1	60	—	—
United Brewery and Soft Drink Workers	1	50	—	—
Sub-total	—	6,264	—	—
Employees Association	1	67	—	—
No Union	40	4,860	—	—
Total	88	11,191	—	—

*Note: Membership, and job loss as a percentage of membership, are not shown for those unions with only one closure.

Closures can also be categorized by size of company, as measured by the number of employees (see Table 54). Companies with 50-99 employees constitute two-thirds of the closures, but only one-third of the job loss, while companies with more than three hundred employees, which constituted less than 4 percent of the closures, also caused close to one-third of the job loss. This suggests that any plant closure strategy must pay particular attention to large closures, given their disproportionate impact on job loss.

TABLE 54
CLOSURES AND JOB LOSS BY SIZE, 1976-1986

Size in Number of Employees	Number of Companies	Percentage of Total	Number of Jobs Lost	Percentage of Total
50-100	59	67.3	4,006	35.8
101-300	25	28.4	3,904	34.9
301 or more	4	4.6	3,281	29.3
Total	88	100.0	11,191	100.0

Effects of Plant Closures

Not only have the number of closures and workers affected in Manitoba been high, but also the effects of these closures have been very adverse. The literature on plant closures in the United States clearly spells out their consequences.[6] At least one-third of those who lose jobs suffer long-term unemployment. Table 55 suggests similar results in Canada. And job loss due to closure has a discriminatory impact: older workers, women, and those with lower levels of formal education have more difficulty finding work.[7] Those who do find new jobs suffer reduced income. This is so especially in better-paying unionized sectors like meat packing, but also applies to low-wage, "secondary" industries like the garment industry.[8] This may lead to loss of homes, savings or other personal assets, which in turn results in stress and frequent deterioration in physical and mental health.[9]

For the community, closures cause reduced purchasing power, which may lead to further layoffs or even closures in suppliers or retailers, plus reduced tax revenue and increased social service expenditures for local authorities, which may in turn lead to a reduced ability to provide needed public services. In short, the *real* cost of plant closures is very high indeed. Professor Paul Grayson calculated a part of the real cost of the December 1981 closure of SKF, Canada Ltd., in Scarborough, Ontario. By February 1984, lost wages and pensions totalled $3.5 million for those still unemployed, $2.1 million for those re-employed, and $1.5 million had been paid out in unemployment insurance — a total of $7.1 million. This, he said, is a conservative estimate: it includes neither welfare payments nor increased medical costs. And this was only for the 310 people at SKF:

> When the cost of job loss for this 310 is multiplied by the hundreds of thousands of others who have lost their positions because of corporate decisions to rationalize production for the good of the company, the economic cost is staggering.[10]

Studies of the effects of closures and layoffs in Manitoba are few and incomplete, in that they do not include data on *all* the factors treated in other such studies, but in general they are consistent with the experience elsewhere. Brad McKenzie studied Thompson, comparing various socioeconomic indicators in the first quarter of 1978 with the first quarter of 1977. Between May 1977 and October 1978 INCO laid off 1,200 workers, resulting in a 30 percent reduction of Thompson's labour force, and a 20 percent reduction in population.[11] No other significant social changes occurred during this period, so changes in the indicators would appear to be a function of job loss.

TABLE 55
UNEMPLOYMENT RATES AMONG FORMER EMPLOYEES
OF CLOSED ENTERPRISES*

Company	Location	Months from Closure	% Labour Unemployed
Firestone	Whitby	18	20.2
Norwich Eaton	Paris	15	32.0
Armstrong Cork	Lindsay	15	37.3
Harlequin Books	Stratford	12	39.5
Union Carbide	Toronto	6	66.7
Rockwell	Parry Sound	21	27.0
MacMillan Bloedel	Toronto	18	30.3
Celanese Millhaven	Cambridge	9	82.9
Western Automotive	Toronto	21	11.1
Co-op Health Services	Toronto	12	10.0
Courtaulds-Caravelle	Cornwall	15	20.8
Sheller Globe	Deseronto	12	47.4
Square D Co.	Mississauga	27	26.9
Blue Bell	Carleton Place	9	52.2
Bendix Automotive	Windsor	21	49.4
General Bakeries	Hamilton	21	39.6
Agincourt Motor Hotel	Toronto	12	24.0
Laura Secord	Toronto	9	51.4
Pecters	Belleville	18	30.6
Roper Corporation	Ingersoll	21	15.8
Greb Industries	Kitchener	21	41.5

*Note: All data as of March 1982.
Source: Paul Grayson, *Corporate Strategy and Plant Closures: The SKF Experience* (Toronto: Our Times Publishing Ltd., 1985), 169.

McKenzie found dramatic increases in public expenditures for income support, crime, and social service referrals, as shown in Table 56. A questionnaire was also mailed to approximately five hundred Thompson residents in July 1978. Some 27 percent of respondents reported reduced household income, and more than 40 percent that stress in their lives had increased in the last year. McKenzie concluded that

> job reductions cause significant increases in income support payments and that resulting stress contributes to increased Criminal and non-Criminal Code offenses, incidents of crisis related to personal depression, and increased family and marital breakdowns [and that] the magnitude of these costs are [*sic*] considerable.

Yet he added that

> this study found little evidence that decision-makers are taking serious notice of the major policy changes required to offer protection to workers and families affected by forces in the workplace.[12]

McKenzie also conducted a telephone survey of former Swift's employees in the summer of 1981, approximately eighteen to twenty months after the December 1979 Swift's closure.[13] His analysis is based on 168 analyzed questionnaires, which represented 38 percent of the 450 hourly employees. He found that 15 percent of the respondents still had no work. He also found a total loss of income (based on 119 workers who responded to this question) of $878,259, or an average of $7,388 per worker. This figure does not include severance pay (84 percent reported receiving severance pay), or unemployment insurance, which averaged $3,025 per worker. Thus, each worker lost on average a net amount of $4,363, excluding severance pay, in the period following the closure.

TABLE 56
THE EFFECTS OF JOB LOSS IN THOMPSON

	First Quarter 1977	First Quarter 1978	% Change
A. Income Support:*			
Unemployment Insurance Recipients	244	421	+72
Unemployment Insurance Costs	$329,888	$602,030	+82
Unemployment Insurance Costs per 1000 of Population	$ 18,638	$ 37,393	+101
Welfare Applicants	572	692	+21
Welfare Payouts	$ 44,900	$ 65,304	+45
Welfare Costs per 1000 of Population	$ 2,537	$ 4,056	+60
B. Crime:**			
Criminal Code Offenses	414	526	+27
Criminal Code Offenses per 1000 of Population	23.4	32.7	+40
Non-Criminal Code Offenses (mainly liquor related)	795	1,032	+32
Juvenile Offenders	73	129	+77
C. Social Service Referrals:			
Cases of Child Abuse	1	6	—
Children Taken into Care	19	33	+74
Voluntary Family Counselling Services	26	31	+19
Referrals to Hospital, Women's Crisis Centre or Telecare due to Depression or Suicide	23	50	+117
Referrals due to Marital Problems	102	137	+34

Notes: *Unemployment and welfare costs are understated. A very significant cost factor was
exported to other constituencies because many of the unemployed left Thompson;
**There was no evidence of tighter policing nor improved collection reporting of data
to account for these increases. Further, while these Thompson crime incidences were
rising, Criminal Code offenses for Manitoba as a whole declined by 6.5%.

Source: Prepared from data in Brad McKenzie, "INCO and Thompson: An Analysis of the Social
Impact of Job Cutbacks," paper delivered to the Annual Conference, Canadian Rural
Social Work Forum, Thunder Bay, Ontario.

This is consistent with reports of a telephone survey of former Swift's employees conducted 15-16 January 1980 by Leitold and St. Yves, members of the Joint Manpower Adjustment Committee set up at Swift's. The minutes of a 17 January 1980 meeting of that committee report that

> Mr. Leitold indicated there was considerable verbal abuse given to both he and Mr. St. Yves during the course of their survey and that many employees had indicated they would not accept jobs in the $5.00 to $6.00 salary [sic] range nor would they be prepared to accept shift work.

Minutes of the 19 December 1979 committee meeting state that "Mr. Trudel [of the Canada Employment Commission] reported that approximately 50% of the jobs that had been submitted to him were in the $6.00 or less category."[14] Most hourly employees at Swift's had been earning about $8.00; a $6.00 job represents a 25 percent cut in gross wages.

When asked whether personal stress had increased or decreased in their new jobs, 40 percent of the Swift's workers surveyed by McKenzie reported no change, but 39 percent reported an increase (19 percent a little, 20 percent a lot). More positively, 36 percent of respondents reported more job satisfaction, 27 percent reported less, and 19 percent reported no change, while 36 percent reported better working conditions, 18 percent reported worse, and 27 percent reported no change.[15]

These figures are consistent with the findings of Al Patterson in his 1982 study of former employees of Swift's, the *Tribune* and Maple Leaf Mills. Patterson mailed a questionnaire in May-June 1982, and got a 29.4 percent response rate. He found that "71.6% (159/122) ... rated their present jobs as good as or better than those they lost." This is a surprising figure since "on the basis of constant dollars, success in the job market after the shutdowns was low. That is, 68.8% (130/189) of the respondents earn less now than on the jobs lost." His findings also led him to conclude, consistent with findings elsewhere, that "older and less educated workers are the ones hardest hit by plant closings."[16]

Of the 825 employees at Canada Packers who lost their jobs in 1987 or 1988, 350 (40 percent) were 50 years of age or over. An age profile of Swift's employees at the time of closure revealed that 45 were aged 18-30 years, 121 were 31-45 years, and 95 (approximately 36 percent) were in the "age-disadvantaged" range of 45-65. Further, "on a sampling of 50 employees laid off the average education was grade 8."[17]

Although the literature is not completely consistent on the effects of closures,[18] there is much evidence that closures cause significant personal hardship, in the form of extended periods of unemployment, income loss, de-skilling, and family and health problems, plus significant societal cost, in the form of additional job losses through the multiplier effect, reduced government revenue and increased government expenditure, and higher incidences of social problems such as crime. What little evidence has been gathered in Manitoba suggests that closures have had such adverse consequences.

Plant Closure Legislation in Manitoba

Despite the magnitude of the problem, and the severity of its consequences, legislative remedies for Manitoba closures are few and inadequate. The main federal instrument for dealing with closures is the Canada Industrial Adjustment Service (IAS), formerly called the Manpower Consultancy Service (MCS). The IAS uses joint consultation, via the establishment of industrial adjustment committees comprised of equal numbers of management and labour representatives plus a neutral chair, to respond to "manpower adjustment problems" such as closures.

The IAS has serious limitations. The establishment of a committee at the time of a closure is voluntary: if management chooses not to cooperate, there is no committee. Thus, adjustment committees are seldom used. In Manitoba, about twelve such committees are established per year. But since the program's emphasis has shifted in the last three years from a concentration on "crises," like closures, to a concentration on technological change and plant expansion,[19] only a small proportion of closures benefit from the IAS.

The "benefits" are few, because committees have little power. They cannot require companies to open their books and justify decisions to close or move, nor can they require that proposed recommendations be implemented. They can do only what management and labour can mutually agree upon, which effectively gives management a veto.

In the case of closures, committees confine themselves to trying to find new jobs for laid-off workers, providing information about retraining opportunities and mobility grants, and offering financial guidance and counselling for stress-related psychological problems. Keeping a plant open is not considered. Such is a "political" issue, beyond the committees' mandate.[20]

But even in this narrowed realm, the performance of these committees is uninspiring. In the case of the Swift's closure, for example, workers lost $8.00 per hour jobs; the committee offered jobs paying $6.00 or less to about one-half of those laid off. According to Walter Pascoe, chief union steward at Swift's and a member of the committee:

> it didn't work out … the jobs we could come up with were all low-paying jobs that the employees didn't want. Can you imagine making $8.00 an hour and being asked to work for $4.50?[21]

The same case applied when Kimberley Clark closed: jobs were found at $5.00 to $6.00 per hour, well below the preclosure rates, and workers would not take them.

Patterson's study found that only 13.2 percent of the respondents at Swift's and Maple Leaf Mills (17/129) found the adjustment committees useful,[22] a finding consistent with the comment of a Manitoba Department of Labour official that often "not a heck of a lot gets done."[23] Brad McKenzie's conclusion in his study of Thompson seems correct:

> Programs which include Counselling and Manpower Adjustment Committees are sometimes created in cases where large plant shutdowns have occurred. While these efforts are oriented to locating new employment, and assisting workers in relocating, they have proven to be of limited effectiveness, and do nothing to reduce the net effect of lost positions to the general economy.[24]

Provincial legislation is equally ineffectual. Recent changes to the Employment Standards Act, 35.1(1) increase the advance written notice employers must give for mass layoffs: ten weeks if the number terminated does not exceed 100; fourteen weeks if the number terminated is between 101 and 300; and eighteen weeks for 301 workers or more. The previous notice period had been eight weeks for 50-100 employees, twelve weeks for 100-300, and fourteen weeks for more than 300. As already shown, this provision is frequently circumvented. Nor is the notification period close to the one year called for by the MFL and the NDP.

The legislation also empowers the provincial minister of labour to establish a joint planning committee of not less than two representatives each of management and labour, plus any other persons considered suitable.[25] The purpose of such committees is

> to develop on a cooperative basis an adjustment program to eliminate the necessity for the termination of employment or to minimize the impact of such termination on the affected employees and to assist those employees in obtaining other employment.[26]

This provision is superior to the IAS, in that a committee may be established without management's approval, and may question the necessity for closure. However, its powers are limited by the provision that the "adjustment program" shall be established "on a cooperative basis." Nothing is compulsory. The committee can act only on a consultative basis, giving management a veto. Committees cannot examine a company's books, nor require a company to justify its actions, and are likely to be indistinguishable from the industrial adjustment committees. Committees established by similar legislation in Québec have been referred to as "funeral committees."[27]

Why is There No Plant Closure Strategy?

Government inactivity on plant closures is easy to explain in the case of the Conservatives. When former Conservative Industry Minister J. Frank Johnston was criticized for the inadequacy of the reporting system for closures he replied: "What do you want us to do? Put an ad in the paper saying: 'please warn us if you are going broke'?"[28] Johnston had earlier revealed his ignorance of the dynamics of plant closures by stating that "I don't think anyone closes a plant if it is making a profit."[29] In fact, profitable plants are frequently closed, as a result of rationalization.

The NDP government's inactivity on plant closures is harder to explain. After the announcement of the Swift's closure Howard Pawley, then Leader of the Opposition, called upon Premier Sterling Lyon "to immediately have a legislative committee fully investigate the closure,"[30] and Rod Murphy, NDP MP for Churchill, concurred, saying "Manitoba appears to be suffering from an unproportionally [sic] high number of plant closures."[31]

Plant closure legislation is party policy,[32] and the NDP promised legislation during its 1981 election campaign. Yet when such legislation was finally introduced in 1986, it consisted only of slightly longer notice periods and the provision for joint planning committees.

It appeared, early in the first Pawley administration, that plant closure legislation would be enacted. Campaign promises were made in the fall of 1981. The December 1982 Throne Speech promised a major review of labour legislation, to begin in April 1983 and to include plant closure. The subsequent Labour Law Review held public hearings in June-July 1983,[33] shortly after several major closures — the Shell Refinery,

CAE Aircraft, Kimberley Clark — had stimulated concern, as evidenced by Muriel Smith's reference to the latest ''chilling list of branch plant closures.''[34] But the sources from which the government sought advice on the issue were advisory bodies structured so as to ensure that tough plant closure legislation would not be recommended. Two such advisory bodies were the ad hoc Scotten Committee, and the Labour Management Review Committee.

The Labour Law Review was organized such that plant closure legislation and technological change were passed to a separate interdepartmental committee headed by Cliff Scotten, senior adviser to Premier Howard Pawley. Scotten's committee was a weak body, hastily drawn together in ad hoc fashion and pressed for time. All its members were full-time civil servants, and Scotten himself was especially burdened with work. The commitee was not high-powered — its members were middle-level civil servants — and in any event it appears to have been split on the issue of plant closures. Even had the committee not been split, middle-level bureaucrats are an unlikely source of strong recommendations on a controversial policy issue. The committee concluded that there were insufficient data available on the magnitude and the details of the problem of plant closures, and that an ''army of researchers'' would be needed to rectify this lack of data.[35] Only one researcher was made available. The result was a weak report.[36]

The Labour-Management Review Committee (LMRC) also examined technological change and plant closure legislation. Comprised of equal numbers of labour and management representatives, the LMRC operates on a consensual basis, making only those recommendations to cabinet which are mutually agreed upon. It forms part of the consensual machinery through which labour policy is processed, and by which management is afforded a veto.Thus the business community insists that all labour law recommendations be channelled through the LMRC, arguing that ''proposals for change submitted by that Committee would have the advantage of mutuality and would enjoy the confidence of the labour relations community.''[37] The LMRC struck a subcommittee to study plant closure legislation. The subcommittee met for two years, working out the details of a proposal, and culminated its efforts with a weekend meeting at Hecla Island. An agreement was reached which, while not ideal, was satisfactory to the labour representatives. One final meeting was scheduled to finalize the proposal, and it was agreed that the consensus achieved after so much effort could not be undone by any representative not present at the Hecla Island meeting. This agreement notwithstanding, at the final meeting in Winnipeg a management representative from the garment industry who was not at Hecla scuttled the entire proposal. In the end, no recommendation was made to cabinet.[38]

Although the minister of Labour wrote to the LMRC in July 1986, requesting that consideration again be given to plant closure legislation,[39] there is little likelihood of the LMRC recommending tough plant closure legislation, since management maintains its veto, and since the business community has made its views on plant closure legislation well known. The Winnipeg Chamber of Commerce has recommended that ''the Government encourage an economic environment which will keep businesses operating effectively rather than imposing any more restrictive legislation on employers and employees,''[40] the Manitoba Chambers of Commerce have added that ''plant closures must be allowed to happen at minimum cost and with minimum restrictions,''[41] and the Manitoba branch of the Canadian Manufacturers' Association (CMA) has argued that job loss due to plant closures ''is adequately dealt with under Section 35 of the Employment Standards Act-Group Terminations,'' so that no further legislation is ''necessary or desirable.''[42]

Though such statements are contrary to NDP policy on closures, the former NDP government's strategy on labour legislation was generally to move on issues around which a consensus had been reached, and where a consensus had not been reached, to work to develop one.[43] This strategy was consistent with the business community's insistence that labour law recommendations be channelled through consensual machinery like the LMRC. Given that the LMRC affords management a veto, the outcome regarding plant closure legislation was preordained.

The NDP government felt it necessary to use such consensual machinery because capital is mobile in a way that labour is not. Capital can choose to locate or expand in Manitoba, or not to, and must therefore be induced to invest. This is done in large part by creating a ''good business climate.'' As the Manitoba branch of the CMA stated, any plant closure legislation ''would only act as a further deterrent for prospective employers opening up manufacturing operations in Manitoba.''[44] In fact, however, it may be that closures create a ''good business climate'':

> Compelling evidence exists that the layoffs created by plant closings can actually improve the business climate. The swelling of the ranks of the unemployed creates a reserve of malleable workers and even potential strikebreakers.[45]

The perceived need to create a good business climate was accentuated when, shortly after taking office in 1981, the NDP government realized that Manitoba had been experiencing a net disinvestment since the mid-1970s, especially in manufacturing (see Table 57).[46] This ''scary prognosis'' led to a cabinet fight, the outcome of which was a commitment to a consensual approach to labour legislation. It was feared that tough labour legislation would accelerate closures, and given the process of disinvestment already underway, the province would have nothing with which to replace closed businesses.

Thus, although the NDP looked at many options for plant closure legislation,[47] especially in 1983, it made only the minor legislative modifications already described. It also examined various other options — venture capital, purchasing policy,[48] the identification and promotion of Manitoba ''sun-rise industries,'' the attraction of Hong Kong capital, the promotion of small business and entrepreneurship — which constituted a ''pro-active'' policy to attracting capital to Manitoba. But such measures served to reinforce the desire to avoid plant closure legislation, since such legislation would impede attempts to attract capital.

Consequently, the government neither introduced plant closure legislation nor developed a plant closure strategy. Minister of Cooperative Development Jay Cowan described the government's thinking on plant closures by saying that change has to be managed well to be effective, and therefore governments have to establish a limited agenda for change, which means setting priorities. Plant closures were not a priority and were therefore the type of issue that was ''incident-driven,''[49] meaning that the government responded in ad hoc fashion to closures when announced.

TABLE 57

NET STOCK, FIXED CAPITAL IN MANUFACTURING,
MANITOBA AND CANADA, 1970-1985

End of Year	Total Manufacturing Industries, Canada (Millions of Constant 1971 Dollars)	Index Number 1975 Base Year	Total Manufacturing Industries, Manitoba (Thousands of Constant 1971 Dollars)	Index Number 1975 Base Year
1970	28,170.3		790,494	
1971	29,304.3		794,556	
1972	30,221.3		795,684	
1973	31,562.4		809,799	
1974	33,364.0		841,915	
1975	34,954.0	100.0	851,213	100.0
1976	36,154.5	103.4	847,663	99.6
1977	37,307.3	106.7	841,635	98.9
1978	38,102.9	109.0	834,105	98.0
1979	39,093.7	111.8	834,150	98.0
1980	40,615.3	116.2	836,408	98.3
1981	42,671.8	122.1	863,758	101.5
1982	43,815.1	125.4	856,259	101.7
1983	43,927.9	125.7	845,710	99.4
1984	43,962.6	125.8	834,607	98.0
1985	44,527.0	127.4	829,973	97.5

Source: Statistics Canada, unpublished data, Science, Technology and Capital Stock Division.

The absence of a strategy was attributable not only to the government's response to the pressures exerted by the needs of the ''business climate,'' but also to the *absence* of pressure from the labour movement in favour of such a strategy. The MFL has passed resolutions calling for plant closure legislation, and made a submission — along with seven other labour organizations — to the Labour Law Review. At its 1980 convention the MFL stated that if tough plant closure legislation — including one year's notice and the opening of a company's books — were not implemented, it would ''undertake an effective opposition to the closure or layoff, which shall include sitdowns and physical occupation of the plant or company, if necessary.''[50] Bernard Christophe of the Manitoba Food and Commercial Workers said the labour movement had had enough of committees such as that at Swift's, which were limited to helping workers find other jobs, and called for the physical occupation of plants that shut down.[51] Yet no plants have been occupied, no rallies have been staged, and no outcry has been raised at the abandonment of effective plant closure legislation. Unions have not even been successful in building protection against plant closures into their collective agreements (see Table 58). Why is this so?

TABLE 58

COLLECTIVE AGREEMENT PROVISIONS RELATED TO CLOSURES, 1985

	Number of Employees	% of Total	Number of Agreements	% of Total
1. Advance Notice of Termination (or pay in lieu) to Employees				
No provision	48,463	68.0	385	65.0
One week or less	4,448	6.2	40	6.8
Two to eight weeks	11,265	15.8	94	15.9
Varies with different groups of employees	6,169	8.7	59	10.0
Graduated by length of service	312	.4	6	1.0
Mentioned but not specified	409	.6	7	1.1
Other	160	.2	1	.2
Total	71,226	100.0	592	100.0
2. Supplemental Unemployment Benefit (Sub) Plans				
No provision	69,890	98.1	587	99.2
Provision exists	1,336	1.9	5	.8
Total	71,226	100.0	592	100.0
3. Severance Pay and Lay-Off Benefit Plans (Other than Sub)				
No provision	43,154	60.0	474	80.1
Severance pay plan	25,706	36.1	106	17.9
Lay-off benefits	431	.6	5	.8
Severance pay and lay-off benefit plan	1,935	2.7	7	1.2
Total	71,226	100.0	592	100.0

Source: Manitoba Labour, *Collective Agreement Analysis Data Base Guide, 1985.*

The answer, it seems, is that an NDP government demobilizes the labour movement. Rather than pressure an NDP government to promote its interests, labour seeks to cooperate with it, entering willingly into the consensual machinery through which labour legislation is processed. This strategy is attractive to labour: it ensures that labour's voice is heard and that some gains are made, at least in areas where management does not exercise its veto. Such gains may be significant but the price is high, since such an approach precludes the mobilization of labour, and a demobilized labour movement is unable to exert the pressure needed to win victories in more contentious areas, where capital would have to be confronted. Thus, under an NDP administration, labour is limited to gains at the margin, while gains which would require confronting capital, like plant closure legislation, are made impossible by the very machinery which negotiates the marginal gains. Ironically, therefore, plant closure legislation — which it is possible to achieve, which exists elsewhere (France, Italy, Norway, Sweden and West Germany have strong plant closure laws or the equivalent), which can be justified not only ethically but also socially and economically, and which would serve the interests of the very people the NDP seeks to represent — cannot be won from a Conservative administration, given its ideology, and cannot be won from an NDP administration, also given its ideology. The case of plant closure legislation in Manitoba is an example of the limitations of social democracy. Yet social democracy need not be this limited.

A Plant Closure Strategy

The thrust of this chapter is not that there are easy solutions to the plant closure problem — there are not. Capital can choose to invest in Manitoba, or not to, creating a hard economic reality which it is utopian to deny, and the provincial budget is severely squeezed, leaving little fiscal capacity for innovation.[52] The plant closure problem cannot be completely solved as long as our society is organized on the basis of profit, since the search for profit causes much of the problem in the first place. However, a partial solution is possible.

The first requirement is legislative change to require longer notice. Adequate notice is the basis of a plant closure strategy, since the response to a closure requires time to prepare. Research must be done, corporate and industry financial data must be assembled and analyzed, legal issues must be considered, and workers must be involved.

The second requirement is the establishment of a plant closure review agency, mandated to investigate closures. Investigations should include a social audit by a commission including labour and community representatives, with powers to examine a company's books, to determine causes and *real* costs of closures, and to determine if a plant could be kept open under different ownership arrangements. When it could, the agency would provide or mobilize the technical expertise — financial, legal, organizational — and the necessary funding.

The idea of a closures unit was considered by labour and NDP government officials, but nothing came of it. For example, the MFL held talks with several departments about the government's establishment of a ''SWAT'' team to move in when a closure was threatened, to see if a workers' takeover was possible. In the end it was placed on a ''back burner'' because both sides had other priorities.[53]

In many cases, investigation of a closure is likely to reveal that no response is desirable. No good purpose is served in intervening indiscriminately to save uneconomic plants in dying industries.[54] But in some cases a plant about to be closed is still viable. It may have been operating profitably, but not profitably enough for its parent corporation, or it may have been mismanaged, so that improved management would make it viable. And a social audit may reveal that the *real* costs to the community of a closure are much higher than the costs of keeping the plant in operation.[55]

In such cases it may be possible to keep the plant open under new ownership, of which several variations are possible. Another owner, group of investors, or even a private/community consortium, may be found or mobilized. Local ownership is advantageous, since Manitoba-based capital is generally less mobile than capital domiciled elsewhere.[56] Or the employees may buy the plant; this has already proven successful in saving Greb Shoes and Dawsteel. Or a workers' cooperative may be established, as was done successfully to save jobs at Vent-Air.

The track record of employee buyouts to prevent closures in other jurisdictions is mixed and it is sometimes argued that buyouts are detrimental to the interests of workers — they may be a way of de-unionizing a plant, or getting employees to accept a cut in pay.[57] But this need not necessarily be so, and a purpose of the plant closure review agency would be to ensure that buyouts occur only when they will benefit workers, as they sometimes do. In the United States, for example,

> an estimated 60 companies have been bought by their employees in an effort to prevent a planned shutdown of the facility. Of these only two — involving 50 employees — have ended in financial failure. . . . Employee ownership is said to have saved approximately 50,000 jobs directly and thousands more in related or support firms.[58]

Finally, a plant closure strategy would be much more effective if it were part of a broader industrial strategy. Some have even argued that plant closure strategies simply will not work in the absence of an industrial strategy.[59] The NDP government had no industrial strategy. Although job creation efforts were coordinated by the Economic and Resource Committee of cabinet, and the Jobs Fund, the allocation of resources was not based on a strategy. The Jobs Fund drew money from existing departments, which then "bid" for it by proposing programs oriented to job creation, the money being allocated to those programs deemed most likely to create jobs. Thus the initiative for program proposals continued to rest with traditional departments, and job creation was not pursued via a coherent strategy, but rather via a series of discrete programs. The strategy was in the programs. What are they? Industry, Trade and Technology boasts "a comprehensive range of financial incentive programs,"[60] with no indication that they are part of a strategy. The only "strategy" was the government's reliance on what amounted to a state-led megaprojects thrust, centred on the Limestone hydroelectric project and various large urban development programs related to Winnipeg's Core Area Initiative and the North Portage Development Program. These created a substantial number of construction jobs, and at least some related activity, but their job creating capacity was short term (see Chapter 12). It seems fair to say, then, that under the former NDP government, Manitoba had no industrial strategy within which to situate a plant closure strategy, nor indeed did it have a plant closure strategy.

Conclusion

The preceding elements, preferably with but even without an industrial strategy, constitute the rudiments of a viable plant closure strategy. Such a strategy would consist, at a minimum, of improved government monitoring of closures, with powers to examine a company's books, to conduct public social audits to determine the real costs of closures, and to effect a plan to keep a plant open when warranted. These measures would not "solve" the problem of plant closures, for this is not possible given capitalist relations of production. Thus a plant closure strategy would also have to include improved provisions for severance pay, and retraining and relocation allowances. Nor is this a socialist strategy. "Socialism in one province" is not possible. Thus the challenge is to develop a strategy that can fit within these constraints, and yet is bold enough to effect gains for working people.

Regrettably, Manitoba's NDP government did not meet this challenge. It abandoned meaningful action in response to closures, and did not even establish the means by which to identify those closures which occurred. Social democracy is limited; it need not be *this* limited.

NOTES

1. Statistics Canada, *Domestic and Foreign Control of Manufacturing, Mining and Logging Establishments in Canada*, 1981, Catalogue # 31-401, Table 2, 35.

2. This finding is consistent with Paul Grayson, "Global Chess: Who Owns the Pieces?," *Our Times* (November 1984): 14-15, and with John Elleen and G. Ashley Bernardine, *Shutdown: The Impact of Plant Shutdown, Extensive Employment Terminations and Layoffs on the Workers and the Community* (Toronto: Ontario Federation of Labour, 1971), 171-91. However, it is inconsistent with the findings of Fred Caloren in *Layoffs, Shutdowns and Closures in Ontario Manufacturing, Mining and Trade Establishments, January 1971-June 1972* (Ottawa: University of Ottawa, 1974). Caloren found that country of control did not make any difference to the propensity to closure.

3. Jack Alexander, Canadian Paperworkers Union, interview with author, 16 September 1986. Alexander claims that management made this admission to the union. See also *Winnipeg Free Press* (hereafter *WFP*), 26 February 1983.

4. See, for example, the *Globe and Mail*, 29 November 1983.

5. See, for example, the *Winnipeg Sun*, 2 March and 12 May 1982.

6. See, for example, Barry Bluestone and Bennett Harrison, *The Deindustrialization of America* (New York: Basic Books, 1982), especially pages 49-81. For a review of case studies of American closures, see William Haber, Louis A. Ferman and James R. Hudson, *The Impact of Technological Change: The American Experience* (Kalamazoo, Michigan: The W.E. Upjohn Institute for Employment Research, 1953), and J.P. Gordus, P. Jarley and Louis A. Ferman, *Plant Closings and Economic Dislocation* (Kalamazoo, Michigan: The W.E. Upjohn Institute for Employment Research, 1981).

7. Bluestone and Harrison, *Deindustrialization*, 51.

8. Louis S. Jacobson, "Earnings Loss of Workers Displaced From Manufacturing Industries," in William G. Dewold, ed., *The Impact of International Trade and Investment on Employment* (n.p.: General Publishing Office, 1978); and Louis S. Jacobson, "Earnings Loss Due to Displacement" (Working paper CRC-385, The Public Research Institute of the Centre for Naval Analysis, April 1979); and Bluestone and Harrison, *Deindustrialization*, 55-61.

9. Sidney Cobb and Stanislaw Kasl, *Termination: The Consequences of Job Loss* (Washington, D.C.: Department of Health, Education and Welfare, 1977). Cobb and Kasl have published numerous other studies relating health to job loss. See also Robert L. Aronson and Robert B. McKersie, *Economic Consequences of Plant Shutdowns in New York State* (Ithaca, N.Y.: Cornell University, 1980).

10. Paul Grayson, *Corporate Strategy and Plant Closures: The SKF Experience* (Toronto: Our Times Publishing Ltd., 1985), 168.

11. Brad McKenzie, "INCO and Thompson: An Analysis of the Social Impact of Job Cutbacks" (paper delivered to the Annual Conference, Canadian Rural Social Work Forum, Thunder Bay, Ontario, 26 May 1981).

12. Ibid., 25-26.

13. The following information was taken from Brad McKenzie's as yet unpublished notes on the results of the survey.

14. Swift's Joint Manpower Adjustment Committee, "Minutes" (19 December 1979)

15. McKenzie, unpublished notes.

16. Al Patterson, "A Study of Three Plant Closings in Winnipeg" (paper presented at ASAC Conference, University of British Columbia, 1983, pages 6, 9-10).

17. Swift's, "Minutes."

18. See Grayson, *Corporate Strategy*, 200-01, for a discussion.

19. Barry Meyer, Industrial Adjustment Service Officer for Manitoba, interview with author, 20 August 1986.

20. Ibid.

21. *WFP*, 4 February 1981.

22. Patterson, "A Study," 4.

23. Manitoba Department of Labour official who wished not to be identified, interview with author, 19 August 1986.

24. McKenzie, "INCO and Thompson," 28.

25. Employment Standards Act, 35.1(7.2).

26. Ibid., 35.1(7.12).

27. Jean Sexton, *Blue Collar Workers Displaced by Complete and Permanent Plant Shutdowns: The Quebec Experience* (Québec: Université Laval, Département des Relations Industrielles, 1974).

28. *WFP*, 18 December 1980.

29. Ibid., 15 September 1979.

30. Howard Pawley to Sterling Lyon, 10 October 1979. I am grateful to Bruno Zimmer of the United Food and Commercial Workers for allowing me access to his file on the Swift's closure, in which a copy of this letter was found.

31. *WFP*, 27 October 1979.

32. Recommendations at the 23rd Annual Convention in February 1986 included one year's notice of closures; a committee to find alternatives to closure; one week's severance pay per year of service if closure is inevitable; and a closure tax to establish a fund to supplement lost income once severance pay is exhausted until employees find suitable jobs. Previous conventions had also called for access by the union and government to the company's books, and a provincial government capital fund to assist workers in establishing workers' cooperatives.

33. "Compendium of Recommendations Made to the Labour Law Review, Public Hearings," Winnipeg, June and July 1983.

34. *WFP*, 2 March 1983.

35. Member of the Scotten Committee who wished not to be identified, interview with author, 12 September 1986.

36. The report was an internal document, and has not been made available to me. However, it appears not to have made much of an impact. Eugene Kostyra, then minister of Industry, Trade and Technology, claims not even to have known of the existence of the Scotten Committee. Eugene Kostyra, interview with author, 29 August 1986.

37. "Presentation to the Premier of Manitoba and Cabinet Representatives on Behalf of the Manitoba Chambers of Commerce on Labour Law," 25 May 1984.

38. Jack Alexander, interview with author, 15 September 1986. Mr. Alexander was a member of the plant closure subcommittee.

39. Eugene Laye, United Steelworkers of America, interview with author, 15 September 1986.

40. "The Winnipeg Chamber of Commerce Resolution on Plant Closings," undated.

41. "Presentation to the Premier," 25 May 1984.

42. "A Submission by the Canadian Manufacturers Association, Manitoba Branch, to the Labour Law Review Office re the Labour Relations Act," July 1983.

43. Kostyra, interview.

44. "A Submission by the Canadian Manufacturers Association," July 1983.

45. Bluestone and Harrison, *Deindustrialization*, 74.

46. This analysis was offered by Muriel Smith, minister of Economic Development in the first Pawley administration. Interview with author, 26 September 1986.

47. The government looked carefully at notice and financial disclosure provisions, the latter particularly in the case of the Kimberley Clark closure, at which time it found that it had no legal authority to go beyond the province to gain access to corporate information. Smith, interview.

48. Purchasing policy was used, for example, in the recent case of Burroughs Canada, which threatened to close its Winnipeg plant at a cost of 300 jobs, and was "dissuaded" from doing so when awarded a $30 million, four-year contract for the supply of information-management systems to Manitoba hospitals. As is so often the case in plant closures, the Burroughs threat followed only a month after the merger of Burroughs Corp. and Sperry Inc. *WFP*, 8, 9 and 11 October 1986.

49. Jay Cowan, minister of Cooperative Development, interview with author, 14 October 1986. Cliff Scotten, senior policy adviser to Premier Pawley, said the same in an interview.

50. *WFP*, 14 November 1980.

51. Ibid., 24 November 1986.

52. See, for example, James A. McAllister, *The Government of Edward Schreyer* (Kingston and Montréal: McGill-Queen's University Press, 1984), especially pages 47-53; and Neil Tudiver, Chapter 14 in this volume.

53. Gary Russell, Manitoba Federation of Labour, interview with author, 5 September 1986. See also Jack Quarter, "Worker Cooperatives in English Canada: A Movement in the Making," *Working Papers* 2, no. 6 (1984): 56.

54. This makes it all the more essential that a plant closure strategy include better provisions regarding severance pay, retraining and relocation.

55. See Leon Muszynski, *The Deindustrialization of Metropolitan Toronto: A Study of Plant Closures, Layoffs and Unemployment* (Toronto: Social Planning Council of Metropolitan Toronto, 1985), 108.

56. N.E. Cameron, J.M. Dean and W.S. Good, *The Manufacturing Sector in Manitoba*, Economic Council of Canada Discussion Paper No. 254, March 1984.

57. See, for example, George Hewison, "Worker Co-ops not an Industrial Strategy," *Canadian Tribune*, 26 January 1987.

58. Linda Wintner, *Employee Buyouts: An Alternative to Plant Closings* (New York: The Conference Board, 1983), 4.

59. Professor Paul Grayson, personal correspondence, 3 June 1987.

60. Manitoba, Department of Industry, Trade and Technology, *Annual Report* (1984-85), 3.

Some Costs of Unemployment in Manitoba   12

Jeremy Hull

Unemployment in Manitoba is a largely hidden problem. Its extent is masked by official statistics which simply identify a transitional population which will shortly either become employed or give up looking for a job. The impact of unemployment is cushioned for most Manitobans by its unequal distribution; if you live in the north, or the inner city, if you are poorly educated and young, Native, or female you are more likely to be out of work or underemployed. Others experience much lower levels of risk.

In this chapter I will examine the unequal distribution, and some of the social costs, of unemployment in Manitoba. It will be seen that, to some extent, our large institutions tend to act as "holding pens" for the unemployed. The numbers in our prisons, our mental institutions, and our postsecondary training institutions tend to increase during periods of high unemployment. Those unemployed who have the advantages of education or family resources are more able to make use of the universities and colleges; those without these advantages are more likely to end up in prison or on welfare.

While the former Manitoba NDP government of Howard Pawley reduced the level of unemployment somewhat through job creation activities, most of the jobs created were temporary. In the longer run a more substantial approach to job creation, one which addresses the problem of inequality, will be required. It will be shown that the cost of such an approach would be partially offset by the savings in social allowance payments, unemployment insurance payments, and maintenance of inmates in jails. If a more thorough analysis of the many social costs of unemployment were done, it is likely that these offsetting costs would be even higher. On the other hand, the quality of the jobs created through most government programs, including most jobs created by such activities as the Manitoba Jobs Fund and the Winnipeg Core Area Initiative, has been poor. They have often been short term, have been dominated by construction and low-paid service occupations, and have done little to improve the range of jobs open to women and Natives in Manitoba.

Inequality And Unemployment In Manitoba

The prairie provinces have been fortunate in comparison to the rest of Canada in the levels of unemployment experienced. Between 1946 and 1975, the Prairies had the lowest unemployment rate of any region of Canada in every year except 1970. However, this has not meant that the economy has been booming throughout the period; rather, the pattern on the Prairies has been to export the unemployed to Ontario and British Columbia during the periodic downturns in the agricultural sector. Thus population growth has been depressed when unemployment rates were higher. Within the prairie provinces, Manitoba has had a relatively balanced and stable economy. Unlike Saskatchewan, Manitoba has a significant manufacturing sector, and has not experienced the extremes of boom and bust as frequently or severely as the other prairie provinces.

Nevertheless, unemployment has been a problem. In Manitoba in 1983, there were on average 48,000 people officially unemployed, and the unemployment rate reached 9.4 percent. These statistics understate the severity of the unemployment problem. As unemployment goes up, the number of "labour force participants" — people who are either working or actively looking for a job — goes down (see Figure 12). While labour force participation rates change more slowly than unemployment rates it can be seen from the figure that when one line goes down, the other line usually goes up. According to official definitions, only those who are actively seeking a job are counted among the unemployed. People who have not had success getting a job simply drop out of the labour market and also out of the unemployment statistics.

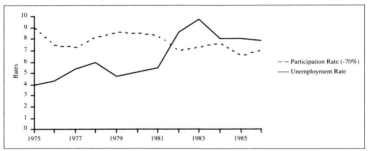

Figure 12. Labour Force Participation and Unemployment Rates, Manitoba Men, 1975-1986
Source: Statistics Canada, *The Labour Force*, 1985 (#71-201); Manitoba Labour Market, Employment and Immigration.

Those who are not working and want a job, but who have given up looking for one, are considered the "hidden unemployed." If this group is added to the officially unemployed, the unemployment rate increases by 2 to 4 percent (see Figure 13). Thus, while the official unemployment rate peaked at 9.4 percent in Manitoba in 1983, when the hidden unemployed are included it reached 12.1 percent. Moreover, the Labour Force Survey, on which most monthly and annual unemployment statistics are based, does not cover residents of Indian reserves where unemployment is very high.

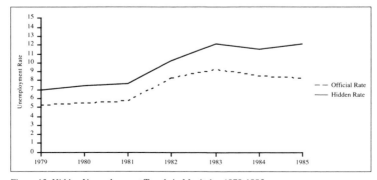

Figure 13. Hidden Unemployment Trends in Manitoba, 1979-1985
Source: Statistics Canada, *Labour Force Survey*, March 1979 – March 1985.

Unemployment and Women

As shown in Figure 14, unemployment rates are usually higher for women than men. Manitoba men and women have generally had unemployment rates which were about 1 to 2 percent lower than overall rates for Canada. From the figure it is apparent that during the high unemployment period of 1982-83, men's unemployment rates were above those of women, both in Manitoba and in Canada generally. The reversal of the normal pattern seems to be the result of two factors. First, during periods of high unemployment a relatively large proportion of the unemployed are job losers — those who have been laid off or dismissed. In 1975 this group made up 30 percent of the unemployed; by 1982 it had reached 55 percent.[1] It is likely that the majority of those laid off or dismissed would be men, partly because men are in the majority in the total labour force, and partly because the industries most affected by layoffs, such as manufacturing, have higher proportions of male workers. Other industries which have a majority of female workers, such as the service sector, continued to experience an increase in employment during the recession. Second, there was an increase in part-time employment during the recession, part of a long-term trend of increased reliance by employers on part-time workers. In Manitoba there are more than twice as many women as men in part-time jobs; accordingly, more women than men were hired for part-time work during the recessionary period. Table 59 summarizes employment growth over the 1975-86 period.

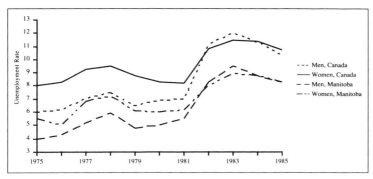

Figure 14. Unemployment Rate Trends, By Sex, Canada and Manitoba, 1975-1985 Averages
Source: Statistics Canada, *Labour Force Survey*, Cat.: 71-201.

Between 1975 and 1986, full-time employment in Manitoba grew by 13 percent, from 363,000 to 410,000. During the same period, part-time employment grew by 54 percent, from 54,000 to 83,000. Even during the recessionary period the number of part-time jobs continued to grow. Over this three-year period, full-time employment fell by 7,000 jobs, while part-time employment rose by 8,000, an 11 percent increase. When asked by the Labour Force Survey why they were working part-time, 7 percent of workers in 1975 said it was the only work they could only find. By 1983 this proportion had more than tripled to 23 percent of part-time workers.[2] This indicates that the unemployment figures understate the unemployment problem by failing to identify underemployment, that is, those workers who are seeking full-time work but are forced to settle for part-time work.

TABLE 59
PART-TIME AND FULL-TIME EMPLOYMENT GROWTH BY SEX,
MANITOBA, 1975-1986
(Thousands)

	Men		Women		Total	
Period	Full-Time	Part-Time	Full-Time	Part-Time	Full-Time	Part-Time
Employed:						
1975	252	15	111	39	363	54
Growth:						
1975-80	3	3	22	14	25	17
1980-83	-13	2	6	6	-7	8
1983-86	13	3	16	1	19	4
1975-86	3	8	44	21	47	29
Employed:						
1986	255	23	155	60	410	83
12 Year						
Growth Rate:	1%	53%	40%	54%	13%	54%

Sources: Statistics Canada, *Labour Force Annual Averages, 1975-1983*, Cat.: 71-529; Statistics Canada, *Historical Labour Force Statistics*, Cat.: 71-201.

Family Status

Family status is also believed to have an effect on labour force activity. Part of the reason for women's relatively low levels of labour force participation is thought to be the social expectation placed on them to care for young children in the home. In particular, female single parents experience very low participation rates and high unemployment, as shown below.

TABLE 60
LABOUR FORCE ACTIVITY BY SEX AND MARITAL STATUS, CANADA, 1983

	Men		Women	
Marital Status	Unemployment Rate (%)	Participation Rate (%)	Unemployment Rate (%)	Participation Rate (%)
Single	21.0	69.5	13.6	64.0
Married	8.3	81.6	10.5	52.3
Other	16.0	59.1	12.2	36.1
All	12.1	76.7	11.6	52.6

Source: Statistics Canada, *Labour Force Annual Averages, 1975-1983*, Cat.: 71-529.

While women's unemployment rates were lower than men's in Canada in 1983, Table 60 shows that married women's unemployment rates were higher than those of married men. Moreover, the "other" category, which includes those who are divorced, separated and widowed as well as all single parents, has a very low female labour force participation rate. Accordingly, very few women in this group have jobs, and income among this population is extremely low on average (for a discussion of issues concerning Native single parents in Manitoba, see Chapter 9).

In Manitoba, female heads of households and spouses have higher unemployment rates than their male counterparts, even when the overall female unemployment rate is lower than that of men (see Table 61). On the other hand, female children, other relatives, and unattached individuals have lower unemployment rates than their male counterparts. In terms of labour force participation rates, women's rates are much lower than men's for all family status groups. The gap between men's and women's labour force participation is greatest among spouses and heads of households, and smallest among children fifteen years of age or older living at home.

TABLE 61
LABOUR FORCE ACTIVITY BY FAMILY STATUS AND SEX, MANITOBA, 1983

Family Status	Men		Women	
	Unemployment Rate (%)	Participation Rate (%)	Unemployment Rate (%)	Participation Rate (%)
Head	8.2	81.5	13.3	57.0
Spouse	9.9	84.8	10.4	51.8
Child	23.6	65.0	16.6	59.5
Relative	25.7	63.3	15.9	37.9
Unattached Individual	15.1	73.3	8.4	50.3
All	12.1	76.7	11.6	52.6

Source: Statistics Canada, *Labour Force Annual Averages, 1975-1983*, Cat.: 71-529.

Effects of Educational Attainment

Educational attainment and age both have a major impact on unemployment rates. Generally, the higher the level of education, the greater the likelihood of participating in the labour force and of being employed. Those with less than a grade 11 education face the greatest risk of being unemployed; the completion of high school and especially the completion of university lead to lower unemployment rates. High levels of unemployment are also found among the younger age groups. These factors combine to make those under the age of twenty-five with less than grade 11 educational attainment especially vulnerable to unemployment (see Table 62).

Regional and Ethnic Patterns of Unemployment

Unemployment affects some regions and groups within the province much more severely than others. Those who live in the northern part of the province, on Indian reserves, in Winnipeg's inner city, or who are of Native ethnic backgrounds have the greatest likelihood of being unemployed. For example, Statistics Canada identifies four major economic regions within Manitoba: Winnipeg, the interlake, the north, and the remainder of the south. Of these, Winnipeg consistently has the highest level of unemployment, and the southern region consistently has the lowest.[3] In 1983, unemployment in these regions was: Winnipeg, 10.7 percent; northern, 9.3 percent; interlake, 7.0 percent; southern, 6.8 percent.

TABLE 62

UNEMPLOYMENT RATES BY AGE AND EDUCATIONAL ATTAINMENT,
MANITOBA, 1981

Educational Attainment	Age Group					
	15-19 (%)	20-24 (%)	25-34 (%)	35-44 (%)	45+ (%)	Total (%)
< Grade 9	20.6	15.7	9.1	5.9	4.2	6.4
Grades 9-10	15.3	13.4	7.0	3.6	3.6	7.5
Grades 11-13	6.2	6.5	4.6	2.8	3.4	4.8
Some Post secondary	10.2	6.8	4.2	3.0	2.9	4.4
University Degree	—	6.4	2.9	2.0	1.4	2.8
All	10.2	7.9	4.7	3.3	3.4	5.1

Source: Unpublished Indian and Northern Affairs Canada customized data based on the *Census of Canada, 1981*.

Although these figures suggest that unemployment is only slightly more severe in the northern part of the province than elsewhere, the true unemployment picture in the north is quite different. Northern Manitoba is generally seen as divided between the more industrialized centres, such as Thompson, The Pas, Flin Flon, and Lynn Lake, and the smaller, more isolated communities. While the larger centres are based on the mining and forestry industries and have a significant demand for labour, the smaller communities base their livelihood on fishing, hunting and trapping, as well as small-scale employment in local government and services.[4] Most residents of the smaller communities are Native, while most residents of the larger communities are not. When these two population groups are compared striking differences emerge, as shown below. These differences are the result, in part, of the much greater mobility among the labour force in the industrialized communities.[5] During times of unemployment or layoffs, workers in the mining industry, for example, tend to move elsewhere to seek employment. For this reason, Native unemployment rates remain higher. In northern Manitoba in 1981, Native men were five times as likely to be unemployed as non-Native men, while Native women were 3.5 times as likely to be unemployed (see Table 63).

TABLE 63

NATIVE AND NON-NATIVE LABOUR FORCE ACTIVITY
IN NORTHERN MANITOBA, 1981

Group	Unemployment Rate (%)	Labour Force Participation Rate (%)
Native Men	20.1	55.2
Native Women	16.1	31.8
Non-Native Men	4.0	78.8
Non-Native Women	4.6	65.8

Source: Department of Regional Industrial Expansion, "Human Resource Circumstances in Manitoba's North" (Winnipeg: DRIE, 1986).

Unemployment is higher on reserves than elsewhere in Manitoba, and Natives living on reserves in 1981 also had much lower labour force participation rates than those living off reserves (see Table 64). These low participation rates, combined with high unemployment rates, meant that only a minority of Native men were actually employed.

For example, with only 49.1 percent of the Native men on-reserve participating in the labour market, and with 24.3 percent of those participants unemployed, *only 37.2 percent of Native men on reserves were employed in 1981. Among Native women living on reserves, only 19.7 percent had jobs.* Native men living off-reserve had a labour force participation rate which was 50 percent higher than that of Native men living on-reserve, and Native women's labour force participation rate was almost twice as high off-reserve as on-reserve.

TABLE 64

NATIVE AND NON-NATIVE LABOUR FORCE ACTIVITY BY SEX
AND ON/OFF RESERVE RESIDENCY, MANITOBA, 1981

| | Native | | Non-Native | |
| | Unemployment Rate (%) | Participation Rate (%) | Unemployment Rate (%) | Participation Rate (%) |
Group				
Men				
On-Reserve	24.3	49.1	6.1	85.4
Off-Reserve	17.3	75.1	3.7	82.0
All Men	20.6	60.3	3.7	82.0
Women				
On-Reserve	13.8	22.8	7.5	52.9
Off-Reserve	16.6	43.0	5.1	53.9
All Women	15.7	33.4	5.1	53.9

Source: Unpublished Indian and Northern Affairs Canada customized data based on the *Census of Canada, 1981.*

Low Native employment rates reflect several factors. First, low educational levels among Natives, and particularly among those living in northern and isolated communities, tend to increase unemployment rates and reduce labour force participation rates. Second, the official definition of unemployment and labour force participation excludes those who have not actively contacted an employer during the previous four weeks. However, in many isolated communities there are very few jobs to be had; thus, many quit looking for jobs which for the most part do not exist. Third, in northern Manitoba many people are engaged in seasonal work such as fishing or trapping. Some of this work is done on a commercial basis, but much of it is done for the direct value of the product to the individual's family. Although they are not working for much of the year, those involved in harvesting these resources for their own use or the use of their families may not be identified as either employed or unemployed.

In addition to northern and on-reserve residents, residents of Winnipeg's inner city face especially high levels of unemployment and low levels of labour force participation, particularly if they are young or of Native ancestry. In 1981, those living in the inner city had an unemployment rate of 7.2 percent, more than three times the unemployment rate of those living in the remainder of Winnipeg (2.3 percent). As Table 65 shows, the highest levels of unemployment were experienced by young Native men living in the inner city (38.0 percent), and the lowest labour force participation rates were experienced by Native women in the inner city over the age of twenty-five (34.3 percent).

It can be concluded that place of residence within Manitoba is closely related to labour force participation rates, and that this is especially true among the Native population. Moreover, as will be seen below, the economic and social isolation of the Native population works in combination with low levels of education to make paid employment participation doubly difficult to obtain.

TABLE 65

NATIVE AND NON-NATIVE LABOUR FORCE ACTIVITY BY SEX, AGE GROUP, AND INNER CITY RESIDENCY, WINNIPEG, 1981

Group	Inner City		Remainder of Winnipeg	
	Unemployment Rate (%)	Participation Rate (%)	Unemployment Rate (%)	Participation Rate (%)
Non-Native Men				
15-24	16.9	81.8	6.4	95.9
25+	10.4	71.9	1.9	83.1
Total	12.1	74.3	2.6	85.0
Non-Native Women				
15-24	14.7	77.1	4.1	86.3
25+	6.2	49.8	3.9	53.4
Total	8.9	56.0	4.0	58.1
Native Men				
15-24	38.0	62.1	15.3	100.0
25+	22.6	70.7	5.7	83.5
Total	28.7	67.3	7.6	88.7
Native Women				
15-24	31.8	42.7	6.7	59.4
25+	23.4	34.3	7.6	51.7
Total	26.8	37.3	6.9	53.5

Source: Unpublished *Census of Canada, 1981* tabulation prepared for the Winnipeg Core Area Initiative Office.

Educational Attainment Among the Native Population

Perhaps the most important factor affecting Native employment is the educational level of the population, which is substantially below provincial norms. As shown in Table 66, more than 70 percent of the Native population has less than a grade 11 educational level.

The impact of educational levels among the northern Native population is especially pronounced, and is seen not so much in unemployment rates as in participation rates. As educational levels increase, so do participation and employment rates. As Table 67 shows, this relationship is quite consistent for Natives living in isolated areas of Manitoba. Figure 15 graphically shows how, as educational levels increase, Native labour force employment rates begin to approach those of non-Natives. (The employment rate is the percentage of the population aged fifteen or older which is employed; educational attainment categories refer to those found in Table 67.) This suggests that one of the most effective developmental activities that can be pursued by governments

and Native organizations is the improvement of educational achievement among both
Native children and adults.

TABLE 66

NATIVE AND NON-NATIVE EDUCATIONAL ATTAINMENT, MANITOBA, 1981

	Proportion of the Population	
Educational Attainment	Native (%)	Non-Native (%)
< Grade 9	47.2	20.5
Grades 9-10	25.2	17.5
Grades 11-13	11.8	25.0
Some Postsecondary	14.4	29.2
University Degree	1.3	7.7

Source: Unpublished Indian and Northern Affairs Canada customized data based on the *Census
of Canada, 1981.*

TABLE 67

LABOUR FORCE ACTIVITY IN ISOLATED AREAS OF MANITOBA BY
EDUCATIONAL ATTAINMENT AND ETHNICITY, 1981*

Educational Attainment	Unemployment Rate		Participation Rate		Employment Rate	
	Native (%)	Other (%)	Native (%)	Other (%)	Native (%)	Other (%)
< Grade 5	17.0	10.0	19.6	42.3	16.3	38.5
Grades 5-8	19.3	10.0	29.9	61.0	24.0	54.9
Grades 9-10	22.7	5.9	36.8	65.4	27.9	61.5
Grades 11-13 without certification	18.0	5.6	48.8	69.2	40.0	65.4
Grades 11-13 with certification	20.0	4.2	65.2	88.9	52.2	77.8
Non-university with trades certificate	19.4	6.5	67.9	75.6	54.7	70.7
Some University	16.7	5.4	72.7	71.2	60.6	67.3
University Degree	6.3	0.0	100.0	100.0	93.8	87.1
Total	18.8	5.8	33.5	71.1	27.3	67.0

*Note: Isolated areas include Indian reserves and unorganized Crown lands which are more
than 350 kilometers from the nearest regional centre, or which have no all weather
access road.

Source: Unpublished Indian and Northern Affairs customized data based on the *Census of
Canada, 1981.*

Some Costs Of Unemployment

Over the past decade a body of research has developed which attempts to test
empirically the widely accepted idea that higher levels of unemployment lead to an
increase in a variety of social problems. Among the areas investigated have been the
relationship of unemployment to income, crime rates, suicide rates, mortality rates,
incarceration rates and admission to mental hospitals. A brief review of some of these
investigations follows.

Unemployment and Health

In a study of entrants to New York state mental hospitals from 1852 to 1960, Harvey
Brenner concluded that "in New York State, for over 127 years, economic changes are

probably the single most important cause of mental hospitalization."[6] He also found that, during the 1900-60 period, as employment decreased mortality due to a variety of causes increased, including heart disease, infant deaths, homicide and suicide.[7]

TABLE 68

PREVALENCE OF HEALTH PROBLEMS BY MAJOR ACTIVITY, CANADA, 1978-1979

Type of Problem	Major Activity			
(Selected Problems)	Working (%)	Housekeeping (%)	Inactive for Health Reasons (%)	Inactive for Other Reasons (%)
Mental Disorders	2.9	9.3	24.3	9.0
Hypertension	5.6	15.3	24.3	18.1
Heart Disease	2.4	6.0	32.1	13.4
Headache	5.4	10.4	9.5	2.4
Anemia	1.2	5.2	4.9	1.6
Slight Disorders	4.3	9.5	16.9	11.5
Hearing Disorders	3.9	4.6	21.2	14.4
At Least One Problem	55.1	72.2	100.0	72.9

Source: Statistics Canada, *The Health of Canadians* (Ottawa: Statistics Canada, 1983).

However, O.B. Adams, who examined Canadian mortality and unemployment rates from 1950 to 1977, found that when unemployment *increased*, mortality *decreased*, but heart disease and psychiatric first admissions to hospitals *increased*.[8] Adams emphasized that indicators of social inequality, such as income distribution and income inequality, were more clearly correlated with mortality rates than unemployment rates.

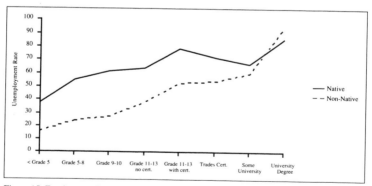

Figure 15. Employment Rates in Isolated* Regions of Manitoba, by Ethnicity, 1981
*Note: No road access/350 km to urban centre.
Source: Indian and Northern Affairs customized 1981 Census data.

The Canadian Health Survey carried out in 1978-79 examined, among other things, the relationship between health and "major activity." As Table 68 shows, those who were inactive or who were housekeeping (that is, unemployed) were much more likely to experience health problems. The Canada Health Survey also reported that men who were unemployed or not participating in the labour force were more than three times as likely to have frequent symptoms of anxiety and depression, and that unemployed and non-participating women were almost twice as likely as employed women to suffer these symptoms. Those who were working were also found to have a more positive outlook as compared to those who were inactive for health or other reasons.

Grayson found that employees at two factories were traumatized by the shutdown of their plants and the loss of their jobs. More than two years after the closure, over one-half of the former employees and their spouses considered the experience to be as devastating as divorce or the death of a spouse.[9] In comparison with other Ontario residents, former employees and their spouses had a much lower feeling of psychological well-being.

In Edmonton, researchers found that the sharp rise in unemployment in 1982-83 was associated with significantly lower levels of satisfaction among former workers with their health, nonwork activities, and standard of living.[10] The unemployed were more likely than others to feel depressed and powerless.

In order to examine the relationship between unemployment and mental health in Manitoba, a time-series analysis of first admissions to mental hospitals was carried out. This analysis was limited to the 1967-77 period because of unavailability and inconsistency of data concerning admissions to mental hospitals.[11] The analytical technique used was to detrend the data using a linear regression trend line, and then to analyze the correlation between detrended unemployment rates and detrended data concerning the rate per 100,000 of psychiatric first admissions to hospitals. Correlations were examined for a series of possible lag periods from zero to five years, and the correlations were tested for significance.

Psychiatric first admissions were found to be highly correlated with unemployment rates ($r = .90$) if no lag between unemployment and admissions was assumed. Figure 16 illustrates the relationship between these two variables, and it will be noticed that in each year that unemployment rates reach a low point (1969 and 1974), first admissions also reach a low point. The regression model suggested that when unemployment increased by 1 percent, psychiatric first admissions increased by 24 per 100,000 people, or by about 240 per year in Manitoba. These findings, although based on a short time period, are consistent with the results of Adams's analysis of Canadian data for the 1950-77 period. Adams found that both male and female psychotic first admissions increased in years when the average annual duration of unemployment also increased.

Effects of Unemployment on Educational Attainment

Unemployment is commonly seen as a result, in part, of low levels of education, and the information presented above tends to confirm this belief. On the other hand, children of unemployed parents are in turn less likely to succeed in school, thereby perpetuating the problem of unemployment into the next generation, and increasing the social costs of poorly educated children for years to come. Table 69 shows the educational attainment of children aged 15-24 who were living with their parents at the time of the 1981 Census of Canada. (The census does not contain educational data for those under the age of fifteen.) Those whose parent (father or single parent) had not worked over the previous eighteen months were more than twice as likely to have less than a grade 9 education, considered to be the minimum education required for functional literacy in Canada.

TABLE 69

COMPARISON OF THE EDUCATIONAL SUCCESS OF CHILDREN, 15-24,
NOT ATTENDING SCHOOL AND LIVING IN CENSUS FAMILIES,
BY THE LABOUR FORCE STATUS OF THE PARENT,* CANADA, 1981

Child's Educational Attainment	Parent Had Worked Since Jan. 1, 1980		Parent Had Not Worked Since Jan. 1, 1980	
	#	%	#	%
< Grade 9	64,595	7.5	36,105	18.0
Grades 10-11	196,120	22.7	50,355	25.2
Grades 11-13 (without certificate)	196,925	22.8	35,845	17.9
Grades 11-13 or Higher (with certificate)	406,570	47.0	77,780	38.9
Total	864,210	100.0	200,085	100.0

*Note: "Parent" refers to the father in two-parent families; otherwise it is the single parent.
Source: Unpublished Indian and Northern Affairs customized data based on the *Census of Canada, 1981.*

Those suffering long-term or chronic unemployment are even more marginalized than those in low wage and low status jobs. The education of their children suffers as a result, and (as shown in Figure 10, Chapter 9) this is accentuated when longer term unemployment is combined with Native ethnicity. (In this figure quintile "0" represents those where the father or single parent had not worked since 1 January 1980.)

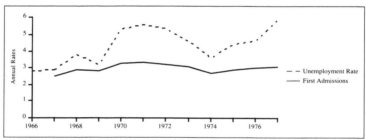

Figure 16. Unemployment Rates and Psychiatric First Admissions/1,000, Manitoba, 1966-1977

Source: F.H. Leary, 1983; Statistics Canada, Cat.: 83-204.

Unemployment and Postsecondary School Attendance

As Figure 17 illustrates, postsecondary enrollments in Manitoba have generally parallelled unemployment rates. Unemployment peaked in 1971, 1978, and 1983 in Manitoba, and postsecondary enrollments peaked in 1971, 1976, and 1983. A multiple regression analysis of this relationship was carried out, which controlled for the upward tendency in enrollments and unemployment rates over the period by including the year as an independent variable. The resulting regression model suggests that with a 1 percent increase in unemployment, postsecondary enrollment will increase by 850 students. Since the cost to government of providing postsecondary training to one full-time student was $3,779 in 1981,[12] the additional cost borne by government during periods of high unemployment is substantial. (A true estimate of these costs would require more detailed analysis of full-time and part-time university and community college costs, and would have to be based on incremental costs rather than an average cost per student.)

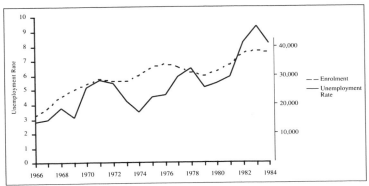

Figure 17. Post-Secondary Enrolments and Unemployment Rates, Manitoba, 1966-1984

Source: Statistics Canada, *Labour Force Survey*, Cat.: 71-201, various years.
  Statistics Canada, *Education in Canada*, Cat.: 81-229, various years.
  Statistics Canada, *Historical Convention of Education Statistics*, Cat.: 81-568.

Unemployment, Crime Rates, and Incarceration

Research has been carried out relating unemployment to crime rates and incarceration. One of the most influential studies was by Ivan Jankovic, who described two alternative concepts of how the punishment of criminals is organized.[13] The prevailing assumption, that punishment is simply a response to crime or a measure to prevent crime, was challenged by Jankovic. Instead, he tested the idea that punishment is not simply a response to crime, but is rather an outgrowth of the social and economic structure. Pointing out that one of the most striking characteristics of advanced capitalist countries is the oversupply of labour in relation to labour market demand, he proposed that imprisonment, along with the welfare system, act as a way of regulating the size of the surplus labour force. As the economy improves and requires more workers, he hypothesized, there will be fewer people imprisoned; as the economy deteriorates and the numbers of the unemployed grow, there will be more people put in jail. Moreover, he predicted that the rate of imprisonment would bear no relationship to the amount of crime which occurred.

His research, which was based on an analysis of federal, state and county prison admissions, unemployment rates and crime rates, confirmed his major hypotheses. He found that admissions to California state prisons during the 1947-74 period were correlated to unemployment rates as well as population growth, but were not correlated to changes in criminal activity. For every one thousand additional unemployed workers, he found that there were four additional admissions to state prisons.

Some research of this kind has also been done in Canada. Brown has described how relief camps during the 1933-36 period in Saskatchewan were a means of defusing and isolating potentially militant unemployed single men in what amounted to a type of imprisonment.[14] Looking at imprisonment data in eastern Manitoba during the 1918-39 period, Kellough, Brickey and Greenaway also found that imprisonment was used as a means of repressing political dissent.[15] They found that imprisonment increased both during times of economic depression and during periods of economic expansion. In addition, they found that the lowest social classes were more likely to serve their full terms of imprisonment than others.

More recently, Montgomery has conducted an extensive time series analysis of Canadian data on unemployment and incarceration since 1945.[16] He found a strong correlation between unemployment and admissions to penitentiaries in eight provinces (excluding Newfoundland and Québec). This correlation was equally strong whether he examined the two variables in the same year, or lagged the unemployment rates by one or two years. He concludes that the data provide partial support for the Marxist theory of imprisonment as a means of controlling conflict. While the correlation between these two variables may be spurious, in that both trends may be caused by some other factor, Montgomery argues that it is difficult to identify such a causal factor to account for the correlation, and that none has yet been suggested.

On the other hand, the relationship of unemployment to *crime rates* has not been supported by the research which has been done in Canada and elsewhere. To begin with, official crime statistics are a doubtful measure of the level of crime, since they are affected by the levels of policing and reporting which are themselves variable. However, research into the crime-unemployment relationship has been inconsistent. Grainger points out that this relationship has been the subject of study for over one hundred years, that research has become increasingly sophisticated, but that the relationship has yet to be clarified.[17] He concludes that "the aggregate search for a connection between these variables should stop." However, he suggests that study of the relationship between an individual's circumstances (including unemployment and crime) are warranted, noting that previous studies have shown that approximately 40 percent of those who commit crimes are unemployed at the time the crime is committed.

Further evidence of the correlation between unemployment or poverty and incarceration in Manitoba can be found in the high proportion of Native inmates in Manitoba's prisons (see Table 70). In 1981, 21.4 percent of those convicted of federal crimes and admitted to either federal or provincial institutions were of Native ancestry, but only 6.5 percent of Manitoba's population was Native. Natives were almost four times as likely to be incarcerated for federal offences as non-Natives.

TABLE 70

NATIVE AND NON-NATIVE INCARCERATION RATES, MANITOBA, 1981

Group	Admissions to Federal and Provincial Institutions	Total Population	Rate per 100,000
Native	112	66,280	1,690
Non-Native	411	1,013,703	434

Sources: J. Hull, "An Overview of Socio-Economic Conditions Among the Registered Indian Population of Manitoba" (Draft manuscript prepared for Indian and Northern Affairs Canada, May 1985), Table 10.2; *Statistics Canada Daily*, February 1, 1983.

The conclusion is that there is a clear relationship between incarceration and unemployment identified both in Canadian and American research. This research shows that admissions to prisons increase during periods of high unemployment, and suggests that this is in part a reflection of the state's need for social control during periods of political unrest, and in part a response to poor labour market conditions. Imprisonment disproportionately affects those who are poor or in lower socioeconomic classes, including many who are unemployed. The high proportion of Native inmates of prisons in Manitoba is probably a reflection of their high levels of poverty, unemployment and social inequality.

Unemployment Insurance and Social Allowance Payments

Unemployment Insurance Commission (UIC) benefits and welfare payments also increase during periods of high unemployment. As shown in Figure 18, unemployment rates and benefits are closely parallel. A multiple linear regression analysis of benefit payments and unemployment was done, which included an independent variable for the year to account for the general upward trend in both unemployment and benefits. Benefits were converted to constant 1981 dollars using the consumer price index. The resulting equation suggests that an increase of 1 percent in the annual average unemployment rate results in increased UIC payments of $24 million in Manitoba (in 1981 dollars).

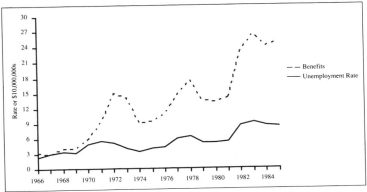

Figure 18. Unemployment Rates and U.I.C. Benefits Paid, Manitoba, in $1981, 1966-1985
Source: Statistics Canada, Cat.: 71-201; 73-202S.

In order to identify the possible relationship between unemployment rates and social allowance payments, a time series analysis was carried out, using data from the Manitoba Public Accounts Annual Reports (1970-86). While a complete study of the issue is beyond the scope of this chapter and would require much more detailed analysis than is provided here, some areas of the social services and health budgets were found to be correlated to unemployment rates (see Figures 19 and 20). Overall, Manitoba's Health and Welfare expenditures over the period (converted into 1981 dollars) showed a weak positive correlation with unemployment rates. When Social Allowance (welfare) payments were examined separately, a stronger correlation was found, significant at the 90 percent level of probability. The linear regression equation, which controlled for the effect of upward trends over time, found that with a 1 percent increase in the unemployment rate, social allowance expenditures increased by $4.8 million.

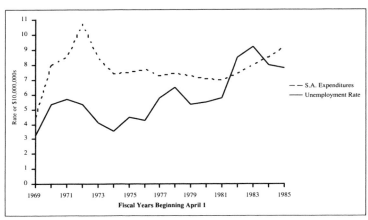

Figure 19. Unemployment Rate and Social Assistance Payments in $1981, Manitoba, 1969/70-1985/86

Source: Statistics Canada, *The Labour Force*, Cat.: 71-201; Manitoba Public Accounts, 1969/70-1985/86.

An even stronger correlation was found between unemployment rates and provincial expenditures on municipal aid. This regression model, significant at the 99 percent level of probability, suggested that with each 1 percent increase in unemployment rates, provincial expenditures on municipal aid increase by $4.2 million (also in 1981 dollars). While further analysis is required to refine these statistical models, the initial indication is that, as expected, welfare payments increase substantially during periods of high unemployment.

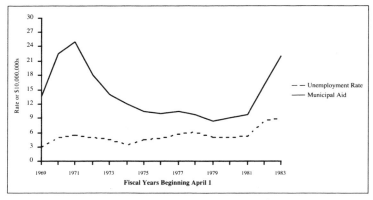

Figure 20. Unemployment Rate and Municipal Aid Expenditures in $1981, Manitoba, 1969/70-1983/84

Source: Statistics Canada, *The Labour Force*, Cat.: 71-201; Manitoba Public Accounts, 1969/70-1983/84.

Unemployment and Other Social Services

A number of other approaches have been taken to examine the effects of unemployment. One study of the effects of a major cutback in employment by INCO in Thompson compared the frequency or rate of a number of social indicators before and after the cutback occurred.[18] Such areas as welfare and unemployment insurance expenditures, crime and delinquency rates, social service referrals, and other indicators all showed a marked increase from one year to the next. Based on a follow-up analysis of these same indicators two years after the initial data were collected, McKenzie concluded that the cutback in employment had a lasting effect on the social costs borne by the city of Thompson (see Table 56, Chapter 11).

Increases in child welfare problems and violence within the family are also believed to result from increased levels of unemployment. A recent study of workloads and socioeconomic conditions at Winnipeg's Northwest Child and Family Services Agency established a number of links between general socioeconomic conditions in specific service areas, the nature of the clients and cases dealt with by the child welfare workers, and the amount of time spent on the cases by these workers. It was found that areas which had high levels of poverty produced much more demand for child welfare services.[19]

One measure of socioeconomic conditions which was examined was the proportion of families where there were no labour force participants. As Table 71 shows, this proportion was closely correlated with the per capita hours of child welfare work in each service area. This study also showed that those child welfare cases involving families receiving welfare took 50 percent more staff time on average than other cases handled by the Northwest Agency.

TABLE 71

CORRELATION BETWEEN DEMAND FOR CHILD WELFARE SERVICES AND PERCENTAGE OF FAMILIES WITH NO LABOUR FORCE PARTICIPANTS IN THE NORTHWEST CHILD AND FAMILY SERVICES REGION OF WINNIPEG, 1987

Service Area	Hours of Child Welfare Work Generated/Person Living in Area Over a 22 Day Period (Feb./Mar. 1987)	Percentage of Families with No Labour Force Participants (1981)
A	0.23	31
B	0.12	26
C	0.05	13
D	0.03	11
E	0.07	19

Sources: "Analysis of Socio-Economic Conditions and Child and Family Services in the Northwest Region of Winnipeg," Study prepared for the Northwest Child and Family Services Agency by the Working Margins Consulting Group, Winnipeg, May 15, 1987, 43; Statistics Canada, *Census of Canada, 1981, Winnipeg Census Tracts,* Cat.: 95-981.

Unemployment and Income

It is important to keep in mind the essential problem unemployment creates: lack of income. Poverty is linked to several negative conditions, and insofar as poverty is the result of being without work, unemployment is a contributing if indirect cause of these same negative conditions. At the same time, not all who are unemployed are poor. Those who are wealthy investors, and those who are second or third income earners in a family, may fall into this category.

The National Council of Welfare has documented the relationship between family poverty and employment by examining poverty rates in relation to the labour force activity of the head of the household.[20] Where the heads of the households were employed on a full-time basis in 1983, 4.7 percent of families had incomes below the poverty line; where the household heads were employed on a part-time basis, 23.7 percent of families were living in poverty; and where the heads of the households did not work, 32.4 percent of the families were living in poverty. Second, the rate of poverty among families where the head of the household was not participating in the labour market in 1983 (27.8 percent) was almost three times as high as among families where the household head was a labour force participant (10.3 percent). As the National Council of Welfare notes, "Families whose heads were out of work at some point during 1983 were twice as likely to be poor as those in which no member was unemployed."[21] In addition, the more weeks the head of the household worked, the less likely that the family would be poor, as Table 72 shows.

TABLE 72
POVERTY RATE BY WEEKS WORKED BY HEAD OF HOUSEHOLD, CANADA, 1983

Weeks Worked	Poverty Rate (%)	Number of Poor Families
0	32.4	411,200
1-9	43.3	49,900
10-19	38.1	80,400
20-29	22.4	75,800
30-39	17.2	42,500
40-48	12.4	39,700
49-52	5.5	223,600

Source: National Council of Welfare, *Poverty Profile 1985*, 40.

The National Council of Welfare also found that the likelihood of poverty increased for unattached individuals who were not participating in the labour force, who were working part time, or who were working fewer weeks during 1983. Rates of poverty among unattached individuals, however, were much higher than among families, with almost two-thirds of those individuals who were not in the labour force being poor.

Job Creation In Manitoba

Given the negative consequences of unemployment, what has the record of private- and public-sector job creation been in Manitoba? One way of looking at this question is to compare Manitoba's record to that of the rest of Canada (see Table 73). Manitoba's unemployment rate is consistently below the Canadian average, but apart from this no clear pattern emerges from this comparison. For the 1966-73 period, Manitoba's level of unemployment was relatively high, at more than 80 percent of the Canadian average. From 1974-76, Manitoba was in the most favourable position relative to Canada, with unemployment rates which were less than 70 percent of the Canadian average. Since 1977, Manitoba's rates have been slightly higher in relative terms, at 72 to 79 percent of the national average. There is virtually no difference in the years in which the two political parties were in power. During the NDP years, 1970-77 and 1982-85, Manitoba's unemployment rate averaged 77.9 percent of the national rate. During the

Conservative years, 1966-69 and 1978-81, Manitoba's rate was 77.8 percent of Canada's.

TABLE 73

COMPARISON OF UNEMPLOYMENT RATES, MANITOBA AND CANADA, 1966-1986

Year	Manitoba (%)	Canada (%)	Ratio: (Man./Can.)
1966	2.8	3.4	.82
1967	3.0	3.8	.79
1968	3.9	4.5	.87
1969	3.2	4.4	.73
1970	5.3	5.7	.93
1971	5.7	6.2	.92
1972	5.4	6.2	.87
1973	4.6	5.5	.84
1974	3.6	5.3	.68
1975	4.5	6.9	.65
1976	4.7	7.1	.66
1977	5.9	8.1	.73
1978	6.5	8.3	.78
1979	5.3	7.4	.72
1980	5.5	7.5	.73
1981	5.9	7.5	.79
1982	8.5	11.0	.77
1983	9.4	11.9	.79
1984	8.3	11.3	.73
1985	8.1	10.5	.77

Source: Statistics Canada, *The Labour Force*, Cat.: 71-201.

While unemployment shows no clear trends, employment growth indicates that there was some improvement in Manitoba after the NDP was reelected in 1981 (see Figure 21). From 1976-81, employment in Manitoba grew at a lower rate than in Canada as a whole. However, employment growth has been stronger in Manitoba in three of the five years between 1982 and 1987.

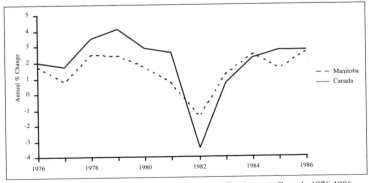

Figure 21. Comparison of Manitoba and Canada, Annual Employment Growth, 1976-1986

Source: Statistics Canada, Labour Force Annual Averages, 1975-1983, and the *Labour Force Survey*, 1984, 1985, 1988, Statistics Canada.

In recent years significant job creation has taken place in Manitoba through two major public-sector initiatives: hydroelectric construction in northern Manitoba and the

Core Area Initiative in Winnipeg. The largest number of jobs which have resulted from these two projects have been in construction occupations. The construction of the Limestone hydroelectric station, started in 1986, involved a peak level of employment of more than 1,200 workers in August of 1986.[22] However, over the course of the year the level of employment was generally far below that level, and only a few dozen permanent jobs will be required to operate the facility once it is completed. Between 1982 and January 1986 the Winnipeg Core Area Initiative created 2,000 person-years of work in construction jobs. Again, these have been temporary and seasonal jobs. During the same time period the Core Area Initiative also created 1,730 person-years of work in nonconstruction occupations, of which 915 are considered to be permanent jobs on the basis that they had been retained for a twelve-month time period.[23]

In addition to these major initiatives, the provincial NDP government launched the Manitoba Jobs Fund in 1983. This is a vehicle for economic development and job creation which takes in a variety of activities. Over a three-year period the fund, which totaled $275 million in expenditures, created 15,550 person-years of employment. Many of the jobs created, however, were temporary or part-time jobs. More than 50 percent of the jobs created in 1983-84, and more than 40 percent in 1984-85 were in the construction trades.[24] Many of the jobs were also part of Careerstart, the provincial government's major youth training program.[25]

In light of the severe inequities in access to employment that have been identified above, it is also important to ask whether these job creation activities on the part of governments have improved the employment opportunities of women, Natives, youth and other marginalized segments of the labour force. A recent report on the Manitoba Jobs Fund showed that in its first two years, only 24 percent of the jobs created were filled by women, and that women were "overwhelmingly concentrated in low-paying female job ghettos."[26] On the other hand, the hydroelectric construction in the north has involved a major affirmative action program which has resulted in large numbers of northern Native residents being trained and hired. While problems remain with respect to Native training and hiring on this project, and while the extent of training and employment of women in the traditionally male construction trades has not been great, the main issue is whether northern communities and individuals will benefit from the project in the longer run. Finally, the Core Area Initiative also has had specific affirmative action objectives. A recent evaluation of its success in this regard has concluded that, for the most part, the project has not succeeded in operationalizing its affirmative action hiring goals.[27]

Alternative approaches to job creation may be more effective than those most often pursued by government. One relatively new approach in Canada is to provide financial support to groups of workers wishing to own and operate their own businesses. Based on research in Canada, the United States and Europe, employee ownership, which can take a number of forms, can be effective when there is a significant personal investment in the business by individual employee-owners, and when the business is structured to provide for a high degree of employee participation in management decisions.

In Manitoba an Employment Cooperatives Program, providing financial and technical support to worker cooperatives, was organized under the Department of Cooperative Development in 1985. Such cooperatives are required to be democratic in structure, and to demonstrate financial viability as well as membership commitment. Although the program has not been in operation long, a small number of employee-owned cooperatives has now been established. Some of these were conversions of existing businesses from a corporate structure to a cooperative structure, while others were newly formed businesses or buy outs of existing businesses.

A Comparison Of Costs

The above discussion has shown that there are a number of social and personal costs to unemployment, some of which have been quantified, but many of which are difficult or impossible to quantify. These costs include: reduced income of individuals and increased risk of poverty among individuals and families; increased likelihood of hospitalization for mental illness; increased government expenditures on social services, in particular unemployment insurance and welfare; increased likelihood of a number of health problems; increased levels of depression and anxiety among the unemployed and others; increased likelihood of incarceration and associated increases in government expenditures; increased levels of postsecondary educational enrollments and associated increases in government expenditures; reduced levels of educational success among children of unemployed parents, resulting in long-term social costs.

On the other side of the ledger we can examine the cost of job creation, as identified in government job creation programs. One measure of this cost is provided by the Department of Regional Industrial Expansion (DRIE), which is in the business of creating jobs. The cost to DRIE of job creation over the 1975-86 period has averaged about $11,000 per job.[28] This underestimates the total cost since it does not include DRIE administrative costs, since other government funding is often involved in job creation projects (either direct funding, tax incentives, or other subsidies), and since not all of these businesses are successful in the longer run. As Silver has found in his study of plant closures, many businesses which are closed have recently received government grants of various kinds (see Chapter 11).

Moreover, job creation costs vary widely according to the type of industry involved and the nature of the jobs. For example, the creation of permanent jobs in the manufacturing sector may require an investment of more than $100,000 per job.[29] Jobs which are created in the service sector cost much less to create because of lower capital costs. Cheapest are the temporary jobs typically funded by government make-work programs. However, if permanent jobs cost more to create, they also provide more social benefits. A temporary job reduces UIC and welfare expenditures for a year, but a permanent job reduces these expenditures year after year.

The Manitoba government has also been involved in job creation through the Jobs Fund. Over the 1983-86 period its programs created or retained an estimated equivalent of 15,550 full-time jobs at a cost of $275.8 million, for an average cost of $17,736 per job created or retained.[30] Again, this is not the total cost of creating permanent jobs. First, a number of the jobs were "retained" rather than created. Second, the degree of permanence of these jobs is not known; the Manitoba government does not have any follow-up data concerning how long these jobs continue. For example, under the Jobs and Training Program companies agree to keep subsidized employees on staff after the subsidy period runs out, but there is no way of telling to what degree this has actually happened. In addition, the program is intended to "leverage" investment by the private sector and by other levels of government. Again, the total government investment is unknown.

It is clear that, based on the present state of information, it is impossible to compare the costs of unemployment in Manitoba to the costs of job creation. However, a sense of the order of magnitude of these two factors can be gained through the following calculations. If it costs government about $17,000 to create one person-year of work (as it did in the 1985-86 fiscal year under the Jobs Fund programs), and if it is necessary to create about 5,000 jobs to reduce the level of unemployment by 1 percent, the total cost is $85 million. On the other hand, by reducing unemployment by 1 percent, about $24 million (in 1981 dollars) will be saved in unemployment insurance benefits, $9 million will be saved in social allowance payments and aid to municipalities, and there will be additional savings in the areas of education, hospitalization, and social services. When converted into 1985 dollars, the savings in UIC and welfare payments *alone* amount to over $40 million. It is known that some proportion of our hospitalization costs, the costs of running prisons, and our postsecondary education costs should be added to this $40 million. In addition, the multiplier value of the jobs created should be taken into account. That is, each job which is directly created may result in one or more jobs being created elsewhere in the economy. To the extent that *permanent* jobs are created, probably at a significantly higher cost than $17,000 per job (and if these jobs do not displace other jobs), the savings to the government and to society in general will continue year after year. If permanent jobs are *not* created, the welfare and unemployment insurance costs will instead continue to drain the government's coffers.

Conclusion

The research done for this and other studies largely supports the view that unemployment is a traumatic experience for the individuals involved, affecting their income, self-worth, family life and a variety of other areas. There are clearly social costs, both financial and human, to high levels of unemployment. Within Manitoba, a relatively well-off province in terms of unemployment levels, the burden of unemployment is not shared equally. The Native population living in either the inner city or in isolated rural areas of the province suffers very high unemployment levels, as do younger adults with little formal education. The division of the population into more favoured and more marginalized segments, which is characteristic of the general distribution of jobs and income, can also be seen in the various institutions into which the unemployed seem to flow during periods of high unemployment. The welfare system, the prisons, the hospitals, and the postsecondary educational institutions all help to absorb the unemployed as their numbers increase during economic downturns. The more marginalized groups enter the prisons in disproportionate numbers, while those with a social and educational advantage are more likely to enter postsecondary schools.

Unemployment and its consequences are therefore intimately bound up with the general problem of socioeconomic inequality. The structuring of unemployment in this way seems to be a mechanism of social control. When different status groups within society face the problem of unemployment and loss of income, they have different options available to them. Accordingly, the unemployed do not see themselves as a single group with a common problem. Moreover, the transient state of unemployment, as defined in official statistics, helps both to minimize the problem of unemployment as a public issue, and to prevent the formation of a stable group of the unemployed who can make common cause and press for political or economic reform.

Organizers have to recognize the diversity of the unemployed population. Organizational activities need to be aimed at specific segments of the unemployed in order to address their needs. Skilled and experienced workers, for example, might be an appropriate group with which to launch a worker-owned and managed enterprise, funded in part by government or socially oriented investment funds. Job reentry and training activities would be more appropriate for the chronically unemployed, assisting them to take advantage of postsecondary training opportunities. A guaranteed income may be a more effective and universal approach to income support than unemployment insurance, given the wide variation in conditions of employment and participation rates of different segments of the population.

An effective approach to ensuring access to employment would unify the various segments of the unemployed by providing an integrated range of activities from training through job creation, using a variety of mechanisms. The glue holding the system together would be the overriding principle that all segments of the population will be ensured access to productive work and a reasonable income. Those in training programs would be assured that upon successful completion of their training they would either be placed in existing jobs, or that permanent jobs would be created for them to fill. Both training and job creation would be designed to reduce inequality by assisting victims of intentional or systemic discrimination as a first priority.

The cost-benefit analysis of job creation done here is quite incomplete, but it does point to certain conclusions. There are substantial savings from job creation, but when the jobs created are temporary these savings are probably less than the annual cost of job creation. Permanent job creation can be much more expensive, but it increases the offsetting benefits to government and to society in two ways. First, the annual savings in welfare and other social costs are repeated year after year. Second, the creation of permanent jobs can be used to create wealth for society (if the jobs are productive), which then can be used to pay back the original cost of job creation. Permanent jobs also have a greater multiplier effect, increasing the demand for various products and services, and creating other jobs in the process. Therefore, permanent job creation is clearly preferable to temporary job creation.

In Manitoba, job creation has often been tied to megaprojects, such as hydroelectric development or downtown redevelopment. Many of the jobs created have been temporary and of marginal quality, and many job creation programs have been oriented towards the small-business sector. For example, the Winnipeg Core Area Initiative has created large numbers of low wage jobs in the service sector. These jobs are typically insecure and experience high turnover rates.

It is inappropriate to see job creation as a short-term response to high unemployment rates, in part because unemployment rates are themselves artificial. Rather, job creation should be part of a long-term plan of social and economic investment. This plan should be guided by the need to invest in our collective future, to reduce inequality in access to goods and services, and to maximize our investment in human resources. Job creation, as part of such a plan, would result in significant and permanent savings in the cost of social services, along with an overall increase in wealth. This is clearly a more radical approach than the NDP in Manitoba has been willing to take.

NOTES

1. Statistics Canada, *Labour Force Annual Averages, 1975-83* (Ottawa: Statistics Canada, 1984).

2. Ibid.

3. Ibid.

4. See Jeremy Hull, "Human Resources for Northern Flood Development; A Study of Eight Communities in Northern Manitoba" (unpublished study prepared for the Northern Flood Committee, April 1984).

5. For evidence of this, see Jeremy Hull, *Human Resources for Northern Flood Development* (Winnipeg: Northern Flood Committee, 1984), 27.

6. Harvey Brenner, *Mental Illness and the Economy* (Cambridge: Harvard University Press, 1973), 243.

7. Harvey Brenner, *Time Series Analysis of Relationships Between Selected Economic and Social Indicators* (Washington, D.C.: U.S. Government Printing Office, 1971).

8. O.B. Adams, *Health and Economic Activity, 1950-1977* (Ottawa: Statistics Canada, 1981).

9. J. Paul Grayson, "Plant Closures and Political Despair," *Canadian Review of Sociology and Anthropology* 23, no. 3 (1986): 331-49.

10. Harvey Krahn, Graham Lowe and Julian Tanner, "The Social-Psychological Impact of Unemployment in Edmonton" (Edmonton: Population Research Laboratory, University of Alberta, 1984).

11. The data source was Statistics Canada, *Mental Health Statistics*, Catalogue # 83-204 (Ottawa: Statistics Canada, 1977).

12. Statistics Canada, *Education in Canada: A Statistical Review for 1982-83*, Catalogue # 81-229 (Ottawa: Statistics Canada, 1983), 188.

13. Ivan Jankovic, "Labour Market and Imprisonment," *Crime and Social Justice* 8 (Fall/Winter, 1977): 17-31.

14. Lorne Brown, "Unemployment Relief Camps in Saskatchewan, 1933-1936," *Saskatchewan History* 23 (1970): 81-104.

15. D.G. Kellough, S.L. Brickey and W.K. Greenaway, "The Politics of Incarceration: Manitoba, 1918-1939" (paper delivered at the 14th Annual Conference, Atlantic Association of Sociologists and Anthropologists).

16. Randal Montgomery, "Time Series Analysis of Imprisonment in the Context of the Conflict-Consensus Debate on Social Control," *Ciminometrica* 1 (1985): 50-73.

17. R. Grainger, "Unemployment and Crime: A Critique of Methodology" (unpublished report prepared for the Solicitor General, Ottawa, October 1980).

18. Brad McKenzie, "INCO and Thompson: An Analysis of the Social Impact of Job Cutbacks" (paper delivered to the annual conference, Canadian Rural Social Work Forum, Thunder Bay, Ontario, 26 May 1981).

19. "Analysis of Socio-Economic Conditions and Child and Family Services in the Northwest Region of Winnipeg" (study prepared for the Northwest Child and Family Services Agency, Working Margins Consulting, May 1987).

20. National Council of Welfare, *Poverty Profile 1985* (Ottawa: National Council of Welfare, 1985).

21. Ibid., 42.

22. "Evaluation and Monitoring of the Limestone Training and Employment Agency, Report II" (Churchill Research Centre, December 1986).

23. Stewart Clatworthy, Winnipeg Core Area Initative Office, personal communication, 10 June 1987.

24. Sheila Gordon, "Women in the Labour Force: A Case Study of the Manitoba Jobs Fund" (report to the government of Manitoba, prepared by the Manitoba Advisory Council on the Status of Women, 1987), 121.

25. Ibid., 117-20.

26. Ibid., 4.

27. Clatworthy, personal communication.

28. Letter from D. Lynn Gates, DRIE, to J. Silver, 1 October 1986.

29. See Chan F. Aw, *A Dual Labour Market Analysis: A Study of Canadian Manufacturing Industries* (Ottawa: Labour Canada, 1980), 41.

30. Information provided by Laureen Bader, Manitoba Jobs Fund Office, 4 November 1986.

13 Manitoba's Clothing Industry in the 1980s: Change and Continuity

Parvin Ghorayshi

Manitoba's clothing industry has become highly polarized. While a few large plants use sophisticated computer technology, the more numerous small shops still work with comparatively simple and old technology. The clothing industry has entered the modern era, but it still preserves many characteristics of its past.

The purpose of this chapter is to provide a short description of the clothing industry in Manitoba, from its origins in the wheat and railway boom at the turn of the century, to the rapid restructuring and modernization of the 1970s and 1980s. The focus is on the industry's uneven development, on changes in the labour process brought about by computer-based technology, and on the characteristics of its largely female and immigrant labour force. For the garment workers, while much has changed, much remains the same.[1]

The Beginning

Manitoba's first clothing factory was the Winnipeg Shirt and Overall Company established in 1899.[2] From this time standardized garment styles were produced and specialized workers employed in a factory setting.[3] By 1943, though the growth rate had fluctuated, there were 129 establishments.[4] Around 1957, the growth rate began to decrease and the number of establishments declined steadily to 81 in 1982.

The Winnipeg clothing industry was founded originally to provide work clothes for farm and railway workers. Thus the end of the great wheat and railway boom adversely affected the industry, as did the reduced demand during the Depression.[5] Both world wars brought new opportunities, with many of the factories devoting themselves to the production of military uniforms, canvas, parachutes and other types of war supplies.[6] By the 1980s, Manitoba continued to be known for the production of outerwear, workwear, sportswear and jeans,[7] but the industry had also become a supplier of fashion garments for both men and women.

The clothing industry has always been characterized by its small size and low level of capital investment.[8] As late as 1978, capital investment in this industry was low compared to other firms in the manufacturing sector: "to establish an apparel manufacturing plant in terms of cost per employee is about 40% of the average for all manufacturing and about 10% in the case of high technology industry."[9]

Pressure for capitalization came from both inside and outside the industry.[10] Since the 1950s, in response to competition from overseas, the industry has capitalized and rationalized, and has entered what Ray Winston, an industry spokesman, calls "the high technology era."[11] By the 1970s, there were a number of firms with large capital, such as Silpit Industries and Monarch Wear of Canada.[12] And recently there has been a jump in the rate of capitalization, which has brought mergers and polarization within the industry.[13] By 1980, large establishments controlled most of the production and work force in the industry.

From its beginning, the clothing industry has been a major source of employment for poorly educated working-class immigrant women of Jewish, Ukrainian, Polish, German and Russian origin.[14] Not only did women work inside the shop, many were also producing garments at home; homeworking has been a common feature of this industry.[15]

Wages were low, women were underpaid, and homeworkers were paid less than inside workers. Plants were in low-cost vacant buildings, available after the decline of Winnipeg as a wholesale centre and not designed for factory production. Many buildings did not meet the requirements set down in the statutes and did not provide essential basic services.[16] With its hazardous working conditions, low wages, and its work force dominated by poorly paid female working-class immigrants, the industry earned the name of "sweatshop."

In the 1980s, Winnipeg's warehouse district continued to be the centre of the garment industry.[17] Some firms moved to the suburbs and established new plants, but many remained in their original places. Some tried to change their "sweatshop" image, but working conditions, the nature of the work force, and the structure of pay preserved many characteristics of the past.

The 1980s

Manufacturing is an important but far from dominant part of Manitoba's economy. In 1980, manufacturing output accounted for 14 percent of the gross provincial product and 9.4 percent of total employment[18]; the clothing industry, with 6,828 employees, accounted for 11.7 percent of total manufacturing employment, second to food and beverages.[19]

Manitoba follows Québec and Ontario in terms of the number of clothing manufacturers in Canada. Although known as a centre for production of outerwear, work clothes and sportswear, the industry has now become part of the world of high fashion. Some names synonymous with Manitoba fashion are Wescott, Tan Jay, Gemini Fashion, and the Sterling Stall Group. Twenty years ago no one thought that Manitoba fashions would invade the sophisticated New York scene. Merchandise is now exported to other places in Canada, as well as to the United States and Europe.

The Manitoba clothing industry is integrated into the world market, which has an important role in producing our domestic condition. The clothing industry in advanced capitalist countries faces a general economic crisis.[20] Clothing markets are over-saturated, and developing economies are taking a large share of the world's export of clothing.[21] In the postwar period the centre of production shifted away from traditional locations like Britain to Japan, to centrally planned economies and to developing countries. While the developed western market economies' share of world production of clothing declined from 70.2 percent in 1963 to 52.3 percent in 1980, that of Japan, the planned economies and developing countries increased from 29.8 percent to 47.7 percent.[22] Clothing imports into Canada reflect this worldwide shift, having increased from 65 million units in 1981 to 237 million units in 1984.[23] Since 1956, strong international competition has come from Hong Kong, India, Japan, Pakistan, Taiwan, the Republic of China and the Republic of Korea.[24] These countries are characterized by vast labour resources, low wages and export subsidies.[25]

Manitoba's clothing industry, like its counterparts elsewhere, has developed several basic responses to the crisis. There has been a conscious attempt to reduce costs through mechanization, reallocation of some phases of production to less developed capitalist economies, more extensive use of subcontracting and small shops, direct marketing by establishing retail stores, and direct import and export of garments. In short, the rise of multinationals, the drive of the developing countries to industrialize, and the new international division of labour have all played important roles in producing the domestic condition in Manitoba.

In what follows, we will see how integration into the global market economy has intensified the existing uneven structure of the industry. On the one hand, a few large firms have undergone a rapid process of technological change, employ large numbers of workers, and are characterized by an extensive division of labour. On the other hand, most of the firms remain small, and shops based on subcontracting not only have survived, but are playing a major role. They provide the flexibility that capital needs in the face of the crisis. Most of these small shops do not use modern technology. They rely on the larger firms for their survival. The uneven capitalist development, together with the industry's exceptional reliance on female immigrant workers, have important implications for our understanding of the structure of this industry.

Uneven Development

In Manitoba, as elsewhere, firms in the clothing industry range from a few large establishments to a large number of small enterprises. As Table 74 shows, only twenty firms hire one hundred or more employees, and a very large proportion of firms (45.2 percent) have less than twenty workers. We can see from Table 75 that only two firms hire over five hundred workers. Compared to some other manufacturing sectors, the garment industry has a large percentage of shops of less than twenty employees.[26] It is important to notice that these small shops are increasing both in number and proportion, while there is a continuous decrease in the total number of garment establishments.[27] In 1972, 35.4 percent of the clothing firms had less than twenty employees, but in 1982 their proportion went up to 45.2 percent.[28] In many of these small shops, the employees work alongside the employer, and a large proportion of such shops are contractors.[29]

Apart from variations in the size of the firms, the clothing establishments can be divided into inside shops and outside shops. In inside shops, the owner or manager runs the firm while all aspects of the operation, from designing, purchasing fabric, cutting, sewing, to selling are done by the employees. Outside shops are operated by contractors or subcontractors who manage small production units, hire homeworkers, or do the work themselves.[30] The contractor can receive work from a manufacturer and assign all or part of it to the homeworkers. In 1982, there were nine clothing contractors reported in Manitoba,[31] but for reasons explained later the actual numbers are higher.

TABLE 74

GARMENT FIRMS IN MANITOBA BY EMPLOYMENT SIZE,
IN NUMBER AND PERCENTAGE, 1982

Size by Number of Employees	Number	Percentage
0-19	42	45.2
20-49	19	20.4
50-99	12	12.9
100-199	13	14.0
199+	7	7.5
Total	93	100.0

Source: Cameron, Dean and Good, *The Manufacturing Sector in Manitoba.*

Despite the predominance and persistence of small shops, the industry has been undergoing a process of concentration and centralization. The number of firms in the clothing industry has been declining since the 1950s. By 1982, as can be seen from Table 76, there were only eighty-one firms, a 31 percent decrease since 1966. During this time, the value of shipments increased by 380 percent,[32] but they have been handled by a smaller number of firms. Both production and employment tend to be concentrated in large firms.[33] In 1982, about 50 percent of the total factory shipments were attributable to ten companies, the largest of which include Tan Jay, Wescott Fashions, Silpit Industries and the Sterling Stall Group. In 1986, Nygard International, Wescott Fashions, and Freed and Freed of Canada were listed among the top one hundred Manitoba businesses, with annual sales of $200, $44, and $25 million respectively. As we can see from Table 75, these firms also hire a large number of employees.

TABLE 75

CLOTHING MANUFACTURERS WITH OVER 100 EMPLOYEES, 1984

500+ Employees	100-199 Employees
Nygard International	ACME Garment Ltd.
Wescott Fashions	Century 21 Apparel Ltd.
	Gemini Outwear Ltd.
200-499 Employees	National Cloaks Ltd. (Sterling Stall Group)
Dylex Ltd.	Richlu Sportswear Manufacturing Ltd.
Freed and Freed of Canada	Western Gloves Works Ltd.
MWG Apparel Corporation	Standard Knitting Ltd.
Olympic Pants and Sportswear	
Rice Sportswear Ltd.	

Source: Manitoba Government, unpublished data.

Many large clothing establishments in Manitoba operate internationally. They have plants in many parts of Canada, as well as offshore activities.[34] Tan Jay, for example, has plants in Winnipeg, Montréal, and Ontario, research and design facilities in New York and Los Angeles, and extensive offshore operations throughout the Orient.[35] Some, like Freed and Freed, Tan Jay and Dylex, are suppliers of clothing to major retail and specialty stores all over North America and Europe. Some, such as Tan Jay and Knit-Rite, have reduced their dependence on retailers by opening their own retail stores. These large companies have a large share of the clothing market. As Francis has correctly stated, ''one dollar out of every ten spent on clothing in this country is earned by Dylex.''[36]

TABLE 76
NUMBER OF FIRMS AND NUMBER OF WORKERS IN THE CLOTHING INDUSTRY,
1972-1982

Year	Number of Firms	Number of Workers
1982	81	6,468
1981	87	7,058
1980	96	6,828
1979	94	6,852
1978	93	6,119
1977	86	5,571
1976	96	6,439
1975	97	6,552
1974	105	6,905
1973	105	7,604
1972	110	7,361

Source: Statistics Canada, *Manufacturing Industries of Canada, National and Provincial Areas*, Cat.: 31-203.

Uneven development of Manitoba's clothing industry shows that capitalism has not developed simply and straightforwardly in this sector and has not destroyed all ''outdated'' forms of production.[37] The modern industry has incorporated other systems of production.[38] Capital in this industry has acquired an international character, but small firms, subcontractors and homeworkers continue to play a pivotal role.

As we have seen, to rationalize operations, and more particularly to offer a complete line without necessarily producing it all, some clothing manufacturers have turned to direct imports. Some have organized their own distribution and retail networks, and a number of firms are maintaining the production capacity that will satisfy an average demand for their product, passing on to the contractors any excess demand which may occur. These developments have been made possible by the increasing utilization of computers which can provide information on all aspects of production and circulation. The new technology allows many aspects of production to be carried out through local, national or international subcontracting.[39] The existing information and communication systems are capable of transmitting not only written or numerical messages, but also garment patterns in just a few seconds.

It is important to emphasize that the clothing industry is very sensitive to seasonal changes and to changes in style. Specialization exists for standardized products with little sensitivity to seasonal production and changes in fashion, such as jeans and men's shirts, but a significant proportion of garment products remain sensitive to changes in style and season. Subcontracting and small shops provide the flexibility essential for coping with peaks in demand or changes in style, while making use of cheap female immigrant labour.

There is a shortage of information on contract labour and homeworkers, partly because in many cases the operation is more or less clandestine. An ILGWU representative believes that the minimum wage in Manitoba is low and does not necessitate resorting to homeworkers. The common belief is that homework in the garment industry is not significant. However, one of the homeworkers I interviewed received the garment pieces through her neighbour and did not know how many more, like her, worked at home. As well, two of the plants that I visited relied on homework directly or indirectly. In the glove factory, homeworkers outnumbered inside workers.[40]

The garment industry is the largest employer of homeworkers in Canada.[41] It has been reported that with the crisis facing the industry, homework has gained in importance in Canada.[42] According to the International Labour Organization's research estimate, in Canada as a whole one-third of all clothing workers are employed on the basis of subcontracting.[43]

In short, what we are observing in the Manitoba garment industry is in line with the major tendencies which are shaping the industry everywhere. Small firms are increasing in number, but large firms account for most of the production and employment. The already polarized clothing manufacturing industry is becoming more concentrated and centralized, but small shops and contractors provide the flexibility that large capital needs to enhance accumulation and face competition.[44] Large manufacturers do not have to produce all lines of garments or employ a large number of workers on the main factory floor. Instead, they reduce overhead costs and relegate the risk of changes in fashion, and ups and down in demand, to small shops, subcontractors and homeworkers. In this process, the company retains complete managerial control over the design and finishing of garments, but delegates unskilled operations to small producers. As we will see in the following section, technology has played an indispensable role in the overall rationalization of production.

The Role of Technology

It is widely believed that the clothing industry is labour intensive and has a high labour cost compared to other manufacturing sectors. Even today, it is estimated that labour in this industry accounts, on average, for between 25 percent[45] and 35 percent of the total cost price.[46] However, in the last two decades, by investing heavily in advanced technology, the industry has attempted to reduce labour costs and increase its competitiveness. The garment industry has undergone rapid technological innovations. Microtechnology is changing the organization of labour and production. The introduction of numerically controlled sewing machines has brought substantial changes. Straight seams can now be stitched automatically. Many operations have now become machine feeding rather than sewing. An operator made this point very clearly:

> I do not make clothes, I feed the machine. You see, put all these three parts together, put it in this box, and put the box in the machine. The finished collar comes from the other side.

This process is very similar to taking a xerox copy. There are machines for sewing buttons, zips, trimming and the like. Machines are now computer programmed to perform a particular operation. Tape-controlled sewing machines are used for embroidery. Laser systems and numerically controlled cutting devices cut rapidly and precisely many layers of garments. Many garment manufacturers have installed material handling equipment which is taking the place of the old "line system." Under this system, bundles of garments flow in an orderly fashion from one operator to another: "All parts of a garment are tied in the same bundle with a 'ticket' that specifies the 'operations' that have to be done to complete the garment. Each operation has a number and each type of garment has a rate for each operation."[47] It has been argued that eventually a "central computer will pre-program machinery to automatically change from one line to another — say from skirts to pants — without a shutdown. Machine operators would still be needed, but a computer would record their output in units, enabling us to better judge productivity."[48] However, as yet the industry is not tied into a central computer and there are impediments to full mechanization. For the most part, sophisticated equipment is available for material distribution. The central task of separating and picking up fabrics from a stack and guiding them through the sewing process remains entirely dependent on manual work. The physical variations in fabrics make it extremely difficult to devise machines capable of accurately identifying a single ply.[49] Moreover, despite the advantages, the implementation of advanced technology has not been widespread. The vast majority of small firms either cannot afford the cost of high technology, or find reliance on cheap labour more profitable.[50] As a result, new technology has been mainly adopted by large and medium-sized firms, and only in certain lines of production.

As early as 1965, Monarch Wear, at the time one of the leading clothing manufacturers in Winnipeg, used the keraton permanent press system as well as a tex-o-graph machine to reduce pattern size and reduce cloth costs.[51] It also had an IBM 360 which did invaluable work in accounting, order processing, projection of sales, preparing production reports and many other jobs. Since then the industry, with the help of the government, has spent millions of dollars to upgrade its technology, investing $60 million from 1977-82, according to the Manitoba Fashion Institute.

Government programs have helped and encouraged this technological transformation. For instance, Tan Jay received $1,442,086 from the Department of Economic and Regional Expansion in the late 1970s,[52] and it is estimated to have received $4.3 million in federal grants between 1982 and 1985.[53] High-priced government contracts have benefited the larger companies, such as J. Freed's clothing industry, which received a $3 million contract from the federal government.[54] As well, the Manitoba Fashion Institute, an umbrella organization which promotes the interests of the garment industry, was heavily subsidized by the government.

Government assistance to this industry has been crucial and has taken many forms: direct grants, wage subsidies, tax shelters, low business taxes, import restriction and subsidized training programs. The industry relied heavily on Canada Manpower industry-based training programs to train sewing machine operators. The industry has enjoyed substantial subsidies to set up plants outside Winnipeg, hiring unemployed Canadians and offering sewing courses.[55] A case in point has been the various levels of government involvement in creating jobs for Natives. Plants were established on the Swan River and Peguis reserves. Monarch Wear of Canada, Rice Sportswear and

Gemini Sportswear were among firms that were financially supported by the government to set up plants and hire Natives.[56] Regardless of this assistance, government does not control the mobility of capital. In 1985, Tan Jay announced that it was moving its Winnipeg-based national sales operations to Toronto.[57]

At present, the Manitoba garment industry stands in the forefront of technological development and is equipped with the most advanced machinery.[58] However, in Winnipeg as elsewhere, new technology has been adopted mainly by the large and successful companies whose names appear in Table 75.[59] Several of these firms are using computerized pattern grades, robotically fed sewing machines, electronically controlled laser cutters, and other advanced technology. For the most part, the majority of the small firms rely on old, often obsolete equipment.[60] The managers of all the small shops that I have visited were very explicit that they did not plan to mechanize and could not afford the new technology. In many of these small firms, straight knives and band knives are used for cutting, patterns are made by hand, and many other aspects of production rely heavily on labour-intensive methods.[61]

In shops with sophisticated equipment, technology is used to speed up the line and increase productivity; workers are encouraged to do the job well and quickly. Here, the manager sets the speed and "tries to limit the scope for the labour power to vary."[62] As one worker noted:

> you have to meet, at least, the average speed set by the manager. If not, you'll get a notice to speed up ... the pace is too fast and the rate keeps changing. ... Some girls cannot keep up, they are let go. ... You have to work like crazy.

The new technology has intensified the uneven development within this industry. It has increased the power of the large firms and made it possible for them to expand their market share by responding speedily and efficiently to changes in the market.[63] It has also intensified the division of labour and has reduced the time and knowledge needed for the production of a particular operation. For instance, computerized pattern graders can complete in ten minutes what skilled workers would take ten days to do.[64] Furthermore, through effective fragmentation of the labour process, technology has facilitated and extended the scope of subcontracting.[65]

Sexual and Ethnic Division of Labour

Despite tecnological changes, the nature of the work force and of working conditions has not changed much. Immigrant women continue to be the core of the work force. In 1981, 70 percent of workers in the clothing industry came from a non-English speaking background.[66] However, there has been a shift in the ethnic origin of the garment workers. Whereas in the 1920s and 1930s the work force was dominated by Jewish, Ukrainian and other Eastern European immigrants, 60 percent of the workers now come from countries such as Vietnam, China, India, the Philippines and Pakistan, while a few are Native Canadians.[67] The mother tongue of over 66 percent of the workers is neither English nor French.[68] The Manitoba garment industry is almost totally concentrated in

Winnipeg, which has the highest concentration of the immigrants who serve as a source of cheap labour.

TABLE 77

PRODUCTION WORKERS AS A PERCENTAGE OF TOTAL GARMENT WORKERS,
AND PROPORTION OF FEMALE WORKERS AS A
PERCENTAGE OF PRODUCTION WORKERS, 1972-1982

Year	Production Workers as a % of All Garment Workers	Female Workers as a % of All Production Workers
1982	90.3	82.9
1981	89.7	83.6
1980	89.9	81.3
1979	90.0	82.0
1978	88.5	81.4
1977	88.3	84.7
1976	90.7	82.0
1975	90.1	83.8
1974	89.9	84.0
1973	90.9	84.4
1972	89.8	84.2

Source: Statistics Canada, *Manufacturing Industries of Canada, National and Provincial Areas*, Cat.: 31-203.

Although women account for 42.4 percent of the employed work force, only 13.3 percent of them are in the manufacturing sector.[69] However, women form 80.7 percent of the work force in the clothing industry.[70] Women hold low administrative positions and account for over 75 percent of production workers. Table 77 shows that 90.3 percent of workers in 1982 were in production-related jobs, of whom 82.9 percent were female workers. The production work itself tends to be divided into what are perceived as skilled positions such as cutting and tailoring, usually held by men, and semiskilled and unskilled positions such as pressers, machine operators and so on, held by women.[71] As well, higher paid and hourly paid jobs tend to be held by male workers. Female workers are paid far less than male garment workers for doing the same work. As a male operator put it:

> Oh, yes. Women do get paid less than me. My job is seen as skilled work, and I have a higher pay than a simple machine operator. I get paid $6.10 per hour, but my sister-in-law does the same job in another shop for this company and only makes $4.75.

The industry is known for discriminating against women,[72] and women have raised their voices many times in this regard.[73]

The Workers and Their Work Experiences

In general, the workers employed in the clothing industry have ''low mobility'' and a weak position in the labour market. Many face a constant threat of unemployment. Most are married, older and have little education. In 1981, 67.2 percent of the sewing machine operators in Manitoba were married, 66.7 percent were over the age of thirty, and close to 12 percent were over fifty-five years of age. Approximately 66 percent had not finished high school.[74] Women are aware of their limitations in the labour market:

I have no education, no skill, no training.... I have been here for 15 years.... I am too old [49].... I make good money, $9.50 an hour.... I cannot make this money anywhere else....

For women in the clothing industry, as for most women in the paid work force, the double day of work is a fact of life. Work does not end when they leave the factory. Women are, for the most part, responsible for their children's care and for basic domestic chores. They often leave their factory work to raise their children. Many continue to work with the help of family and friends. Their family ties, ethnic ties and work experiences often intersect.[75] For many of these women, factory work is compounded with many other tasks:

It is hard to work when you have a kid.... When my children get sick, I don't know how I concentrate.... I am lucky, I have a sister who helps.

I am a presser.... I spend all day standing in steaming heat.... When I get home, I am exhausted.... I cook, vacuum, wash.... I do most of the chores in the weekend, but there is always something to do ... the kids get sick ... there is the family.

Despite the perception prevalent in the industry, that women's income is secondary to the family,[76] the paid work of these women is crucial for the survival of their families. Economic necessity is the main reason for working in the factory. Family obligations and the increasing need for two incomes are cited as the major reasons for being in the paid labour market:

I am the oldest child.... My father does not have a steady job.... The only thing I knew was sewing.... Besides, I always liked to make clothes.... The pay is o.k., I guess. I could get education, but I have to work.

I need this job. My husband works in the food processing factory. One paycheque does not go far. We have two kids and my mother-in-law lives with us. We also send money back home [the Philippines] for my folks. You see, life is difficult out there.

Of course, there are some who choose to work for social reasons:

My husband says, "don't go to work, we can manage," but I like to go out, make some money and meet people.... In the house, I wash, clean, cook.

The employees here are tied to their jobs by more than a "cash nexus." A look at the recruitment practice within this industry makes this point clearly. There are advertisements in the ethnic papers, as well as lists of those employees who were laid off or left for personal reasons. The most common method of finding a job in this industry is through family and friends of existing workers and employers. The smaller firms rely almost exclusively on the latter method for finding the required workers:

My brother-in-law found me this job. He knows the boss.... He is good to me. He gives me "better" pieces.... When he has a rush order, he comes to me first....

Sometimes, I have to work double shifts. . . . There are times that, I think, I should say something, but I know the boss will take the phone and talk to my brother-in-law.

Insofar as a job is found through friendship connections, it would not do to complain because it could involve those who have introduced the worker and reflect badly on them.[77] Moreover, although the distribution of tasks and rates of pay have been greatly standardized, the uneven development of the industry means that there are still variations in pay, especially in many small shops. Some piece work jobs are considered better than others, as they are easier to work with or are better paid. There is a "constant battle" between workers for favours from the boss to secure the better paying piece work positions.[78]

Paternalism is prevalent in the smaller shops, where employers have face-to-face interaction with their employees:

I know all these girls personally. If they have any problem, I go to them and they can always speak to me. . . . They all know that they can count on me. . . .

Employers try to create the feeling of a "family network," by gestures such as bringing women a yearly birthday cake or by showing concern for their family members.

TABLE 78
AVERAGE WEEKLY EARNINGS IN MANUFACTURING AND IN THE
GARMENT INDUSTRY IN MANITOBA, 1972-1980

Year	(1) Average Weekly Earnings in Manufacturing ($)	(2) Average Weekly Earnings for Production Garment Workers ($)	Column 2 as % of Column 1 (%)
1972	135.37	79.94	59.1
1973	145.81	86.42	59.3
1974	161.23	99.77	61.9
1975	186.58	116.50	62.4
1976	208.75	129.73	62.1
1977	227.95	144.42	63.4
1978	243.97	155.04	63.5
1979	265.26	178.27	67.2
1980	293.16	189.44	64.6

Source: Statistics Canada, *Employment, Earnings and Hours*, Cat.: 72-002.

Salaries for a large number of workers in the industry remain close to the minimum wage. Affirmative action and equal pay legislation have not helped them much. Garment workers continue to have the lowest average hourly wage rates within the manufacturing sector.[79] Table 78 compares average weekly pay in manufacturing as a whole with that of production workers in the clothing industry. Garment worker's weekly pay between 1972 and 1980 ranged from 59 percent to about 67 percent of the average worker's wage in the manufacturing sector. This low wage level and lack of mobility, as one machine operator has stated, could be one of the reasons that very few men work on the shop floor:

> The wage is low. . . . A man cannot support a family by working in the needle trade
> . . . . Besides the industry does not offer much. . . . It is not a career.

Government has played a crucial role in the ghettoization of immigrant women in this industry by importing cheap immigrant labour.[80] From 1966 to 1970, Mr. Klapman of Gemini Fashions was appointed by the provincial Conservative government to recruit employees for the industry. He made three trips to Italy, and three to the Philippines to bring 1,700 workers. In addition, 1,000 trained operators were admitted for employment in the Manitoba garment industry from 1973 to 1978.[81] As well, many immigrant women are channelled into this industry by the help of employment counsellors:

> I have never worked before. . . . I started to look for job when my husband was laid off. . . . It took me three months. . . . It was 1975. . . . A friend told me to go to the manpower. . . . I could not type . . . I did not want to work in a hotel. . . . When the officer found that I can sew, he arranged a factory work for me. . . . I thought, I'll stay a short while . . . but I am in this job for over ten years.

Immigrant women are regarded as "good" and "flexible" workers who benefit from having a job in the garment industry. In general, it is perceived that:

> These women find little difficulty to make a reasonable wage. . . . They do not have a good knowledge of English. . . . This job allows them to familiarize themselves with the new culture, gain skill and rely on themselves.

The industry has always cited the shortage of labour as its major problem,[82] and has pressured the government to import immigrant workers.[83] The underlying assumption is that Canadians are not interested in working in the garment industry, ignoring low wage levels and often bad working conditions. The disadvantaged position of immigrant women in the Manitoba labour market and lack of alternatives have forced them to settle for wages that most Canadians refuse to accept. Moreover, due to language problems workers are not aware of their rights. They tend to congregate in shops where a supervisor or some workers speak their native language.[84] This creates different cliques of workers which hampers collective action:

> You go to the lunchroom. Filipinos sit with their own, Vietnamese sit with their own. . . . Mostly, they speak their own language.

The Method of Production and the Condition of Work

Regardless of the level of technological development and the size and type of the firm, the piece rate system remains the main method of production. The assembly of garments relies heavily on Taylorist scientific management. The tasks are based on a series of specialized and often simple operations. Under this system the division of labour is very advanced, especially with the application of modern technology. Each operation is characterized as a particular type of job such as neck binding, labelling or hemming. Each job has a certain time period of training and a particular level of skill attached to it. The garment is divided into working parts. Through time-study the industrial engineer determines the exact time and the rate of pay for each piece. The rate of pay and the alloted time for each piece may change with the change in style and technology. In such cases, a temporary time allotment and pay rate will be introduced to allow workers to familiarize themselves with the new product. After about two weeks the industrial engineer will time each worker to establish an average.

Each worker receives detailed instructions on what she/he is to accomplish, as well as the means to be used in doing the work and the exact time alloted to the production of a particular piece. If an operator sews the piece in the alloted time, she makes 100 percent, which is usually equivalent to about the minimum wage. Some benefit from this system more than others:

> The young girls find piece work fair. . . . I have worked in the factory too long. I am old now [55], my back hurts and I cannot work too fast. . . . The boss always tells me how fast the others are.

The piece rate, as Marx observed, "tends to develop on the one hand that individuality, and with it the sense of liberty, independence and self control of labourers, on the other hand, their competition one with another."[85] This system of production integrates workers into the labour process as individuals rather than as members of a class. The system of reward and punishment is based on individual work and competition rather than collective work. Many garment workers prefer piece work. Many accept the ideology that the "good" (fast) worker is rewarded by the piece rate system. They believe that having the same hourly wage for all would lower their individual take-home salary:

> With piece work you can make more money. . . . You work faster, you have more production and you get more. . . . Yes, I like the piece work. . . . This way everybody gets her share. It is up to you.

This system of production keeps workers from uniting to fight for a decent wage and work pace.[86] There is constant pressure to work faster. Those who speed up and go beyond the average will receive incentive pay. Those who are not fast enough will receive a warning. Modern technology is increasingly using the piece rate system to minimize costs and to boost productivity. A very high level of stress is associated with this type of production:

> As far as the employers are concerned, this is just a job with not much skill. . . . But all the time you are sitting on the chair and have to concentrate. . . . You are expected to produce. You cannot choose to go on with your own pace. . . . When the day is over you are dead.

Despite changes, there continue to be many problems associated with the working conditions and the work environment. While some large companies have established new plants, many remain in their original warehouse buildings. Some provide adequate services and have air conditioning, proper lights and ventilation, but many lack basic facilities. Overall, shops are crowded with bundles of clothes, the level of noise is high, and machine operators are sitting in rows trying to increase their output by working at a great pace. Most of the workers I have talked to complained of back pain, extreme heat, and high levels of dust and noise. Added to all these is the social isolation of the occupation itself, where every minute is translated into dollars:

> It is always work, home. It is very hard to talk during work. . . . After work, there is your husband, kid, shopping. . . . Girls come and go. . . . They cling to their own language.

According to the Fashion Institute, ''in the past five years, the industry has changed to such an extent that it retains little resemblance of its former self.''[87] As I have argued, drastic technological changes have taken place, mainly in the larger plants. But by and large, the working conditions, characteristics of the work force and structure of pay greatly resemble ''the former self'' of the industry.

Labour's Response

Garment workers respond both individually and collectively to the increasing rationalization in the clothing industry. At an individual level workers make sure that they get their fair share, keeping careful track of how many pieces they have completed, and making sure that mistakes made at other levels of the operation are not blamed on them. Many leave the job whenever they find a chance. The garment industry has one of the highest rates of turnover in the manufacturing sector.[88]

TABLE 79

LOCAL UNIONS, MEMBERSHIP AND COLLECTIVE AGREEMENTS OF EACH REPORTING ORGANIZATION IN MANITOBA, 1981

Union	Number of Locals	Membership	Women Members	Employers	Collective Agreements
Amalgamated Clothing and Textile Union (AFL-CIO/CLC)	2	1,944	1,755	25	6
International Ladies Garment Workers' Union (AFL-CIO/CLC)	1	1,510	1,327	7	7
United Garment Workers of America (AFL-CIO/CLC)	1	588	518	4	3
Total	4	4,042	3,600	36	16

Source: Statistics Canada, *Corporations and Labour Unions Returns Act*, Cat.: 71-202.

Membership in unions has been the major form of collective response. As can be seen from Table 79, there are three unions operating in the Manitoba garment industry: the Amalgamated Clothing and Textile Union (ACTU), the ILGWU, and the United Garment Workers of America (UGWA). Of those workers who are unionized, 48.1 percent belong to ACTU, over 33 percent are members of ILGWU, and the rest are in UGWA. It is important to emphasize that in 1981, 42.8 percent of the workers in the clothing industry were not unionized. To this figure we must add those who are home-workers.

The union organization parallels that of the industry. Small unions compete among themselves. The division among unions operating in this sector, together with the general weakness of the CLC vis-à-vis its affiliates, has curtailed their capacity to respond to the crisis which faces both the industry and the workers.

They have been perceived as business unions.[89] The ILGWU representative I spoke to believes that the unions have been slow to take up the specific problems and needs of their members, who are mainly women and immigrants. The tone was set by Sam Herbst, the first union organizer in Winnipeg's needle trade, who stated: "I am a great believer in piece work. I established it in Winnipeg in the cloak industry."[90] For the most part, the clothing unions have not questioned the process of rationalization and restructuring of capital in this sector. "Rather, they have continued to accept the clothing industry's definition of what is at issue — namely low-wage import competition which the government should deal with by continuing its import restraint program."[91]

Since 1980, the ILGWU in Winnipeg has experienced a rebirth of militant leadership. However, according to the ILGWU representative:

> Our union is still fighting for bread and butter issues: seniority, job security, wages, and lay offs. We are not able to fight on health and safety issues — the union is in the process of finding out just what the dangers are.

Under this leadership, the ILGWU began to challenge some of the traditional employers' practices in Winnipeg.[92] For instance, in 1984 more than one hundred members of Local 286 went on strike for eighteen days, asking for wage increases. Similarly, in 1981 about ninety workers in Knit-Rite Mills walked off the job demanding a wage scale.[93] The industry found it difficult to deal with this new leadership.[94]

The structure of the industry and the characteristics of the work force have had a great impact on the effectiveness of union organization. Large companies, such as Tan Jay, can use their power and facilities to undermine the union in more ways than just by threatening to move. For instance, during the strike of 1981 the company offered "safe transportation, as long as necessary to and from work," and staffed phones with people speaking Filipino, Vietnamese and other languages to provide workers with information.[95] In addition, the tight network existing among employers makes it hard for workers to raise their voices. There are instances of workers being denied employment after being fired by another garment firm.[96]

It must be remembered that a significant proportion of the work force still falls outside the scope of trade union action. This is due, in large part, to difficulties in reaching workers scattered in small shops.[97] As well, the dominance of small shops in this sector means that the paternalistic and personal ties between workers and employers often make workers reluctant to join the union. In some cases, union membership could threaten their already fragile employment status and low level of earnings.

Women's double day of work and their patriarchal family relations also stand in the way of their union activities. Women's participation in the union could be curbed by their husband's political and ideological stand: "When we were on strike, I picketed. My husband did not like it. . . . We had a fight . . . he was about to divorce me. . . . He thinks I should keep quiet."

In general, women's union involvement tends to be limited due to economic dependence on their husbands, a patriarchal family ideology, the double day of work, lack of a common language and lack of sensitivity by the union about issues concerning immigrant women.[98] Added to these problems is the fact that the piece rate system, the dominant form of production in this industry, promotes individualism and enhances competition among workers, which makes workers hard to organize. Although women recognize that a new militancy has emerged within the ILGWU leadership, they are very critical of the union, as well as being ignorant of the benefits of their union membership.

Conclusion

In response to growing competition and the crisis facing the clothing industry, large and medium-sized firms have rationalized their production process and adopted advanced technology in an attempt to reduce costs and increase competitiveness. The already unevenly developed garment industry has become more polarized. In the 1980s in Manitoba, a few large firms with sophisticated technology produced for the international market and employed most of the workers. Small firms did not have advanced technology, but survived and predominated numerically. The small shops, contractors and homeworkers remained important in this industry, as they provided the flexibility that capital needs in its process of accumulation. These small firms, by and large, depended on their relationship with large firms for their survival.

Despite major changes in the structure and the labour process of the clothing industry, many of its past features are preserved. The work force remains predominantly female and immigrant, with a weak position in the labour market. The industry continues to have one of the lowest levels of wages in the manufacturing sector. The sexual and ethnic division of labour in the industry have been perpetuated by a number of factors: the work force's lack of mobility, government and industry programs, and the unions' insensitivity to issues concerning immigrant women.

The uneven structure of the industry has produced variations in working conditions. While some plants are equipped with basic facilities, many lack elementary services. By and large, shops are crowded, the pace of production is too fast, and isolation and stress are associated with the method of production. The high rate of turnover, one of the major problems of this industry, reflects the dissatisfaction of the work force with present working conditions.

The uneven development within this industry and the unique characteristics of the work force have left their impact on the latter's organization. It is true that clothing unions are slow in taking up the problems of their members and do not question the process of rationalization. However, the predominance of small shops and the power of large employers have limited the effectiveness of unions. In addition, women's double day of work, their dependence on patriarchal family relations, their weak position in the market, and the paternalism prevalent in the industry make it difficult for them to be active union members.

NOTES

1. A large part of this chapter is based on my first-hand study of the garment industry in Winnipeg. I visited fifteen shops — five with over 200 employees, five with 51-199 workers and the rest in the range of 10-50. Most were located in the warehouse district of Winnipeg; three were in the suburbs. I interviewed the managers of these firms, as well as a total of twenty-five employees, one of whom was male. I have also talked to two of the union representatives. The project was carried out in April 1984 and December 1985. I thank all these people for their cooperation.

2. *Manitoba Business Journal* 4, no.2 (October/November 1967). Note that in 1884 there were some companies which could be put in the apparel industry. *Henderson Directory, 1884*, lists a few companies that produced hats, caps, boots, and so forth.

3. W. Lazer, "An Analysis and Evaluation of the Marketing of Textile Clothing by Western Canadian Manufacturers" (Ph.D. dissertation, Ohio State University, 1956).

4. Ibid. See also *Manitoba Gazette* 32, no. 45 (1903); 37, no. 3 (1908); 38, no. 42 (1909); 39, no. 32 (1910); 42, no. 41 (1913); 44, nos. 4, 31, 48 (1915). In general, the average lifespan of the clothing firm was short. As some of the firms were established, others failed and ceased to exist.

5. J. Gray, *The Winter Years* (Toronto: Macmillan, 1966); R.C. Bellan, "The Development of Winnipeg as a Metropolitan Centre" (Ph.D. dissertation, University of Michigan, 1958), 240.

6. Bellan, "The Development of Winnipeg," 240; Canada, *Report of the Wartime Prices and Trade Board* (Ottawa: King's Printer, 1944); Canada, *The Canada Yearbook*, (Ottawa: Statistics Canada, 1954).

7. As of 1982, close to one-half of the industry's total shipments fell into this category.

8. G.W. Swan, and E.R. Siddall, *Industrial Inquiry Commission*, (Winnipeg: Manitoba Department of Labour, 1957).

9. Manitoba, *Apparel — Manitoba Industry Sector Development Proposal* (Winnipeg: Department of Industry and Tourism, 1978).

10. In 1960, government warned the industry that it would suffer if it did not respond to the changing social and economic needs. Manitoba Department of Industry and Commerce, *Report of the Commission on Targets for Economic Development: Apparel Industry* (Winnipeg: Department of Industry and Commerce, 1969).

11. Ray Winston, Director of the Manitoba Fashion Institute, interview with author.

12. *Manitoba Gazette* 100, no. 1 (1971); 102, no. 7 (1973).

13. The projection has been that this trend will continue. Manitoba, *Apparel*.

14. Swan and Siddall, *Industrial Inquiry Commission*.

15. Ibid., 30, 81.

16. Ibid., 32.

17. With only a few exceptions, the entire industry is located in Winnipeg. Almost all factories are Canadian owned, and in some cases are managed by the second or third generation. Jim O'Shea, Sterling Stall Group, interview with author.

18. N.E. Cameron, J.M. Dean and W.S. Good, *The Manufacturing Sector in Manitoba* (Ottawa: Economic Council of Canada, 1984).

19. But with 12.5 percent of total shipments, it has seventh place in the manufacturing sector. Manitoba, *Manitoba Ten Year Economic Review, 1971-1980* (Winnipeg: Department of Economic Development and Tourism, n.d.).

20. F. Frobel, J. Heinrichs and O. Kreye, *The New International Division of Labour* (Cambridge: Cambridge University Press, 1980).

21. R. Cavendish, *Women on the Line* (London: Routledge and Kegan, 1982).

22. Canada, *Clothing Inquiry: A Report to the Minister of Industry* (Ottawa: Textile and Clothing Board, 1977); Canada, *Textile and Clothing Inquiry: Report to the Minister of Regional Industrial Expansion*, (Ottawa: Textile and Clothing Board, 1985).

23. Canada, *Textile and Clothing Inquiry* (1985).

24. Canada, *Textile and Clothing Inquiry* (Ottawa: Textile and Clothing Board, 1979).

25. The estimated hourly wage for production workers in clothing in 1978 in American dollars is: India 0.4, Taiwan 0.14, Korea 0.12, Hong Kong 0.23, United Kingdom 0.56, Ireland 0.52, Japan 0.61, United States 1.00, France 1.00, Canada 0.98, Italy 1.01, West Germany 1.41, Belgium 1.35, Sweden 1.67, Netherlands 1.46. F. Clairemonte and J. Cavanagh, *The World in Their Web: The Dynamics of Textile Multinationals* (New York: Zed Press, 1981).

26. See Cameron, Dean and Good, *The Manufacturing Sector.*

27. Ray Winston, interview with author. Mr. Winston estimated that this trend will continue. See also, Manitoba Fashion Institute, *A Five Year Plan for the Manitoba Fashion Industry, 1972-76* (Winnipeg: n.p., 1976).

28. Statistics Canada, *Manufacturing Industries of Canada, National and Provincial Areas*, Catalogue # 31-203 (Ottawa: Statistics Canada, 1982).

29. J.E. Newall, *A Report by the Sector Task Force on the Canadian Textile and Clothing Industries* (Ottawa: Queen's Printer, 1978).

30. Two of the small shops I visited fall into this category.

31. Statistics Canada, *Manufacturing Industries of Canada.*

32. Ibid.

33. According to Peter Nygard, 75 percent of garment workers were employed by eight firms. See, Winnipeg Chamber of Commerce, "The Winnipeg Chamber of Commerce Presents an Outstanding Canadian: Peter Nygard" (February 1981).

34. M. Henry, "Manitoba Fashion Institute: Stability and Progress," *Winnipeg Free Press*, 5 June 1976.

35. D. Read, "Tan Jay Chief Seeks Large Role for West on Garment Industry Aid," *Winnipeg Free Press*, 21 October 1981; D. Bain, "Peter Nygard: A Weaver of Golden Threads," *Enterprise* (May-June 1980).

36. D. Francis, *Controlling Interest: Who Owns Canada?* (Toronto: Macmillan, 1986).

37. A.F. Rainnie, "Combined and Uneven Development in the Clothing Industry: The Effects of Competition on Accumulation," *Capital and Class* 22 (1984): 144.

38. R. Samuel, "Workshop of the World," *History Workshop Journal* 3 (1977).

39. OECD, *Textile and Clothing Industries: Structural Problems and Policies in OECD Countries* (Paris: OECD, 1983).

40. Based on the author's interview and visits to plants.

41. L.C. Johnson and R.E. Johnson, *The Seam Allowance: Industrial Sewing in Canada* (Toronto: Women's Educational Press, 1982); L. McQuaig, "The Ever So Humble and Low Pay at Home," *Maclean's*, 10 November 1980.

42. Canada, *Textile and Clothing Inquiry* (1985), 62.

43. International Labour Organization (ILO), *Contract Labour in the Clothing Industry* (Geneva: ILO, 1980).

44. Rainnie, "Combined and Uneven Development"; A.L. Friedman, *Industry and Labour: Class Struggle at Work and Monopoly Capitalism* (London: Macmillan, 1977).

45. ILO, *Contract Labour*.

46. Canada, *Textile and Clothing Inquiry* (1985), 39.

47. L. Lamphere, "Fighting the Piece-rate System: New Dimensions of an Old Struggle in the Apparel Industry," in A. Zimbalist, ed., *Case Studies on the Labour Process* (New York: Monthly Review Press, 1979).

48. R. Mahon, "Canadian Labour in the Battle of Eighties," *Studies in Political Economy* 11 (1983).

49. OECD, *Textile and Clothing Industries*, 22.

50. Ibid., 23.

51. G. Kilvert, "From Work Pants to Tight Pants," *Winnipeg Free Press*, 27 January 1968.

52. "Gemini Grant," *Winnipeg Tribune*, 15 December 1978; "Tan Jay Grants," *Winnipeg Tribune*, 17 August 1979; Manitoba, *Supplement to Style: Manitoba Fashion Industry* (Winnipeg: Department of Industry and Commerce, 1971); "Tan Jay Given $1.4 Million," *Winnipeg Free Press*, 19 June 1978.

53. "Nygard, NDP Trade Charges on Office Move," *Winnipeg Free Press*, 17 May 1985.

54. Manitoba, *Supplement to Style*.

55. Manitoba Fashion Institute, *Five Year Plan*; Manpower Consultative Services and Metro Winnipeg, CEC Personnel, "Manitoba Apparel Industry Labour Supply and Demand" (June 1978); J. McMannus, "Tan Jay Chief Lauds Cooperation in Manitoba Garment Industry," *Winnipeg Free Press*, 12 December 1972; J. McMannus, "Local Garment Plants Hire Filipino Women," *Winnipeg Free Press*, 12 November 1968; A. Lepp, D. Millar and B. Roberts, "Women in the Winnipeg Garment Industry, 1950s-1970s," in M. Kinnear, ed., *First Days, Fighting Days: Women in Manitoba History* (Regina: Canadian Plains Research Center, 1987).

56. Manitoba Fashion Institute, "Manpower Supply and Training Within a Policy and Strategy for the Clothing Industry" (1974), 12.

57. "Tan Jay Sales HQ to Toronto," *Winnipeg Free Press*, 29 May 1985.

58. Canada, *Textile and Clothing Inquiry* (1980), 67-68.

59. Wescott has spent $1.9 million to expand its production facilities. See "Wescott Set to Expand Fife St. Plant," *Winnipeg Sun*, 4 September 1981. Sterling Group spent $2 million between 1980 and 1984 to computerize the shop floor. See W. Dennison, "High Tech Knits Well into Garment Industry," *Winnipeg Free Press*, 5 October 1984. Gemini Fashions implemented a $2 million efficiency program and computerized certain lines. See P. Sullivan, "Roof Caving in on Canadian Garment Industry," *Winnipeg Sun*, 6 May 1982. Tan Jay spent $6 million from 1971 to 1981 for plant and equipment. See Winnipeg Chamber of Commerce, "The Winnipeg Chamber of Commerce Presents an Outstanding Canadian."

60. See B. Hoel, "Collective Clothing 'Sweatshops,' Asian Female Labour and Collective Organization," in J. West, ed., *Work, Women and the Labour Market* (London: Routledge and Kegan, 1982).

61. As late as 1969, the Targets for Economic Development report found divergent patterns in the trade. On the one hand, small firms were facing declining capitalization, conservative management, shrinking markets and bankruptcies. By contrast, some large firms had aggressive management moving into export markets and were capitalizing. Manitoba, *Report of the Commission on Targets for Economic Development* (Winnipeg: Department of Industry, Trade and Commerce, 1969). This uneven pattern of development is still present in the 1980s.

62. A.L. Friedman, *Industry and Labour*.

63. S. Mitter, "Industrial Restructuring and Manufacturing Homework: Immigrant Women in the U.K. Clothing Industry," *Capital and Class* 27 (1986).

64. Mahon, "Canadian Labour," 61.

65. Mitter, "Industrial Restructuring," 48.

66. Statistics Canada, *Census of Population*, Catalogue # 92-918 (Ottawa: Statistics Canada, 1981).

67. Ibid.

68. Ibid.

69. Manitoba, *Manitoba Labour Market Information Bulletin* (1984).

70. Statistics Canada, *Manufacturing Industry of Canada*, Catalogue # 31-203.

71. See C. McLaren, "Women Paid Less for Same Work, Right Inquiry," *Winnipeg Free Press*, 18 December 1982; Hoel, "Contemporary Clothing."

72. Swan and Siddall, *Industrial Inquiry Commission*.

73. McLaren, "Women Paid Less"; T. Goldstein, "Knit-Rite's Lower Pay to Women Argued," *Winnipeg Free Press*, 24 February 1983.

74. Statistics Canada, *Census of Population*, Catalogue # 93-967 (Ottawa: Statistics Canada, 1981).

75. See C. Gannage, *Double Day, Double Bind: Women Garment Workers* (Toronto: Women's Press, 1986).

76. Swan and Siddall, *Industrial Inquiry Commission*; Manitoba Fashion Institute, *A Discussion Paper on the Manitoba Apparel Industry Manpower Program* (Winnipeg: Manitoba Fashion Institute, 1978).

77. See Hoel, "Contemporary Clothing."

78. See S. Arnapoulos, "Don't Stop, Not for a Second," *Montreal Star*, 28 April 1974.

79. Statistics Canada, *Employment, Earnings and Hours*, Catalogue # 72-002 (Ottawa: Statistics Canada, 1986).

80. Swan and Siddall, *Industrial Inquiry Commission*.

81. W. Kroeker, "Fashion Industry Plans to Honour Veteran Garment Manufacturer," *Winnipeg Free Press*, 30 April 1971; Manitoba, *A Review and Analysis of Manpower Shortages in Manitoba's Apparel Industry* (Winnipeg: Department of Labour and Manpower, Department of Economic Development, 1979), 13.

82. Swan and Siddall, *Industrial Inquiry Commission*; Manitoba Fashion Institute, *Five Year Plan*; Manitoba Fashion Institute, *Discussion*.

83. Manitoba Fashion Institute, *Discussion*.

84. See W. Ng, "Organizing Workers in the Garment Industry," *Rikka* 7, no. 1 (Spring 1980).

85. K. Marx, *Capital: Volume 1* (New York: International Publishers, 1967), 555.

86. See Ng, "Organizing Workers."

87. Manitoba Fashion Institute, *Five Year Plan*, 6.

88. A sample survey in 1975 showed a turnover rate of up to 150 percent. Manitoba, *Review and Analysis of Manpower Shortages*. As well, a study done by the Manitoba Fashion Institute showed a turnover rate of over 67 percent for female machine operators in 1974. See Manitoba Fashion Institute, "Manpower Supply and Training Within a Policy and Strategy for the Clothing Industry" (March 1974).

89. See Gannage, *Double Day*.

90. Swan and Siddall, *Industrial Inquiry Commission*, 92.

91. Mahon, "Canadian Labour," 162.

92. A. Coyle, "Tough," *Winnipeg Free Press*, 4 August 1981.

93. "Union Angry at Tan Jay Over Letter Sent to Strikers," *Winnipeg Free Press*, 14 August 1981.

94. B. Cole, "Union Firing Raised," *Winnipeg Free Press*, 27 October 1983.

95. "Union Angry," *Winnipeg Free Press*, 14 August 1981.

96. B. Cole, "Tan Jay Striker Alleges Blacklist," *Winnipeg Free Press*, 12 August 1981.

97. See ILO, *Contract Labour*.

98. See A. Cumsille et al., "Triple Oppression: Immigrant Women in the Labour Force," in L. Briskin and L. Yanz, eds., *Union Sisters in the Labour Movement* (Toronto: The Women's Press, 1983).

SECTION SIX

Constraints and Alternatives

A provincial social democratic government is not only limited in what it can do by capital mobility and the pressure of the business lobby, it is also limited by the terms of Confederation. The responsibilities assigned by the constitution to the provinces (health, education, welfare) are increasingly costly, while the sources of revenue on which the provinces can draw are limited, and to a considerable extent regressive. The revenue shortfall is partially made up by federal transfers, but these have recently declined as a proportion of total Manitoba revenue, as the neoconservative federal government tries to solve its own fiscal squeeze by passing the burden along to the provinces.

This fiscal squeeze, and the details of budgets, taxes and borrowing requirements, should not be seen merely as technical matters. They are political. An examination of state budgets reveals the underlying class relations and power configurations of which budgets, taxes and fiscal management are but an expression. For example, Tudiver, in his examination of Manitoba's sources of revenue, shows that the contribution of corporate taxes to Manitoba's total revenue has been falling fairly steadily since the early 1950s, while the contribution of personal taxes has been rising. Working people have been paying an increasing, and corporations a decreasing, share. Tudiver shows too that the total annual value of tax expenditures (more commonly called tax breaks or loopholes), both in Manitoba and federally, exceeds the total annual deficit. Most of these tax expenditures are intended to encourage investment — though there is little evidence that they do so. Consequently, those with the most money to invest derive the most benefit, and vice versa.

The choices facing a provincial government attempting to solve its revenue shortfall are limited. One response is to cut expenditures. The bulk of the provincial budget is spent on health, education and welfare. Thus expenditure cuts are borne disproportionately by the less well-to-do. A second response is to raise taxes. But most provincial taxes are relatively regressive, and thus again the load is borne disproportionately by the less well-to-do. A third response is to borrow, but the cost of doing so ultimately cuts into the ability to make expenditures, and further, the greater the need to borrow, the greater is the conservative influence of finance capital on provincial policy. This is the fiscal vise in which any provincial government is placed.

Manitoba performed relatively well within these constraints when NDP governments were in office. Expenditures were pared, but less than elsewhere; taxes were raised, but primarily in progressive ways; and borrowing increased, but not to the extent that the damage outweighed the benefits. The result has been that in fiscal management in general, and taxation in particular, Manitoba's NDP governments have generally been as progressive as, and sometimes more progressive than, other provinces — but not by much. They did not find a way to overcome the fiscal constraints.

Fiscal realities accentuate the limits of provincial social democratic politics. Public spending cannot, given these circumstances, be used as a solution to all problems. This places severe constraints on NDP governments for whom politics is primarily about enacting legislation and increasing public spending. The result is that the financial squeeze is added to the forces pushing Manitoba's NDP governments ever closer to the centre of the political spectrum. Movement is needed toward a different conception of politics, one which relies less on legislative enactments and public spending, and more on mobilizing and ultimately empowering ordinary people. Unfortunately, as Tudiver concludes, the NDP has no vision of an alternative politics.

This is made clear in the chapter by Loxley. Like St. Onge, Hull and Falconer, Loxley examines people who have been marginalized by the uneven development of capitalism — in this case the underdevelopment of Manitoba's largely Native north. He describes the Schreyer government's refusal to consider the implementation of an imaginative and well-conceived plan aimed at promoting an integrated, self-sustaining northern economy. The plan was scrapped before it was even tried. In fact, Loxley argues, there may never have been any intention to implement the plan. Megaprojects built around natural resources have continued to pass for a northern development strategy.

The failure of NDP governments to meet the needs of northerners is not peculiar to the Schreyer government. Murray Dobbin has described in detail the very similar failures of successive NDP governments in Saskatchewan,[1] and Moses Okimaw has documented the case of the Pawley government's inadequate response to the needs of Manitoba's Gods River Indian Band.[2]

What explains such NDP failures? Leaving aside the pervasive effects of racism, which may play a part, much of the answer seems to be related to the NDP's sense of politics. The NDP's is not a politics of struggle and empowerment, of involving people in solving their own problems. Thus the ''great northern plan'' described by Loxley was alien to the NDP. Without a vision of such a politics, or such an alternative, the NDP is confined to adjustments at the margins. This makes for better government than that offered by its Conservative opponents, but it prevents the tackling at their roots of more fundamental problems.

NDP failures cannot be mentioned without also identifying the role of the Left in influencing the NDP. During the period when the Left had its greatest influence — the period described by Loxley — there was some success in shaping the theory of a northern development alternative, but little, if any, success in translating it into reality. This suggests that, while the NDP has been ineffective in the absence of political mobilization, the Left has been ineffective in its efforts to create the conditions, both within and outside of government, for the implementation of its program.

NOTES

1.   Murray Dobbin, *The One-And-A-Half Men* (Vancouver: New Star Books, 1981).
2.   Moses Okimaw, ''Gods River and the Manitoba Government,'' *Canadian Dimension* 22, no. 2 (1988): 4-12.

Constraints and Opportunities With Provincial Budgets: The NDP Experience

14

Neil Tudiver

When first elected in 1969, the NDP government set out lofty goals for social and economic equality. As John Loxley points out in the next chapter, some objectives were met. Most were barely approached.

Distribution of income was not significantly improved, despite successive NDP commitments to narrow income disparities. The NDP was also determined to transform government finances into active instruments of social democratic policy. Taxation schemes could release the burden on low income people by taking more from those at the top. Heavy individual tax loads might be transferred back to corporations.

These objectives were far from modest. Truly redistributive welfare systems are virtually nonexistent in the capitalist world. Transfers usually occur *within* classes, not between them. Benefits for one segment of the working class are typically taken from another. The overall effect of state policies has been "to direct very substantial sums in the postwar epoch away from the personal sector as a whole towards the corporate sector."[1] For example, Canadian income taxation has imposed greater taxes on individuals and reduced them for corporations.

To improve distribution of income or wealth, NDP governments would have to reform social and economic policy in such areas as taxation, legislation and regulation, government intervention in production and distribution, or reduction of salary inequities within the provincial public sector.

This chapter begins to assess NDP accomplishments in these areas, in light of NDP policies and the constraints which operate upon them. Social policies have aimed for reforms to improve the lot of Manitoba's poor, Natives, women, and other groups subject to systematic discrimination. Some important gains were achieved, yet they have been limited by major constraints: conservative federal government policies within a confederation which allows fiscal domination over the provinces; the restraining influence of finance capitalists over the province's borrowing capacity;[2] threats from industrial and commercial capitalists to leave the province if taxation or labour legislation are too unfavourable; and limitations of the NDP's own ideology in the area of economic reforms.

The main focus of this chapter is on structures of public finance from 1965 to 1985, a span of three Conservative and three NDP governments. This is important because the nature of government revenues and expenditures, and their relationship, are major determinants of social and economic inequality. NDP policies are examined on their own, and in relation to experience with Conservative governments.

A central thesis of the chapter concerns federal-provincial fiscal relations. Like other provinces, Manitoba is caught by the compromise of Confederation. Under the BNA Act, provinces received restricted powers to raise revenue, consistent with their minimal responsibilities for health, education and welfare; the principal authority to shape government finances went to the federal government. Provinces now confront the mismatch between their service responsibilities and their fiscal authority. They determine most of the expenditures for social policy, but income taxation, which has a large bearing on social policy, is shaped mainly by the federal government. This mismatch was not changed by the 1982 Constitution Act.

Manitoba's major dilemma concerns revenues, since the proportion it controls is shrinking. To increase the share through consumption taxes or fees is regressive. Using income tax is also regressive under the present system since it discriminates in favour of high incomes.

Even if a province uses a surcharge on high incomes, as Manitoba has done, it is undermined by federally controlled tax expenditures. Provinces other than Québec cannot determine factors such as Registered Retirement Savings Plan (RRSP) deductions, capital gains exemptions, dividend tax credits, interest income deductions, or personal exemptions. All these are *regressive*; the tax saving rises with income.

Examination of the structure of public finance reveals relatively little change between 1965 and 1985. The NDP's major accomplishments were in the area of social programs and marginal changes to taxation to reduce income inequality. Economic policies have been less successful, since the NDP has been committed to work within existing structures. The chapter concludes with a discussion of alternative sources of provincial revenue. Truly viable alternatives would require some alteration to existing economic structures. Important opportunities have been lost due, in part, to a lack of social democratic vision.

Public Finance: Setting the Context for Social Policy

Social policy analysis usually examines the activities of elected ministers and their officials in the social welfare apparatus.[3] Their decisions have substantial impact. Income security programs can affect the life conditions of countless families surviving at the margins of subsistence. Job creation programs can provide gainful employment for thousands who are ejected from labour markets. Supports for labour force participation — day care, or programs in skills training and employment counselling — can help people overcome barriers to staying in the labour force. Affirmative action is crucial for groups systematically excluded from jobs of their choosing. Much can also be gained from restructuring conventional services. Community health centres, women's health clinics, and occupational health programs can transform traditional services to address fundamental health care needs.

Programs like these are essential components of state policies to address inequality. Without them, hundreds of thousands of Canadians would have little recourse beyond the mercies of employers, the benevolence of churches, or the handouts of private charities.

Yet in total they fall far short of reshaping the inequality pie. Social welfare spending, at best, helps to maintain people whose incomes are at the bottom. It shuffles money among competing demands of myriad interest groups. From the vast pool of economically disadvantaged people, advances for some are at the expense of others. Social policy decisions may alter the size of slices in the welfare pie, but the pie does not expand. Evidence suggests expenditures on social welfare are *shrinking*, to the benefit of corporations and the military.[4]

Public Finance Decisions

Public finance decisions can have far greater influence on income distribution and concentration of wealth than social service programs. The *forms* of taxation used to raise revenue are terribly important. Taxes on liquor, tobacco, general sales, or property are more burdensome on lower income people than taxes on income or wealth. Taxing individuals' incomes is more regressive than taxing corporate income.[5] Licence and user fees have other undesirable consequences, since they allocate services based on ability to pay.

And there are hidden revenues and taxes. Examples are electricity charges kept significantly below the rates of other provinces, or automobile insurance charges held below market rates by a Crown monopoly. These are forms of hidden expenditure, in that they represent foregone revenue. Benefits from charging less than prevailing rates accrue to consumers of electricity and drivers of automobiles. Were the higher market rates charged, the additional revenues of the Crown agencies could be distributed differently.

Public finance sets an environment for decision making about social programs. We can examine this in three areas. First, much about relations between the state and capital is uncovered through examining how governments raise revenue and target expenditure. Second, taxation patterns show us the effects of government policies on income. Third, limits to government action are revealed through examination of fiscal policies.

Public Aid to Private Capital

The Canadian state is a major benefactor for capital. Through subsidies and technical assistance, vast sums are spent on private industry. Provision of infrastructure such as transport and energy provides considerable indirect support. Corporations also receive immense benefits from low rates of taxation and from tax expenditures. Tax expenditures reduce income tax otherwise payable. They include tax credits for investment or research and development, tax deferrals, incentive write-offs for spending in designated regions or industries, and deemed nontaxable income.

State assistance to capital enjoys a long tradition in Canada. Government support was crucial to the rise of almost every major industry.[6] Contemporary evidence on government's generosity to business is furnished by the Nielson Task Force, commissioned by the federal government in September 1984 to suggest means to eliminate waste and improve efficiency. For 1985, it tallied 212 programs which subsidized and serviced business, at a total estimated cost of $16.4 billion. The equivalent of 68,000 civil servants at full-time compensation were employed to service the programs. This pro-business group concluded that "Giving with both hands' [subtitle of report] refers to an *overly rich, overlapping industrial incentive system* that according to the team needs rationalizing."[7] (emphasis added)

A recent example of unnecessary corporate aid illustrates a widespread problem. For its $180 million acquisition of Versatile Farm Equipment Ltd. of Winnipeg in early 1987, Ford Motor Company of Canada received a $45.5 million loan from the federal government. Ford may use the entire principal until 1997, when repayments begin in ten annual installments. The 10 percent annual interest is reduced by the amount Ford spends on research and development. Kenneth Harrigan, Ford's president, stated that his company would have purchased Versatile without federal assistance. He noted that the money "was available, and we picked it up."[8]

TABLE 80

PROVINCIAL INCOME TAXES
AMOUNT AND PERCENTAGE OF TOTAL PROVINCIAL REVENUE, 1965-1985
(Thousands)

Year	Individuals ($)	Individuals (%)	Corporations ($)	Corporations (%)	Total ($)
1965	24,287	14.6	15,508	9.3	165,872
1966	32,385	15.4	22,872	10.9	210,709
1967	39,955	13.7	20,534	7.0	292,332
1968	53,728	15.5	22,259	6.4	346,526
1969	64,555	18.1	24,830	6.9	357,332
1970	81,226	19.7	31,687	7.7	412,395
1971	116,194	24.1	32,540	6.8	481,168
1972	119,355	22.3	34,712	6.5	535,667
1973	139,637	22.5	46,593	7.5	620,566
1974	159,859	20.7	48,850	6.3	772,832
1975	203,908	22.2	79,207	8.6	920,421
1976	257,231	24.2	62,095	5.8	1,061,470
1977	279,405	23.7	108,494	9.2	1,178,587
1978	325,243	25.2	89,637	6.9	1,290,547
1979	383,154	24.7	98,320	6.3	1,550,819
1980	370,107	20.5	95,096	5.3	1,805,983
1981	412,869	21.0	111,739	5.7	1,968,405
1982	514,312	23.6	114,886	5.3	2,180,821
1983	631,158	26.2	54,157	2.2	2,408,960
1984	596,126	21.3	110,930	4.0	2,797,155
1985	586,872	20.1	129,631	4.4	2,924,647

Source: Manitoba Department of Finance, *Public Accounts*, Vol. 1 and 2 (Winnipeg: Queen's Printer, 1966-1986).

A recent review of expenditure management in Manitoba documented $91 million of assistance to business for 1986-87, including direct subsidies, tax expenditures and budgets for special agencies.[9] Total spending on assistance to industry is considerably higher, as it also includes the entire budget of departments such as Industry, Trade and Technology, plus portions of spending in departments like Consumer and Corporate Affairs.

The income tax system also favours corporations over individuals. Between 1951 and 1984, total corporate income taxes fell from 23.6 percent of total government revenue, to 8.7 percent, while individuals' contribution rose from 21.1 percent to 38.3 percent.[10] Manitoba trends are similar. In 1965, individual income taxes were 1.5 times total corporate taxes. By 1985 the factor had *tripled* to 4.5 (see Table 80).

The Effects of Tax Policies on Income Distribution

Fiscal policy can alter income distribution. In principle, the harsh inequities of capitalist economies can be tempered by progressive taxation. Federal income taxation policies are progressive in principle: they are supposed to redistribute money from higher-income to lower-income groups. Rates of income tax rise gradually, so people with greater earnings should incur higher rates of taxation.

Recent studies confirm the opposite.[11] The system is *regressive.* The poor endure heavier tax burdens than the rich, due to the heavy taxes on consumption as well as very significant income tax reductions for the wealthy.

TABLE 81
PROVINCIAL REVENUES AND EXPENDITURES, 1965-1985
(Thousands of Dollars)

Year	Total Revenue	Total Expenditure	Surplus (Deficit)
1965	165,872	150,906	14,966
1966	210,709	195,442	15,267
1967	292,332	291,641	691
1968	346,526	345,565	961
1969	357,332	355,932	1,400
1970	412,395	394,270	18,125
1971	481,168	460,906	20,262
1972	535,667	532,836	2,831
1973	620,566	567,628	52,938
1974	772,832	698,984	73,848
1975	920,421	871,990	48,431
1976	1,061,470	1,072,485	(11,015)
1977	1,178,587	1,197,704	(19,117)
1978	1,290,547	1,191,233	99,314
1979	1,550,819	1,621,768	(70,949)
1980	1,805,983	1,850,737	(44,754)
1981	1,968,405	2,057,913	(89,508)
1982	2,180,821	2,431,864	(251,043)
1983	2,408,960	2,843,608	(434,648)
1984	2,797,155	3,226,104	(428,949)
1985	2,924,647	3,407,180	(482,533)

Source: Manitoba Department of Finance, *Public Accounts*, Vol. 1 and 2 (Winnipeg: Queen's Printer, 1966-1986).

Taxes on consumption burden low-income people since they ignore ability to pay. Poor people, because they must spend a higher proportion of their disposable income on consumption, pay a higher sales tax rate than wealthier people. Taxes on property tend to maintain or increase inequities since they are based on assessed valuation rather than income. Yet recent initiatives (1988) by the Conservative federal government aim both to increase the rate of the federal sales tax and to apply it to a broader range of goods and services. A federal sales tax on food is even contemplated.

Massive federal tax expenditures undermine the progressive rate structure. Tax expenditures include deductions for payments to RRSPs or pension plans, credits for spending on designated investments, elimination of taxes on capital gains, dividend tax credits, exemptions for marriage and children, and others. Recent federal budgets have increased these regressive expenditures. For example, the maximum allowance for RRSP deductions will rise considerably, thereby benefiting higher income taxpayers.

Provinces are virtually powerless to alter this inequity, since the federal government shapes income taxation. Except for Québec, provincial income tax is calculated as a percentage of basic federal tax payable.[12] All federal measures, progressive or not, are built into provincial income tax schemes.

For 1986, Manitoba's total tax expenditures were $390 million on personal and $55 million on corporate income tax, enough to eliminate 91 percent of the budgeted $490 million deficit (see Table 81). Since 1983, they have increased by 20 percent on personal and 48 percent on corporate income tax. Some expenditures seem contrary to NDP policy: $1,000 investment income deduction ($19.5 million); personal deductions for capital gains and dividend income ($48.9 million); and deductions for corporate capital gains ($12.8 million).[13]

Taxation's effect on income distribution is negligible. Differences between pre-tax and post-tax income distribution are slight. This situation has remained stable since World War II.[14]

Limits on Provincial Government Fiscal Capacity

Sources of provincial revenue are in four categories: direct taxes; taxes on consumption; transfers from other governments; licenses and fees.[15] Most revenue is shaped by federal policies, including *potentially* progressive taxes such as income tax. To increase revenue, provinces are left to choose from mainly regressive options: raising taxes on sales, liquor, tobacco or gasoline; boosting the cost of licenses and user fees; or engaging in business ventures which generate public income. Unless new forms of revenue are captured, a province reinforces inequality by raising its conventional taxes. With some exceptions, the NDP has not been very successful in transforming these circumstances.

Manitoba's four major revenue sources appear in Table 82, which shows a steady decline in provincially controlled sources. Revenue from licenses, fees and miscellaneous income dropped from 12.6 percent of total revenue in 1965 to 4.4 percent in 1985. Taxes on consumption fell from 34.1 to 27.4 percent. This could be seen as *favourable* since these taxes tend to increase disparities of income and wealth. Their relative decline should reduce inequities. But from a province's fiscal perspective the trend is disheartening, as it marks reduced provincial autonomy over revenue. Revenue under direct provincial control fell from 51.3 percent of the total to 37.3 percent.

Shrinking provincial autonomy over revenue has several causes. First, the federal government determines a rising portion of the total, a trend which is covered in the next section. Second, the main revenues under provincial control are declining relative to federal influence. Third, most provincial revenue comes from consumption taxes: 74 percent in 1965; 86 percent in 1985. These are difficult to raise because they are regressive and highly visible. Fourth, license and user fees have dropped to a small portion of the total: 12 percent in 1965; 4.4 percent in 1985. Even large increases in these items would have a small impact on the budget. Fifth, the province has lost flexibility to tax individual wealth. When the federal Estate Tax was phased out in 1973, Manitoba initiated a succession duty and gift tax. It peaked in 1978, at $8.8 million, before the Conservatives dropped it in 1979. It would be difficult to resurrect such taxes, especially since they do not exist in any other province.[16]

TABLE 82

SOURCES OF PROVINCIAL REVENUE, 1965-1985
(Thousands of Dollars)

Year	Direct Taxes ($)	(%)	Taxes on Consumption ($)	(%)	Other Governments ($)	(%)	License Fees & Miscellaneous ($)	(%)	Total Revenue ($)
1965	47,509	28.6	56,565	34.1	40,956	24.7	20,842	12.6	165,872
1966	64,338	30.5	72,856	34.6	48,919	23.2	24,596	11.7	210,709
1967	69,920	23.9	76,231	26.1	123,537	42.3	22,644	7.7	292,332
1968	84,693	24.4	114,850	33.1	115,768	33.4	31,215	9.0	346,526
1969	99,570	27.9	139,284	39.0	89,678	25.1	28,800	8.1	357,332
1970	124,682	30.2	151,304	36.7	99,292	24.1	37,117	9.0	412,395
1971	160,872	33.4	156,734	32.6	126,151	26.2	37,411	7.8	481,168
1972	163,686	30.6	166,498	31.1	149,360	27.9	36,814	6.9	535,667
1973	197,067	31.8	200,770	32.4	176,186	28.4	41,770	6.7	620,566
1974	237,361	30.7	231,689	30.0	215,066	27.8	46,716	6.0	772,832
1975	320,121	34.8	263,253	28.6	237,475	25.8	54,572	5.9	920,421
1976	345,194	32.5	298,486	28.1	314,604	29.6	53,935	5.1	1,061,470
1977	427,814	36.3	349,019	29.6	336,926	28.6	64,828	5.5	1,178,587
1978	454,106	35.2	366,225	28.4	402,418	31.2	67,798	5.3	1,290,547
1979	527,385	34.0	341,246	22.0	588,493	37.9	93,695	6.0	1,550,819
1980	518,183	28.7	428,132	23.7	772,437	42.8	87,231	4.8	1,805,983
1981	584,167	29.7	456,418	23.2	837,814	42.6	90,006	4.6	1,968,405
1982	682,394	31.3	539,222	24.7	842,622	38.6	91,586	4.2	2,180,821
1983	777,539	32.3	594,137	24.7	929,586	38.6	107,698	4.5	2,408,960
1984	888,041	31.7	731,294	26.1	1,056,678	37.8	121,142	4.3	2,797,155
1985	877,083	30.0	800,304	27.4	1,118,451	38.2	128,809	4.4	2,924,647

Source: Manitoba Department of Finance, *Public Accounts*, Vol. 1 and 2 (Winnipeg: Queen's Printer, 1966-1986).

The corporate capital tax, introduced by the NDP in 1976-77, brought some flexibility to provincial finances. Although a small sum, at $24.5 million in 1985, it established the principle of taxing capital.[17]

The Constraints of Confederation: Federal Control of Provincial Revenue

Federal influence over the provinces has increased. Federal transfers accounted for 24.7 percent of Manitoba's revenue in 1965 and 38.2 percent in 1985. Also, a province cannot determine how incomes are taxed. As shown in Table 83, transfer programs and income taxes combined leave 62.7 percent of provincial revenue under federal control, up from 48.7 percent in 1965.

The nature of federal transfers has also been changing. In 1966-67 a major infusion of new money came with the Canada Assistance Plan (CAP), by which the federal government paid 50 percent of provincial welfare costs. In 1977-78 Established Programs Financing (EPF) was instituted. Through EPF the federal government provided block funding to support provincial expenditures on health and higher education. By 1985 EPF alone, at $405.2 million, accounted for 13.9 percent of provincial revenue.

TABLE 83
FEDERAL COMPONENTS OF PROVINCIAL REVENUE, 1965-1985
(Thousands of Dollars)

Year	Income Tax		Other Federal Transfers		Total Federal Components		Total Revenue
	($)	(%)	($)	(%)	($)	(%)	($)
1965	39,795	24.0	40,956	24.7	80,751	48.7	165,872
1966	55,257	26.2	48,919	23.2	104,176	49.4	210,709
1967	60,489	20.7	123,537	42.3	184,026	63.0	292,332
1968	75,987	21.9	115,768	33.4	191,755	55.3	346,526
1969	89,385	25.0	89,678	25.1	179,063	50.1	357,332
1970	112,913	27.4	99,292	24.1	212,205	51.5	412,395
1971	148,734	30.9	126,151	26.2	274,885	57.1	481,168
1972	154,067	28.8	149,360	27.9	303,427	56.6	535,667
1973	186,230	30.0	176,186	28.4	362,416	58.4	620,566
1974	208,709	27.0	215,066	27.8	423,775	54.8	722,832
1975	283,115	30.8	237,475	25.8	520,590	56.6	920,421
1976	319,326	30.1	314,604	29.6	633,930	59.7	1,061,470
1977	387,899	32.9	336,926	28.6	724,825	61.5	1,178,587
1978	414,880	32.1	402,418	31.2	817,298	63.3	1,290,547
1979	481,474	31.0	588,493	37.9	1,069,967	69.0	1,550,819
1980	465,203	25.8	772,437	42.8	1,237,640	68.5	1,805,983
1981	524,608	26.7	837,814	42.6	1,362,422	69.2	1,968,405
1982	629,198	28.9	842,622	38.6	1,471,820	67.5	2,180,821
1983	685,315	28.4	929,586	38.6	1,614,901	67.0	2,408,960
1984	707,056	25.3	1,056,678	37.8	1,763,734	63.1	2,797,155
1985	716,503	24.5	1,118,451	38.2	1,834,954	62.7	2,924,647

Source: Department of Finance, *Public Accounts*, Vol. 1 and 2 (Winnipeg: Queen's Printer, 1966-1986).

The other main federal transfer is comprised of equalization payments, which are designed to redress regional imbalances. The federal government shifts funds to assure that poorer provinces can provide services comparable to wealthier provinces. From 1970 to 1980 equalization rose from $42.1 million to $366.1 million, a rate of growth (770 percent) which was more than double that for Manitoba's total revenue (340 percent). Between 1980 and 1985 it fell from 20.3 percent of provincial revenue to 16.3 percent.[18]

Even though their powers to shape revenue are declining, provinces still have some room to manoeuver. In 1985 Manitoba controlled over 37.3 percent of its revenues, including sales taxes; taxes on liquor, tobacco and gas, and fees for licenses, admission to parks and other services to consumers. Although substantial in size, their scope is limited to consumption taxes and fees. In 1965, collections of $76 million financed 47 percent of provincial expenditures (Tables 82 and 83). In 1985, collections of $929 million covered only 27 percent.

Income taxes, supposedly the main vehicle for progressive taxation, are shaped almost entirely by federal policy. In principle, they should exact more from the wealthy and less from the poor, making it possible for taxation to improve income distribution. Unfortunately, this has not been achieved.

Federal transfers financed much of provincial expenditure growth between 1965 and 1980. Manitoba benefited from the additional resources, but spending became more dependent on federal funds. When the rising tide of federal transfers began to ebb in the late 1970s, Manitoba experienced serious fiscal problems. Demands on spending soared while growth in revenue stagnated.

In 1978 the federal government changed the structure of transfers. Almost 50 percent of expenditures on health and higher education had been covered on an unconditional basis. With the introduction of EPF in 1978, federal increases became tied to the GNP rather than actual costs. From 1978, provinces had to pay for the difference between increases in actual cost and rises in GNP.[19]

As Manitoba entered the 1980s, health and education spending gradually outstripped federal transfers. Some of the shortfall in EPF financing of health and education was made up by increasing tax points, that is, the rate of provincial income taxation. All provinces except Québec set their income taxes as a percentage of the federal income tax. By 1986, Manitoba's income tax rate had grown to 54 percent of the federal income tax.[20]

Federal belt tightening hit the provinces in the 1980s. Growth in transfers fell from an average annual compounded rate of 21.6 percent (1965-80) to 7.7 percent (1980-85). Income tax declined from 17.8 percent growth to 9 percent. Provincial revenues were devastated, with consequent rapid rises in the deficit from $89.5 million in 1981 to $434.6 million in 1983. Unemployment reached its highest level in 1982, at 8.5 percent, and remained over 8 percent through 1985 (see Table 73 in Chapter 12).

The General Shape of NDP Policy

Manitoba's NDP works within existing economic structures. It aims to *improve* the capitalist economy, not *transform* it. Labour market opportunities are improved with programs in job creation, career education and employment training, and expansion of day-care facilities. Labour market conditions receive attention in the form of legislation for workplace health and safety, public-sector pay equity, and provision of first collective agreements. Innovations in social welfare programs aim to ameliorate conditions of targeted groups in need. Family law legislation has established greater equity in treatment of marital property.

With the exception of Autopac, the government monopoly for automobile insurance, NDP policies do not challenge normal business operations.[21] Even lucrative opportunities have been rejected. Eric Kierans, hired in 1972 to recommend resource policies, noted:

> By turning over the management of their resources to the private sector the government has given up all but $15.6 million of a total flow of profits of $192 million in three years.[22]

Kierans, a Liberal, argued that Manitoba should capture economic rents, or excess profits, from metal mining. For 1970 he appraised this sum at $60 million. His counsel was not heeded.

The NDP did embark on some ventures in production. But the business achievements of some Crown corporations were doubtful.[23] Enterprises like Saunders Aircraft and Flyer Industries made bad investment decisions, compounded by inferior management. They seemed indistinguishable from private companies on employment practices, marketing strategies or production decisions. They followed conventional models for industrial relations, with many of the attendant problems experienced in the private sector.[24] Production decisions were led by market considerations. They were based on exchange, that is, whatever will sell in existing markets. Production for use has not been a significant concern.[25]

Using public enterprise as an engine of progressive economic growth did not easily fit in Manitoba's brand of social democracy. The cabinet was cautious, apparently concerned with maintaining a balance of public and private investment. The role of public enterprise was minor in relation to the dominant role of private enterprise. This position was stated by Premier Schreyer in 1971:

> We continue to believe that the greatest majority of enterprise should properly remain in private hands. But we are prepared to seek a better balance of the various forms of government involvement.[26]

Achieving *balance* was a hallmark of the Schreyer governments.[27] It was evident in two ways.

First, social and economic policies were balanced with other provinces. For example, Manitoba's tax credit schemes, offering relief from sales and property taxes, were similar to sales tax rebates in Ontario. Autopac, the provincial auto insurance scheme, followed paths paved by Saskatchewan's NDP. The Crown-owned monopoly was established despite stiff opposition. It enjoyed enough popular support to survive unscathed from attacks by Sterling Lyon's right-wing Conservative government.

Second, NDP policies were balanced *internally*. Changes were incremental: adding to or subtracting from existing conditions without challenging their fundamental nature. For example, the minimum wage of $1.25 in late 1968, just before the NDP took office, was 50 percent of average wages in Manitoba. It was raised gradually to reach $2.95, or only 51 percent of average wages, in December 1977, despite a commitment in the party's 1969 platform to increase the minimum wage.[28]

Balance also occurs in comparing total revenues and expenditures, which are similar in NDP and Conservative eras. Income distribution was largely unchanged. Structures of inequality were not challenged. Yet marginal improvements occurred within the structures. These assertions are scrutinized in the following sections.

NDP Fiscal Policies

NDP governments have been conventional in their fiscal policies, and similar to the Conservatives. For example, between 1965 and 1980 annual changes in expenditure and revenue were balanced by governments of both parties. Average annual increases in revenue of $109.3 million were close to the expenditure rises of $113.3 million. The compounded annual rate of revenue growth was 17.3 percent, compared to 18.2 percent for expenditures (see Table 84). Per capita spending in Manitoba has been consistent with national trends, averaging slightly higher under the NDP than the Conservatives (see Table 85). Per capita spending by the Conservatives between 1965 and 1969 averaged 89.5 percent of per capita spending for all the provinces. The NDP raised it to 91.1 percent during 1969-77. It fell to 88 percent for the Conservative years of 1977-81, and climbed to 89.5 percent with the NDP in 1981 and 1982.

TABLE 84
CHANGES IN REVENUE AND EXPENDITURE, MANITOBA, 1965-1985
(Thousands)

Period	Increase in Revenue			Increase in Expenditure			Accumulating Surplus (Deficit) During Period ($)
	Total ($)	Annual Amount ($)	Average[1] (%)	Total ($)	Annual Amount ($)	Average (%)	
1965-69 (PC)	191,460	47,885	21.2	205,026	51,257	23.9	33,285
1969-77 (NDP)	821,255	102,657	16.1	841,772	105,222	16.4	186,303
1977-80 (PC)	623,396	209,132	15.3	653,033	217,678	15.6	(16,389)
1965-80	1,640,111	109,341	17.3	1,699,831	113,322	18.2	203,199
1980-85 (NDP)	885,562	177,112	10.1	1,556,443	311,289	13.0	(1,686,681)

Note: [1] The increase is calculated as a percentage, compounded annually.
Source: Compiled from Table 82.

The Schreyer governments of 1969-77 appear as fiscal conservatives compared to the Pawley administrations after 1981. Budgets were balanced. The provincial treasury took in $186 million more than it paid out on current account.

Most new debt was for hydroelectric construction. Schreyer, who held this portfolio, was intensely committed to renewable resource development. He maintained low electricity prices for domestic use in southern Manitoba, and cheaper rates for large industrial consumers and export markets. Hydroelectric construction moved steadily along the province's northern rivers. In its wake Native fishing grounds were flooded. By 1977, Manitoba Hydro accounted for 60 percent of total provincial debt.[29]

Pawley's governments ran up substantial deficits. This was due to declining federal transfers rather than a departure from fiscal conservatism. During the 1970s, Manitoba received substantial federal funding.[30] Growth in federal transfers has declined since 1981. Spending for job creation and economic stimulation increased the accumulated debt by $1.68 billion in the Pawley government's first five years. From 1982 to 1986, Manitoba's growth in public investment has been higher than any other province. It rose by 55.9 percent, compared to a drop of 9.9 percent for Canada.[31]

Most of Manitoba's investment is devoted to hydroelectric construction in the north. Although thousands of new jobs have been created, the long-term costs may outweigh the benefits.[32] Employment is short-lived, since the completed systems require a small operating work force. The new high-wage jobs are welcome to workers and unions in construction trades, as relief from high unemployment elsewhere in Manitoba. Manitoba Hydro's employment policies have also improved recently. Before 1981 the huge projects did not substantially improve Manitobans' employment, since most of the skilled jobs were filled by a migrant labour force. Current policies call for employment of northerners first, and other Manitobans second. Where necessary, training programs are offered to raise employees' skills. Even so, Native communities throughout the north can be adversely affected. Some have lost their fishing grounds through flooding. Others are losing their most valued workers to hydroelectric construction.

TABLE 85

MANITOBA GOVERNMENT SPENDING, 1965-1983

Year	Total Spending		Per Capita Spending	
	Amount ($000)	As % of All Prov	Amount	As % of All Prov
1965	2,458	4.4	2,547	89.2
1966	2,629	4.2	2,730	87.1
1967	2,854	4.2	2,964	89.4
1968	3,154	4.3	3,248	91.2
1969	3,435	4.2	3,509	90.5
1970	3,647	4.2	3,710	91.2
1971	3,948	4.2	3,996	90.7
1972	4,369	4.1	4,408	90.2
1973	5,205	4.2	5,226	91.9
1974	6,167	4.1	6,124	91.0
1975	6,967	4.1	6,871	92.7
1976	7,964	4.1	7,793	91.9
1977	8,396	3.9	8,175	89.1
1978	9,292	3.9	8,975	88.6
1979	10,396	3.8	10,113	88.2
1980	11,303	3.7	11,027	86.5
1981	13,158	3.7	12,825	88.7
1982	13,983	3.8	13,523	90.0
1983	15,048	3.7	14,386	89.0

Note: Average per capita percentages are: 1965-69 (89.5%); 1970-77 (91.1%); 1978-81 (88.0%); 1982-83 (89.5%).

Source: Statistics Canada.

Private investment has also been strong in Manitoba, compared to Canada and the other provinces. Between 1982 and 1986 Manitoba's growth rate of 61 percent matched that of Ontario and Québec. Canada's stood at 21.7 percent, and all other provinces were considerably lower.

These expenditures have helped to keep Manitoba's unemployment low compared to national averages. Yet there is little appreciable difference on this score between the NDP and the Conservatives (see Table 73 in Chapter 12). Unemployment rates are still high for Manitoba. "Real" unemployment is between 50 and 100 percent above official rates. Women have fared worse than men (see Table 86). (For further analysis of these issues, see Chapter 12.)

TABLE 86

OFFICIAL & ESTIMATED REAL EMPLOYMENT RATES, MANITOBA, 1975-1985

(Percentage)

Year	Official Unemployment			Part-Time Employment[1]			Estimated Real Unemployment[2]		
	Male	Female	Total	Male	Female	Total[3]	Male	Female	Total
1975	4.0	5.5	4.5	5.4	24.6	12.4	4.9	12.9	8.3
1976	4.4	5.0	4.7	5.4	24.6	12.6	5.3	12.4	8.9
1977	5.4	6.7	5.9	5.7	24.3	13.0	6.4	14.0	9.9
1978	6.0	7.4	6.5	6.0	24.8	13.4	7.0	14.4	10.5
1979	4.7	6.3	5.3	5.9	25.4	13.7	5.7	13.9	9.4
1980	5.1	6.1	5.5	6.3	26.8	14.6	6.2	14.1	9.9
1981	5.6	6.5	5.9	6.3	25.2	14.3	6.7	14.1	10.2
1982	8.6	8.2	8.5	6.7	27.1	15.5	9.7	16.3	13.2
1983	9.7	9.0	9.4	6.9	27.1	15.4	10.9	17.1	14.0
1984	7.9	8.9	8.3	7.1	26.7	15.5	9.1	16.9	13.0
1985	7.9	8.5	8.1	6.7	26.0	14.9	9.0	16.3	12.6

Notes: [1]Part-time includes everyone employed less than 30 hours a week, and *who consider themselves to be part-time.* In 1981, 1.9 million Canadian workers were in this category. A further 1.3 million were employed 30-34 hours per week. Yet the official number of part-time workers was only 1.48 million. This was because an estimated 432,000 workers employed less than 30 hours per week did not consider themselves working part-time. As Julie White notes, the part-time estimate should include those employed 30-34 hours a week who consider themselves to be part-time. See Julie White, *Women and Part-Time Work* (Ottawa: Canadian Advisory Council on the Status of Women, 1983). [2]These percentages are obtained by adding the official unemployment rate and the percentage of part-time workers who would prefer to work full-time. The percentages of men (approximately one-third) and women (approximately 30 percent) part-time workers who would prefer full-time jobs was obtained from surveys done by Statistics Canada. See *Women In Canada: A Statistical Report* (Ottawa: Supply & Services Canada, 1984). The estimate is probably understated, since it should also include discouraged workers. [3]Part-time employment is a percentage obtained by dividing the numbers who are in part-time employment by their numbers in the labour force.

Source: Statistics Canada, *Women in Canada: A Statistical Report* (Ottawa: Supply and Services Canada, 1989).

Some Specific Policy Initiatives

Tax credit programs are an NDP measure to reduce income inequity by moderating undesirable consequences of existing taxes. The property tax credit program pays a partial rebate of property taxes to homeowners and renters. It is designed to reduce a regressive tax. The minimum credit is deducted directly on the annual tax bill. Amounts above this are calculated on the income tax form. The cost of living credit program provides a modest cash payment to low-income families. It is also calculated on the income tax form.

Property tax credit was introduced in 1972 and a cost of living credit in 1974 (see Table 87). A minimum property tax credit of $50 was set in 1972. Those at low incomes received more, to a ceiling of $140. These have been raised periodically, to current levels of $325 minimum and $525 maximum ($625 for seniors). Payments above the minimum are still targeted to low-income families.

The lowest-income people received token amounts above the minimum property tax credit in 1974.[33] Approximately 100,000 people received no credit since only the highest-income member of a family could apply.[34] The benefit of property tax credits for low-income families depends on the spread between minimum and maximum payment. As the maximum rises above the minimum, the portion of total benefits going to families with low incomes also increases. When introduced, the ratio between maximum and minimum was 2.8:1 (140:50); the current ratio is 1.6:1 (525:325) overall, and 1.9:1 (625:325) for seniors.

TABLE 87

SELECTED PROVINCIAL EXPENDITURES, 1968-1985

(Thousands of Dollars)

| Year | Tax Credits[1] | Social Allowances | | | CRISP[4] | Day Care | Legal Aid | WAP[5] |
		Direct Payments[2]	Munic Assist[3]	Child Maint				
1968		17,478	3,825					
1969		21,088	4,435					
1970		20,973	5,404					
1971		30,504	9,149					
1972		39,286	10,587	5,082				
1973	236	52,105	8,097	7,092				
1974	42,177	43,853	6,653	8,488				1,747
1975	56,978	40,677	6,283	10,492			1,047	2,361
1976	77,191	47,057	5,941	14,771		1,152	2,250	2,565
1977	104,997	51,828	6,162	17,021		2,861	2,777	2,918
1978	126,982	53,390	6,916	15,654		3,770	3,022	3,018
1979	137,094	58,615	7,179	17,831		4,207	3,282	2,922
1980	142,824	62,669	6,875	19,689		4,321	3,389	1,794
1981	169,238	66,895	8,035	22,256	678	5,693	4,745	1,926
1982	151,865	74,392	9,326	24,339	6,195	8,527	5,054	2,361
1983	172,467	89,550	17,944	29,831	6,372	11,236	6,830	4,106
1984	180,821	103,085	26,244	29,427	6,684	13,554	8,116	3,919
1985	191,780	114,537	34,700	28,942	6,114	16,699	7,962	3,908

Notes: [1]Includes property tax credit and cost-of-living tax credit programs. [2]Provincial income security, or welfare, payments. [3]Municipal Assistance; provides payments to municipal social assistance, or welfare, agencies. [4]Child Related Income Support Program. [5]Work Activity Projects, a rehabilitation employment program. The program was renamed in 1984 to Human Resource Opportunity Centres.

Source: Manitoba Department of Finance, *Public Accounts*, Vol. 1 and 2 (Winnipeg: Queen's Printer, 1964-1986).

The program's redistributive impact could be improved by raising the maximum payment. Total cost need not rise: higher maximum payments to low-income people could be financed by lowering the minimum. For 1987-88, eliminating the minimum would have reduced credits on a graduated basis for family incomes between $20,000 and $52,500 ($30,000-$63,500 for seniors).[35] Savings could be used to raise the maximum.

The cost-of-living tax credit is supposed to reimburse some of the provincial sales taxes paid by low-income families. It was modelled after Ontario's sales tax credit program.[36] It is more progressive than the property tax credit, as it is entirely income tested.

By 1977 the combined tax credit programs were returning $105 million to taxpayers' pockets, approximately 80 percent of it to families with income below the median.[37] Payments grew to $192 million by 1985, but declined to 5.6 percent of gross expenditures from 8.8 percent in 1977.

Provincial tax changes have been relatively modest. The 5 percent sales tax introduced in 1967 was increased to 6 percent in 1983. A surtax on incomes above $25,000 was introduced by the NDP in 1976, eliminated by the Conservatives in 1978, reinstated by the NDP in 1982, and increased in 1987.

Corporate income taxes have increased for banks and large businesses, and declined for smaller companies.[38] The net effect on the corporate sector is negligible. As a proportion of total provincial income, Manitoba's corporate income taxes have declined steadily, while individuals have contributed an increasing share (Tables 80 and 81).

In 1982 the NDP introduced a levy on payrolls, similar to Québec's, to finance health and education.[39] It is apparently more fair than health care premiums, eliminated in 1970 for Manitoba, but still assessed in Ontario, Alberta and British Columbia. The levy also recaptured some federal revenue, since the federal government is taxed on its payrolls in Manitoba.[40] The total levy in 1985 was $111 million, 3.8 percent of total revenue.

Since the levy is targeted at employees' remuneration it is treated as a form of taxed employee benefit. The method of collection is similar to employers' contributions for Canada Pension Plan or Unemployment Insurance. Employers will attempt to reduce their remuneration accordingly.

As noted in the introduction, Manitoba's fiscal policies are still shaped by the compromise of Confederation. Like other provinces, Manitoba confronts the mismatch between its service responsibilities and its fiscal authority.

Alternative Sources of Provincial Revenue

The provincial government's public finance dilemma stems from its commitment to maintain reasonable levels of expenditure in the face of insufficient revenue. Without alternative forms of revenue, the province is locked into choosing among narrow options. Three directions seem possible: increase deficits, raise taxes, or reduce expenditures. Each is politically undesirable.

Deficits create problems because major American investment houses peg their bond ratings to the deficit, which in turn affects Manitoba's cost of borrowing. Raising taxes is also touchy. Part of the rise in a regressive tax on individuals must be offset for low incomes; increased burdens on a sector of the business community are usually tempered with some concessions; the impact on net receipts from the federal government must be carefully monitored. Capital mobility is also an issue. Large corporations tend to play provinces off against each other in comparing rates of taxation, incentives for investment, labour and other legislation, and the general climate of government policies towards business. Expenditure reductions may be of two sorts. First are government programs, the majority of which are in health, education and social services. Cuts here are unkind and unpopular. Reducing tax expenditures is more desirable, but it is subject to limited provincial influence due to federal control over most taxation policy and the threats of capital mobility.

Revenue-raising options are thus limited. They include rises in consumption taxes. Based on 1986-87 estimates, each 1 percent increase in sales tax would raise an extra $85 million. Although some of this money should be returned to low-income consumers via tax credits, it is the single largest source of revenue increase. Other options which fit the existing framework include: raising the payroll levy, now at 1.5 percent; increasing the capital and income taxes on banks and large corporations; and negotiating with the federal government for a greater share of taxes.

Another regressive step is to increase lottery and casino revenue. Gambling tends to tax the poor. The last NDP government announced a trial increase in casino gambling. Casino revenue is granted to charity and public service organizations.

The recent review of taxation advocated a surtax on net instead of taxable income.[41] This has appeal, since it would by-pass federal tax expenditures such as personal exemptions and deductions for interest income and capital gains. It would also disallow deductions for pension income, medical expenses, education and charitable donations.[42]

Tales of Lost Opportunity

NDP policies have precluded serious consideration of alternatives to working within the existing framework. When revenue was available, public spending supported progressive policies. Yet with few exceptions, traditional structures of government revenue generation have been used.

The NDP has rarely pursued industrial or regional economic planning, nor has it pursued a more comprehensive industrial strategy. Instead, the NDP has left capitalist markets intact. When opportunities emerged, the government usually backed off.

Provincial mining policy is an example. Contrary to Eric Kierans's recommendations, the Schreyer governments neither nationalized nor extracted more of the excess profits from mining companies like INCO and Falconbridge Nickel. Far from extracting more of the economic rents from mining, NDP governments have followed their Conservative predecessors by improving benefits for the companies. INCO's smelter in Thompson has enjoyed subsidized Manitoba Hydro rates since its inception. Considerable infrastructure has been financed publicly for Sherrit Gordon Mines near Leaf Rapids, and for the Falconbridge mine at Manibridge near Wabowden. Most of the major mining operations have been exempted from local taxes. They have paid negotiated fees instead.

The Falconbridge mine at Manibridge provided many of the benefits corporate guests have come to expect from host provincial governments. For extracting Manitoba's valuable mineral resources, and employing workers in unsafe conditions, Falconbridge received generous concessions from the province. It was allowed to create a separate residential village at Clarke Lake adjacent to the mine, despite pleading from the nearby community of Wabowden to use its facilities. The lake had supported a Wabowden resident in a small commercial fishing operation. This was banned, in favour of sport fishing for Falconbridge employees resident at Clarke Lake. Wabowden already had a political structure in place, plus physical infrastructure for housing, some recreational facilities and a school. The community would have benefited from spending by the company and its workers.[43] An expanded tax base would have allowed financing of projects to create a more secure economy for the small town, and to improve the quality of life for its residents. Instead of being on Wabowden's tax rolls, Falconbridge was allowed to pay grants to the province. Wabowden received an annual $75,000, with no inflation provision for the five-year duration of the lease.[44]

Social Democratic Vision?

In a preface to remarks on the first Pawley government, Errol Black noted that "NDP governments of recent years have shown little inclination to challenge established interests."[45] Perhaps the only time the Manitoba NDP launched a significant challenge was with Autopac. Since then, it has shied away from fundamental reforms. Significant opportunities were not taken.

The former NDP government tabled a rather progressive budget for 1987-88 (16 March 1987). It used virtually all the tax options outlined in the "Current Limitations" section. There was much to applaud in the budget, which planned to raise an extra $277 million over the 1986-87 fiscal year, directed mainly for health, education, social welfare, agriculture, and reduction of the deficit. The government was maximizing its options to maintain employment and most services, and bring improvements to some.

But, as noted in the introduction, the NDP is also limited by its own ideology and history. Income from taxation must be maximized because alternative sources of revenue were not created. During highly profitable periods in the 1970s, sectors like mining of nonrenewable resources were allowed to retain most of their surpluses. Options to nationalize the mines were not taken. Some innovative services were provided to miners and their families.[46]

Other opportunities to convert private profit into public revenue have also been neglected. For example, the Winnipeg Gas Company, now owned by InterCity Gas Corporation, was granted a twenty-five-year renewal on its monopoly to distribute natural gas in Winnipeg when the old lease expired in 1981. Such an institution, which is providing a public service, ought to be nationalized by the provincial government. In 1987 the NDP government launched discussions with InterCity Gas to purchase the Winnipeg Gas Company for conversion to a public utility. Negotiations with the company eventually broke down. The Winnipeg Gas Company continues its monopoly as a private company operating for profit.

As early as 1971 the NDP committed itself to structural change. For example, *Guidelines for the Seventies* included a proposal to create government-owned Treasury Branches, to "stem the drain of financial resources from Manitoba and make capital more accessible to local development."[47] There was a 1970 commitment to study the feasibility of establishing "a Crown corporation to manufacture drugs in Manitoba."[48] Reforms to the pricing and distribution of pharmaceuticals were investigated between 1971 and 1974, prior to the 1975 Pharmacare program. Neither commitment was met. McAllister estimates that by fiscal year 1977-78, Pharmacare was paying $7.9 million in inflated prices for prescription drugs.[49] Estimates are not available on the costs and foregone opportunities of the phantom Treasury Branches.

Although the NDP identified significant structural reforms, it did not deliver. McAllister astutely sums up the NDP's economic accomplishments:

> In summary, the Schreyer government did move in the direction of increased government involvement in the economy, just as Liberal, Conservative, Social Credit, and Parti Québécois governments almost everywhere else in Canada and most governments in the western world increased their participation in the economy. But the NDP government moved only the minimum distance possible into the domain of the private sector. Indeed, it was willing to incur tremendous costs to the public sector to avoid a loss of electoral support.[50]

Since 1974 the NDP has moved rightward, even from the modest social democratic alternatives posed in the heady days of its first term in office. During economic expansion, when provincial budgets were growing, it was possible to initiate some important social reforms. In later periods the province was squeezed by the federal government's fiscal restraints. Its revenue base also suffered, as did its residents, from declining employment growth in the private sector.

In the current parlance of fiscal management, little seems left of the visions in *Guidelines for the Seventies*. Such may be the inevitable dilemma with social democratic management of capitalist economies. Yet the soil of Canadian society hungers for the seeds of a new vision for the future. The NDP has grown from its roots in the dusty plains of Saskatchewan. Not since 1933 has it offered a vision to equal the terms and conditions of the Regina Manifesto. Some new beginnings are in order.

NOTES

1. Ian Gough, *The Political Economy of the Welfare State* (London: Macmillan, 1979), 114.

2. This refers to the system of bond rating. Manitoba's rating is determined by the major American investment houses. Each drop in the rating, from AA downward, indicates that investment in the province is more risky. The cost of borrowing will rise because higher interest rates must be offered. There is also a political cost, in that lowered bond ratings do not sit well with the electorate.

3. The "apparatus" includes: government departments concerned with social services, income security, health, and education; committees of cabinet which initiate and/or review social policies; other bodies which are formally consulted in the processes of policy formation. The term is here used in a broad sense, to include the stages of policy formation as well as implementation.

4. For evidence on this argument, see Canadian Union of Public Employees, *Special Peace Issue, The Facts* 6, no. 4 (May 1984); Ernie Regehr and Mel Watkins, "The Economics of the Arms Race," in Ernie Regehr and Simon Rosenblum, eds., *Canada and the Nuclear Arms Race* (Toronto: James Lorimer and Company, 1983).

5. As corporate income flows to owners of capital, it is more unevenly distributed than wages and salaries. With lower corporate income taxes, the wealthier owners of capital benefit far more than the poor.

6. Several major studies have documented the history of state assistance to industry. See the following: R.T. Naylor, *The History of Canadian Business, 1867-1914* (Toronto: James Lorimer and Company, 1975); Tom Traves, *The State and Enterprise: Canadian Manufacturers and the Federal Government, 1917-1931* (Toronto: University of Toronto Press, 1979); Robert Chodos, *The CPR: A Century of Corporate Welfare* (Toronto: James Lorimer and Company, 1973).

7. The seventeen-member study team which examined assistance to business was made up of ten government officials, five business executives, one business consultant and one trade union representative — only three were women. See Canada, Task Force on Program Review (Nielson), *Services and Subsidies to Business: Giving with Both Hands* (Ottawa: Supply and Services Canada, 1985).

8. Geoffrey York, "Ford to Purchase Winnipeg Tractor Maker," *Toronto Globe and Mail*, 16 February 1987.

9. See Michael B. Decter, *Expenditure Management: A Review and Recommendations for Reform* (Winnipeg: The October Group, 1986). The estimated tax expenditures of $21.4 million cover an exemption on the provincial health and education levy and the lower tax rate for small business. The total tax expenditure to business is considerably higher since it includes the impact of all corporate tax deductions on provincial income taxes.

10. Canada, Department of Finance, *Economic Review, April 1985* (Ottawa: Supply and Services, 1985).

11. See the following: A.W. Djao, *Inequality and Social Policy: The Sociology of Welfare* (Toronto: John Wiley and Sons, 1983); Canada, National Council of Welfare, *The Hidden Welfare System Revisited: A Report by the National Council of Welfare on the Growth in Tax Expenditures* (Ottawa: Supply and Services Canada, 1979); National Council of Welfare, *Social Spending and the Next Budget* (Ottawa: Supply and Services Canada, 1989); David Ross, *The Canadian Fact Book on Income Distribution* (Ottawa: Canadian Council on Social Development, 1980).

12. *Basic federal tax* is the amount obtained by applying the federal income tax rates to *taxable income*. Taxable income results from subtracting all allowable federal deductions from *total income*.

13. Data on tax expenditures and the 1986 projected deficit are from Manitoba, *The Manitoba Budget Address 1986* (Winnipeg: Queen's Printer, 1986).

14. For comprehensive studies on tax expenditures, see National Council of Welfare, *The Hidden Welfare System*. See also David Ross, *The Canadian Fact Book on Income Distribution* (Ottawa: Canadian Council on Social Development, 1980). For a study of postwar income distribution by quintile, see Leo Johnson, *Poverty in Wealth* (Toronto: New Hogtown Press, 1974).

15. Direct taxes include individual and corporate income taxes. Taxes on consumption include the provincial sales tax, tobacco tax, gasoline and oil taxes, and profits from Liquor Board sales. Licenses and fees include such items as automobile licenses, fees for using provincial parks, and all other user and license fees.

16. A province which taxes transfers of wealth on its own would probably experience capital outflow, fear of which makes such a move unlikely.

17. Manitoba's corporate capital tax rates rank third among the provinces, behind Saskatchewan and Québec. All provinces except Alberta, Prince Edward Island and New Brunswick impose some form of tax on private capital. Data are from Michael B. Decter, *Taxation: A Review and Recommendations for Reform* (Winnipeg: The October Group, 1986), 34.

18. Percentages are calculated from Manitoba Public Accounts. Manitoba has argued that it suffered more than any other province from changes to equalization in 1982. See Decter, *Taxation*.

19. According to the Manitoba government, between 1977-78 and 1984-85, health and higher education requirements in the province grew at an average annual rate which was 3.5 percent above the rate of growth in the GNP. See Manitoba Finance, *The Manitoba Budget Address*.

20. Decter, *Taxation*, xi. For 1986-87, Manitoba's rate of 54 percent on basic federal tax was the fourth highest, after Newfoundland (60 percent), New Brunswick (58 percent) and Nova Scotia (56.5 percent). Alberta was lowest (43.5 percent), while Québec cannot be compared as it collects its own taxes directly. Data are from Decter, *Taxation*, 19.

21. Even with Autopac the government was cautious. Private insurance agents, who represented a voting constituency, retained rights to sell supplementary automobile insurance as well as the basic coverage. Basic coverage could easily be handled through the mail and the Autopac claims centres. The agents were also compensated for the loss of part of their business. See James A. McAllister, *The Government of Edward Schreyer: Democratic Socialism in Manitoba* (Montréal and Kingston: McGill-Queen's University Press, 1984).

22. Eric Kierans, *Report on Natural Resources Policy in Manitoba* (Winnipeg: Government of Manitoba, 1973).

23. For commentary on the Schreyer government's approach to equity participation in business enterprises, see McAllister, *Government of Edward Schreyer*.

24. The Schreyer government did investigate industrial democracy. It placed worker representatives on the boards of some Crown corporations. While a laudable beginning, it was not pursued further. Formal placement of workers on a board is insufficient to substantially reform the policies and management practices of a corporation.

25. For an alternative working model see the approach of the Greater London Council's (GLC) Technology Program. The GLC has promoted products which are socially useful and employ the talents of its labour force. For the principles upon which GLC plans are based, see Hilary Wainwright and Dave Elliott, *The Lucas Plan: A New Trade Unionism in the Making?* (London: Allison and Busby, 1982).

26. Quoted in Paul Beaulieu, *Ed Schreyer: A Social Democrat in Power* (Winnipeg: Queenston House Press, 1977), 6.

27. See McAllister, *Government of Edward Schreyer*. The NDP was in power under Schreyer for two terms (1969-77). It is often labelled the Schreyer government because of his strong personal stamp on the two administrations. Some observers argue that Schreyer's popular image carried the NDP to victory. See also Nelson Wiseman, *Social Democracy in Manitoba: A History of the CCF/NDP* (Winnipeg: University of Manitoba Press, 1983).

28. Approximately 10 percent of Manitoba's labour force receives the minimum wage. See McAllister, *Government of Edward Schreyer*, 57-58.

29. The government argued that the dams would produce electrical power for future generations, financed in part by export earnings from short-run excess capacity. Increasing the debt for Manitoba Hydro was politically safer than general debt. The province's bond rating is not affected by Manitoba Hydro's self-sustaining debt, which is repaid from business income. General debt repayment relies on tax revenue.

30. This was from CAP, EPF, and National Equalization. Sectoral agreements were also signed, providing between 50 and 60 percent federal funding, such as the Northlands Agreement, the Fund for Rural Economic Development (FRED) agreement for the Interlake region of Manitoba, and special ARDA.

31. It dropped in every other province except Nova Scotia (up 2 percent) and Prince Edward Island (up 21.1 percent).

32. For analysis of costs and benefits of recent Manitoba Hydro investment, see John Loxley and George Chuchman, "Is Limestone a Lemon? Manitoba Mega Projects," *Canadian Dimension* 19 (May/June 1985): 4-7.

33. Filers with incomes below $2,000 received $27 above the minimum. The largest spread went to filers with incomes between $5,000 and $8,000 who averaged $37 above the minimum. See McAllister, *Government of Edward Schreyer*, 56.

34. Ibid.

35. Decter, *Taxation*. He estimates that the tax saved by eliminating the minimum would be $54 million for 1987-88 and $23 million annually thereafter.

36. McAllister, *Government of Edward Schreyer*, 56. He provides confirmation from the 1977 budget address of the minister of finance.

37. Ibid.

38. The rate for large businesses rose to 17 percent by 1986. The small business rate dropped to 10 percent by 1982. Capital tax on banks reached 3 percent in 1986.

39. The levy is 1.5 percent of total annual gross payroll. Not all employers or payrolls are taxed. Anything less than $50,000 is exempt. The amount between $50,000 and $75,000 is subject to a reduced rate.

40. This observation was provided in personal correspondence by a well-informed observer.

41. See Decter, *Taxation*.

42. This option shows the provincial limits on income tax options. A province cannot choose preferred deductions by item. By using net income some undesirable deductions are by-passed. Some favoured ones may also be eliminated.

43. More than $1 million was spent by the company on facilities at its village. This included a recreational complex, which Wabowden lacked at the time. Wabowden eventually built one for $250,000. The facility at Clarke Lake was abandoned when the company mothballed the site. Because of their location, most employees of the company tended to shop in Thompson rather than Wabowden. Figures and observations are from unpublished studies of the Manibridge mine.

44. Wabowden did receive some short-term cash benefits from the mine. They were not, however, tied to the needs of the community, nor to the additional costs incurred for services provided to 25 employees who lived in a trailer court which Wabowden established and serviced. Employment benefits were rather meager. Of 180 employees, only 10 were long-term residents of the community. Of the 170 who migrated to the region for employment, 25 located in Wabowden. The remaining 145 resided in the company village at Clarke Lake. Data taken from an internal study of the Manibridge mine experience.

45. Errol Black, "The NDP in Manitoba," *Canadian Dimension* 19 (May/June 1985): 3-4.

46. The most shining example of innovations in this regard is the townsite development at Leaf Rapids. Instead of allowing a fairly (sub)standard mining town to emerge under corporate control, the NDP took over development of the townsite from inception. The result was a model community designed to optimize northern living conditions. It included above-standard housing and recreational facilities as well as a town centre with amenities not usually available in mining towns.

47. Quoted in McAllister, *Government of Edward Schreyer*, 7, from *Guidelines for the Seventies*, 137. Although a Treasury Branch Act was passed in 1975, the legislation was never implemented.

48. Quoted in McAllister, *Government of Edward Schreyer*, 68.

49. Ibid., 69.

50. Ibid., 69-70.

15   Economic Planning Under Social Democracy

John Loxley

In recent years considerable attention has been focussed on the type of planning required to build feasible socialism, that is, a socialism realizable within the lifetime of the current younger generation. There is a growing consensus that centralized material planning, while perhaps imperative in the earlier years of structural transformation, is cumbersome, unwieldy and far too autocratic as a method of planning a sophisticated economy en route to socialism. Thus, observers are giving sympathetic consideration to blends of direct controls, and the use of market forces.[1] Western socialists are debating the minimal kinds of planning models, institutions and techniques required to make market economies responsive to minimal social demands of workers.[2]

This debate does not concern directly the nature of planning under social democracy, but it is felt that some planning initiatives undertaken by the NDP governments of Edward Schreyer, while not being in any sense fully implemented, are relevant to the broader debate about planning in the transition to socialism. In particular, they suggest what kind of planning might be possible in Canada, and point to important lessons of dangers to be avoided. In many respects, this experience suggests the feasibility of a type and degree of planning which goes well beyond that being advocated by some European socialists.

The Organization of Planning Under the Schreyer Government

The nominal importance attached to planning by the Schreyer government (1969-77) is evident from the planning structure it created. The afternoon sessions of weekly cabinet meetings were designated "Planning Sessions," during which cabinet became a (planning) committee-of-the-whole to which a series of cabinet subcommittees reported. The principal subcommittee in the area of economic affairs was the Resource and Economic Development (RED) subcommittee. Chaired by one of the strongest ministers, Sid Green, representing the Department of Mines, Resources and Environmental Management, this committee comprised the ministers of Industry and Commerce, Northern Affairs, Agriculture and Co-operatives, and the minister responsible for the Public Insurance Corporation. Planning activities related to municipalities were also channelled through this committee until, towards the end of the second Schreyer government, a new Land Use Planning Committee was created.

The RED subcommittee was serviced by a secretary, who had full deputy minister status, and about a dozen staff with technical skills in economics, finance, engineering, land-use planning and computer programming. The RED secretariat formed part of the planning secretariat of cabinet, the secretary of which was a senior deputy minister and, usually, a close political confidante of the premier (see Figure 22).

Servicing such a powerful group of ministers and having reasonably direct channels of communication to the premier, the RED secretariat had considerable influence among line department deputies and their staff. This influence was strengthened by the RED secretariat acting as the point of contact with the federal government on all matters related to Department of Regional Economic Expansion (DREE) cost-sharing agreements, the principal means by which the federal government sought to influence provincial economic policy. The RED secretary or his designate could also sit on all interview boards for senior appointments in line departments in the area of economic policy and/or analysis.

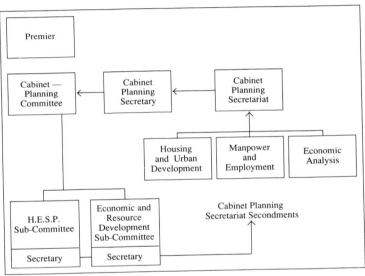

Figure 22. Organization of Planning Under the Schreyer Governments

There was one other permanent subcommittee of cabinet, the Health, Education and Social Policy subcommittee (HESP) and three ad hoc subcommittees, Manpower and Employment (MECS), Urban Affairs, and Provincial Employment and Winter Works. Professional staff were again grouped around the subcommittee specialization reporting immediately to a secretary (HESP) or assistant secretary (MECS) who in turn was responsible to the planning secretary. An elaborate planning structure was created, therefore, within executive council, one which was interposed between line departments and the cabinet.

The Nature of Planning Under the Schreyer Government

The logic of the planning secretariat was to provide the NDP government with a politically sympathetic check and evaluation of material flowing to cabinet from line departments, the senior staff of which, for the most part, had been hired by previous governments. A strong central agency was needed, therefore, in part as an alternative to a clean sweep of the senior levels of the bureaucracy which the NDP, with its deep attachment to parliamentary democracy and the associated traditions of civil service impartiality, refused to undertake. This distrust of many line department officials also necessitated that the secretariat be a source of new ideas for policy initiatives. The publication of the three-volume *Guidelines for the Seventies*, discussed below, was a major, but by no means the sole, expression of planning secretariat creativity during this time.

Planning was conceived, therefore, in very narrow terms to mean policy planning. This was stated explicitly in the "General Manual of Administration" which specified the functions of the planning secretariat as those of carrying out "policy analysis, review and assessment of alternatives."[3] More specifically, the RED subcommittee functions were defined as follows:

> (a) reviews, considers, develops, recommends on significant or major matters concerning current and future policies affecting economic and resource development, either on its own initiative or by referral from the Executive Council or from any member thereof.
>
> (b) makes subsequent recommendations to the entire Cabinet.[4]

Predominantly, and certainly until 1975, the RED secretariat served to "police" line departments by examining their submissions to cabinet. In effect, it scrutinized new program or project proposals in light of declared NDP policy, and from the point of view of economic analysis. This generated resentment against the secretariat by departmental staff who saw it as an obstacle to be by-passed. Secretariat staff were also bright, brash, unconventional in dress, and generally well to the Left of the NDP ideologically. None of these traits endeared them to the older, senior level bureaucracy, nor indeed to several of the RED ministers or their own senior NDP appointees. They were tolerated because of their abilities, because of their location in executive council, because of the recognized need for the policing function and, less frequently as time went by, for their contribution to policy formulation.

Much of the RED subcommittee's work consisted, therefore, of an "after-the-fact" reaction to line department initiatives, and often involved diverting submissions sent directly to the cabinet secretary on Monday intended for discussion at cabinet on Wednesday. At best, this meant redirecting the submission to an RED subcommittee meeting at which RED staff would submit a written critique. Line department ministers and staff found this almost as intimidating as facing the chairman of the subcommittee, whose acerbic debating tone and critical intellect were generally to be avoided. In this respect, the secretariat and the committee were performing much more of a control than a planning function, a similar function in the area of economic analysis to that performed by the management committee in the area of budgets.

The distancing of the secretariat from line departments also characterized the one major constructive initiative undertaken by it to this time, the preparation of *Guidelines for the Seventies*, published in 1973.[5] This document represented an important policy statement for the government as a whole, encompassing not just economic and regional policy, but also policy in the large and complex area of social services. Yet, in spite of its all-encompassing nature and importance to overall government policy, it appears to have been the product almost entirely of centrally located advisors. This is readily apparent from the objectives of the *Guidelines* which would seem to flow, logically, from a left-wing critique of capitalism. Thus, the *Guidelines* sought to rectify unequal access to power, inequalities of income and wealth, economic instability and especially unemployment, sectoral and regional imbalances, the concentration and centralization of business, and problems of alienation faced by workers.[6] To meet these objectives, a whole series of policies and programs were outlined, each of which would be consistent with the four basic principles on which the *Guidelines* were built: the maximization of the general well-being of all Manitobans; more equitable distribution of the benefits of development; a "stay option" under which no Manitoban would be coerced for economic reasons into leaving the province or his/her place of residence; and greater public participation in government and development decisions.[7]

The *Guidelines* were considered to represent "a comprehensive, rational framework for progressive development planning."[8] It was envisaged that much of that planning would take place at the local or community level, in furtherance of the stay option and participation principles. Furthermore, the local planning of job creation was considered vital to meeting the employment objectives which, remarkably, foresaw guaranteed employment for all Manitobans by the latter half of the decade.[9]

It is not clear from the *Guidelines* just how far the planners felt it would be necessary to go, in terms of changing property relationships and interfering with market forces, if their ambitious objectives were to be met. A significant role was sketched out for Crown corporations, which would not be used simply to rescue insolvent private companies, but instead would move aggressively into profitable ventures. They would, in particular, enter "industries characterized by monopoly control" or by barriers to entry, and could act to support small-scale local businesses by providing a variety of services which would either not be available or else available only at exorbitant charges.[10] A clear emphasis against monopoly, rather than against private enterprise, underlay these recommendations, as it did the proposal to establish treasury branches, which were seen as competitors to private monopoly banks. Indeed, along with cooperatives and local development corporations, the small-scale private sector was to be encouraged. What was not clear was the balance between different ownership vehicles, and while one is left with the impression that the planners envisaged *extensive* public and cooperative sector intervention, the *Guidelines* are so vague that they would be entirely consistent with minimal intervention of this sort, in effect filling in a few of the holes left by the private sector (both monopoly and "competitive") and the market.

For all their shortcomings, which will be analyzed later, the *Guidelines* did provide a generally progressive policy framework within which planners could operate. In themselves, however, they did nothing to help create a coherent government economic planning machinery; quite the contrary, given their origins within a relatively isolated central agency.

After 1975, a number of initiatives were undertaken by the planning secretariat, and by the RED secretariat in particular, to change the nature of economic planning and to build a more constructive relationship with line departments. To begin with, formal guidelines were circulated to departments, outlining clearly the issues to be addressed in submissions to the RED subcommittee. This reduced the incidence of referrals back to departments for additional information and analysis, helped create greater uniformity and relevance in the quality of submissions and, to some degree, reduced friction. The subsequent development of benefit-cost appraisal *pro formas* was also well received by line departments. Moreover, RED staff began to assist line departments in the conception and preparation of submissions, becoming both supportive and pro-active rather than seemingly obstructive and negative. In consequence, RED subcommittee meetings became less of a forum for debate among bureaucrats and allowed ministers greater input. In addition, RED staff worked closely with line department staff in the preparation of a series of draft federal-provincial agreements for negotiation with DREE. This enabled the secretariat to influence programing in a constructive manner.

The Northern Manitoba Development Strategy

It was, in fact, under the umbrella of such an exercise, and in the context of improved working relationships with line departments, that the secretariat launched its most ambitious and innovative planning initiative — the Northern Manitoba Development Strategy. In preparation for the renewal of the Federal-Provincial Northlands Agreement, which covered essentially non-status Indian, non-urban communities in the north, the secretariat sought to develop a comprehensive development plan for the area. Drawing on the principles and objectives of the *Guidelines for the Seventies*, what distinguished this exercise from others, both in Manitoba and elsewhere in Canada, was an attempt to introduce an explicit strategy of development with which all government expenditures and programs would be consistent. The essence of this strategy was *convergence*, the maximum use of local resources (both human and nonhuman) to meet local demands and needs. In practical terms this entailed the physical and financial planning of investment and production to maximize backward, forward and final demand linkages. It called for the maximum utilization of northern labour and expertise on all government programs and in the delivery of all government services, and it put an explicit priority on communal or cooperative ownership of the means of production. Participation by northerners was a fundamental characteristic of the strategy, taking the form of the specification of needs, the determination of investment priorities, the choice of personnel for training, employment and management roles, and the creation and nurturing of community enterprises.[11]

For over a year all line departments *and* Crown corporations were required to draw up plans applying the principles of convergence to their particular activities and any future programing they intended to finance under the Northlands Agreement. These were vetted by sectoral working groups and eventually by senior staff representing the secretariat and the Department of Northern Affairs. By the end of the exercise, comprehensive and internally consistent plans had been developed for the north, embracing economic, social and cultural aspects and laying out as fully as possible the physical, human and financial implications.

To facilitate this and similar exercises that might be carried out at a later date for other parts of the province, the secretariat gained approval for a series of broad, supportive policy measures from the RED subcommittee. The first of these acknowledged that the massive purchasing power of the provincial government could legitimately be used to encourage local enterprises pursuing goals which were socially much broader than pure profit maximization. The implication was that in the government procurement process, the lowest bidder need not be accepted. The second specified the circumstances in which state subsidization of community-based enterprises might be justified and the maximum limits of such subsidization. This was tied into the social cost-benefit *pro forma* mentioned earlier. Third, the case was made and accepted for the RED secretariat and subcommittee to have a legitimate role in the analysis of line department draft budgets, assessing the conformity of planned expenditures with accepted policy, and the soundness of those expenditures in terms of economic analysis. This opened the way for central scrutiny of budgets for consistency with the strategy; in principle, this was a major step forward from pure paper planning.

Participation of northerners and specifically of Natives in this exercise was to be achieved by involving three groups which represented them, the Northern Association of Community Councils, the Manitoba Indian Brotherhood, and the Manitoba Metis Federation. Each was to be given funds to hire a planner, to participate in planning meetings and to be forwarded *all* background materials for comment and input. Community input was achieved by analysis of the tapes and records of a series of earlier meetings between communities and government officials. A Community Participation Working Group held extensive meetings in six northern communities, while the Department of Northern Affairs hired Natives to act as liaison officers between communities and the government. Provision was made in the strategy for the funding of local economic and social planning capabilities while support was given, more specifically, for communities to plan the future organization of their school administration. Support was also given for community representatives to meet on a regional basis to develop collective input into planning and implementation. Northern MLAs, as elected representatives of northern people, were also involved intimately in all stages of the planning exercise. It is evident that the definition of participation went well beyond the narrow bounds of parliamentarianism and, to facilitate this, that the exercise presupposed an unusual degree of access to information by communities and their representatives.

Subsequent to the northern strategy the RED secretariat also prepared two other important planning documents. The first of these was a Rural Development Strategy, the second an Industrial Strategy for the Province. Inspired by the convergence approach, these documents specified in some detail the types of linkages that could theoretically be developed to build or strengthen an integrated provincial economy and to encourage greater regional balance. They were to serve later as a model for work on a national industrial strategy by the federal NDP, which indeed drew on some of the people who had worked on the provincial strategies. Unlike the northern plan, however, these proposals did not go beyond strategic outlines; they were not project- or community-specific and did not make detailed physical, financial or personnel projections. Above all, they were not linked to the government budget (which, in any case, is much less influential in these areas than it is in the northern region), nor were they accompanied by implementation schedules or proposals for implementation vehicles. They were, therefore, indicative plans, although they specified some of the policy instruments the government might adopt to help realize them.

Assessment of Planning Under the Schreyer Government

In spite of the publication of *Guidelines for the Seventies*, and cabinet approval of the northern strategy and the rural and industrial strategies, there can be no denying that the NDP government "certainly did not transform or radically alter the social and economic fabric of the province."[12] The impact of these and other planning initiatives was minimal and the explanation for this is to be found in the nature of the politics of social democracy.

The essence of social democratic politics is reformism, a basic acceptance of the capitalist system combined with reform designed to curb some of the more gross excesses. Without challenging the property relations underlying capitalism, there are severe limits to what can be achieved in terms of income or wealth redistribution, economic stabilization, and the other laudable goals of the *Guidelines*. Indeed, the hallmark of the Schreyer government was its extreme incrementalism, the adoption of social reform programs which "were almost always within bounds that threatened no one."[13] Schreyer himself saw the mandate of the NDP as "a qualified mandate . . . the mandate to undertake programs of social reform of a moderate kind."[14] By the time the *Guidelines* were published the government had exhausted most of its provocative initiatives, such as Autopac, the reduction of Medicare premiums, the introduction of property tax credits, and the creation of new funding agencies for farmers and the north. Thereafter its program initiatives were, with a few exceptions, such as occupational health and safety, even more marginal and cautious. Moreover, many of its innovations both before and after 1973 were not peculiar to Manitoba or to NDP governments. There were certainly no profound changes in income or wealth distribution under the NDP, no evidence that the stay option reduced in any significant way the trend towards fewer, larger farmers and to rural depopulation, and, far from disappearing, unemployment had almost doubled by the late 1970s to over 4 percent, compared with only 2.3 percent in 1969.[15] This is not to underestimate the importance to select groups of some of the reforms carried out. The poor and the aged did benefit from tax reforms, rent controls, reduced Medicare premiums, access to some education programs, and a new Pharmacare program, but these benefits were not significant enough or widespread enough to threaten the income or wealth of other groups in society.

The record of the NDP in Manitoba illustrates the limits of social democracy. The party, when in power, has never sought to go beyond the mild reform of capitalism. Furthermore, as Miliband and Liebman have said of European social democracy, "it has consistently sought to *limit* the scope and substance of the reforms which it has itself proposed and implemented, in an endeavour to pacify and accommodate capitalist forces, and to demonstrate how much these forces could count on the 'moderation' and 'reasonableness' of their social democratic opponents.''[16] McAllister provides a whole list of areas where the NDP backed away from its own declared program or else diluted that program to placate opposition, for example, restricting the takeover of insurance business to some portion of car insurance only, limited changes to the tax structure, refusal to nationalize resource companies unless they needed financial assistance, and some land banking, public housing and rent controls but no fundamental threat to the huge profits of property developers.[17] In these and many other areas, it is suggested that the government could have gone further. In some instances it was even urged to do so by outside, nonpartisan advisors. For example, the Kierans report advocated significant taxation of mineral rents and the eventual nationalization of profitable mines.[18] Yet the NDP chose not to do so, instead adopting minimal changes "resulting in the least possible dislocation.''[19]

McAllister suggests that this timidity can be explained by the fragility of the NDP's electoral base — the fact that it garnered less than one-half of the popular vote, that it had an ambiguous base in terms of class and ethnicity, and that many people voted for it more because of Schreyer's charisma than for ideological reasons.[20] It seems, however, that McAllister understates the strength of working-class support for the party and overstates the "ethnic coalition" interpretation (for example, by ignoring the support of the urban Anglo-Saxon working class for the NDP).[21] Furthermore, he himself admits that more radical measures in the mineral, insurance and financial areas "would provide massive pools of money for investment in the provincial economy.''[22] Surely the generation and prudent use of these funds might have strengthened working-class and perhaps even broader-based support for the NDP? Moreover, it could plausibly be argued that Schreyer never really tested the limits of reform, but was quite content to stop well before them. Neither, therefore, were the limits of his charismatic appeal put to the test.

It is tempting to explain the limitations of the Schreyer government in terms of the limitations of Schreyer himself. After all, it is widely recognized that the premier tended to dominate decision taking in cabinet. Yet what needs to be explained are the social and political factors which led to such a "safe" candidate being promoted into the leadership. As Miliband and Liebman argue, this type of leadership appears to be a systemic feature of social democratic parties the world over. Their explanation is that the party apparatus is controlled by moderates who sift out undesirables and/or radicals, selecting, co-opting and promoting moderates.[23] In Manitoba, the NDP appears to have achieved this through control of the party by a small elite, and through a caucus and cabinet drawn essentially from the "middle class" — teachers, professionals and small businesspeople. At the same time it failed to build a solid working-class constituency base. This party structure militated against strong policy positions coming from below, and enabled Schreyer and his cabinet to have a disproportionate influence on policy.[24] It is they who sought to build an electoral base *not* centered on the working class, but rather cutting across classes by being all things to all people, and seeking to occupy the political middle ground which elsewhere in Canada is filled by the Liberals. Thus, by the time of its defeat, the Schreyer government had refused to abolish compulsory overtime, had imposed wage controls, had started cutting back on social services, and had run an election program based on tax cuts for the middle class. Many electors seem to have believed that if the choice was between one set of conservative policies or another, they might as well choose the real thing! Therefore, the weak electoral base owes much to the nature of the party itself, its elitism and its reluctance to identify itself with the working class and to commit itself unambiguously to furthering working-class interests.

Thus, while social democratic politics place severe constraints on what planning can achieve, the specific nature of social democracy in Manitoba further limited the scope for planning. The commitment of social democracy to retaining the private-enterprise system essentially intact means that planning for this, the largest sector of the economy, can, *at best, be indicative*. The Manitoba government did not, however, even go this far. It did not attempt indicative planning at the macro-level along the lines, for instance, of the French or British experience. It did not construct a macro-model of the provincial economy or any other plan framework within which to attempt to carry out even Keynesian-type intervention to deal with unemployment. On the contrary, the relationship between the overall budget position and changes in the rate of unemployment was often perverse, in that government fiscal policy served to worsen rather than improve the employment situation. The Department of Finance was not represented on either the RED subcommittee or the MECS committee, so there was no formal policy link between the budgetary situation and overall economic or employment planning at the committee level, although some cooperation took place at the staff level.

The most the government did to alleviate cyclical and seasonal unemployment was to activate special funds under the control of a committee chaired by the premier. The overall amounts devoted to these purposes were arrived at quite arbitrarily and, while the programs aimed to create useful services or infrastructures for communities, they were invariably put together at short notice and were poorly staffed, so that project quality varied enormously. Moreover, projects were not subject to the kind of detailed and systematic scrutiny they received in the RED committee, and often applications were made to this "Winter Works" committee as a means of avoiding the RED committee. To a degree, these monies constituted a political slush fund to be dispensed in the guise of funds for temporary job creation.

This makeshift approach to employment generation was a far cry from the grandiose goals of the *Guidelines* and fell well short of a commitment to full employment. It reflected, in part, a refusal by the government to use systematically the quite considerable powers of the provincial state to address as fully as possible the problem of unemployment. In turn, this can be explained by the ambiguous relationship of the government to the objectives of the *Guidelines*, as discussed later, and to the aversion of the government to any deficit-raising fiscal measures which might affect adversely the province's bond rating on the New York money markets. The reliance of the province on international capital for its hydro-expansion projects placed tight constraints on provincial economic policy through the cost of international borrowing. Yet critics of the government, and the planning secretariat itself, questioned the wisdom of the large-scale hydroelectric development which was based, in the latter years of the Schreyer administration, mainly on dubious premises about the rate of growth of residential heating demand. They also questioned the wisdom of large-scale international borrowing for this purpose, and the sensitivity of government policy to the province's bond rating. In the light of the experience of the later NDP government of Howard Pawley, it is clear that the Schreyer government was particularly conservative in the job creation area, and quite zealous in protecting the province's credit rating. It must be noted, however, that in the mid-1970s the unemployment situation was not acute, because the unemployed were able to ''vote with their feet'' and move to other, more dynamic, areas of Canada. This option was not open in 1982-85, a period which saw, therefore, record provincial deficits and slippage in the bond rating. International considerations were a powerful influence on provincial economic policy as a result of the government's energy and borrowing policies.

The limited and haphazard approach to employment creation in the Schreyer years reflected also the limited levers of macro-economic policy available to a province, and the belief that responsibility for stabilization policy belonged more properly to the federal government. The broader lesson to be drawn from this is, of course, that the Constitution of Canada places strict limits on the potentialities of economic planning at the provincial level, whatever the political complexion of the government in power. There are, for instance, constitutional limits to provincial regulation of trade and capital flows. The civil servants at both levels of government are also often driven by different bureaucratic imperatives so that even building a common or mutually consistent planning framework, let alone common development strategies, is a difficult if not impossible task. Where the governments in power are from different political parties a harmonious approach to planning and strategy is even less likely. This soon became evident in the northern strategy exercise, when the federal government refused to make the effort to calculate the amount and direction of its spending in northern Manitoba or, more importantly, to endorse the convergence approach to development and to reshape its programs along convergence lines in that region. Since the federal government had constitutional responsibility for residents of Indian reserves and, as well, contributed significantly to total spending in the north, this lack of cooperation was critical to the outcome of the strategy exercise.

Elsewhere in the world, indicative planning by social democratic governments has been accompanied also by the planning of investment activities of Crown corporations. In Manitoba, Crown corporations were almost entirely outside the formal planning machinery. The government chose to run them at arm's length along the lines of private business where possible.[25] The most important of these was Manitoba Hydro, with the premier as minister. The investment activities of Manitoba Hydro were so large as to have enormous implications for the provincial economy yet, amazingly, they were not subject to scrutiny by the RED subcommittee or any other cabinet body, nor were they made to tie in with other provincial initiatives. Indeed, the senior staff of Manitoba Hydro actively resisted intervention by planners and, while ostensibly cooperating with the northern strategy, went ahead and built a whole townsite in the north by shipping in materials from southern suppliers. It is a measure of the premier's awareness of what was happening around him or, perhaps, of his commitment to convergent development in the north, that he acquiesced in this move. Manitoba Hydro's blatant disregard for government policy was eagerly seized upon by other branches of government which opposed the convergence strategy on ideological, convenience or other grounds.

Nor did the government ever follow the *Guidelines* in systematically extending Crown corporation activities into profitable ventures. On one occasion, when the author presented to the RED subcommittee a proposal to buy out an extremely profitable agricultural machinery company, whose shares were grossly undervalued, the response was that the province was not in the business of taking over profitable ventures. Many Crown corporations were, instead, money-losing enterprises taken over to preserve jobs.[26] This enabled the Opposition to equate public-sector ownership with incompetence, a stance used with great success in the 1977 election. It is to be emphasized that where formal cost-benefit analysis of such Crown corporations was carried out, as it was in some cases by the RED secretariat, this was only *after* the decision to acquire the companies had been made. Thus, once again, the essentially liberal nature of NDP politics in Manitoba, which dictated that the public sector should not only be small but also that it be operated at arm's length like private business, served to limit the degree and type of planning possible. European-style public-sector investment planning was simply not considered desirable or useful.

Apart from its commitment to the relative status quo in terms of property relationships, the politics of social democracy limit the nature of economic planning in two other important ways. First, the social democratic tradition is very much a Fabian one, with an emphasis on a paternalistic, technocratic elite bestowing political largesse on the mass of ignorant or less capable workers. This political approach gives rise, at best, to planning from above by a group of experts acting *on behalf* of workers but not *with* them or *through* them.[27] Participation in planning is considered important but is interpreted to mean *consultation* at various points in the planning process, or even mere information sharing. It rarely means democratic and popular *control* of the planning process and a concomitant discretion over planning resources, including funds. Rather, it takes the form of co-optation, of rubber-stamping plans drawn up by others, subject to change only after the fact and to a very limited degree. The northern strategy was a classic example of this type of planning despite the best intentions of its authors. Though the plan strategy was premised on local participation and control, the planners were simply unable to shift the locus of planning or control to the local level because of political and bureaucratic resistance. The politics of a shift to this type of planning and development had simply not been thought through sufficiently by the planners.[28]

The limitations imposed on planning by this Fabian tradition are rendered even more severe by social democracy's commitment to *parliamentarianism* as the dominant form of democratic expression.[29] In the Manitoba context in the mid-1970s, this commitment expressed itself in a deep suspicion, and belittling, of bodies representing Natives which were not (like the Northern Association of Community Councils) creatures of the provincial government. There was a refusal to accept their legitimacy as representatives of Natives, which was considered inferior to that of MLAs, and they were accepted and dealt with only reluctantly to defuse potential political opposition. The outcome of this was that they were allowed only token representation in the planning process and given insufficient funding to allow them even to react to government papers on planning *for* their constituency.

Elitism and parliamentarianism combined also to render ineffective the *Guidelines* objective on promoting self-development and self-actualization. Crown corporations and all levels of government retained traditional, hierarchical management forms and no effort was made to address problems of alienation either at the board level or at the level of the work place. Naturally, the private sector remained equally untouched by this *Guidelines* objective.

The question that naturally arises is why there was such a huge gap between the planning rhetoric and formal cabinet policy, in the case of the later northern, rural and industrial exercises, and planning in reality. What needs to be explained is not the paucity of action; hopefully, we have explained that, but rather why the government tolerated such extreme policy statements and such progressive planning initiatives, if it had no intention of implementing them.

The answer lies, once again, in the nature of social democratic politics as they developed in the Manitoba context. In the early years of the NDP government, the party was able to attract a large number of left-wing social democrats and socialists into policy formulation positions. Indeed, as argued above, the political spectrum covered by the party was very large, but the Left gravitated towards policy units of the government from which it attempted to push as hard as it could for reform. As a self-confessed liberal,[30] Schreyer himself had little time for formal planning, but several other ministers, including Sidney Green, were intellectually attracted to the rationality of planning, and supported it both as an intellectual exercise and as a process from which acceptable and "practical" *individual* ideas or policies might result. Schreyer too was able to acquiesce in planning, providing the government was not seen to be *committed* to any particular policy thrusts or, more importantly, to any specific future programing. From this point of view the *Guidelines* were an ideal approach to planning because they involved only the vaguest form of commitments. Likewise the rural and industrial strategies were regarded as sound but nonthreatening, being purely indicative in nature. The northern strategy was quite a different matter. It generated commitments and attempted to establish machinery to ensure that they were kept. It had the support of northern MLAs and some community support, but it met opposition from Winnipeg MLAs who felt that it involved excessive future financial commitments ($245 to $370 million over five years with recurrent costs of about $20 million per year).[31] The premier betrayed his own lack of commitment to the notion of an integrated, multifaceted attack on northern poverty during the discussion of the plan by calling for more modest efforts and preferring, instead, "to shake the trees and see what falls out" in the form of specific projects. Nonetheless, the strategy was accepted in principle by the cabinet, and the secretariat endeavoured to see that it was implemented.

More than any other planning exercise, the northern strategy pushed the state as far as it could go in terms of reform. In some areas this was quite far. One line department put its senior staff through retraining sessions to better handle the new policy directions and, at the same time, reserved all forestry resources within twenty-five miles of northern communities for their exclusive use. Few other departments and agencies were as cooperative, and since the strategy document was merely the first stage of what should have been an ongoing planning commitment, this lack of cooperation prevented the necessary technical refinement of the exercise and the gradual application of convergence principles to all areas of state activity in the north. Part of the opposition was undoubtedly ideological, as the bulk of senior bureaucrats had little sympathy for an exercise considered radical both in its underlying analysis of the causes of northern poverty and in its prescriptions for state and community action. Some of the opposition was most certainly inertial in nature, as both bureaucrats and politicians preferred to stay with the familiar and tended to shy away from untested and potentially risky departures from past practice.

As the government found itself in the midst of a growing fiscal crisis (heightened, it may be added, by earlier NDP reluctance to nationalize profitable private enterprise or to tax, significantly, profits and higher incomes), it became easier to legitimize ideological and bureaucratic opposition to implementing the strategy. Ultimately, therefore, the strategy was managed into nonexistence after some short-lived adverse publicity on the lack of participation of Native northerners in the preparation of the plan. Since the plan itself did not threaten existing private enterprise in the north, but instead sought to influence it along convergent lines and to *limit* future private businesses in favour of community enterprises, it did not generate more widespread political opposition within the province.

The policy and planning units of the government were, therefore, centres of creative initiatives and critical analysis of government policy. The left-wing social democrats and socialists who staffed them reinforced the legitimacy of the NDP as a progressive party but, in reality, had only a marginal impact on government policy. Nevertheless, it is instructive to note that subsequent NDP governments have not drawn on strong central policy units, nor risked associating themselves with ambitious left-wing policy statements of even the most general type. In their new conservatism their rhetoric is now much closer to reality than it was in the past.

In summary, there were a number of factors shaping the nature of economic planning under the Schreyer governments. The first and most important of these was the essential nature of social democratic politics with its general acceptance of private enterprise, its limited ambition in terms of reforming and guiding capitalism, its elitism, and its attachment to the narrowest forms of parliamentary democracy. Each of these placed powerful constraints on what economic planning might hope to achieve and on the forms it might take. But in addition to these *general* political constraints must be added the limitations imposed by the *specific* form taken by social democratic politics in the Manitoba context. The tenuous working-class base of the NDP was acquiesced in by the party, which chose instead to strive for broader class acceptability in an effort to occupy the political ground vacated by the Liberals. The government accordingly adopted a timid approach to public ownership and income redistribution, to state intervention and workers' control, allowing the limited public sector to operate largely as if it were still privately owned, that is, with little or no worker participation on the one level and with little or no state direction or coordination on the other. The possibilities of planning were also constrained by the state's emphasis on hydroelectric development funded by overseas borrowing, since this made economic policy, and especially anticyclical employment policies, sensitive to the province's bond rating on the New York money market. A further important constraint was, and is, imposed by the limitations on provincial economic powers within Confederation.

Planning the Transition to Socialism: The Manitoba Experience

Because of these political constraints, the approaches to planning described earlier did not yield any significant success in practice, so much so that the northern, rural and industrial strategies do not even rate a mention in the literature assessing the NDP government's record.[32] Nevertheless, they were not entirely futile efforts and may have relevance in other contexts. Several Native organizations, for instance, both in northern Manitoba (the God's River and Fox Lake Bands) and in the south (the Southeast Resource Development Council) have subsequently expressed an interest in adopting a convergence strategy in their communities. As well, the industrial and rural strategy exercises formed the analytical base of the federal NDP's national industrial strategy stance at the end of the 1970s. Moreover, the lessons of the northern strategy appear to have great relevance in the current European debate about planning in the transition to socialism.

The most striking lesson to be learned is that dealing with the multifaceted problems of regional development during such a transition will require a planning approach of some sophistication and complexity. In this respect, the recent proposals of Nuti to deal with market economy instability by the more extensive use of future contingent instruments, such as salary indexation, investment *quid pro quos* for salary cuts/freezes, and by the creation of new corporations for national employment, national investment and international trade can be seen to be, at best, useful but merely partial solutions.[33] These would need to be complemented with a whole series of institutional and policy developments, not the least of which would be the formulation of a credible industrial strategy. The essence of Nuti's approach is that these planning institutions would be supportive of essentially private-enterprise initiatives, providing subsidized labour or machinery, but not replacing the private sector. The analysis of the reasons for underdevelopment in northern Manitoba suggest that much more aggressive central intervention is required, in terms of direct provision of capital, coordination of investment, training and marketing, than Nuti envisages. Furthermore, Nuti avoids the whole issue of democracy and participation in this transitional period.

The northern strategy suggests that the obstacles to finding solutions to problems of uneven development are not technical in nature and that a whole range of reasonable alternatives can be generated to market-induced migration or regional poverty. Within a broader socialist or transitional framework, convergent strategies might be feasible technically and financially. They would require that central, regional and community planning machineries be introduced and harmonized, that a blend of market and non-market forces be used in development, and that clear guidelines be adopted for the state subsidization of local activities. Above all, however, the requirements for the successful pursuit of planned convergence are essentially political. The state must be prepared to reject the primacy of private enterprise and the free rein of the market and it must be able to create supportive, nonhierarchical, nonelitist central planning agencies, while at the same time being prepared to devolve decision taking and funding to both regional and community levels.[34] The centralized planning machinery of the Schreyer government was too distanced from those it sought to serve, and the resources of regional and community planners too restricted for successful socialist planning. Finally, it will be necessary to broaden the definition of democracy beyond parliamentarianism, to encompass a diverse range of popularly based organizations. The state must be prepared to accept the legitimacy of such organizations and to work through them as vital complements to whatever parliamentary forms of democracy are adopted in the transitional period. From these and other perspectives the experience of planning in Manitoba is quite useful in suggesting, in concrete terms, the form that planning might take under ''feasible socialism.''

NOTES

1. See Alec Nove, *The Economics of Feasible Socialism* (London: George Allen and Unwin, 1983); Andrew Gamble, ''Capitalism or Barbarism: The Austrian Critique of Socialism,'' in R. Miliband, J. Saville, M. Liebman and L. Panitch, eds., *The Socialist Register 1985/86* (London: Merlin Press 1986), 355-72.

2. D.M. Nuti, ''Economic Planning in Market Economies: Scope, Instruments, Institutions,'' in Miliband et al., *The Socialist Register*, 373-84.

3. Manitoba, ''General Manual of Administration,'' February 1985.

4. Ibid.

5. Manitoba, *Guidelines for the Seventies* (Winnipeg: Government of Manitoba, 1973), volumes 1-3.

6. Ibid., volume 1, especially chapter 6.

7. Ibid., 13.

8. Ibid., 12.

9. Ibid., 60.

10. Ibid., chapter 7.

11. For a detailed discussion and evaluation of the strategy, and of the theory underlying it, see John Loxley, ''The Great Northern Plan,'' *Studies in Political Economy* 6 (Autumn 1981): 151-82.

12. Nelson Wiseman, *Social Democracy in Manitoba: A History of the CCF/NDP* (Winnipeg: University of Manitoba Press, 1983), 139.

13. Ibid.

14. Dave Godfrey and Mel Watkins, eds., *Gordon to Watkins to You: A Documentary: The Battle for Control of our Economy* (Toronto: New Press, 1970), 90.

15. Manitoba Budget Address, 1968, 1978. The general points being raised in this paragraph are also supported by Wiseman, *Social Democracy in Manitoba*, and James A. McAllister, *The Government of Edward Schreyer: Democratic Socialism in Manitoba*, (Montréal and Kingston: McGill-Queen's University Press, 1984).

16. Ralph Miliband and Marcel Liebman, "Beyond Social Democracy," in Miliband et al., *The Socialist Register*, 478.

17. See McAllister, *The Government of Edward Schreyer*, 79.

18. E. Kierans, *Report on Natural Resources Policy in Manitoba* (Winnipeg: Government of Manitoba, 1973).

19. McAllister, *The Government of Edward Schreyer*, 79.

20. Ibid., chapter 6.

21. See Wiseman, *Social Democracy in Manitoba*, 107.

22. McAllister, *The Government of Edward Schreyer*, 79.

23. Miliband and Liebman, "Beyond Social Democracy," 482.

24. See McAllister, *The Government of Edward Schreyer*, chapters 10-12.

25. This approach to Crown corporations was by no means unique to Manitoba at that time. See John Langford, "Crown Corporations as Instruments of Policy," in G. Bruce Doern and Peter Aucoin, eds., *Public Policy in Canada: Organization, Process and Management*, (Toronto: Macmillan, 1979), 255.

26. L. LeVan Hall and D. Gardave, "Public Ownership: The Manitoba Experience," mimeo, October 1986.

27. For an elaboration of this point see Gary Teeple, "Liberals in a Hurry: Socialism and the CCF-NDP," in Gary Teeple, ed., *Capitalism and the National Question in Canada* (Toronto: University of Toronto Press, 1972), 233 ff.

28. Loxley, "The Great Northern Plan."

29. See, for example, Geoff Hodgson, *The Democratic Economy: A New Look at Planning, Markets and Power* (Harmondsworth: Penguin Books, 1984), 165.

30. Godfrey and Watkins, *Gordon to Watkins to You*, 90.

31. Loxley "The Great Northern Plan," 170.

32. They are not mentioned by either McAllister or Wiseman, although McAllister cites an early draft of Loxley, "The Great Northern Plan," in his bibliography, and both authors were certainly aware of these exercises.

33. See Nuti, "Economic Planning in Market Economies."

34. Many of these proposals are quite in line with Nove's *Feasible Socialism*, but convergence strategies appear to go well beyond Nove in terms of the degree of physical planning required and, perhaps, the extent of intervention called for in the market place.

Conclusion: Toward the Future

Jeremy Hull and Jim Silver

Several themes have threaded their way through this book. The foremost is the attention paid by authors to the political struggles which are central to political economy, especially those waged by the Native and Métis inhabitants who were marginalized by the process of primitive accumulation, and those waged along the lines of class and gender in a manner more central to the process of capital accumulation. Other important themes include the emergence in Manitoba early in the century of an agriculturally based, relatively diversified and stable economic structure that has remained largely unchanged since World War I, but which in recent years has not only been restructuring, but has also exhibited signs of fragility; the emergence in recent years of a much wider variety of important political struggles; and the confounding experience of the NDP governments which held office in Manitoba from 1969-77, and from 1981-88. It what manner will these themes be interwoven in the future, and what are the implications for the Left, and for socialist politics in Manitoba?

Given the limits placed on a single province by capital and by our federal system of government, and given the existence of a politically moderate and, until recently, electorally successful social democratic party, what is a feasible socialist politics in Manitoba? Though for socialists in the province this should be a fundamental question, it is seldom posed directly. To the extent that they deal with this question, the chapters in this book, particularly when taken as a whole, are somewhat ambiguous in their view of socialist politics and the NDP. In this conclusion we will try to extrapolate from these chapters in order to reflect on this question.

For many NDP supporters, the party offers as much socialism as is necessary, or at least as much as they think possible. Mainstream social democrats have a ''realistic'' view of parliamentary politics, and of the importance of reelection. Their attention is focussed on the undeniable gains made possible by the election of NDP governments. They do not articulate a vision of a better society, and are staunch defenders of the competent economic management, and very cautious and pragmatic social reform, which are the goals of Manitoba NDP governments. To go beyond such a conception of politics and of the party would, they argue, make reelection more difficult, which in turn would put at risk those moderate yet important gains made possible by the party's cautious and pragmatic politics. Thus, for them, a ''socialist politics'' becomes the defence of NDP programs and the organization of reelection campaigns. Such a politics discourages debate, thus reinforcing the cautious pragmatism of NDP governments, and completing the logical circle.

The NDP is not monolithic, however. A variety of positions and approaches are advocated within the party which differ from the characterization just given. Debates take place over both philosophy and tactics. Many within the party are frustrated by the lack of commitment to socialist principles, and will support more radical alternatives when these appear able to gain popular support. Those on the Left of the party often argue that if an NDP government adopted and advocated more consistently socialist positions, it would be able to generate as much or more support for its policies as it does through its more typical, cautious approach. We concur with this belief.

A major impediment to such a shift, however, is that there is no credible socialist alternative outside of the NDP. The history of the Left in Manitoba, as elsewhere, is full of divisions, infighting and failed organizational efforts. The Left outside the NDP is largely atomized and organizationally incoherent. Thus an NDP government feels little pressure from it, in comparison to that from the vocal and well-organized business community. This in turn results in the Left inside the party being marginalized and rendered less effective than might otherwise be the case.

In short, there does not now exist in Manitoba a realistic Left politics, and thus any criticism of the NDP's cautious pragmatism must also be a criticism of those who would move Left, but who do not have a politics, let alone an organization, by which this might be done. Further, there is a lack of theorizing and debate about what a socialist politics for Manitoba might be. This is not unique to Manitoba. The intellectual Left has relatively little interest in theorizing about a socialist politics generally, and is particularly uninterested in considering socialist politics at the provincial level, where the constraints on political actions are so severe.

Given the absence of a coherent Left alternative, and the depravities of the neo-conservative onslaught in neighbouring western provinces and countries, and given too the relative prosperity and apparent stability of Manitoba's economy, the cautious pragmatic politics of social reform practiced by successive provincial NDP governments makes sense, yields returns, and until recently has won support. The party believes that it has laid claim to the terrain of common sense.

Yet the view which is implicit in many of the chapters in this volume is that, although severely constrained, provincial NDP governments have more room for manoeuvre than they are prepared to use, and that doing more is both necessary and possible. It can even be argued that the NDP government's electoral defeat on 26 April 1988 was largely attributable to its shift since the 1986 budget towards a more neoconservative fiscal agenda, or at least to the sharp increase in taxes and Autopac fees which occurred.[1] What is needed is an imaginative approach to defining a political strategy suitable to the admittedly limited manoeuverability available to a provincial government.

But a logical dilemma confronts those who would argue, as we are doing, that there is a feasible socialism which could be practiced in Manitoba. To go further than the current NDP is prepared to go, and to push up against the limits of what is possible for a provincial government, requires a different conception of politics, one which aims to mobilize and politicize people, and thus to empower them in support of tough, tangible gains. This is a politics which would see a socialist or social democratic party take on a more extraparliamentary role, campaigning around progressive demands, connecting with popular feelings and sentiments, making itself the focal point of people's aspirations, mobilizing and politicizing to build a solid base of support for substantial policy reform in a wide range of areas. But the very base of support which a party with such a conception of politics could build is what is needed in the first place in order to build such a politics.

This is a conception of politics and the role of the party which is at odds with that held by Manitoba's NDP. The party has a history and a culture of pragmatism, and antagonism to radical thought and even debate. Far from mobilizing and politicizing in support of political gains, the party demobilizes and depoliticizes as part of a limited and narrowly conceived parliamentary strategy. And the membership accepts this politics because the gains achieved, while moderate, are significant, and because the alternatives to the Right and the Left are, by comparison, unattractive.

Whether such a politics can continue to win support is less clear, given the dynamics of Manitoba's political economy. The social and economic structure of Manitoba is being transformed. The global restructuring of capital and the related Canada-United States Free Trade Agreement will hasten the process, placing Manitoba's peripheral economy at risk. Although Manitoba's economy has been relatively diversified and strong historically, it is now threatened by declines in manufacturing, agriculture and finance. Beneath the surface appearance of robustness there are signs of increasing fragility — a fragility partially masked by large-scale public investment.

Until the April 1988 election, these structural changes only reinforced support for the relatively beneficial economic policies and cautious social reform of the NDP because, while other governments responded with a neoconservative strategy of spending cuts and union-bashing, Manitoba's NDP government largely maintained public investment and government social programs. Only with the 1986 budget did the NDP government slip towards fiscal conservatism, and even then only on the revenue, not the expenditure side of the budget. Consequently, as measured by traditional economic indicators, Manitoba's economy looks comparatively healthy. This relative economic health was not the result of a socialist, nor even a social democratic strategy. It was more the maintenance of the postwar liberal Keynesian strategy that other governments have abandoned. And it has all the limitations of such a strategy. For example, severe social and economic inequality continues in Manitoba, while the necessity of coming to grips with a planned industrial development strategy is avoided. This liberal strategy will become less and less feasible if, as expected, the traditional sources of the province's economic diversity and stability — agriculture, manufacturing and finance — are gradually restructured and even eroded.

Where, then, are the social forces which could effect a transition to a feasible socialist politics in Manitoba? A proper analysis of this question is beyond the scope of this short conclusion, and the foresight of the editors, but some general comments can be made. First, the current transformation in the social and economic structure of the province is throwing up new social forces and new demands. Any analysis of a socialist politics in Manitoba must be built on a detailed analysis of these emergent social forces. Of particular importance is the changing composition of the working class. Despite much recent literature to the contrary, the working class remains the backbone of any socialist strategy. What the increasing proportions of women and public-sector workers will mean for the politics practiced by the labour movement is impossible to tell. More easy to predict is the likely continuation of labour's links to the NDP, with all the ambiguities and limitations which that entails.

Second, a wide range of progressive popular movements has emerged in recent years. There is at least some evidence to suggest that, while they do not practice a coherent socialist politics, the beginnings of such a politics are implicit in their efforts. This can be seen in many of the submissions to the Macdonald Commission, and in the struggle against free trade, both of which provide at least some evidence of the emergence of a "common sense" consistent with a socialist politics.[2] On the other hand, single-issue politics is inherently limited, and its ability to transcend these limits is dependent upon the existence of a broader movement able to articulate single-issue goals as part of a broader socialist strategy. Without the emergence of such a broad socialist strategy and movement, the progressive potential of the many single-issue movements is likely to remain unrealized.

Third, the increasingly constrained provincial and federal budgets preclude the continued pattern of increasing government expenditures as a response to popular demands. New solutions which extract more taxes from capital and are much more critical of the current array of social expenditures will be, and in fact already are, necessary.

In addition to the pressures created by these underlying dynamics, two crucial steps are necessary for a viable socialist politics to emerge in Manitoba. First, a clear vision of socialist goals must be articulated, and second, the practical steps involved in moving toward those goals must be identified to a much greater degree than in the past. Without these two elements the limitations of the competent and humane, but largely non-socialist NDP, cannot be transcended.

Some of the chapters in this volume have tried, at least implicitly, to suggest both the need for, and the possibility of, a revised conception of policy and politics. They have identified numerous missed opportunities for, and several areas where there is a perceived need for, a more "radical reformism." Loxley, for example, described the failure of the Schreyer government to pursue a more imaginative approach to northern development; Tudiver identified several missed opportunities for generating additional provincial revenue; Falconer offered an important analysis of the urban Native family and made useful suggestions for reform; Hull, Silver and Ghorayshi identified areas where a more radical approach to reform may be desirable.

But however desirable they may be, such individual, more radical reforms are unlikely, given two fundamental shortcomings of Manitoba's NDP. First, the party lacks a broad and coherent strategy for economic and industrial development. Its approach is piecemeal, often reactive, and lacking in vision. Specific, more radical reforms would become much more feasible as parts of a coherent, overall economic and industrial strategy. Second, what makes the development of such a comprehensive economic strategy unlikely is the form of politics which the NDP practices. It is a narrow, cautious, pragmatic version of parliamentary politics, designed to capture and control popular movements rather than inspire popular participation. This form of politics cannot create the popular base needed to sustain more aggressive policy initiatives.

To go beyond this moderate politics requires the creation of an extraparliamentary Left with a different conception of politics. The challenge facing Manitoba socialists — both inside and outside the NDP — is to create a vibrant, extraparliamentary Left, with a politics rooted in peoples' needs and aspirations. To do this requires going beyond simple repetitions of past socialist formulas developed elsewhere for other purposes. It requires building a program of "radical reform" rooted in an understanding of the specifics of Manitoba's political economy and of the political struggles and specific needs of Manitobans. We hope that the chapters in this book can contribute to the development of thinking, debate, and ultimately political action, along such lines.

NOTES

1. Cy Gonick and Jim Silver, "The Manitoba Election: A Neo-Conservative Defeat," *Canadian Dimension* 22, no. 4 (1988): 5-8.

2. See, for example, Daniel Drache and Duncan Cameron, eds., *The Other Macdonald Report* (Toronto: Lorimer, 1985).

Contributors

DONALD A. BAILEY was educated as an historian of Early Modern Europe, has published several articles and reviews on seventeenth-century French history, and has just finished a year as president of the Western Society for French History. This background has been useful for the writing of several papers on constitutional and French-language issues in Canada. Two of these are "The French Presence in Canada: The Case for Optimism," *Canadian Ethnic Studies* 17, no. 3 (1985): 100-19, and "The Judicial Fortunes of French on the Canadian Prairies," *Great Plains Quarterly* 9, no. 3 (Summer 1989): 139-55.

ERROL BLACK is Associate Professor of Economics at Brandon University, where he teaches courses in economics and industrial relations. He has previously published in *Canadian Dimension, Monthly Review, City Magazine, Labour/Le Travail, Relations Industrielles/Industrial Relations, Studies in Political Economy,* and *Contemporary Crises.*

PATRICK FALCONER completed his graduate studies in Public Administration in 1986, and has since worked on issues related to social justice, ecology and urban Native development. He is currently a community development consultant with the Winnipeg Core Area Initiative.

PARVIN GHORAYSHI is Associate Professor of Sociology at the University of Winnipeg. She has written extensively on agriculture in Canada and is the author of the forthcoming book, *Sociology of Work.*

CY GONICK is Professor of Economics at the University of Manitoba. He is founder and a member of the editorial collective of *Canadian Dimension.* He is the author of several books, including *Inflation or Depression* and *The Great Economic Debate.*

JOHN HOFLEY is Professor of Sociology and Associate Dean of Arts and Science at the University of Winnipeg. Before joining the University of Winnipeg in 1971, he was a Shastri Fellow in India and Assistant Professor of Sociology at Carleton University from 1966-70. He was president of the CSAA in 1980-81. His current research interests are in the areas of family and stratification.

JEREMY HULL is currently a partner with the Working Margins Consulting Group. He has a BA in English Literature from the City College of New York, and has written widely on Native issues.

JOHN LOXLEY is Professor and Head of the Economics Department, University of Manitoba. He served as secretary (deputy minister) to the Resource and Economic Development Sub-Committee of Cabinet under the Schreyer government in Manitoba. He is the author of *Debt and Disorder*, co-editor of *Towards Socialist Planning* and

Structural Adjustment in Africa, and is a member of the editorial board of *Studies in Political Economy*.

PAUL PHILLIPS grew up in British Columbia where he attended Victoria College before moving to Saskatoon and the University of Saskatchewan where he obtained his BA and MA in economics. His research there was concentrated on the economic development of the Canadian prairie region. After obtaining his Ph.D. from the London School of Economics he returned to western Canada. Since 1969 he has taught economics at the University of Manitoba. He has published a number of books and articles on Canadian political economy, including *Regional Disparities*.

ÜSTÜN REINART is a television journalist with the CBC. She has been social affairs reporter for "CBC 24 Hours Winnipeg," and covered a wide range of issues related to women and minorities. At present she is writer/broadcaster with "Country Canada."

REG SKENE is Professor of Theatre and Drama at the University of Winnipeg and Chair of the Department of Theatre and Drama. He is the author of *The Cuchulain Plays of W.B. Yeats: A Study*, and for seven years was drama critic of the *Winnipeg Free Press*. He is currently working on a projected two-volume history of theatre in Winnipeg, from 1897 to the present, the first volume of which (1897-1958) is ready for publication.

JIM SILVER is Associate Professor of Political Science at the University of Winnipeg. He is also currently an editor of *Canadian Dimension*.

NICOLE ST.-ONGE teaches history at the Collège Universitaire de St. Boniface. Her major research interests are in Métis history and Marxist theory.

NEIL TUDIVER teaches in the Faculty of Social Work at the University of Manitoba. His current research interests are in Canadian defence policy, and in collective bargaining in Canadian universities.

27   92